PRAISE and WORSHIP

HYMNAL

"They sang praises with gladness, and they bowed their heads and worshipped."

"Sing ye praises with understanding."

II Chronicles 29:30 ; Psalms 47:7

LILLENAS PUBLISHING COMPANY
KANSAS CITY, MISSOURI

✝ fOREWORD ✝

"LET THE WORD OF CHRIST DWELL IN YOU RICHLY IN ALL WISDOM;
TEACHING AND ADMONISHING ONE ANOTHER IN PSALMS AND HYMNS
AND SPIRITUAL SONGS, SINGING WITH GRACE IN YOUR HEARTS TO THE
LORD." Thus St. Paul, of the first Christian century, advised the
church at Colosse.

SINGING, along with preaching of the Word, has always been a part
of the worship of Christian congregations. Singing in the Spirit is the
expression of the deep and holy emotions of the soul of man. By it
the aspirations are ennobled and elevated. The depth of character and the
reality of religious experience possessed by a people are revealed in the
language and spirit of their songs and hymns.

"Praise and Worship" is the rightful successor to "Glorious Gospel
Hymns," which has enjoyed such wide acceptance for many years. Herein is
offered a wide range of hymns and spiritual songs. They have been chosen
by competent musicians and church leaders representing all areas of North
America. Dr. Haldor Lillenas, well-known and highly esteemed author, com-
poser, and editor of music, has given invaluable counsel.

Included in this presentation is a splendid collection of the great hymns
of the Church appropriate for use in morning worship services and on special
occasions. There are many songs adapted to the purpose of Sunday evening
meetings and revivals as well as youth groups and church schools. The num-
ber of responsive readings from the Scriptures is increased.

"Praise and Worship," a gospel hymnal, is hereby offered for use in
all churches in the English-speaking countries.

THE PUBLISHERS

✦ PRAISE AND WORSHIP ✦

1   All Hail the Power of Jesus' Name

EDWARD PERRONET   OLIVER HOLDEN

1. All hail the pow'r of Je - sus' name! Let an - gels pros-trate fall.
2. Ye cho - sen seed of Is - rael's race, Ye ran-somed from the fall,
3. Let ev - 'ry kin - dred, ev - 'ry tribe, On this ter - res - trial ball,
4. Oh, that with yon - der sa - cred throng We at His feet may fall!

Bring forth the roy - al di - a - dem, And crown Him Lord of all.
Hail Him who saves you by His grace, And crown Him Lord of all.
To Him all maj - es - ty as - cribe, And crown Him Lord of all.
We'll join the ev - er - last - ing song, And crown Him Lord of all.

Bring forth the roy - al di - a - dem, And crown Him Lord of all.
Hail Him who saves you by His grace, And crown Him Lord of all.
To Him all maj - es - ty as - cribe, And crown Him Lord of all.
We'll join the ev - er - last-ing song, And crown Him Lord of all.

2   All Hail the Power of Jesus' Name

EDWARD PERRONET

JAMES ELLER

1. All hail the pow'r of Je - sus' name! Let an - gels prostrate fall.
2. Ye cho - sen seed of Is - rael's race, Ye ran-somed from the fall,
3. Let ev - 'ry kin - dred, ev - 'ry tribe, On this ter - res-trial ball,
4. Oh, that with yon - der sa - cred throng We at His feet may fall,

Let an - gels pros-trate fall. Bring forth the roy - al di - a - dem,
Ye ransomed from the fall, Hail Him who saves you by His grace,
On this ter - res - trial ball, To Him all maj - es - ty as - cribe,
We at His feet may fall! We'll join the ev - er - last-ing song,

And crown ———————————————— Him, Crown Him,

And crown Him, crown Him, crown Him, crown Him, And crown Him Lord of
And crown ———————————————— Him, Crown Him,

And crown Him, crown Him, crown Him, Crown ——————

crown Him, crown Him;
crown ——— Him,

all. Crown Him; And crown Him Lord of all!
crown ——————————— Him; And crown Him Lord of all!

3   A Mighty Fortress Is Our God

MARTIN LUTHER

Tr. by Frederick H. Hedge

MARTIN LUTHER

1. A might-y for-tress is our God, A bul-wark nev-er fail - ing:
2. Did we in our own strength con-fide, Our striv-ing would be los - ing,
3. And tho' this world, with dev - ils filled, Should threaten to un - do us,
4. That word a - bove all earth-ly pow'rs, No thanks to them a - bid - eth;

Our help-er He, a - mid the flood Of mor-tal ills pre - vail - ing.
Were not the right Man on our side, The Man of God's own choos - ing.
We will not fear, for God hath willed His truth to tri - umph thro' us.
The Spir-it and the gifts are ours, Thro' Him who with us sid - eth.

For still our an-cient foe Doth seek to work us woe; His craft and pow'r are
Dost ask who that may be? Christ Je-sus, it is He; Lord Sab-aoth is His.
The prince of dark-ness grim, We trem-ble not for him; His rage we can en-
Let goods and kin-dred go, This mor-tal life al - so; The bod - y they may

great, And, armed with cru - el hate, On earth is not his e - qual.
name, From age to age the same, And He must win the bat - tle.
dure, For, lo! his doom is sure. One lit - tle word shall fell him.
kill; God's truth a bid - eth still. His king-dom is for - ev - er.

4   Praise Him! Praise Him!

FANNY J. CROSBY   CHESTER G. ALLEN

1. Praise Him! praise Him! Je-sus, our bless-ed Re - deem - er! Sing, O
2. Praise Him! praise Him! Je-sus, our bless-ed Re - deem - er! For our
3. Praise Him! praise Him! Je-sus, our bless-ed Re - deem - er! Heav'n-ly

Earth, His won-der-ful love pro - claim! Hail Him! hail Him! high-est arch-
sins He suffered, and bled, and died. He, our Rock, our hope of e -
por - tals loud with ho-san-nas ring! Je - sus, Sav-iour, reign-eth for

an-gels in glo - ry; Strength and hon - or give to His ho - ly
ter-nal sal - va-tion—Hail Him! hail Him! Je - sus the Cru - ci -
ev - er and ev - er. Crown Him! crown Him! Proph-et, and Priest, and

name! Like a shep - herd, Je - sus will guard His chil - dren;
fied. Sound His prais - es! Je - sus, who bore our sor - rows!
King! Christ is com - ing! o - ver the world vic - to - rious;

REFRAIN

In His arms He car-ries them all day long.
Love un - bounded, won-der-ful, deep and strong! Praise Him! praise Him!
Pow'r and glo - ry un - to the Lord be - long.

Praise Him! Praise Him!

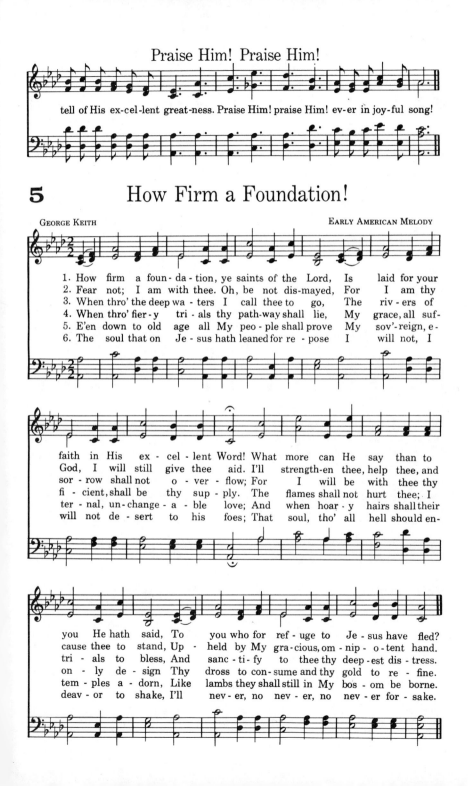

tell of His ex-cel-lent great-ness. Praise Him! praise Him! ev-er in joy-ful song!

5   How Firm a Foundation!

GEORGE KEITH   EARLY AMERICAN MELODY

1. How firm a foun - da - tion, ye saints of the Lord, Is laid for your
2. Fear not; I am with thee. Oh, be not dis-mayed, For I am thy
3. When thro' the deep wa - ters I call thee to go, The riv - ers of
4. When thro' fier - y tri - als thy path-way shall lie, My grace, all suf-
5. E'en down to old age all My peo - ple shall prove My sov'-reign, e -
6. The soul that on Je - sus hath leaned for re - pose I will not, I

faith in His ex - cel - lent Word! What more can He say than to
God, I will still give thee aid. I'll strength-en thee, help thee, and
sor - row shall not o - ver - flow; For I will be with thee thy
fi - cient, shall be thy sup - ply. The flames shall not hurt thee; I
ter - nal, un-change - a - ble love; And when hoar - y hairs shall their
will not de - sert to his foes; That soul, tho' all hell should en-

you He hath said, To you who for ref - uge to Je - sus have fled?
cause thee to stand, Up - held by My gra-cious, om - nip - o - tent hand.
tri - als to bless, And sanc - ti - fy to thee thy deep - est dis - tress.
on - ly de - sign Thy dross to con - sume and thy gold to re - fine.
tem - ples a - dorn, Like lambs they shall still in My bos - om be borne.
deav - or to shake, I'll nev - er, no nev - er, no nev - er for - sake.

6 How Firm a Foundation!

PORTUGUESE HYMN

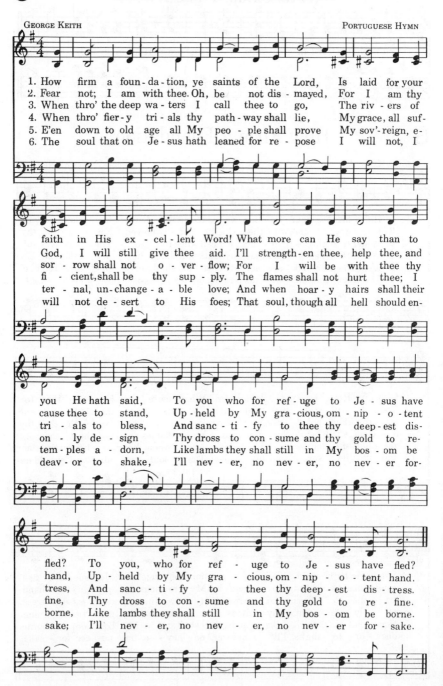

1. How firm a foun-da-tion, ye saints of the Lord, Is laid for your
2. Fear not; I am with thee. Oh, be not dis-mayed, For I am thy
3. When thro' the deep wa-ters I call thee to go, The riv-ers of
4. When thro' fier-y tri-als thy path-way shall lie, My grace, all suf-
5. E'en down to old age all My peo-ple shall prove My sov'-reign, e-
6. The soul that on Je-sus hath leaned for re-pose I will not, I

faith in His ex-cel-lent Word! What more can He say than to
God, I will still give thee aid. I'll strength-en thee, help thee, and
sor-row shall not o-ver-flow; For I will be with thee thy
fi-cient, shall be thy sup-ply. The flames shall not hurt thee; I
ter-nal, un-change-a-ble love; And when hoar-y hairs shall their
will not de-sert to His foes; That soul, though all hell should en-

you He hath said, To you who for ref-uge to Je-sus have
cause thee to stand, Up-held by My gra-cious, om-nip-o-tent
tri-als to bless, And sanc-ti-fy to thee thy deep-est dis-
on-ly de-sign Thy dross to con-sume and thy gold to re-
tem-ples a-dorn, Like lambs they shall still in My bos-om be
deav-or to shake, I'll nev-er, no nev-er, no nev-er for-

fled? To you, who for ref-uge to Je-sus have fled?
hand, Up-held by My gra-cious, om-nip-o-tent hand.
tress, And sanc-ti-fy to thee thy deep-est dis-tress.
fine, Thy dross to con-sume and thy gold to re-fine.
borne, Like lambs they shall still in My bos-om be borne.
sake; I'll nev-er, no nev-er, no nev-er for-sake.

7   The Son of God Goes Forth to War

REGINALD HEBER   HENRY S. CUTLER

1. The Son of God goes forth to war, A king-ly crown to gain;
2. The mar - tyr first, whose ea - gle eye Could pierce be-yond the grave,
3. A glo - rious band, the cho-sen few On whom the Spir - it came!
4. A no - ble ar - my, men and boys, The ma - tron and the maid,

His blood - red ban-ner streams a - far. Who fol -lows in His train?
Who saw his Mas-ter in the sky And called on Him to save;
Twelve val-iant saints, their hope they knew, And mocked the cross and flame;
A - round the Sav-iour's throne re-joice, In robes of light ar - rayed.

Who best can drink his cup of woe, Tri - um-phant o - ver pain;
Like Him, with par - don on his tongue, In midst of mor - tal pain,
They met the ty - rant's brandished steel, The li - on's gor - y mane;
They climbed the steep as - cent of heav'n Thro' per - il, toil, and pain.

Who pa - tient bears his cross be - low, He fol - lows in His train.
He prayed for them that did the wrong. Who fol - lows in his train?
They bowed their necks the death to feel. Who fol - lows in their train?
O God, to us may grace be giv'n To fol - low in their train.

8   The Glorious Hope

SAMUEL MEDLEY   LOWELL MASON

1. Oh, glo-rious hope of per-fect love! It lifts me up to
2. Re-joic-ing now in ear-nest hope, I stand, and from the
3. A land of corn, and wine, and oil; Fa-vored with God's pe-
4. Oh, that I might at once go up; No more on this side

things a-bove; It bears on ea-gles' wings. It gives my
mountain-top See all the land be-low. Riv-ers of
cul-iar smile, With ev-'ry bless-ing blest; There dwells the
Jor-dan stop, But now the land pos-sess; This mo-ment

rav-ished soul a taste, And makes me for some mo-ments feast
milk and hon-ey rise, And all the fruits of par-a-dise
Lord our Right-eous-ness, And keeps His own in per-fect peace,
end my le-gal years, Sor-rows and sins, and doubts and fears,

With Je-sus'priests and kings, With Je-sus' priests and kings.
In end-less plen-ty grow, In end-less plen-ty grow.
And ev-er-last-ing rest, And ev-er-last-ing rest.
A howl-ing wil-der-ness, A howl-ing wil-der-ness!

9 There Is a Name I Love to Hear

F. WHITFIELD

W. H. HAVERGAL

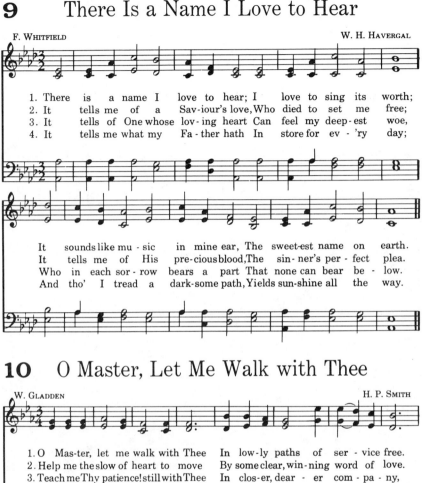

1. There is a name I love to hear; I love to sing its worth;
2. It tells me of a Sav-iour's love, Who died to set me free;
3. It tells of One whose lov-ing heart Can feel my deep-est woe,
4. It tells me what my Fa-ther hath In store for ev-'ry day;

It sounds like mu-sic in mine ear, The sweet-est name on earth.
It tells me of His pre-cious blood, The sin-ner's per-fect plea.
Who in each sor-row bears a part That none can bear be-low.
And tho' I tread a dark-some path, Yields sun-shine all the way.

10 O Master, Let Me Walk with Thee

W. GLADDEN

H. P. SMITH

1. O Mas-ter, let me walk with Thee In low-ly paths of ser-vice free.
2. Help me the slow of heart to move By some clear, win-ning word of love.
3. Teach me Thy patience! still with Thee In clos-er, dear-er com-pa-ny,
4. In hope that sends a shin-ing ray Far down the fu-ture's broadening way,

Tell me Thy se-cret; help me bear The strain of toil, the fret of care.
Teach me the wayward feet to stay, And guide them in the home-ward way.
In work that keeps faith sweet and strong, In trust that tri-umphs o-ver wrong.
In peace that on-ly Thou canst give, With Thee, O Mas-ter, let me live.

11   Take My Life, and Let It Be

FRANCES R. HAVERGAL

CAESAR MALAN

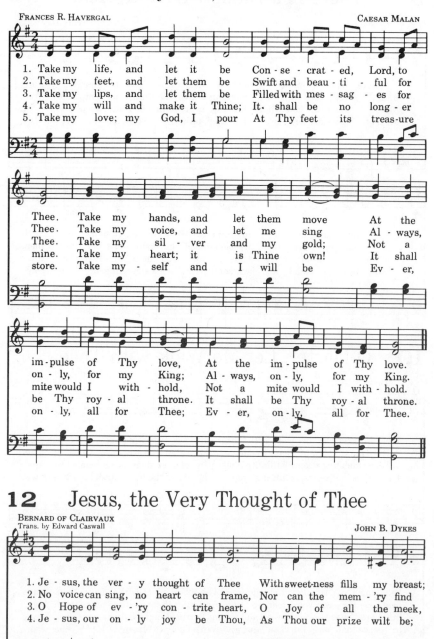

1. Take my life, and let it be Con-se-crat-ed, Lord, to
2. Take my feet, and let them be Swift and beau-ti-ful for
3. Take my lips, and let them be Filled with mes-sag-es for
4. Take my will and make it Thine; It. shall be no long-er
5. Take my love; my God, I pour At Thy feet its treas-ure

Thee. Take my hands, and let them move At the
Thee. Take my voice, and let me sing Al-ways,
Thee. Take my sil-ver and my gold; Not a
mine. Take my heart; it is Thine own! It shall
store. Take my-self and I will be Ev-er,

im-pulse of Thy love, At the im-pulse of Thy love.
on-ly, for my King; Al-ways, on-ly, for my King.
mite would I with-hold, Not a mite would I with-hold.
be Thy roy-al throne. It shall be Thy roy-al throne.
on-ly, all for Thee; Ev-er, on-ly, all for Thee.

12   Jesus, the Very Thought of Thee

BERNARD OF CLAIRVAUX
Trans. by Edward Caswall

JOHN B. DYKES

1. Je-sus, the ver-y thought of Thee With sweet-ness fills my breast;
2. No voice can sing, no heart can frame, Nor can the mem-'ry find
3. O Hope of ev-'ry con-trite heart, O Joy of all the meek,
4. Je-sus, our on-ly joy be Thou, As Thou our prize wilt be;

Jesus, the Very Thought of Thee

But sweet-er far Thy face to see, And in Thy pres - ence rest.
A sweet-er sound than Thy blest name, O Sav - iour of man-kind!
To those who fall, how kind Thou art! How good to those who seek!
Je - sus, be Thou our glo - ry now, And thro' e - ter - ni - ty.

13 Sweetly Resting

MARY D. JAMES

W. WARREN BENTLY

1. In the rift - ed Rock I'm rest - ing; Safe-ly shel - tered, I a - bide.
2. Long pur - sued by sin and Sa - tan, Wea-ry, sad, I longed for rest.
3. Peace which passeth un - der-stand-ing, Joy the world can nev - er give,
4. In the rift - ed Rock I'll hide me Till the storms of life are past;

There no foes nor storms mo-lest me, While with-in the cleft I hide.
Then I found this heav'n-ly shel - ter O - pened in my Sav-iour's breast.
Now in Je - sus I am find - ing; In His smiles of love I live.
All se - cure in this blest ref - uge, Heed-ing not the fierc-est blast.

CHORUS

Now I'm rest - ing, sweet-ly rest - ing, In the cleft once made for me.

Je - sus, bless - ed Rock of A - ges, I will hide my - self in Thee.

14   "Are Ye Able?" Said the Master

EARL MARLATT   HARRY S. MASON

1. "Are ye a - ble," said the Mas-ter, "To be cru - ci - fied with Me?"
2. "Are ye a - ble" to re - mem-ber, When a thief lifts up his eyes,
3. "Are ye a - ble," when the shad-ows Close a - round you with the sod,
4. "Are ye a - ble?" still the Mas -ter Whispers down e - ter - ni - ty.

"Yea," the stur - dy dream-ers an-swered, "To the death we fol - low Thee."
That His par-doned soul is wor - thy Of a place in par - a - dise?
To be - lieve that spir - it tri-umphs, To com-mend your soul to God?
And he - ro - ic spir - its an - swer, Now, as then in Gal - i - lee,

REFRAIN

"Lord, we are a - ble." Our spir - its are Thine. Re - mold them;

make us like Thee, di - vine. Thy guid - ing ra - diance a - bove

us shall be A bea - con to God, To love and loy - al - ty.

15 Saviour, Like a Shepherd Lead Us

DOROTHY ANN THRUPP

WILLIAM B. BRADBURY

1. Sav-iour, like a Shep-herd lead us; Much we need Thy ten-der care.
2. We are Thine; do Thou be - friend us. Be the Guardian of our way;
3. Thou hast promised to re - ceive us, Poor and sin - ful tho' we be;
4. Ear - ly let us seek Thy fa - vor; Ear - ly let us do Thy will.

In Thy pleas-ant pas-tures feed us; For our use Thy folds pre - pare.
Keep Thy flock, from sin de - fend us; Seek us when we go a - stray.
Thou hast mer - cy to re - lieve us, Grace to cleanse, and pow'r to free.
Bless - ed Lord and on - ly Sav - iour, With Thy love our bos-oms fill.

Bless-ed Je-sus, Bless-ed Je-sus, Thou hast bought us, Thine we are;
Bless-ed Je-sus, Bless-ed Je-sus, Hear Thy chil - dren when they pray;
Bless-ed Je-sus, Bless-ed Je-sus, Ear - ly let us turn to Thee;
Bless-ed Je-sus, Bless-ed Je-sus, Thou hast loved us; love us still.

Bless - ed Je-sus, Bless - ed Je-sus, Thou hast bought us, Thine we are.
Bless - ed Je-sus, Bless - ed Je-sus, Hear Thy chil-dren when they pray.
Bless - ed Je-sus, Bless - ed Je-sus, Ear - ly let us turn to Thee.
Bless - ed Je-sus, Bless - ed Je-sus, Thou hast loved us; love us still.

16 My Faith Looks Up to Thee

RAY PALMER • LOWELL MASON

1. My faith looks up to Thee, Thou Lamb of Cal-va-ry,
2. May Thy rich grace im-part Strength to my faint-ing heart,
3. While life's dark maze I tread, And griefs a-round me spread,
4. When ends life's tran-sient dream, When death's cold, sul-len stream

Sav-iour di-vine! Now hear me while I pray, Take all my
My zeal in-spire. As Thou hast died for me, Oh, may my
Be Thou my Guide. Bid dark-ness turn to day; Wipe sor-row's
Shall o'er me roll, Blest Sav-iour, then in love Fear and dis-

guilt a-way; Oh, let me from this day Be whol-ly Thine!
love to Thee Pure, warm, and changeless be, A liv-ing fire!
tears a-way; Nor let me ev-er stray From Thee a-side!
trust re-move; Oh, bear me safe a-bove, A ran-somed soul!

17 Lamp of Our Feet

BERNARD D. BARTON • W. A. SCHULTHES

1. Lamp of our feet, where-by we trace Our path when wont to stray;
2. Bread of our souls, where-on we feed; True man-na from on high:
3. Pil-lar of fire, thro' watch-es dark, Or ra-diant cloud by day;
4. Word of the ev-er liv-ing God; Will of His glo-rious Son;
5. Lord, grant us all a-right to learn The wis-dom it im-parts,

Lamp of Our Feet

Stream from the fount of heav'n-ly grace, Brook by the trav-'ler's way;
Our guide and chart, where-in we read Of realms be-yond the sky;
When waves o'er-whelm our toss-ing bark, Our an-chor and our stay;
With-out thee how could earth be trod, Or heav'n it-self be won?
And to its heav'n-ly teach-ing turn With sim-ple, child-like hearts.

18 Higher Ground

JOHNSON OATMAN, JR.

CHAS. H. GABRIEL

1. I'm press-ing on the up-ward way. New heights I'm gaining ev-'ry day;
2. My heart has no de-sire to stay Where doubts arise and fears dis-may.
3. I want to live a-bove the world, Tho' Sa-tan's darts at me are hurled;
4. I want to scale the ut-most height, And catch a gleam of glo-ry bright;

Still pray-ing as I on-ward bound, "Lord, plant my feet on high-er ground."
Tho' some may dwell where these a-bound, My prayer, my aim, is high-er ground.
For faith has caught the joy-ful sound, The song of saints on high-er ground.
But still I'll pray till heav'n I've found, "Lord, lead me on to high-er ground."

CHORUS

Lord, lift me up and let me stand, By faith, on heav-en's ta-ble-land,

A high-er plane than I have found. Lord, plant my feet on high-er ground.

19 A Blessing in Prayer

E. E. HEWITT

WM. J. KIRKPATRICK

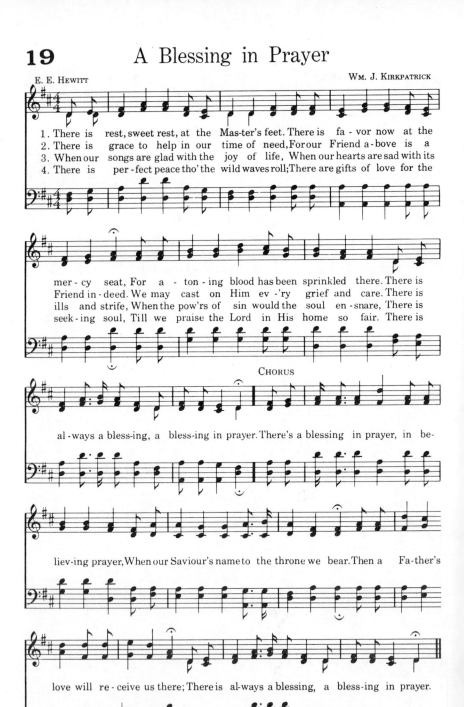

1. There is rest, sweet rest, at the Mas-ter's feet. There is fa - vor now at the
2. There is grace to help in our time of need, For our Friend a-bove is a
3. When our songs are glad with the joy of life, When our hearts are sad with its
4. There is per - fect peace tho' the wild waves roll; There are gifts of love for the

mer - cy seat, For a - ton - ing blood has been sprinkled there. There is
Friend in - deed. We may cast on Him ev -'ry grief and care. There is
ills and strife, When the pow'rs of sin would the soul en -snare, There is
seek - ing soul, Till we praise the Lord in His home so fair. There is

CHORUS

al -ways a bless-ing, a bless-ing in prayer. There's a blessing in prayer, in be-

liev-ing prayer, When our Saviour's name to the throne we bear. Then a Fa-ther's

love will re - ceive us there; There is al-ways a blessing, a bless-ing in prayer.

20 Wonderful Saviour

J. M. H.

J. M. HARRIS

1. Je - sus, my King, my won - der - ful Sav - iour, All of my life is
2. Freedom from sin, oh, won - der - ful sto - ry! All of its stains washed
3. Je - sus, my Lord, I'll ev - er a - dore Thee, Lay at Thy feet my
4. When in that bright and beau - ti - ful cit - y I shall be - hold Thy

giv - en to Thee. I am re - joic - ing in Thy sal - va - tion.
whit - er than snow! Je - sus has come to live in His tem - ple,
treasures of love. Lead me in ways to show forth Thy glo - ry,
glo - ries un - told, I shall be like Thee, won - der - ful Sav - iour,

CHORUS

Thy precious blood now mak - eth me free.
And with His love my heart is a - glow. Won - der - ful Sav - iour, won - der - ful
Ways that will end in heav - en a - bove.
And I will sing while a - ges un - fold.

Sav - iour, Thou art so near, so pre - cious to me! Won - der - ful

Sav - iour, won - der - ful Sav - iour, My heart is filled with prais - es to Thee.

21 Something for Jesus

S. D. PHELPS

ROBERT LOWRY

1. Sav - iour, Thy dy - ing love Thou gav-est me; Nor should I
2. At the blest mer - cy seat, Plead - ing for me, My fee - ble
3. Give me a faith - ful heart, Like - ness to Thee, That each de-
4. All that I am and have, Thy gifts so free, In joy, in

aught with-hold, Dear Lord, from Thee. In love my soul would bow, My
faith looks up, Je - sus, to Thee. Help me the cross to bear, Thy
part - ing day Hence-forth may see Some work of love be - gun, Some
grief, thro' life, Dear Lord, for Thee! And when Thy face I see, My

heart ful - fill its vow, Some off'ring bring Thee now, Something for Thee.
won-drous love de-clare, Some song to raise or prayer, Something for Thee.
deed of kind-ness done, Some wand'rer sought and won, Something for Thee.
ran-somed soul shall be, Thro' all e - ter - ni - ty, Something for Thee.

22 I Worship Thee, O Holy Ghost

W. F. WARREN

From GREATOREX'S "COLLECTION"

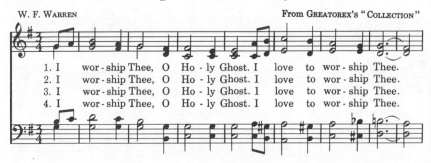

1. I wor - ship Thee, O Ho - ly Ghost. I love to wor - ship Thee.
2. I wor - ship Thee, O Ho - ly Ghost. I love to wor - ship Thee.
3. I wor - ship Thee, O Ho - ly Ghost. I love to wor - ship Thee.
4. I wor - ship Thee, O Ho - ly Ghost. I love to wor - ship Thee.

I Worship Thee, O Holy Ghost

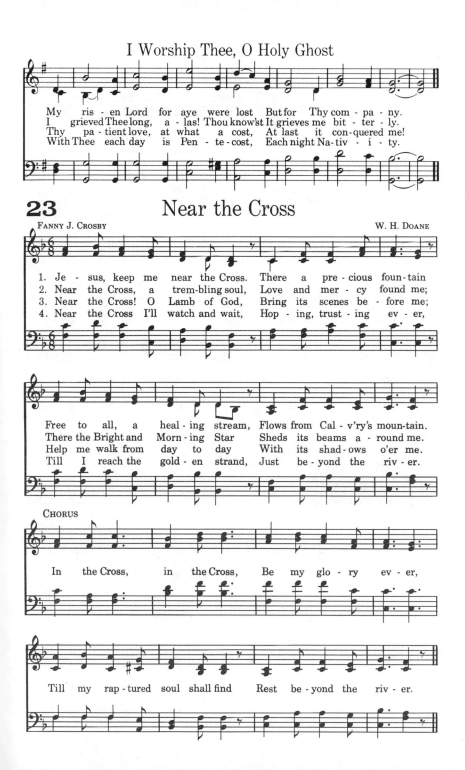

My ris - en Lord for aye were lost But for Thy com - pa - ny.
I grieved Thee long, a - las! Thou know'st It grieves me bit - ter - ly.
Thy pa - tient love, at what a cost, At last it con-quered me!
With Thee each day is Pen - te - cost, Each night Na- tiv - i - ty.

23 Near the Cross

FANNY J. CROSBY

W. H. DOANE

1. Je - sus, keep me near the Cross. There a pre - cious foun - tain
2. Near the Cross, a trem-bling soul, Love and mer - cy found me;
3. Near the Cross! O Lamb of God, Bring its scenes be - fore me;
4. Near the Cross I'll watch and wait, Hop - ing, trust - ing ev - er,

Free to all, a heal - ing stream, Flows from Cal - v'ry's moun-tain.
There the Bright and Morn - ing Star Sheds its beams a - round me.
Help me walk from day to day With its shad - ows o'er me.
Till I reach the gold - en strand, Just be - yond the riv - er.

CHORUS

In the Cross, in the Cross, Be my glo - ry ev - er,

Till my rap - tured soul shall find Rest be - yond the riv - er.

24 Sweet Will of God

MRS. C. H. M.

MRS. C. H. MORRIS

1. My stub-born will at last hath yield-ed; I would be Thine, and
2. I'm tired of sin, foot-sore and wea-ry; The dark-some path hath
3. Thy pre-cious will, O con-qu'ring Sav-iour, Doth now em-brace and
4. Shut in with Thee, O Lord, for-ev-er, My way-ward feet no

Thine a-lone; And this the prayer my lips are bring-ing,
drear-y grown. But now a light has ris'n to cheer me;
com-pass me; All dis-cords hushed, my peace a riv-er,
more to roam; What pow'r from Thee my soul can sev-er?

And this the prayer

rit. — **CHORUS**

"Lord, let in me Thy will be done."
I find in Thee my Star, my Sun.
My soul a pris-oned bird set free.
The cen-ter of God's will my home.

Sweet will of God, still

fold me clos-er, Till I am whol-ly lost in Thee. Sweet will of

God, still fold me clos-er, Till I am whol-ly lost in Thee.

25 Open My Eyes, That I May See

C. H. S.

CHAS. H. SCOTT

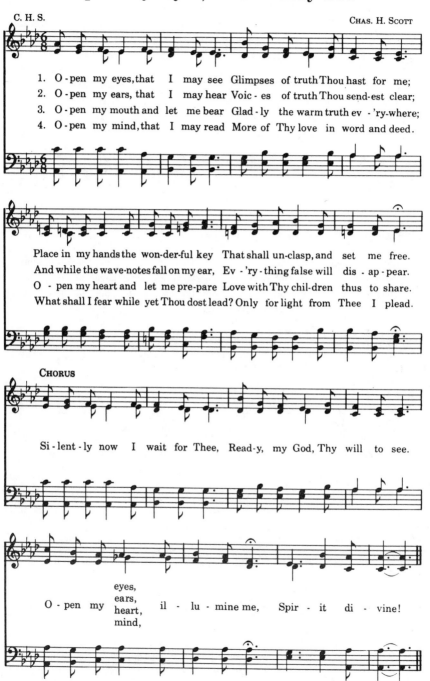

1. O - pen my eyes, that I may see Glimpses of truth Thou hast for me;
2. O - pen my ears, that I may hear Voic - es of truth Thou send-est clear;
3. O - pen my mouth and let me bear Glad - ly the warm truth ev - 'ry-where;
4. O - pen my mind, that I may read More of Thy love in word and deed.

Place in my hands the won-der-ful key That shall un-clasp, and set me free.
And while the wave-notes fall on my ear, Ev - 'ry-thing false will dis - ap-pear.
O - pen my heart and let me pre-pare Love with Thy chil-dren thus to share.
What shall I fear while yet Thou dost lead? Only for light from Thee I plead.

CHORUS

Si - lent - ly now I wait for Thee, Read - y, my God, Thy will to see.

O - pen my { eyes, ears, heart, mind, } il - lu - mine me, Spir - it di - vine!

26 Give Me Jesus

Fanny J. Crosby

Jno. R. Sweney

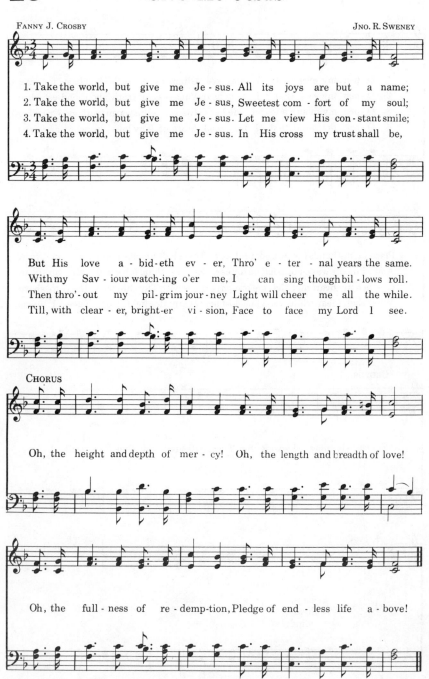

1. Take the world, but give me Je - sus. All its joys are but a name;
2. Take the world, but give me Je - sus, Sweetest com - fort of my soul;
3. Take the world, but give me Je - sus. Let me view His con - stant smile;
4. Take the world, but give me Je - sus. In His cross my trust shall be,

But His love a - bid-eth ev - er, Thro' e - ter - nal years the same.
With my Sav - iour watch-ing o'er me, I can sing though bil - lows roll.
Then thro'- out my pil- grim jour-ney Light will cheer me all the while.
Till, with clear - er, bright-er vi - sion, Face to face my Lord I see.

Chorus

Oh, the height and depth of mer - cy! Oh, the length and breadth of love!

Oh, the full - ness of re - demp-tion, Pledge of end - less life a - bove!

27   Sitting at the Feet of Jesus

J. H.

ASA HULL

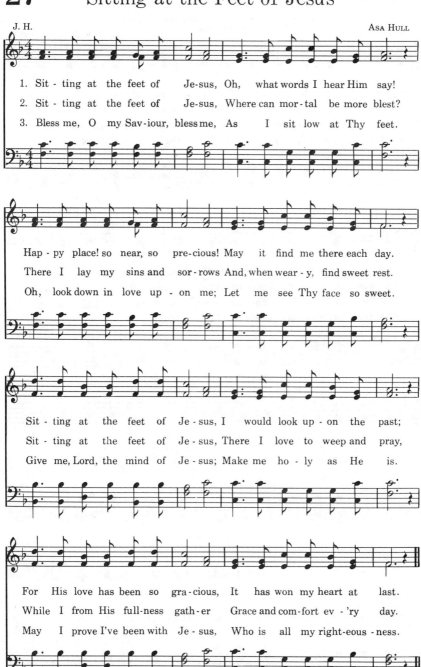

1. Sit - ting at the feet of   Je-sus, Oh,   what words I hear Him say!
2. Sit - ting at the feet of   Je-sus, Where can mor-tal be more blest?
3. Bless me, O my Sav-iour, bless me, As   I sit low at Thy feet.

Hap - py place! so near, so pre-cious! May it find me there each day.
There I lay my sins and sor-rows And, when wear - y, find sweet rest.
Oh, look down in love up - on me; Let me see Thy face so sweet.

Sit - ting at the feet of Je - sus, I would look up - on the past;
Sit - ting at the feet of Je - sus, There I love to weep and pray,
Give me, Lord, the mind of Je - sus; Make me ho - ly as He is.

For His love has been so gra-cious, It has won my heart at last.
While I from His full-ness gath-er Grace and com-fort ev - 'ry day.
May I prove I've been with Je - sus, Who is all my right-eous - ness.

28 Lead Me to Calvary

JENNIE EVELYN HUSSEY   WM. J. KIRKPATRICK

1. King of my life I crown Thee now; Thine shall the glo - ry be;
2. Show me the tomb where Thou wast laid, Ten - der - ly mourned and wept;
3. Let me, like Ma - ry, thro' the gloom Come with a gift to Thee.
4. May I be will - ing, Lord, to bear Dai - ly my cross for Thee;

Lest I for - get Thy thorn-crowned brow, Lead me to Cal - va - ry.
An - gels in robes of light ar - rayed Guard-ed Thee whilst Thou slept.
Show to me now the emp - ty tomb; Lead me to Cal - va - ry.
E - ven Thy cup of grief to share. Thou hast borne all for me.

CHORUS

Lest I for - get Geth - sem - a - ne, Lest I for - get Thine ag - o - ny,

Lest I for - get Thy love for me, Lead me to Cal - va - ry.

29 A Closer Walk with Thee

H. L.

HALDOR LILLENAS

1. Lord, I am plead - ing; hear Thou my prayer. Let me Thy bless - ed
2. Voic - es of earth un - num - bered I hear; Cares and per - plex - ing
3. Strong are the foes that con - quer I must. Long is the way, but
4. Glo - ri - ous Mas - ter, King of my soul, On Thee my bur - dens

fel - low - ship share. From day to day Thy serv - ant I'd be.
prob - lems are near. Trust - ing in Thee, my soul shall be free.
in Thee I trust. In my own strength but weak - ness I see.
glad - ly I roll. Thou art my por - tion e - ter - nal - ly.

CHORUS

Grant me a clos - er walk with Thee. Oh, for a clos - er

walk with Thee! Near to Thy side I ev - er would be. Shield me and

hide me; Con - stant - ly guide me In - to a clos - er walk with Thee.

30   O Day of Rest and Gladness

C. WORDSWORTH   ARR. BY LOWELL MASON

1. O day of rest and glad-ness, O day of joy and light,
2. On thee at the cre - a - tion The light first had its birth;
3. O day of sweet re - flec-tion, Thou art a day of love;
4. New grac - es ev - er gain-ing From this our day of rest,

O balm of care and sad-ness, Most beau - ti - ful, most bright;
On thee for our sal - va-tion Christ rose from depths of earth;
O day of res - ur - rec-tion From earth to things a - bove,
We reach the rest re - main-ing To spir - its of the blest.

On thee the high and low - ly, Bend - ing be - fore the throne, Sing,
On thee, our Lord, vic - to -rious, The Spir - it sent from heav'n; And
When gos - pel light is glow-ing With pure and ra - diant beams, And
To Ho - ly Ghost be prais - es, To Fa - ther and to Son; The

"Ho - ly, Ho - ly, Ho - ly," To the great Three in One.
thus on thee, most glo-rious, A three - fold light is giv'n.
liv - ing wa - ters flow-ing With soul - re - fresh-ing streams.
Church her voice up - rais - es To Thee, blest Three in One.

31   Love Divine

CHARLES WESLEY

JOHN ZUNDEL

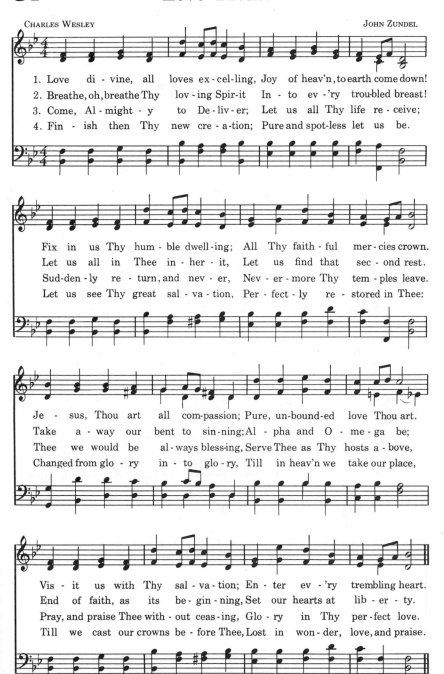

1. Love di - vine, all loves ex - cel - ling, Joy of heav'n, to earth come down!
2. Breathe, oh, breathe Thy lov - ing Spir-it In - to ev - 'ry trou-bled breast!
3. Come, Al - might - y to De - liv - er; Let us all Thy life re - ceive;
4. Fin - ish then Thy new cre - a - tion; Pure and spot-less let us be.

Fix in us Thy hum - ble dwell - ing; All Thy faith - ful mer - cies crown.
Let us all in Thee in - her - it, Let us find that sec - ond rest.
Sud-den - ly re - turn, and nev - er, Nev - er - more Thy tem - ples leave.
Let us see Thy great sal - va - tion, Per - fect - ly re - stored in Thee:

Je - sus, Thou art all com-passion; Pure, un-bound-ed love Thou art.
Take a - way our bent to sin-ning; Al - pha and O - me - ga be;
Thee we would be al - ways bless-ing, Serve Thee as Thy hosts a - bove,
Changed from glo - ry in - to glo - ry, Till in heav'n we take our place,

Vis - it us with Thy sal - va - tion; En - ter ev - 'ry trembling heart.
End of faith, as its be - gin - ning, Set our hearts at lib - er - ty.
Pray, and praise Thee with - out ceas-ing, Glo - ry in Thy per-fect love.
Till we cast our crowns be - fore Thee, Lost in won - der, love, and praise.

32 There's a Wideness

F. W. FABER

LIZZIE S. TOURJEE

1. There's a wide-ness in God's mer-cy Like the wide-ness of the sea;
2. There is wel-come for the sin-ner, And more grac-es for the good;
3. For the love of God is broad-er Than the meas-ure of man's mind;
4. If our love were but more sim-ple, We should take Him at His word;

There's a kind-ness in His jus-tice Which is more than lib-er-ty.
There is mer-cy with the Sav-iour; There is heal-ing in His blood.
And the heart of the E-ter-nal Is most won-der-ful-ly kind.
And our lives would be all sun-shine In the sweet-ness of our Lord.

33 Oh, for a Heart to Praise My God!

CHARLES WESLEY

CARL G. GLAZER

1. Oh, for a heart to praise my God, A heart from sin set free,
2. A heart re-signed, sub-mis-sive, meek, My great Re-deem-er's throne,
3. Oh, for a low-ly, con-trite heart, Be-liev-ing, true, and clean,
4. A heart in ev-'ry tho't re-newed, And full of love di-vine;

A heart that al-ways feels Thy blood So free-ly shed for me!
Where on-ly Christ is heard to speak, Where Je-sus reigns a-lone.
Which nei-ther life nor death can part From Him that dwells with-in!
Per-fect, and right, and pure, and good: A cop-y, Lord, of Thine.

34   Jesus, I'll Go Through with Thee

Mrs. E. E. Williams   H. L. Gilmour

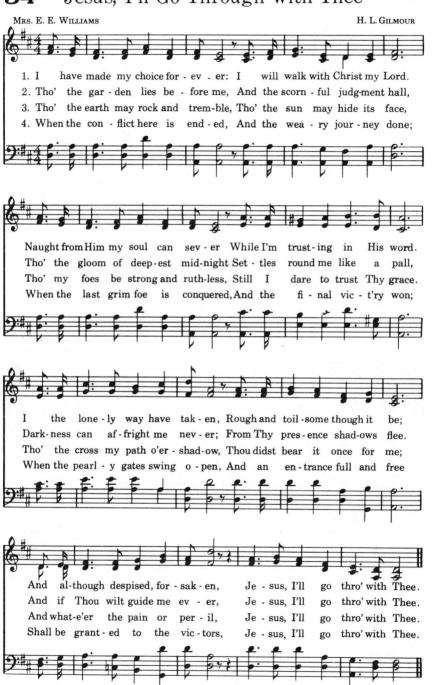

1. I have made my choice for-ev-er: I will walk with Christ my Lord.
2. Tho' the gar-den lies be-fore me, And the scorn-ful judg-ment hall,
3. Tho' the earth may rock and trem-ble, Tho' the sun may hide its face,
4. When the con-flict here is end-ed, And the wea-ry jour-ney done;

Naught from Him my soul can sev-er While I'm trust-ing in His word.
Tho' the gloom of deep-est mid-night Set-tles round me like a pall,
Tho' my foes be strong and ruth-less, Still I dare to trust Thy grace.
When the last grim foe is conquered, And the fi-nal vic-t'ry won;

I the lone-ly way have tak-en, Rough and toil-some though it be;
Dark-ness can af-fright me nev-er; From Thy pres-ence shad-ows flee.
Tho' the cross my path o'er-shad-ow, Thou didst bear it once for me;
When the pearl-y gates swing o-pen, And an en-trance full and free

And al-though despised, for-sak-en, Je-sus, I'll go thro' with Thee.
And if Thou wilt guide me ev-er, Je-sus, I'll go thro' with Thee.
And what-e'er the pain or per-il, Je-sus, I'll go thro' with Thee.
Shall be grant-ed to the vic-tors, Je-sus, I'll go thro' with Thee.

35 God Moves in a Mysterious Way

WILLIAM COWPER

From GREATOREX'S "COLLECTION"

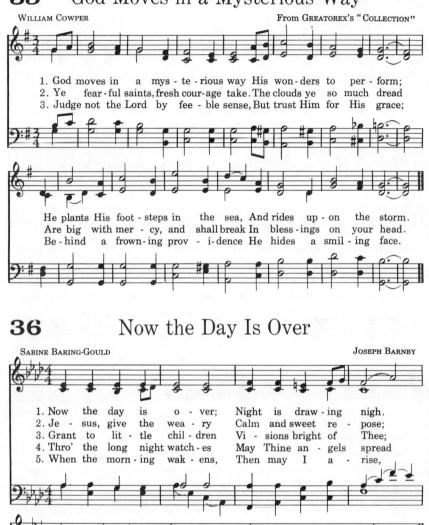

1. God moves in a mys-te-rious way His won-ders to per-form;
2. Ye fear-ful saints, fresh cour-age take. The clouds ye so much dread
3. Judge not the Lord by fee-ble sense, But trust Him for His grace;

He plants His foot-steps in the sea, And rides up-on the storm.
Are big with mer-cy, and shall break In bless-ings on your head.
Be-hind a frown-ing prov-i-dence He hides a smil-ing face.

36 Now the Day Is Over

SABINE BARING-GOULD

JOSEPH BARNBY

1. Now the day is o-ver; Night is draw-ing nigh.
2. Je-sus, give the wea-ry Calm and sweet re-pose;
3. Grant to lit-tle chil-dren Vi-sions bright of Thee;
4. Thro' the long night watch-es May Thine an-gels spread
5. When the morn-ing wak-ens, Then may I a-rise,

Shad-ows of the eve-ning Steal a-cross the sky.
With Thy ten-d'rest bless-ing May our eye-lids close.
Guard the sail-ors toss-ing On the deep, blue sea.
Their white wings a-bove me, Watch-ing 'round my bed.
Pure and fresh and sin-less In Thy ho-ly eyes.

ev'ning Steal a-cross the sky.

37 In Life's Quiet Hours

Copyright 1929 by Lillenas Publishing Co.

FRA MORTON SIMS

HALDOR LILLENAS

1. Of - ten while in med - i - ta - tion On His love so free,
2. Or it may be I have strug-gled Thro' some tri - al sore;
3. Or per-chance while I am wait-ing Still on bend - ed knee,
4. At my work or in my clos - et—Al - most an - y - where—

Comes a mes - sage from my Fa - ther Spo - ken just to me.
When my strug-gling turns to trust - ing, Lo, the tri'l is o'er.
Comes a qui - et rev - e - la - tion Of His love for me.
If in qui - et - ness I lis - ten, I find Je - sus there.

CHORUS

In life's qui - et hours I find Him Wait - ing for my call.

It is there He meets me, greets me, Holds me lest I fall.

38 I Do Not Ask to Choose My Path

J. H. ZELLEY   H. L. GILMOUR

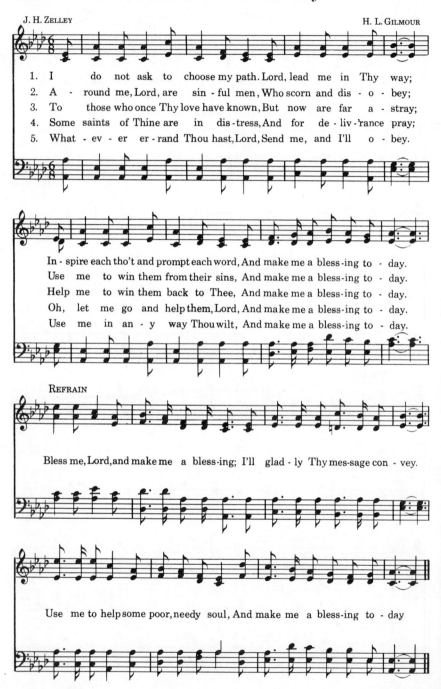

1. I   do not ask to   choose my path. Lord, lead me in Thy   way;
2. A -   round me, Lord, are   sin - ful men, Who scorn and dis - o - bey;
3. To   those who once Thy love have known, But now   are far a - stray;
4. Some saints of Thine are   in dis - tress, And for de - liv - 'rance pray;
5. What - ev - er er - rand Thou hast, Lord, Send me, and I'll   o - bey.

In - spire each tho't and prompt each word, And make me a bless-ing to - day.
Use   me to win them from their sins, And make me a bless-ing to - day.
Help me to win them back to Thee, And make me a bless-ing to - day.
Oh, let me go and help them, Lord, And make me a bless-ing to - day.
Use   me in an - y   way Thou wilt, And make me a bless-ing to - day.

REFRAIN

Bless me, Lord, and make me   a bless-ing; I'll   glad - ly Thy mes-sage con - vey.

Use   me to help some poor, needy soul, And make me a bless-ing to - day

39 The Beautiful Garden of Prayer

ELEANOR ALLEN SCHROLL

J. H. FILLMORE

1. There's a gar-den where Je-sus is wait-ing. There's a place that is
2. There's a gar-den where Je-sus is wait-ing, And I go with my
3. There's a gar-den where Je-sus is wait-ing, And He bids you to

won-drous-ly fair, For it glows with the light of His pres-ence. 'Tis the
bur-den and care, Just to learn from His lips words of com-fort In the
come, meet Him there; Just to bow and re-ceive a new bless-ing In the

REFRAIN

beau-ti-ful gar-den of prayer. Oh, the beau-ti-ful gar-den, the

gar-den of prayer! Oh, the beau-ti-ful gar-den of prayer! There my Sav-iour a-

waits, and He o-pens the gates To the beau-ti-ful gar-den of prayer.

40

Oh, Worship the King

Robert Grant

J. Michael Haydn

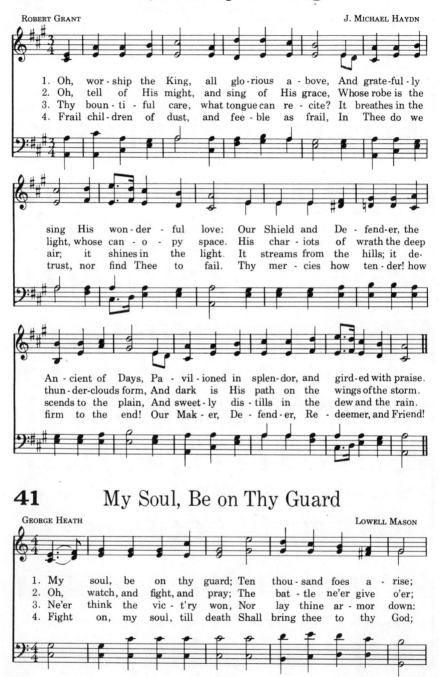

1. Oh, wor-ship the King, all glo-rious a-bove, And grate-ful-ly
2. Oh, tell of His might, and sing of His grace, Whose robe is the
3. Thy boun-ti-ful care, what tongue can re-cite? It breathes in the
4. Frail chil-dren of dust, and fee-ble as frail, In Thee do we

sing His won-der-ful love: Our Shield and De-fend-er, the
light, whose can-o-py space. His char-iots of wrath the deep
air; it shines in the light. It streams from the hills; it de-
trust, nor find Thee to fail. Thy mer-cies how ten-der! how

An-cient of Days, Pa-vil-ioned in splen-dor, and gird-ed with praise.
thun-der-clouds form, And dark is His path on the wings of the storm.
scends to the plain, And sweet-ly dis-tills in the dew and the rain.
firm to the end! Our Mak-er, De-fend-er, Re-deemer, and Friend!

41

My Soul, Be on Thy Guard

George Heath

Lowell Mason

1. My soul, be on thy guard; Ten thou-sand foes a-rise;
2. Oh, watch, and fight, and pray; The bat-tle ne'er give o'er;
3. Ne'er think the vic-t'ry won, Nor lay thine ar-mor down;
4. Fight on, my soul, till death Shall bring thee to thy God;

My Soul, Be on Thy Guard

The hosts of sin are press-ing hard To draw thee from the skies.
Re - new it bold - ly ev - 'ry day, And help di - vine im - plore.
The work of faith will not be done Till thou ob - tain the crown.
He'll take thee, at thy part-ing breath, To His di - vine a - bode.

42   O Jesus, I Have Promised

JOHN E. BODE   ARTHUR H. MANN

1. O Je - sus, I have prom - ised To serve Thee to the end. Be
2. Oh, let me feel Thee near me. The world is ev - er near; I
3. O Je - sus, Thou hast prom - ised To all who fol - low Thee That

Thou for - ev - er near me, My Mas - ter and my Friend. I
see the sights that daz - zle, The tempt - ing sounds I hear. My
where Thou art in glo - ry There shall Thy serv - ant be; And,

shall not fear the bat - tle If Thou art by my side, Nor
foes are ev - er near me, A - round me and with - in. But,
Je - sus, I have prom-ised To serve Thee to the end. Oh,

wan - der from the path-way If Thou wilt be my Guide.
Je - sus, draw Thou near - er, And shield my soul from sin.
give me grace to fol - low, My Mas - ter and my Friend.

43   Safe in the Arms of Jesus

FANNY J. CROSBY

W. H. DOANE

1. Safe in the arms of Je - sus, Safe on His gen - tle breast—
2. Safe in the arms of Je - sus, Safe from cor - rod - ing care,
3. Je - sus, my heart's dear Ref - uge, Je - sus has died for me.

There, by His love o'er - shad - ed, Sweet - ly my soul shall rest.
Safe from the world's temp - ta - tions, Sin can - not harm me there.
Firm on the Rock of A - ges Ev - er my trust shall be.

Hark! 'tis the voice of an - gels, Borne in a song to me,
Free from the blight of sor - row, Free from my doubts and fears!
Here let me wait with pa - tience; Wait till the night is o'er;

O - ver the fields of glo - ry, O - ver the jas - per sea.
On - ly a few more tri - als, On - ly a few more tears!
Wait till I see the morn - ing Break on the gold - en shore.

CHORUS

Safe in the arms of Je - sus, Safe on His gen - tle breast—

Safe in the Arms of Jesus

There, by His love o'er - shad - ed, Sweet - ly my soul shall rest.

44 There Is a Green Hill Far Away

CECIL F. ALEXANDER   GEO. C. STEBBINS

1 There is a green hill far a - way, With - out a cit - y wall,
2. We may not know, we can - not tell What pains He had to bear;
3. He died that we might be for - giv'n, He died to make us good,
4. There was no oth - er good e - nough To pay the price of sin;

Where the dear Lord was cru - ci - fied, Who died to save us all.
But we be - lieve it was for us He hung and suf - fered there.
That we might go at last to heav'n, Saved by His pre - cious blood.
He on - ly could un - lock the gate Of heav'n and let us in.

CHORUS

Oh, dear - ly, dear - ly has He loved, And we must love Him, too;

And trust in His re - deem - ing blood, And try His works to do.

45 I Know I Love Thee Better, Lord

Frances R. Havergal

R. E. Hudson

1. I know I love Thee bet-ter, Lord, Than an - y earth-ly joy;
2. I know that Thou art near-er still Than an - y earth-ly throng;
3. Thou hast put glad-ness in my heart; Then may I well be glad!
4. O Sav-iour, pre-cious Sav-iour mine! What will Thy pres-ence be,

For Thou hast giv-en me the peace Which noth-ing can de - stroy.
And sweet-er is the tho't of Thee Than an - y love-ly song.
With-out the se-cret of Thy love I could not but be sad.
If such a life of joy can crown Our walk on earth with Thee?

CHORUS

The half has nev - er yet been told Of love so full and free!

yet been told

The half has nev-er yet been told. The Blood — it cleanseth me!

yet been told. cleanseth me!

46 The Call for Reapers

J. O. THOMPSON

J. B. O. CLEMM

1. Far and near the fields are teem - ing With the waves of
   ri - pened grain; Far and near their gold is gleam - ing
   O'er the sun - ny slope and plain.

2. Send them forth with morn's first beam - ing; Send them in the
   noon - tide's glare; When the sun's last rays are gleam - ing,
   Bid them gath - er ev - 'ry - where.

3. O thou whom thy Lord is send - ing, Gath - er now the
   sheaves of gold; Heav'n - ward then at eve - ning wend - ing,
   Thou shalt come with joy un - told.

CHORUS

Lord of har - vest, send forth reap - ers! Hear us, Lord; to Thee we cry. Send them now the sheaves to gath - er, Ere the har - vest - time pass by.

47 I Am Thine, O Lord

FANNY J. CROSBY

W. H. DOANE

1. I am Thine, O Lord; I have heard Thy voice, And it told Thy
2. Con - se - crate me now to Thy ser - vice, Lord, By the pow'r of
3. Oh, the pure de - light of a sin - gle hour That be - fore Thy
4. There are depths of love that I can - not know Till I cross the

love to me. But I long to rise in the arms of faith, And be
grace di - vine. Let my soul look up with a stead-fast hope, And my
throne I spend, When I kneel in prayer and with Thee, my God, I com -
nar - row sea; There are heights of joy that I may not reach Till I

clos - er drawn to Thee.
will be lost in Thine.
mune as friend with friend!
rest in peace with Thee.

REFRAIN

Draw me near - er, near - er, bless - ed
near - er, near - er,

Lord, To the cross where Thou hast died. Draw me near - er, near - er,

near - er, bless - ed Lord, To Thy pre - cious, bleed - ing side.

48   I Love Thy Kingdom, Lord

TIMOTHY DWIGHT
AARON WILLIAMS

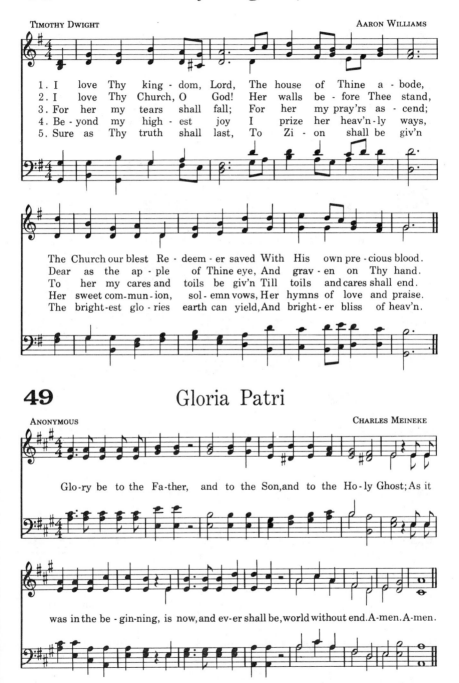

1. I love Thy king - dom, Lord, The house of Thine a - bode,
2. I love Thy Church, O God! Her walls be - fore Thee stand,
3. For her my tears shall fall; For her my pray'rs as - cend;
4. Be - yond my high - est joy I prize her heav'n - ly ways,
5. Sure as Thy truth shall last, To Zi - on shall be giv'n

The Church our blest Re - deem - er saved With His own pre - cious blood.
Dear as the ap - ple of Thine eye, And grav - en on Thy hand.
To her my cares and toils be giv'n Till toils and cares shall end.
Her sweet com-mun - ion, sol - emn vows, Her hymns of love and praise.
The bright-est glo - ries earth can yield, And bright - er bliss of heav'n.

49   Gloria Patri

ANONYMOUS
CHARLES MEINEKE

Glo-ry be to the Fa-ther, and to the Son, and to the Ho-ly Ghost; As it

was in the be - gin-ning, is now, and ev-er shall be, world without end. A-men. A-men.

50 Nearer, My God, to Thee

SARAH F. ADAMS

LOWELL MASON

1. Near - er, my God, to Thee, Near - er to Thee! E'en though it
2. Though like the wan - der - er, The sun gone down, Dark-ness be
3. There let the way ap-pear, Steps un - to heav'n: All that Thou
4. Then, with my wak - ing tho'ts Bright with Thy praise, Out of my
5. Or if on joy - ful wing, Cleav-ing the sky, Sun, moon, and

be a cross That rais - eth me; Still all my song shall be,
o - ver me, My rest a stone; Yet in my dreams I'd be
send-est me In mer - cy giv'n: An - gels to beck - on me
ston - y griefs Beth - el I'll raise; So by my woes to be
stars for-got, Up - ward I fly, Still all my song shall be,

Near-er, my God, to Thee; Near - er, my God, to Thee; Near - er to Thee!

51 Forever Here My Rest Shall Be

CHARLES WESLEY

HUGH WILSON

1. For - ev - er here my rest shall be, Close to Thy bleed-ing side.
2. My dy - ing Sav - iour, and my God, Foun-tain for guilt and sin,
3. Wash me, and make me thus Thine own; Wash me, and mine Thou art;
4. The atone-ment of Thy blood ap - ply, Till faith to sight im-prove;

Forever Here My Rest Shall Be

This all my hope, and all my plea,"For me the Sav-iour died."
Sprin-kle me ev - er with Thy blood, And cleanse,and keep me clean.
Wash me, but not my feet a - lone—My hands, my head, my heart.
Till hope in full fru - i - tion die, And all my soul be love.

52 My Jesus, I Love Thee

WM. R. FEATHERSTONE   A. J. GORDON

1. My Je - sus, I love Thee; I know Thou art mine. For Thee all the
2. I love Thee be - cause Thou hast first lov-ed me, And purchased my
3. I will love Thee in life, I will love Thee in death, And praise Thee as
4. In man-sions of glo - ry and end-less de-light, I'll ev - er a-

fol - lies of sin I re - sign. My gra-cious Re - deem- er, my
par - don on Cal - va - ry's tree. I love Thee for wear - ing the
long as Thou lend-est me breath; And say when the death-dew lies
dore Thee in heav - en so bright; I'll sing with the glit - ter-ing

Sav - iour art Thou. If ev - er I loved Thee, my Je - sus,'tis now.
thorns on Thy brow. If ev - er I loved Thee, my Je - sus,'tis now.
cold on my brow, "If ev - er I loved Thee, my Je - sus,'tis now."
crown on my brow, "If ev - er I loved Thee, my Je - sus,'tis now."

53   Blessed Quietness

MANIE PAYNE FERGUSON

ARR. FROM MARSHALL

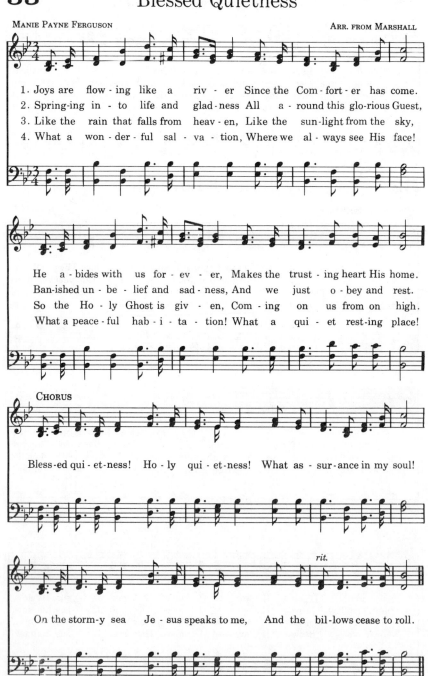

1. Joys are flow-ing like a riv-er Since the Com-fort-er has come.
2. Spring-ing in-to life and glad-ness All a-round this glo-rious Guest,
3. Like the rain that falls from heav-en, Like the sun-light from the sky,
4. What a won-der-ful sal-va-tion, Where we al-ways see His face!

He a-bides with us for-ev-er, Makes the trust-ing heart His home.
Ban-ished un-be-lief and sad-ness, And we just o-bey and rest.
So the Ho-ly Ghost is giv-en, Com-ing on us from on high.
What a peace-ful hab-i-ta-tion! What a qui-et rest-ing place!

CHORUS

Bless-ed qui-et-ness! Ho-ly qui-et-ness! What as-sur-ance in my soul!

rit.

On the storm-y sea Je-sus speaks to me, And the bil-lows cease to roll.

54   A Charge to Keep I Have

CHARLES WESLEY   LOWELL MASON

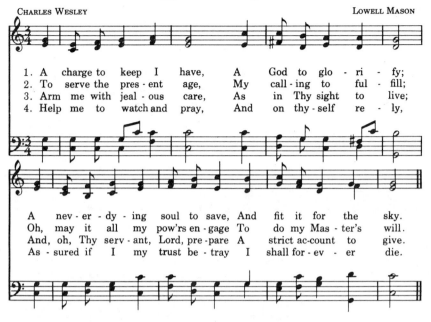

1. A charge to keep I have, A God to glo - ri - fy;
2. To serve the pres - ent age, My call - ing to ful - fill;
3. Arm me with jeal - ous care, As in Thy sight to live;
4. Help me to watch and pray, And on thy - self re - ly,

A nev - er - dy - ing soul to save, And fit it for the sky.
Oh, may it all my pow'rs en - gage To do my Mas - ter's will.
And, oh, Thy serv - ant, Lord, pre - pare A strict ac-count to give.
As - sured if I my trust be - tray I shall for - ev - er die.

55   Majestic Sweetness

SAMUEL STENNETT   THOMAS HASTINGS

1. Ma - jes - tic sweetness sits enthroned Up-on the Saviour's brow; His head with
2. No mor - tal can with Him compare A-mong the sons of men; Fair-er is
3. He saw me plunged in deep dis-tress, And flew to my re - lief; For me He
4. To Him I owe my life and breath And all the joys I have; He makes me
5. Since from His boun-ty I re-ceive Such proofs of love di - vine, Had I a

ra - diant glories crowned, His lips with grace o'er-flow, His lips with grace o'er-flow.
He than all the fair Who fill the heav'nly train, Who fill the heav'nly train.
bore the shameful cross, And car-ried all my grief, And car-ried all my grief.
tri - umph o - ver death, And saves me from the grave, And saves me from the grave.
thousand hearts to give, Lord, they should all be Thine; Lord, they should all be Thine.

56 Come, Thou Fount

ROBERT ROBINSON

ASAHEL NETTLETON

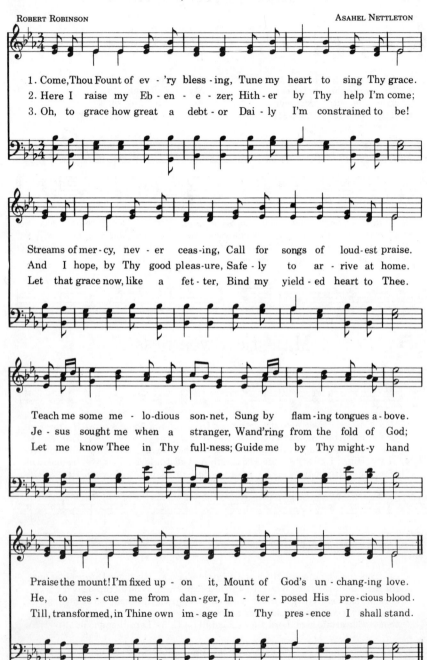

1. Come, Thou Fount of ev - 'ry bless - ing, Tune my heart to sing Thy grace.
2. Here I raise my Eb - en - e - zer; Hith - er by Thy help I'm come;
3. Oh, to grace how great a debt - or Dai - ly I'm constrained to be!

Streams of mer - cy, nev - er ceas-ing, Call for songs of loud-est praise.
And I hope, by Thy good pleas-ure, Safe - ly to ar - rive at home.
Let that grace now, like a fet - ter, Bind my yield - ed heart to Thee.

Teach me some me - lo-dious son-net, Sung by flam-ing tongues a - bove.
Je - sus sought me when a stranger, Wand'ring from the fold of God;
Let me know Thee in Thy full-ness; Guide me by Thy might-y hand

Praise the mount! I'm fixed up - on it, Mount of God's un - chang-ing love.
He, to res - cue me from dan-ger, In - ter - posed His pre-cious blood.
Till, transformed, in Thine own im - age In Thy pres - ence I shall stand.

57 In the Cross of Christ

JOHN BOWRING

ITHAMAR CONKEY

1. In the cross of Christ I glo-ry, Tow'r-ing o'er the wrecks of time.
2. When the woes of life o'er-take me, Hopes de-ceive, and fears an-noy,
3. When the sun of bliss is beam-ing Light and love up-on my way,
4. Bane and bless-ing, pain and pleas-ure, By the Cross are sanc-ti-fied;

All the light of sa-cred sto-ry Gath-ers round its head sub-lime.
Nev-er shall the Cross for-sake me. Lo! it glows with peace and joy.
From the Cross the ra-diance streaming Adds more lus-ter to the day.
Peace is there that knows no meas-ure, Joys that thro' all time a-bide.

58 O God, Our Help in Ages Past

ISAAC WATTS

WILLIAM CROFT

1. O God, our Help in a-ges past, Our Hope for years to come,
2. Un-der the shad-ow of Thy throne Still may we dwell se-cure;
3. Be-fore the hills in or-der stood, Or earth re-ceived her frame,
4. O God, our Help in a-ges past, Our Hope for years to come,

Our Shel-ter from the storm-y blast, And our e-ter-nal Home!
Suf-fi-cient is Thine arm a-lone, And our de-fense is sure.
From ev-er-last-ing Thou art God, To end-less years the same.
Be Thou our Guide while life shall last, And our e-ter-nal Home.

59 In Heavenly Love Abiding

ANNA L. WARING

S. S. WESLEY

1. In heav'n-ly love a - bid - ing, No change my heart shall fear;
2. Wher - ev - er He may guide me, No want shall turn me back;
3. Green pas - tures are be - fore me Which yet I have not seen.

And safe is such con - fid - ing, For noth - ing chang - es here.
My Shep - herd is be - side me, And noth - ing can I lack.
Bright skies will soon be o'er me, Where dark - est clouds have been.

The storm may roar with - out me, My heart may low be laid,
His wis - dom ev - er wak - eth; His sight is nev - er dim.
My hope I can - not meas - ure. My path to life is free.

But God is round a - bout me, And can I be dis - mayed!
He knows the way He tak - eth, And I will walk with Him.
My Sav - iour has my treas - ure, And He will walk with me.

60   The Rock That Is Higher than I

ERASTUS JOHNSON

WILLIAM G. FISCHER

1. Oh, some-times the shadows are deep, And rough seems the path to the goal;
2. Oh, some-times how long seems the day, And some-times how wea-ry my feet!
3. Oh, near to the Rock let me keep If bless-ings or sor-rows pre-vail,

And sor-rows, sometimes how they sweep Like tempests down o-ver the soul!
But toil-ing in life's dust-y way, The Rock's blessed shadow, how sweet!
Or climb-ing the moun-tain way steep, Or walk-ing the shad-ow-y vale.

REFRAIN

Oh, then to the Rock let me fly,
let me fly,
To the Rock that is high-er than I!
is high-er than I!
Oh, then to the Rock let me fly,
let me fly,
To the Rock that is high-er than I!

61

More Love to Thee

Elizabeth Prentiss

W. H. Doane

1. More love to Thee, O Christ, More love to Thee! Hear Thou the prayer I make On bend-ed knee; This is my ear-nest plea:
2. Once earth-ly joy I craved, Sought peace and rest. Now Thee a-lone I seek; Give what is best. This all my prayer shall be:
3. Then shall my lat-est breath Whis-per Thy praise. This be the part-ing cry My heart shall raise; This still its prayer shall be:

More love, O Christ, to Thee; More love to Thee, More love to Thee!

62

Down to the Sacred Wave

S. F. Smith

J. C. Woodman

1. Down to the sa-cred wave The Lord of Life was led; And He who came our souls to save In Jor-dan bowed His head.
2. He taught the sol-emn way; He fixed the ho-ly rite; He bade His ran-somed ones o-bey, And keep the path of light.
3. Blest Sav-iour, we will tread In Thy ap-point-ed way. Let glo-ry o'er these scenes be shed, And smile on us to-day.

63

What a Friend

JOSEPH SCRIVEN

CHARLES C. CONVERSE

1. What a Friend we have in Je-sus, All our sins and griefs to bear!
2. Have we tri-als and temp-ta-tions? Is there trou-ble an-y-where?
3. Are we weak and heav-y-la-den, Cumbered with a load of care?

What a priv-i-lege to car-ry Ev-'ry-thing to God in pray'r!
We should nev-er be dis-cour-aged; Take it to the Lord in pray'r.
Pre-cious Sav-iour, still our Ref-uge! — Take it to the Lord in pray'r.

Oh, what peace we of-ten for-feit, Oh, what needless pain we bear,
Can we find a friend so faith-ful Who will all our sor-rows share?
Do thy friends despise, for-sake thee? Take it to the Lord in pray'r.

All be-cause we do not car-ry Ev-'ry-thing to God in pray'r!
Je-sus knows our ev-'ry weak-ness; Take it to the Lord in pray'r.
In His arms He'll take and shield thee; Thou wilt find a sol-ace there.

64 Meditation

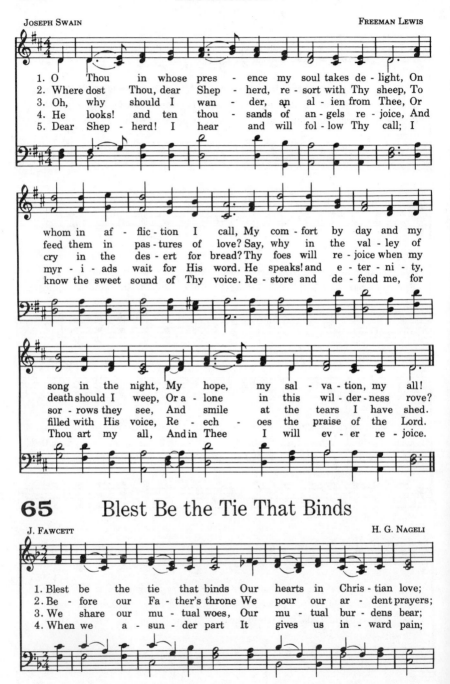

JOSEPH SWAIN

FREEMAN LEWIS

1. O Thou in whose pres - ence my soul takes de - light, On
2. Where dost Thou, dear Shep - herd, re - sort with Thy sheep, To
3. Oh, why should I wan - der, an al - ien from Thee, Or
4. He looks! and ten thou - sands of an - gels re - joice, And
5. Dear Shep - herd! I hear and will fol - low Thy call; I

whom in af - flic - tion I call, My com - fort by day and my
feed them in pas - tures of love? Say, why in the val - ley of
cry in the des - ert for bread? Thy foes will re - joice when my
myr - i - ads wait for His word. He speaks! and e - ter - ni - ty,
know the sweet sound of Thy voice. Re - store and de - fend me, for

song in the night, My hope, my sal - va - tion, my all!
death should I weep, Or a - lone in this wil - der - ness rove?
sor - rows they see, And smile at the tears I have shed.
filled with His voice, Re - ech - oes the praise of the Lord.
Thou art my all, And in Thee I will ev - er re - joice.

65 Blest Be the Tie That Binds

J. FAWCETT

H. G. NAGELI

1. Blest be the tie that binds Our hearts in Chris - tian love;
2. Be - fore our Fa - ther's throne We pour our ar - dent prayers;
3. We share our mu - tual woes, Our mu - tual bur - dens bear;
4. When we a - sun - der part It gives us in - ward pain;

Blest Be the Tie That Binds

The fel-low-ship of kin-dred minds Is like to that a-bove.
Our fears, our hopes, our aims are one, Our com-forts and our cares.
And of-ten for each oth-er flows The sym-pa-thiz-ing tear.
But we shall still be joined in heart, And hope to meet a-gain.

66 Lead On, O King Eternal

ERNEST W. SHURTLEFF

HENRY SMART

1. Lead on, O King E-ter-nal. The day of march has come;
2. Lead on, O King E-ter-nal, Till sin's fierce war shall cease,
3. Lead on, O King E-ter-nal. We fol-low, not with fears;

Henceforth in fields of con-quest Thy tents shall be our home.
And ho-li-ness shall whis-per The sweet A-men of peace;
For glad-ness breaks like morn-ing Wher-e'er Thy face ap-pears.

Thro' days of prep-a-ra-tion Thy grace has made us strong;
For not with swords' loud clash-ing, Nor roll of stir-ring drums;
Thy cross is lift-ed o'er us; We jour-ney in its light.

And now, O King E-ter-nal, We lift our bat-tle song.
With deeds of love and mer-cy, The heav'n-ly King-dom comes.
The crown a-waits the con-quest; Lead on, O God of might.

67   O Sacred Head, Now Wounded

Tr. by J. W. Alexander   Arr. by Lowell Mason

1. O sa-cred Head, now wound-ed, With grief and shame weighed down,
2. What Thou, my Lord, hast suf-fered Was all for sin-ners' gain.
3. What lan-guage shall I bor-row To thank Thee, dear-est Friend,
4. Be near me when I'm dy-ing; Oh, show Thy cross to me;

Now scorn-ful-ly sur-round-ed With thorns, Thine on-ly crown;
Mine, mine was the trans-gres-sion, But Thine the dead-ly pain.
For this Thy dy-ing sor-row, Thy pit-y with-out end?
And, for my suc-cor fly-ing, Come, Lord, and set me free.

O sa-cred Head, what glo-ry, What bliss till now was Thine!
Lo, here I fall, my Sav-iour! 'Tis I de-serve Thy place.
Oh, make me Thine for-ev-er; And, should I faint-ing be,
These eyes new faith re-ceiv-ing, From Je-sus shall not move;

Yet, tho' de-spised and gor-y, I joy to call Thee mine.
Look on me with Thy fa-vor; Vouchsafe to me Thy grace.
Lord, let me nev-er, nev-er Out-live my love to Thee.
For he who dies be-liev-ing Dies safe-ly, thro' Thy love.

68 All That Thrills My Soul

Copyright 1931 by Thoro Harris
Assigned to Nazarene Publishing House

T. H.

THORO HARRIS

1. Who can cheer the heart like Je - sus,   By His pres-ence all di - vine?
2. Love of Christ so free - ly giv - en,   Grace of God be-yond de - gree,
3. Ev - 'ry need His hand sup - ply-ing,   Ev - 'ry good in Him I see;
4. By the crys-tal, flow-ing riv - er   With the ran-somed I will sing,

True and ten - der, pure and pre - cious,   Oh, how blest to call Him mine!
Mer - cy high-er than the heav - en,   Deep-er than the deep-est sea.
On His strength divine re - ly - ing,   He is all in all to me.
And for - ev - er and for - ev - er   Praise and glo - ri - fy the King.

REFRAIN

All that thrills my soul is Je - sus; He is more than life to me (to me);

And the fair - est of ten thou - sand   In my bless-ed Lord I see.

69

When I Survey

Isaac Watts

Arr. by Lowell Mason

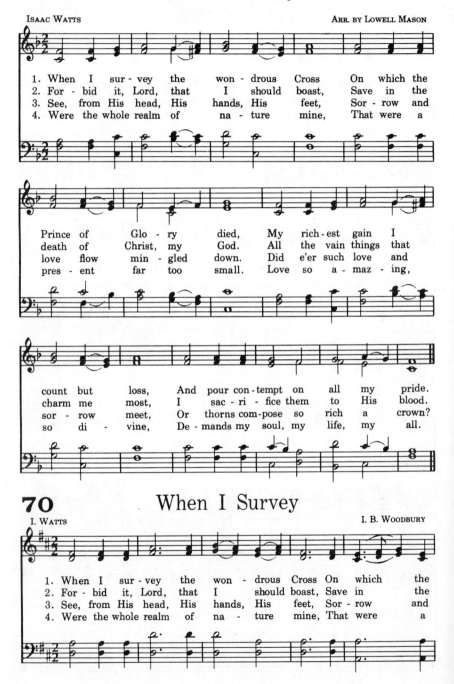

1. When I sur-vey the won-drous Cross On which the
2. For-bid it, Lord, that I should boast, Save in the
3. See, from His head, His hands, His feet, Sor-row and
4. Were the whole realm of na-ture mine, That were a

Prince of Glo-ry died, My rich-est gain I
death of Christ, my God. All the vain things that
love flow min-gled down. Did e'er such love and
pres-ent far too small. Love so a-maz-ing,

count but loss, And pour con-tempt on all my pride.
charm me most, I sac-ri-fice them to His blood.
sor-row meet, Or thorns com-pose so rich a crown?
so di-vine, De-mands my soul, my life, my all.

70

When I Survey

I. Watts

I. B. Woodbury

1. When I sur-vey the won-drous Cross On which the
2. For-bid it, Lord, that I should boast, Save in the
3. See, from His head, His hands, His feet, Sor-row and
4. Were the whole realm of na-ture mine, That were a

When I Survey

Prince of Glo - ry died, My rich - est gain I
death of Christ, my God. All the vain things that
love flow min - gled down. Did e'er such love and
pres - ent far too small. Love so a - maz - ing,

count but loss, And pour con - tempt on all my pride.
charm me most, I sac - ri - fice them to His blood.
sor - row meet, Or thorns com - pose so rich a crown?
so di - vine, De - mands my soul, my life, my all.

71 Here at Thy Table, Lord

MAY P. HOYT   WILLIAM F. SHERWIN

1. Here at Thy ta - ble, Lord, This sa - cred hour, Oh, let us
2. So shall our life of faith Be full, be sweet; And we shall
3. Come then, O ho - ly Christ; Feed us, we pray. Touch with Thy

feel Thee near, In lov - ing pow'r; Call - ing our thoughts a - way
find our strength For each day meet. Fed by Thy liv - ing bread,
pierc - ed hand Each com - mon day, Mak - ing this earth - ly life

From self and sin, As to Thy ban - quet hall We en - ter in.
All hun - ger past, We shall be sat - is - fied, And saved at last.
Full of Thy grace, Till in the home of heav'n We find our place.

72 Sweet Hour of Prayer

W. W. WALFORD

WM. G. BRADBURY

1. Sweet hour of prayer, sweet hour of prayer, That calls me from a world of care
2. Sweet hour of prayer, sweet hour of prayer, The joy I feel, the bliss I share,
3. Sweet hour of prayer, sweet hour of prayer, Thy wings shall my pe-ti-tion bear

And bids me at my Fa-ther's throne Make all my wants and wish-es known!
Of those whose anx-ious spir-its burn With strong desires for thy re-turn!
To Him whose truth and faith-ful-ness En-gage the wait-ing soul to bless;

In sea-sons of dis-tress and grief My soul has of-ten found re-lief,
With such I has-ten to the place Where God, my Saviour, shows His face,
And since He bids me seek His face, Be-lieve His word, and trust His grace,

And oft es-caped the tempter's snare, By thy re-turn, sweet hour of prayer.
And glad-ly take my sta-tion there, And wait for thee, sweet hour of prayer.
I'll cast on Him my ev-'ry care, And wait for thee, sweet hour of prayer.

73   Holy Ghost, with Light Divine

A. REED   L. GOTTSCHALK

1. Ho - ly Ghost, with light di - vine,   Shine up - on   this heart of   mine;
2. Ho - ly Ghost, with pow'r di - vine,   Cleanse this guilt - y heart of   mine;
3. Ho - ly Ghost, with joy   di - vine,   Cheer this   sad - dened heart of   mine;
4. Ho - ly Spir - it, all   di - vine,   Dwell with - in   this heart of   mine;

Chase the shades of night a - way;   Turn my dark - ness in - to day.
Long hath sin with - out con - trol   Held do - min - ion o'er   my soul.
Bid   my man - y woes de - part;   Heal my wounded, bleed - ing heart.
Cast down ev - 'ry i - dol throne;   Reign supreme, and reign   a - lone.

74   Come, Holy Spirit, Dove Divine

ADONIRAM JUDSON   LOWELL MASON

1. Come, Ho - ly Spir - it,   Dove di - vine;   On these bap - tis - mal wa - ters shine,
2. We love Thy name, we   love Thy laws,.   And joy - ful - ly em - brace Thy cause;
3. We sink be - neath Thy   mys - tic flood;   Oh, bathe us in   Thy cleansing blood.
4. And   as we rise, with   Thee to live,   Oh, let the Ho - ly   Spir - it give

And teach our hearts, in   high - est strain,   To praise the Lamb for sin - ners slain.
We love Thy cross, the shame, the pain,   O Lamb of God, for sin - ners slain.
We die to sin, and   seek a grave,   With Thee, beneath the yielding wave.
The seal - ing unc - tion from a - bove,   The breath of life, the fire of   love.

75 Lord, I Hear of Showers of Blessing

ELIZABETH CODNER

WM. B. BRADBURY

1. Lord, I hear of show'rs of bless-ing Thou art scat-t'ring full and free;
2. Pass me not, O God, my Fa-ther, Sin-ful tho' my heart may be.
3. Pass me not, O gra-cious Sav-iour; Let me live and cling to Thee.
4. Love of God, so pure and changeless; Blood of Christ, so rich and free;

Show'rs, the thirst-y land re-fresh-ing. Let some drops now fall on me;
Thou mightst leave me, but the rath-er Let Thy mer-cy fall on me;
I am long-ing for Thy fa-vor; Whilst Thou'rt calling, oh, call me;
Grace of God, so strong and bound-less; Mag-ni-fy them all in me;

E - ven me, e - ven me, Let some drops now fall on me.
E - ven me, e - ven me, Let Thy mer-cy light on me.
E - ven me, e - ven me, Whilst Thou'rt call-ing, oh, call me.
E - ven me, e - ven me, Mag-ni-fy them all in me.

76 This Is the Day the Lord Hath Made

T. A. ARNE

ISAAC WATTS

1. This is the day the Lord hath made; He calls the hours His own.
2. To-day He rose, and left the dead, And Sa-tan's em-pire fell;
3. Ho-san-na to th' a-noint-ed King, To Da-vid's ho-ly Son.
4. Blest be the Lord, who comes to men With mes-sag-es of grace;

This Is the Day the Lord Hath Made

Let heav'n re-joice, let earth be glad, And praise sur-round the throne.
To - day the saints His tri-umph spread, And all His won - ders tell.
Help us, O Lord! De - scend and bring Sal - va - tion from Thy throne.
Who comes, in God His Fa-ther's name, To save our sin - ful race.

77 Blessed Be the Name

CHARLES WESLEY

R. E. HUDSON

1. Oh, for a thou-sand tongues to sing, Blessed be the name of the Lord!
2. Je - sus, the name that charms our fears, Blessed be the name of the Lord!
3. He breaks the pow'r of can-celed sin, Blessed be the name of the Lord!

The glo - ries of my God and King, Blessed be the name of the Lord!
'Tis mu - sic in the sin - ner's ears, Blessed be the name of the Lord!
His blood can make the foul-est clean, Blessed be the name of the Lord!

CHORUS

Bless-ed be the name, Bless-ed be the name, Bless-ed be the name of the Lord!

Bless-ed be the name, Bless-ed be the name, Bless-ed be the name of the Lord.

78 Unsearchable Riches

F. J. C.   J. R. SWENEY

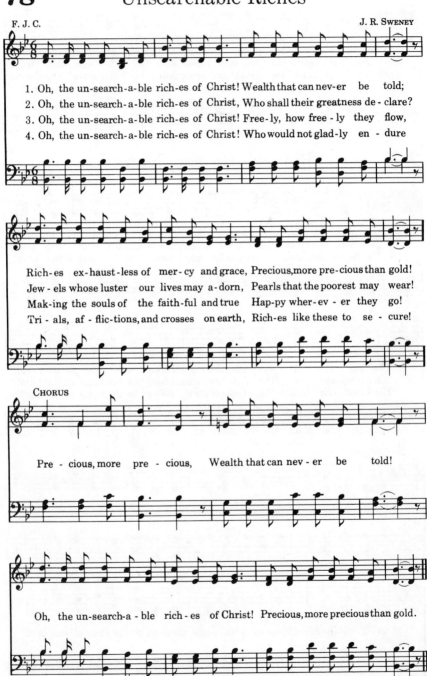

1. Oh, the un-search-a-ble rich-es of Christ! Wealth that can nev-er be told;
2. Oh, the un-search-a-ble rich-es of Christ, Who shall their greatness de - clare?
3. Oh, the un-search-a-ble rich-es of Christ! Free-ly, how free - ly they flow,
4. Oh, the un-search-a-ble rich-es of Christ! Who would not glad-ly en - dure

Rich-es ex-haust-less of mer - cy and grace, Precious, more pre-cious than gold!
Jew - els whose luster our lives may a-dorn, Pearls that the poorest may wear!
Mak-ing the souls of the faith-ful and true Hap-py wher-ev - er they go!
Tri - als, af - flic-tions, and crosses on earth, Rich-es like these to se - cure!

CHORUS

Pre - cious, more pre - cious, Wealth that can nev - er be told!

Oh, the un-search-a - ble rich - es of Christ! Precious, more precious than gold.

79 Oh, for a Faith That Will Not Shrink

William H. Bathurst

Carl G. Glazer

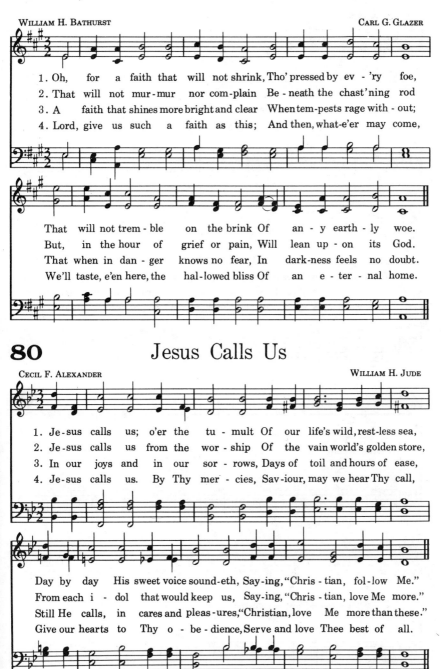

1. Oh, for a faith that will not shrink, Tho' pressed by ev - 'ry foe,
2. That will not mur - mur nor com - plain Be - neath the chast'ning rod
3. A faith that shines more bright and clear When tem-pests rage with - out;
4. Lord, give us such a faith as this; And then, what-e'er may come,

That will not trem - ble on the brink Of an - y earth - ly woe.
But, in the hour of grief or pain, Will lean up - on its God.
That when in dan - ger knows no fear, In dark-ness feels no doubt.
We'll taste, e'en here, the hal - lowed bliss Of an e - ter - nal home.

80 Jesus Calls Us

Cecil F. Alexander

William H. Jude

1. Je - sus calls us; o'er the tu - mult Of our life's wild, rest-less sea,
2. Je - sus calls us from the wor - ship Of the vain world's golden store,
3. In our joys and in our sor - rows, Days of toil and hours of ease,
4. Je - sus calls us. By Thy mer - cies, Sav-iour, may we hear Thy call,

Day by day His sweet voice sound-eth, Say-ing, "Chris - tian, fol - low Me."
From each i - dol that would keep us, Say-ing, "Chris - tian, love Me more."
Still He calls, in cares and pleas - ures, "Christian, love Me more than these."
Give our hearts to Thy o - be - dience, Serve and love Thee best of all.

81 Friendship with Jesus

MAJOR LUDGATE

ARR. FROM FOSTER

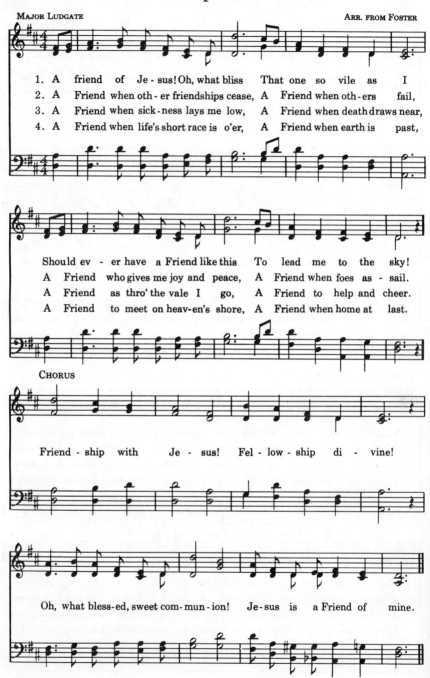

1. A friend of Je-sus! Oh, what bliss That one so vile as I
2. A Friend when oth-er friendships cease, A Friend when oth-ers fail,
3. A Friend when sick-ness lays me low, A Friend when death draws near,
4. A Friend when life's short race is o'er, A Friend when earth is past,

Should ev - er have a Friend like this To lead me to the sky!
A Friend who gives me joy and peace, A Friend when foes as - sail.
A Friend as thro' the vale I go, A Friend to help and cheer.
A Friend to meet on heav-en's shore, A Friend when home at last.

CHORUS

Friend - ship with Je - sus! Fel - low-ship di - vine!

Oh, what bless-ed, sweet com-mun-ion! Je-sus is a Friend of mine.

82 Blessed Hour of Prayer

Fanny J. Crosby

W. H. Doane

1. 'Tis the bless-ed hour of prayer, when our hearts low-ly bend, And we
2. 'Tis the bless-ed hour of prayer, when the Sav-iour draws near With a
3. 'Tis the bless-ed hour of prayer, when the tempt-ed and tried To the
4. At the bless-ed hour of prayer, trust-ing Him, we be-lieve That the

gath-er to Je-sus, our Sav-iour and Friend. If we come to Him in
ten-der com-pas-sion His chil-dren to hear, When He tells us we may
Sav-iour who loves them their sor-row con-fide. With a sym-pa-thiz-ing
bless-ings we're need-ing we'll sure-ly re-ceive. In the full-ness of this

faith, His pro-tec-tion to share,
cast at His feet ev-'ry care. What a balm for the wea-ry! Oh, how
heart He re-moves ev-'ry care.
trust we shall lose ev-'ry care.

CHORUS

sweet to be there! Bless-ed hour of prayer! Bless-ed hour of

prayer! What a balm for the wea-ry! Oh, how sweet to be there!

83 Stand Up for Jesus

G. Duffield   O. J. Webb

1. Stand up, stand up for Je - sus, Ye sol - diers of the Cross. Lift
2. Stand up, stand up for Je - sus. The trum-pet call o - bey; Forth
3. Stand up, stand up for Je - sus—Stand in His strength a - lone. The

high His roy - al ban - ner; It must not suf - fer loss. From
to the might - y con - flict, In this His glo - rious day. "Ye
arm of flesh will fail you — Ye dare not trust your own. Put

vic - t'ry un - to vic - t'ry, His ar - my shall He lead, Till
that are men now serve Him,"A - gainst un - num-bered foes; Let
on the gos - pel ar - mor And,watch-ing un - to prayer, Where

ev - 'ry foe is van-quished And Christ is Lord in - deed.
cour - age rise with dan - ger, And strength to strength op - pose.
du - ty calls or dan - ger, Be nev - er want-ing there.

84   This Is My Father's World

MALTBIE D. BABCOCK   FRANKLIN L. SHEPPARD

1. This is my Fa-ther's world, And to my lis-t'ning ears All
2. This is my Fa-ther's world. The birds their car-ols raise; The
3. This is my Fa-ther's world. Oh, let me ne'er for-get That,

na - ture sings, and round me rings The mu - sic of the spheres.
morn-ing light, the lil - y white De - clare their Mak - er's praise.
though the wrong seems oft so strong, God is the Rul - er yet.

This is my Fa - ther's world; I rest me in the thought Of
This is my Fa - ther's world. He shines in all that's fair; In the
This is my Fa - ther's world. The bat - tle is not done; Je -

rocks and trees, of skies and seas—His hand the won - ders wrought.
rus - tling grass I hear Him pass; He speaks to me ev -'ry - where.
sus, who died, shall be sat - is - fied, And earth and heav'n be one.

85 Hail, Thou Once Despised Jesus!

JOHN BAKEWELL

FRANCOIS H. BARTHELEMON

1. Hail, Thou once de-spis-ed Je-sus! Hail, Thou Gal-i-le-an King!
2. Pas-chal Lamb, by God ap-point-ed, All our sins on Thee were laid.
3. Je-sus, hail! enthroned in glo-ry, There for-ev-er to a-bide!
4. Worship, hon-or, pow'r, and bless-ing Thou art wor-thy to re-ceive;

Thou didst suf-fer to re-lease us; Thou didst free sal-va-tion bring.
By al-might-y love a-noint-ed, Thou hast full a-tone-ment made;
All the heav'n-ly hosts a-dore Thee, Seat-ed at Thy Fa-ther's side.
Loud-est prais-es, with-out ceas-ing, Meet it is for us to give.

Hail, Thou ag-o-niz-ing Sav-iour, Bear-er of our sin and shame!
All Thy peo-ple are for-giv-en Thro' the vir-tue of Thy blood.
There for sin-ners Thou art plead-ing; There Thou dost our place pre-pare,
Help, ye bright an-gel-ic spir-its; Bring your sweet-est, no-blest lays;

By Thy mer-its we find fa-vor; Life is giv-en thro' Thy name.
O-pened is the gate of heav-en; Peace is made 'twixt man and God.
Ev-er for us in-ter-ced-ing Till in glo-ry we ap-pear.
Help to sing our Sav-iour's mer-its; Help to chant Immanuel's praise!

86

Arise, My Soul, Arise

CHARLES WESLEY

LEWIS EDSON

1. A - rise, my soul, a - rise. Shake off thy guilt - y fears.
2. He ev - er lives a - bove For me to in - ter - cede;
3. Five bleed - ing wounds He bears, Re - ceived on Cal - va - ry;
4. The Fa - ther hears Him pray, His dear a - noint - ed One;
5. My God is rec - on - ciled; His par - d'ning voice I hear.

The bleed - ing Sac - ri - fice In my be - half ap - pears.
His all - re - deem - ing love, His pre - cious blood to plead.
They pour ef - fec - tual prayers, They strong - ly plead for me.
He can - not turn a - way The pres - ence of His Son.
He owns me for His child; I can no long - er fear.

Be - fore the throne my Sure - ty stands, Be - fore the throne my
His blood a - toned for all our race, His blood a - toned for
"For - give him, oh, for - give," they cry. "For - give him, oh, for-
His Spir - it an - swers to the Blood, His Spir - it an - swers
With con - fi - dence I now draw nigh, With con - fi - dence I

Sure - ty stands; My name is writ - ten on His hands.
all our race, And sprin - kles now the throne of grace.
give," they cry, "Nor let that ran - somed sin - ner die."
to the Blood, And tells me I am born of God,
now draw nigh, And, "Fa - ther, Ab - ba, Fa - ther," cry.

87 Hiding in Thee

WM. O. CUSHING

IRA D. SANKEY

1. Oh, safe to the Rock that is high - er than I,
2. In the calm of the noon - tide, in sor - row's lone hour,
3. How oft in the con - flict, when pressed by the foe,

My soul in its con - flicts and sor - rows would fly. So
In times when temp - ta - tion casts o'er me its pow'r; In the
I have fled to my Ref - uge and breathed out my woe! How

sin - ful, so wea - ry, Thine, Thine would I be. Thou
tem - pests of life, on its wide, heav - ing sea, Thou
of - ten, when tri - als like sea - bil - lows roll, Have I

CHORUS

blest "Rock of A - ges," I'm hid - ing in Thee.
blest "Rock of A - ges," I'm hid - ing in Thee. Hid - ing in Thee,
hid - den in Thee, O Thou Rock of my soul.

Hid - ing in Thee, Thou blest "Rock of A - ges," I'm hid - ing in Thee.

88 There Is a Fountain

WILLIAM COWPER

LOWELL MASON

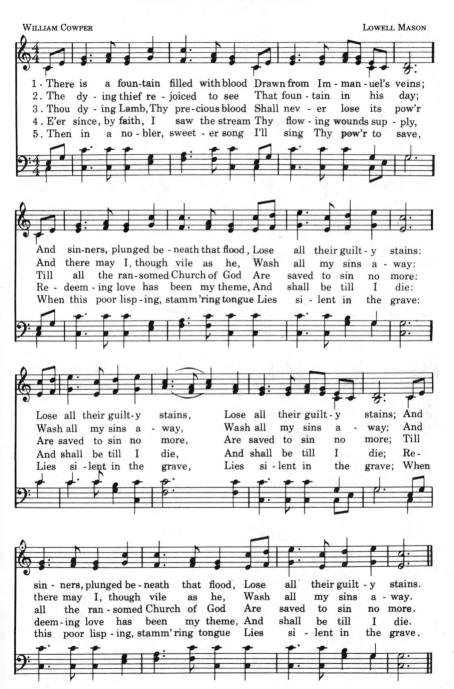

1. There is a foun-tain filled with blood Drawn from Im - man - uel's veins;
2. The dy - ing thief re - joiced to see That foun - tain in his day;
3. Thou dy - ing Lamb, Thy pre-cious blood Shall nev - er lose its pow'r
4. E'er since, by faith, I saw the stream Thy flow - ing wounds sup - ply,
5. Then in a no - bler, sweet - er song I'll sing Thy pow'r to save,

And sin-ners, plunged be - neath that flood, Lose all their guilt - y stains:
And there may I, though vile as he, Wash all my sins a - way:
Till all the ran - somed Church of God Are saved to sin no more:
Re - deem - ing love has been my theme, And shall be till I die:
When this poor lisp - ing, stamm'ring tongue Lies si - lent in the grave:

Lose all their guilt-y stains, Lose all their guilt - y stains; And
Wash all my sins a - way, Wash all my sins a - way; And
Are saved to sin no more, Are saved to sin no more; Till
And shall be till I die, And shall be till I die; Re -
Lies si - lent in the grave, Lies si - lent in the grave; When

sin - ners, plunged be - neath that flood, Lose all their guilt - y stains.
there may I, though vile as he, Wash all my sins a - way.
all the ran - somed Church of God Are saved to sin no more.
deem - ing love has been my theme, And shall be till I die.
this poor lisp - ing, stamm'ring tongue Lies si - lent in the grave.

89 Near to the Heart of God

Copyright 1931 by Lorenz Publishing Co. Renewal. Used by permisson

C. B. McA.

C. B. McAfee

1. There is a place of qui-et rest, Near to the heart of God;
2. There is a place of com-fort sweet, Near to the heart of God;
3. There is a place of full re-lease, Near to the heart of God;

A place where sin can-not mo-lest, Near to the heart of God.
A place where we our Sav-iour meet, Near to the heart of God.
A place where all is joy and peace, Near to the heart of God.

REFRAIN

O Je-sus, blest Re-deem-er, Sent from the heart of God,

Hold us, who wait be-fore Thee, Near to the heart of God.

90 Jesus Shall Reign

ISAAC WATTS

JOHN HATTON

1. Je-sus shall reign wher-e'er the sun Does his suc-
2. To Him shall end-less pray'r be made, And end-less
3. Peo-ple and realms of ev-'ry tongue Dwell on His
4. Let ev-'ry crea-ture rise and bring His grate-ful

Jesus Shall Reign

ces - sive jour - neys run; His king-dom spread from
prais - es crown His head; His name like sweet per-
love with sweet - est song, And in - fant voic - es
hon - ors to our King; An - gels de - scend with

shore to shore, Till moons shall wax and wane no more.
fume shall rise With ev - 'ry morn - ing sac - ri - fice.
shall pro - claim Their ear - ly bless - ings on His name.
songs a - gain, And earth re - peat the loud A - men!

91   When Morning Gilds the Skies

TR. BY EDWARD CASWALL

JOSEPH BARNBY

1. When morn - ing gilds the skies, My heart a - wak - ing cries,
2. The night be - comes as day When from the heart we say,
3. In heav'n's e - ter - nal bliss The love - liest strain is this,
4. Be this, while life is mine, My can - ti - cle di - vine,

May Je - sus Christ be praised! A - like at work and pray'r,
May Je - sus Christ be praised! The pow'rs of dark - ness fear,
May Je - sus Christ be praised! Let earth, and sea, and sky,
May Je - sus Christ be praised! Be this th' e - ter - nal song

To Je - sus I re - pair. May Je - sus Christ be praised!
When this sweet chant they hear, May Je - sus Christ be praised!
From depth to height re - ply, May Je - sus Christ be praised!
Thro' all the a - ges long, May Je - sus Christ be praised!

92 All the Way My Saviour Leads

FANNY J. CROSBY

ROBERT LOWRY

1. All the way my Sav-iour leads me. What have I   to ask be - side?
2. All the way my Sav-iour leads me, Cheers each winding path I   tread,
3. All the way my Sav-iour leads me. Oh, the full - ness of His love!

Can I doubt His ten - der mer - cy Who thro' life has been my Guide?
Gives me grace for ev -'ry tri - al, Feeds me with the liv - ing bread.
Per - fect rest to me is prom - ised In my Fa - ther's house a - bove.

Heav'n-ly peace, di - vin - est com - fort, Here by faith in Him to dwell!
Tho' my wea - ry steps may fal - ter, And my soul a - thirst may be,
When my spir - it, clothed, im - mor - tal, Wings its flight to realms of day,

For I know, what-e'er be - fall me, Je - sus do - eth all things well.
Gush-ing from the Rock be - fore me, Lo! a spring of joy I   see.
This my song thro' end-less a - ges— Je - sus led me all the way;

For I know, what-e'er be - fall me, Je - sus do - eth all things well.
Gush-ing from the Rock be - fore me, Lo! a spring of joy I   see.
This my song thro' end-less a - ges— Je - sus led me all the way.

93 Sun of My Soul

JOHN KEBLE

PETER RITTER

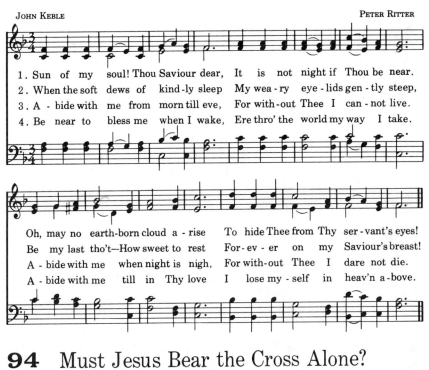

1. Sun of my soul! Thou Saviour dear, It is not night if Thou be near.
2. When the soft dews of kind-ly sleep My wea-ry eye-lids gen-tly steep,
3. A-bide with me from morn till eve, For with-out Thee I can-not live.
4. Be near to bless me when I wake, Ere thro' the world my way I take.

Oh, may no earth-born cloud a-rise To hide Thee from Thy ser-vant's eyes!
Be my last tho't—How sweet to rest For-ev-er on my Saviour's breast!
A-bide with me when night is nigh, For with-out Thee I dare not die.
A-bide with me till in Thy love I lose my-self in heav'n a-bove.

94 Must Jesus Bear the Cross Alone?

THOMAS SHEPHERD

GEORGE N. ALLEN

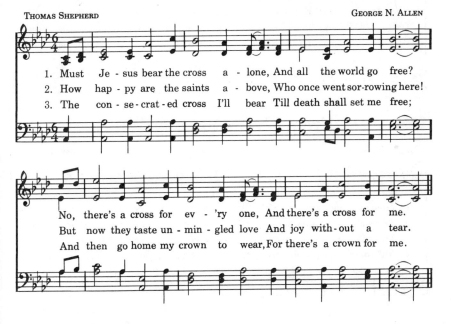

1. Must Je-sus bear the cross a-lone, And all the world go free?
2. How hap-py are the saints a-bove, Who once went sor-rowing here!
3. The con-se-crat-ed cross I'll bear Till death shall set me free;

No, there's a cross for ev-'ry one, And there's a cross for me.
But now they taste un-min-gled love And joy with-out a tear.
And then go home my crown to wear, For there's a crown for me.

95 Lo! He Comes, with Clouds Descending

ALT. FROM J. CENNICK

HENRY SMART

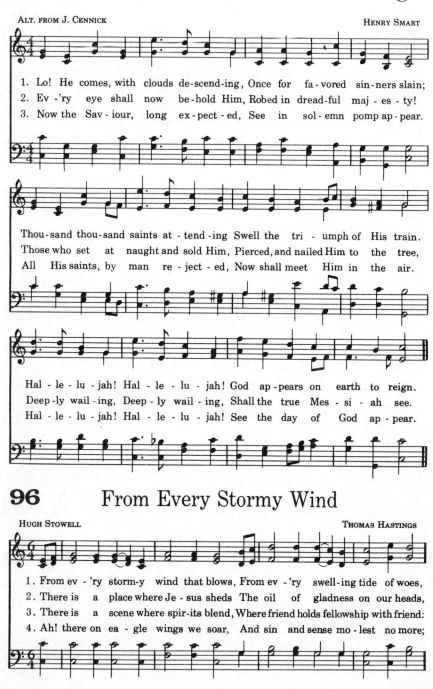

1. Lo! He comes, with clouds de-scend-ing, Once for fa-vored sin-ners slain;
2. Ev-'ry eye shall now be-hold Him, Robed in dread-ful maj-es-ty!
3. Now the Sav-iour, long ex-pect-ed, See in sol-emn pomp ap-pear.

Thou-sand thou-sand saints at-tend-ing Swell the tri-umph of His train.
Those who set at naught and sold Him, Pierced, and nailed Him to the tree,
All His saints, by man re-ject-ed, Now shall meet Him in the air.

Hal-le-lu-jah! Hal-le-lu-jah! God ap-pears on earth to reign.
Deep-ly wail-ing, Deep-ly wail-ing, Shall the true Mes-si-ah see.
Hal-le-lu-jah! Hal-le-lu-jah! See the day of God ap-pear.

96 From Every Stormy Wind

HUGH STOWELL

THOMAS HASTINGS

1. From ev-'ry storm-y wind that blows, From ev-'ry swell-ing tide of woes,
2. There is a place where Je-sus sheds The oil of gladness on our heads,
3. There is a scene where spir-its blend, Where friend holds fellowship with friend:
4. Ah! there on ea-gle wings we soar, And sin and sense mo-lest no more;

From Every Stormy Wind

There is a calm, a sure re-treat: 'Tis found be-neath the mer-cy - seat.
A place than all be-sides more sweet: It is the Blood-bought mer-cy-seat.
Tho' sun-dered far, by faith they meet A-round the com-mon mer-cy - seat.
And heav'n comes down our souls to greet, While glo - ry crowns the mer-cy - seat.

97 Jesus Is My Refuge

H. C. B.

HUGH C. BENNER

1. Je - sus is my Ref - uge In the storm of sin;
2. Je - sus is my Ref - uge In the storm of life;
3. Je - sus is my Ref - uge For all time to come;

Par - don, peace, and cleans - ing Are mine as I trust in Him.
Strength and grace suf - fi - cient He gives in the rag - ing strife.
Safe to heav - en's por - tals He pi - lots His loved ones home.

CHORUS

Je - sus is my Ref - uge; Nev - er - fail - ing Ref - uge;

Blest, e - ter - nal Ref - uge— Ref - uge of my soul.

98 He Leadeth Me

Joseph H. Gilmore

William B. Bradbury

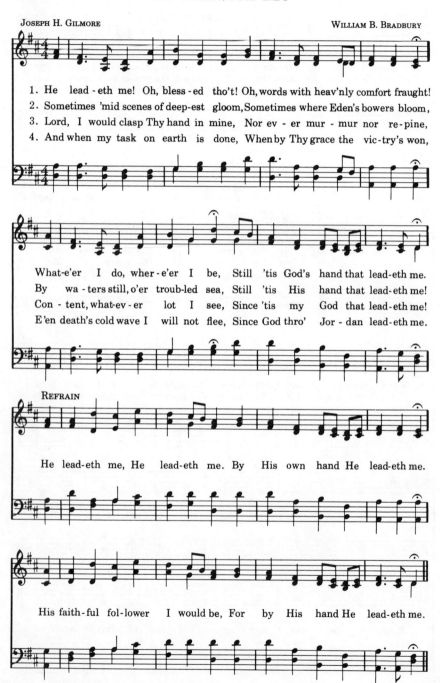

1. He lead-eth me! Oh, bless-ed tho't! Oh, words with heav'nly comfort fraught!
2. Sometimes 'mid scenes of deep-est gloom, Sometimes where Eden's bowers bloom,
3. Lord, I would clasp Thy hand in mine, Nor ev - er mur - mur nor re-pine,
4. And when my task on earth is done, When by Thy grace the vic-try's won,

What-e'er I do, wher-e'er I be, Still 'tis God's hand that lead-eth me.
By wa-ters still, o'er troub-led sea, Still 'tis His hand that lead-eth me!
Con-tent, what-ev-er lot I see, Since 'tis my God that lead-eth me!
E'en death's cold wave I will not flee, Since God thro' Jor-dan lead-eth me.

REFRAIN

He lead-eth me, He lead-eth me. By His own hand He lead-eth me.

His faith-ful fol-lower I would be, For by His hand He lead-eth me.

99 Nearer the Cross

FANNY J. CROSBY

MRS. J. F. KNAPP

1. "Near-er the Cross!" my heart can say; I am com-ing near-er. Near-er the
2. Near-er the Chris-tian's mer-cy seat, I am com-ing near-er. Feasting my
3. Near-er in prayer my hope as-pires; I am com-ing near-er. Deep-er the

Cross from day to day, I am com-ing near-er. Near-er the Cross where
soul on man-na sweet, I am com-ing near-er. Strong-er in faith, more
love my soul de-sires; I am com-ing near-er. Near-er the end of

Je-sus died, Near-er the foun-tain's crim-son tide, Near-er my Sav-iour's
clear I see Je-sus, who gave him-self for me. Near-er to Him I
toil and care, Near-er the joy I long to share, Near-er the crown I

wound-ed side, I am com-ing near-er. I am com-ing near-er.
still would be. Still I'm com-ing near-er. Still I'm com-ing near-er.
soon shall wear, I am com-ing near-er. I am com-ing near-er.

100 O Zion, Haste

MARY A. THOMSON

JAMES WALCH

1. O Zi - on, haste, thy mis - sion high ful - fill - ing,
2. Be - hold how man - y thou - sand still are ly - ing
3. Pro - claim to ev - 'ry peo - ple, tongue, and na - tion
4. Give of thy sons to bear the mes - sage glo - rious;

To tell to all the world that God is Light; That He who
Bound in the dark - some pris - on house of sin, With none to
That God, in whom they live and move, is love: Tell how He
Give of thy wealth to speed them on their way; Pour out thy

made all na - tions is not will - ing One soul should per - ish,
tell them of the Sav - iour's dy - ing, Or of the life He
stooped to save His lost cre - a - tion, And died on earth that
soul for them in pray'r vic - to - rious; And all Thou spend - est

REFRAIN

lost in shades of night.
died for them to win. Pub - lish glad ti - dings, Ti - dings of
man might live a - bove.
Je - sus will re - pay.

peace; Ti - dings of Je - sus, Re - demp - tion and re - lease.

101 Sweeter than All

JOHNSON OATMAN, JR.

J. HOWARD ENTWISLE

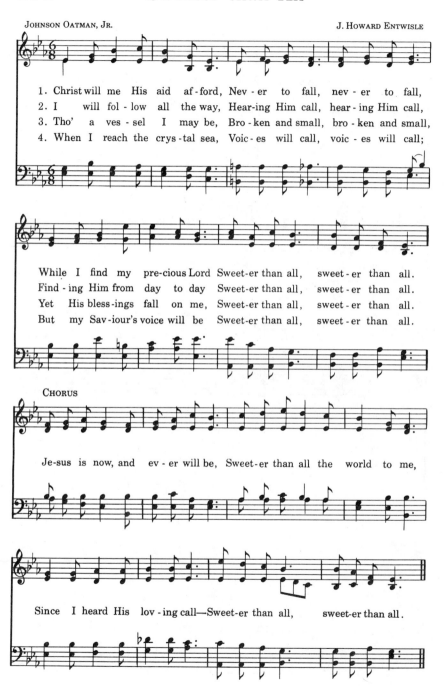

1. Christ will me His aid af-ford, Nev - er to fall, nev - er to fall,
2. I will fol - low all the way, Hear-ing Him call, hear - ing Him call,
3. Tho' a ves - sel I may be, Bro - ken and small, bro - ken and small,
4. When I reach the crys-tal sea, Voic - es will call, voic - es will call;

While I find my pre-cious Lord Sweet-er than all, sweet - er than all.
Find - ing Him from day to day Sweet-er than all, sweet - er than all.
Yet His bless-ings fall on me, Sweet-er than all, sweet - er than all.
But my Sav-iour's voice will be Sweet-er than all, sweet - er than all.

CHORUS

Je-sus is now, and ev - er will be, Sweet-er than all the world to me,

Since I heard His lov - ing call—Sweet-er than all, sweet-er than all.

102   I Gave My Life for Thee

Frances R. Havergal

P. P. Bliss

1. I gave My life for thee; My pre - cious blood I shed,
2. My Fa - ther's house of light, My glo - ry - cir - cled throne,
3. I suf - fered much for thee, More than thy tongue can tell,
4. And I have brought to thee, Down from My home a - bove,

That thou might'st ran-somed be, And quick-ened from the dead.
I left for earth - ly night, For wan - d'rings sad and lone.
Of bit - t'rest ag - o - ny, To res - cue thee from hell.
Sal - va - tion full and free, My par - don and My love.

I gave, I gave My life for thee. What hast thou giv'n for Me?
I left, I left it all for thee. Hast thou left aught for Me?
I've borne, I've borne it all for thee. What hast thou borne for Me?
I bring, I bring rich gifts to thee. What hast thou brought to Me?

I gave, I gave My life for thee. What hast thou giv'n for Me?
I left, I left it all for thee. Hast thou left aught for Me?
I've borne, I've borne it all for thee. What hast thou borne for Me?
I bring, I bring rich gifts to thee. What hast thou brought to Me?

103 The Hallowed Cross

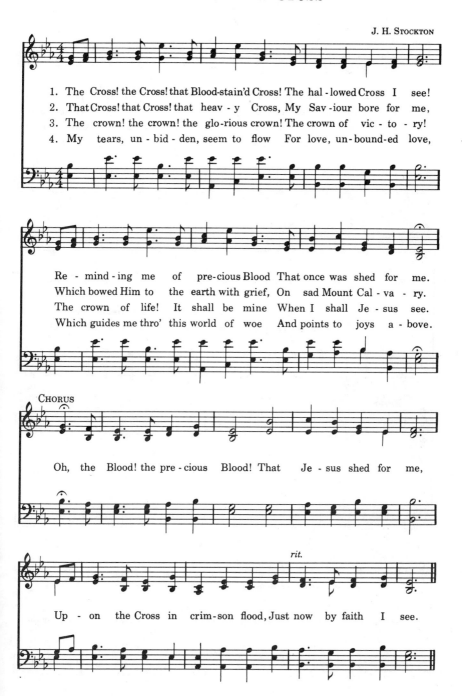

1. The Cross! the Cross! that Blood-stain'd Cross! The hal-lowed Cross I see!
2. That Cross! that Cross! that heav-y Cross, My Sav-iour bore for me,
3. The crown! the crown! the glo-rious crown! The crown of vic-to-ry!
4. My tears, un-bid-den, seem to flow For love, un-bound-ed love,

Re-mind-ing me of pre-cious Blood That once was shed for me.
Which bowed Him to the earth with grief, On sad Mount Cal-va-ry.
The crown of life! It shall be mine When I shall Je-sus see.
Which guides me thro' this world of woe And points to joys a-bove.

CHORUS

Oh, the Blood! the pre-cious Blood! That Je-sus shed for me,

rit.

Up-on the Cross in crim-son flood, Just now by faith I see.

104 More About Jesus

E. E. Hewitt   Jno. R. Sweney

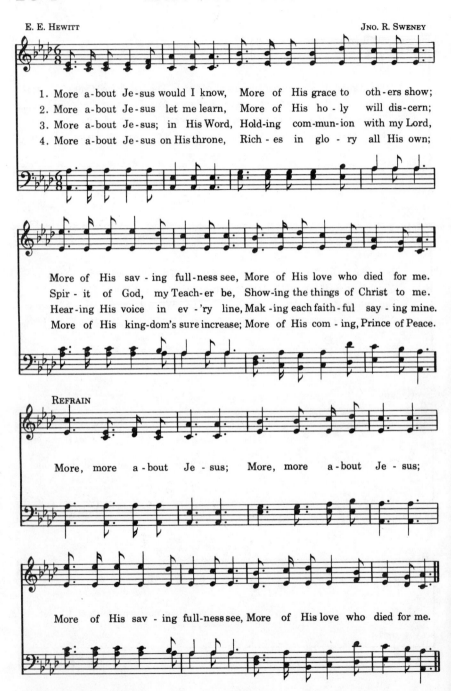

1. More a-bout Je-sus would I know, More of His grace to oth-ers show;
2. More a-bout Je-sus let me learn, More of His ho - ly will dis-cern;
3. More a-bout Je-sus; in His Word, Hold-ing com-mun-ion with my Lord,
4. More a-bout Je-sus on His throne, Rich - es in glo - ry all His own;

More of His sav - ing full-ness see, More of His love who died for me.
Spir - it of God, my Teach-er be, Show-ing the things of Christ to me.
Hear-ing His voice in ev -'ry line, Mak-ing each faith-ful say - ing mine.
More of His king-dom's sure increase; More of His com - ing, Prince of Peace.

REFRAIN

More, more a -bout Je - sus; More, more a -bout Je - sus;

More of His sav - ing full-ness see, More of His love who died for me.

105 Beneath the Cross of Jesus

ELIZABETH C. CLEPHANE

FREDERICK C. MAKER

1. Be-neath the cross of Je-sus I fain would take my stand,
2. Up-on the cross of Je-sus Mine eyes at times can see
3. I take, O Cross, thy shad-ow For my a-bid-ing place.

The shad-ow of a might-y rock With-in a wea-ry land;
The ver-y dy-ing form of One Who suf-fered there for me.
I ask no oth-er sun-shine than The sun-shine of His face;

A home with-in the wil-der-ness; A rest up-on the way,
And from my smit-ten heart, with tears, These won-ders I con-fess:
Con-tent to let the world go by, To know no gain nor loss,

From the burn-ing of the noon-tide heat And the bur-den of the day.
The won-der of His glo-rious love, And my un-wor-thi-ness.
My sin-ful self my on-ly shame, My glo-ry all the Cross.

106 The Great Physician

WM. HUNTER

J. H. STOCKTON

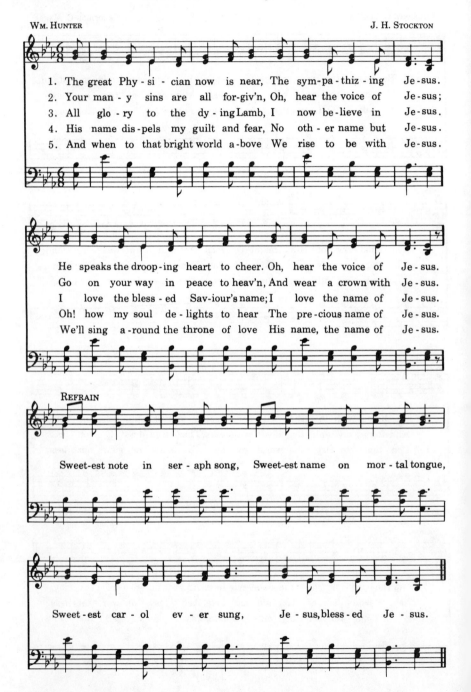

1. The great Phy - si - cian now is near, The sym-pa - thiz - ing Je - sus.
2. Your man - y sins are all for-giv'n, Oh, hear the voice of Je - sus;
3. All glo - ry to the dy - ing Lamb, I now be - lieve in Je - sus.
4. His name dis-pels my guilt and fear, No oth - er name but Je - sus.
5. And when to that bright world a - bove We rise to be with Je - sus.

He speaks the droop-ing heart to cheer. Oh, hear the voice of Je - sus.
Go on your way in peace to heav'n, And wear a crown with Je - sus.
I love the bless - ed Sav-iour's name; I love the name of Je - sus.
Oh! how my soul de - lights to hear The pre - cious name of Je - sus.
We'll sing a - round the throne of love His name, the name of Je - sus.

REFRAIN

Sweet-est note in ser - aph song, Sweet-est name on mor - tal tongue,

Sweet - est car - ol ev - er sung, Je - sus, bless - ed Je - sus.

107 I Will Praise Him

M. J. H.

Mrs. M. J. Harris

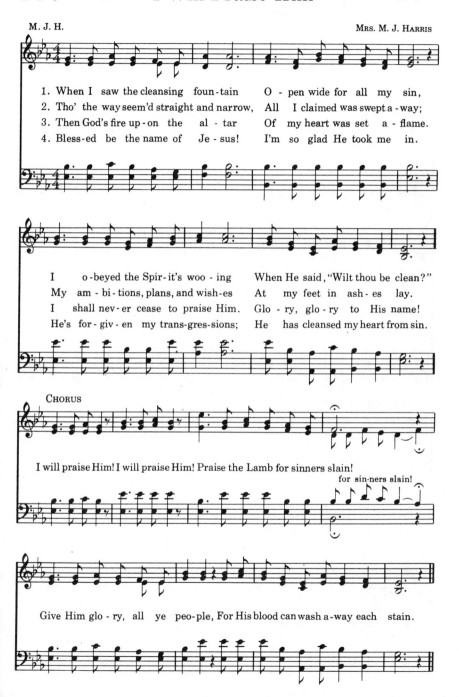

1. When I saw the cleansing foun-tain O - pen wide for all my sin,
2. Tho' the way seem'd straight and narrow, All I claimed was swept a-way;
3. Then God's fire up-on the al - tar Of my heart was set a - flame.
4. Bless-ed be the name of Je - sus! I'm so glad He took me in.

I o-beyed the Spir-it's woo - ing When He said, "Wilt thou be clean?"
My am - bi-tions, plans, and wish-es At my feet in ash-es lay.
I shall nev-er cease to praise Him. Glo - ry, glo - ry to His name!
He's for-giv-en my trans-gres-sions; He has cleansed my heart from sin.

Chorus

I will praise Him! I will praise Him! Praise the Lamb for sinners slain!

for sin-ners slain!

Give Him glo - ry, all ye peo-ple, For His blood can wash a-way each stain.

108 Open the Windows of Heaven

C. E. P.

CHAS. EDW. POLLOCK

1. Lord, send Thy Spir - it down, Like a re - fresh - ing show'r;
2. With-in thy vine - yard here, Let streams of grace de - scend;
3. Re - vive Thy work once more, As in the days of old,
4. We have to-geth - er met In Thy most ho - ly name;

And let His in - flu - ence be felt With Pen - te - cos - tal pow'r.
Re - fresh-ing all the parch-ed ground, A fruit - ful har - vest send.
When near three thousand pre-cious souls Were add - ed to the fold.
Thy prom -ise to be with and bless We right - ful -ly can claim.

CHORUS

O - pen the win-dows of heav-en, O Lord; send a re-fresh-ing show'r;

Quick-en each drooping, fam-ish-ing soul; Show forth Thy won-der-ful pow'r.

109   Jesus, I My Cross Have Taken

HENRY F. LYTE   ARR. FROM MOZART

1. Je - sus, I my cross have tak - en, All to leave and fol - low Thee;
2. Let the world de - spise and leave me; They have left my Sav-iour, too.
3. Go, then, earth-ly fame and treasure! Come, dis - as - ter, scorn, and pain!
4. Know, my soul, thy full sal-va—tion; Rise o'er sin, and fear, and care:

Na - ked, poor, de - spised, for - sak - en, Thou from hence my all shalt be.
Hu - man hearts and looks de - ceive me; Thou art not, like man, un - true.
In Thy serv - ice, pain is pleasure; With Thy fa - vor, loss is gain.
Joy to find in ev - 'ry sta - tion Something still to do or bear.

Per - ish ev - 'ry fond am - bi - tion, All I've sought, and hoped, and known;
And while Thou shalt smile up - on me, God of wis - dom, love, and might,
I have called Thee, "Ab - ba, Fa - ther"; I have stayed my heart on Thee.
Think what Spir - it dwells with - in thee, What a Fa - ther's smile is thine,

Yet how rich is my con - di - tion—God and heav'n are still my own!
Foes may hate and friends may shun me; Show Thy face, and all is bright.
Storms may howl, and clouds may gath - er; All must work for good to me.
What a Sav - iour died to win thee. Child of heav'n, shouldst thou repine?

110   Oh, Sweet Rest!

C. F. O.

Rev. J. Trumbauer

1. For the peo - ple of God a rest doth re - main. Press
2. Oh, how long I'd been pray-ing to find this sweet rest, To
3. Oh, at last I have found it, this bless - ed sweet rest. 'Tis
4. Now the Sav - iour is wait-ing. Oh, what will you give? And

on, pre - cious souls, till the rest you ob - tain. 'Tis the
cease from my la - bor and lean on His breast. I am
Christ in His full-ness, the Bless - er, pos - sessed; And no
what will you suf-fer, this rest to re - ceive? Will you

rest Je - sus prom - ised, so hap - py and blest: The
wea - ry, dear Je - sus. How soon may it be? Low
more wea - ry wait - ing for Je - sus to come, For
give up for - ev - er, count all things but loss, To

joy of His pres - ence, a per - fect sweet rest.
down in the val - ley I'm wait - ing for Thee.
Christ dwell-eth in me; my heart is His home.
gain this great treas - ure, and die at the Cross?

Oh, Sweet Rest!

CHORUS

Oh, sweet rest! Oh, sweet rest! 'Tis the rest of the

soul, so hap-py and blest. By faith in His prom-ise I

lean on His breast. My soul from its la-bor has found its sweet rest.

111 'Tis Midnight

WILLIAM B. TAPPAN

WILLIAM B. BRADBURY

1. 'Tis midnight; and on Ol-ive's brow The star is dimmed that late-ly shone.
2. 'Tis midnight; and from all re-moved, The Sav-iour wrestles lone with fears;
3. 'Tis midnight; and for oth-ers' guilt The Man of Sor-rows weeps in blood;
4. 'Tis midnight; and from heav'nly plains Is borne the song that an-gels know;

'Tis midnight; in the gar-den now The suff'ring Sav-iour prays a-lone.
E'en that dis-ci-ple whom He loved Heeds not his Master's grief and tears.
Yet He that hath in an-guish knelt Is not for-sak-en by His God.
Un-heard by mor-tals are the strains That sweetly soothe the Sav-iour's woe.

112 Living for Jesus

C. F. W.

C. F. WEIGLE

1. Liv - ing for Je - sus, oh, what peace! Riv - ers of pleas - ure
2. Liv - ing for Je - sus, oh, what rest! Pleas-ing my Sav - iour,
3. Liv - ing for Je - sus, ev - 'ry - where, All of my bur - dens
4. Liv - ing for Je - sus, till at last In - to His glo - ry

nev - er cease. Tri - als may come, yet I'll not fear.
I am blest. On - ly to live for Him a - lone,
He doth bear. Friends may for-sake me; He'll be true.
I have passed; There to be - hold Him on His throne,

CHORUS

Liv - ing for Je - sus, He is near.
Do - ing His will till life is done! Help me to serve Thee
Trust-ing in Him, He'll guide me through.
Hear from His lips, "My child, well done!"

more and more. Help me to praise Thee o'er and o'er; Live in Thy

Living for Jesus

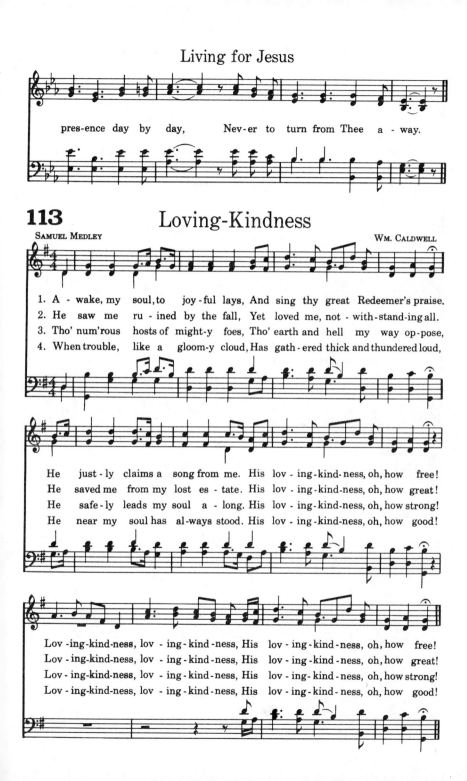

pres-ence day by day, Nev-er to turn from Thee a - way.

113 Loving-Kindness

Samuel Medley

Wm. Caldwell

1. A - wake, my soul, to joy-ful lays, And sing thy great Redeemer's praise.
2. He saw me ru - ined by the fall, Yet loved me, not - with-stand-ing all.
3. Tho' num'rous hosts of might-y foes, Tho' earth and hell my way op-pose,
4. When trouble, like a gloom-y cloud, Has gath - ered thick and thundered loud,

He just - ly claims a song from me. His lov - ing-kind-ness, oh, how free!
He saved me from my lost es - tate. His lov - ing-kind-ness, oh, how great!
He safe - ly leads my soul a - long. His lov - ing-kind-ness, oh, how strong!
He near my soul has al-ways stood. His lov - ing-kind-ness, oh, how good!

Lov -ing-kind-ness, lov - ing-kind-ness, His lov - ing-kind-ness, oh, how free!
Lov - ing-kind-ness, lov - ing-kind-ness, His lov - ing-kind-ness, oh, how great!
Lov - ing-kind-ness, lov - ing-kind-ness, His lov - ing-kind-ness, oh, how strong!
Lov - ing-kind-ness, lov - ing-kind-ness, His lov - ing-kind-ness, oh, how good!

114 Take the Name of Jesus with You

LYDIA BAXTER

W. H. DOANE

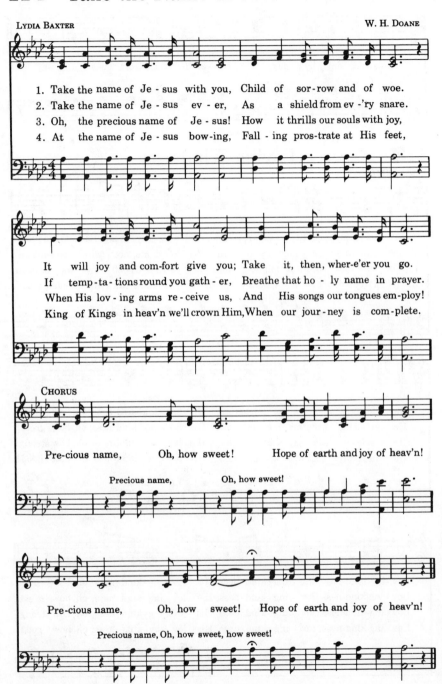

1. Take the name of Je - sus with you, Child of sor-row and of woe.
2. Take the name of Je - sus ev - er, As a shield from ev -'ry snare.
3. Oh, the precious name of Je - sus! How it thrills our souls with joy,
4. At the name of Je - sus bow-ing, Fall - ing pros-trate at His feet,

It will joy and com-fort give you; Take it, then, wher-e'er you go.
If temp - ta - tions round you gath - er, Breathe that ho - ly name in prayer.
When His lov - ing arms re - ceive us, And His songs our tongues em-ploy!
King of Kings in heav'n we'll crown Him, When our jour - ney is com - plete.

CHORUS

Pre-cious name, Oh, how sweet! Hope of earth and joy of heav'n!

Precious name, Oh, how sweet!

Pre-cious name, Oh, how sweet! Hope of earth and joy of heav'n!

Precious name, Oh, how sweet, how sweet!

115 Under the Blood

E. E. HEWITT

WM. J. KIRKPATRICK

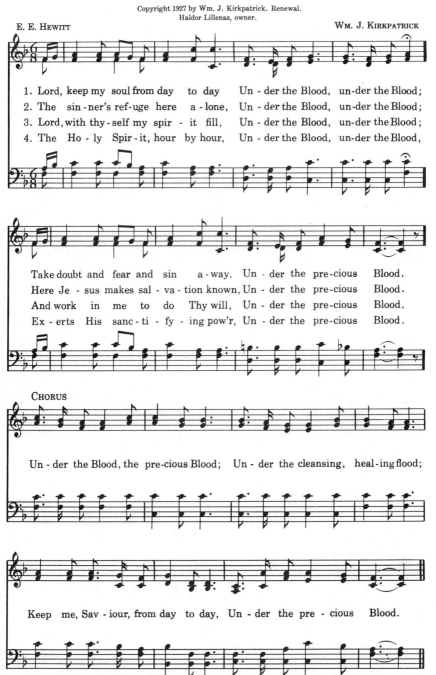

1. Lord, keep my soul from day to day Un-der the Blood, un-der the Blood;
2. The sin-ner's ref-uge here a-lone, Un-der the Blood, un-der the Blood;
3. Lord, with thy-self my spir-it fill, Un-der the Blood, un-der the Blood;
4. The Ho-ly Spir-it, hour by hour, Un-der the Blood, un-der the Blood,

Take doubt and fear and sin a-way, Un-der the pre-cious Blood.
Here Je-sus makes sal-va-tion known, Un-der the pre-cious Blood.
And work in me to do Thy will, Un-der the pre-cious Blood.
Ex-erts His sanc-ti-fy-ing pow'r, Un-der the pre-cious Blood.

CHORUS

Un-der the Blood, the pre-cious Blood; Un-der the cleansing, heal-ing flood;

Keep me, Sav-iour, from day to day, Un-der the pre-cious Blood.

116 Every Bridge Is Burned Behind Me

JOHNSON OATMAN, JR.

GEO. C. HUGG

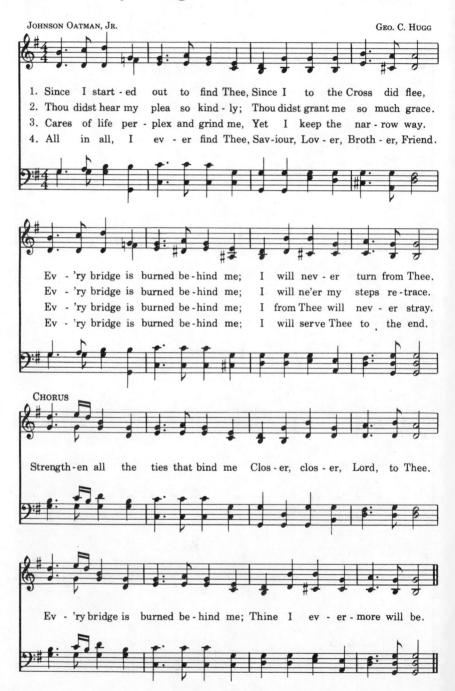

1. Since I start-ed out to find Thee, Since I to the Cross did flee,
2. Thou didst hear my plea so kind-ly; Thou didst grant me so much grace.
3. Cares of life per-plex and grind me, Yet I keep the nar-row way.
4. All in all, I ev-er find Thee, Sav-iour, Lov-er, Broth-er, Friend.

Ev - 'ry bridge is burned be-hind me; I will nev-er turn from Thee.
Ev - 'ry bridge is burned be-hind me; I will ne'er my steps re-trace.
Ev - 'ry bridge is burned be-hind me; I from Thee will nev-er stray.
Ev - 'ry bridge is burned be-hind me; I will serve Thee to the end.

CHORUS

Strength-en all the ties that bind me Clos-er, clos-er, Lord, to Thee.

Ev - 'ry bridge is burned be-hind me; Thine I ev-er-more will be.

117 Jesus, Lover of My Soul

CHARLES WESLEY

S. B. MARSH

1. Je - sus, Lov - er of my soul, Let me to Thy bos - om fly,
2. Oth - er ref - uge have I none; Hangs my help - less soul on Thee.
3. Thou, O Christ, art all I want; More than all in Thee I find.
4. Plen - teous grace with Thee is found, Grace to cov - er all my sin;

While the near - er wa - ters roll, While the tem - pest still is high!
Leave, ah, leave me not a - lone; Still sup - port and com - fort me!
Raise the fall - en, cheer the faint, Heal the sick, and lead the blind.
Let the heal - ing streams abound, Make and keep me pure with - in.

Hide me, O my Sav - iour, hide, Till the storm of life is past.
All my trust on Thee is stayed, All my help from Thee I bring;
Just and ho - ly is Thy name; I am all un - right-eous - ness.
Thou of life the foun - tain art; Free - ly let me take of Thee;

Safe in - to the ha - ven guide. Oh, re - ceive my soul at last!
Cov - er my de - fense - less head With the shad - ow of Thy wing.
False and full of sin I am; Thou art full of truth and grace.
Spring Thou up with - in my heart; Rise to all e - ter - ni - ty.

118 Let All the People Praise Thee

Mrs. C. H. M.

Mrs. C. H. Morris

1. Oh, mag - ni - fy the Lord with me, Ye peo - ple of His choice.
2. Oh, praise Him for His ho - li - ness, His wis - dom, and His grace;
3. Had I a thou - sand tongues to sing, The half could ne'er be told

Let all to whom He lend - eth breath Now in His name re - joice.
Sing prais - es for the pre - cious Blood Which ran - somed all our race.
Of love so rich, so full and free, Of bless - ings man - i - fold,

For love's blest rev - e - la - tion, For rest from con - dem - na - tion,
In ten - der - ness He sought us; From depths of sin He brought us;
Of grace that fail - eth nev - er, Peace flow - ing as a riv - er

For ut - ter - most sal - va - tion, To Him give thanks.
To Him, to Him give thanks.
The way of life then taught us. To Him give thanks.
To Him, to Him give thanks.
From God, the glo - rious Giv - er. To Him give thanks.
To Him, to Him give thanks.

Let All the People Praise Thee

CHORUS

Let all ____ the peo-ple praise Thee. Let all ____ the peo-ple
Let all the peo - ple praise Thee, Lord. Let all

praise Thee! Let all ____ the peo-ple praise Thy name for-
Let all

ev - er and for-ev - er - more, for - ev - er-more. O Lord! Let more.

119 Jesus, Thine All-victorious Love

CHARLES WESLEY

C. G. GLASER, ARR. BY LOWELL MASON

1. Je - sus, Thine all - vic - to - rious love Shed in my heart a - broad;
2. Oh, that in me the sa - cred fire Might now be - gin to glow,
3. Oh, that it now from heav'n might fall, And all my sins con - sume!
4. Re - fin - ing Fire, go thro' my heart; Il - lu - mi - nate my soul;
5. My stead-fast soul, from fall - ing free, Shall then no long - er move,

Then shall my feet no long - er rove, Root - ed and fixed in God.
Burn up the dross of base de - sire, And make the moun-tains flow!
Come, Ho - ly Ghost, for Thee I call; Spir - it of Burn-ing, come!
Scat - ter Thy life thro' ev - 'ry part, And sanc-ti - fy the whole.
While Christ is all the world to me, And all my heart is love.

120   Is Not This the Land of Beulah?

Anonymous   J. W. Dadmun

1. I am dwell-ing on the moun-tain, Where the gold-en sun-light gleams
2. I can see far down the moun-tain, Where I wan-dered wea-ry years,
3. I am drink-ing at the foun-tain, Where I ev-er would a-bide;
4. Tell me not of heav-y cross-es, Nor the bur-dens hard to bear,
5. Oh, the Cross has won-drous glo-ry! Oft I've proved this to be true.

O'er a land whose won-drous beau-ty Far ex-ceeds my fond-est dreams;
Of-ten hin-dered in my jour-ney By the ghosts of doubts and fears;
For I've tast-ed life's pure riv-er, And my soul is sat-is-fied.
For I've found this great sal-va-tion Makes each bur-den light ap-pear;
When I'm in the way so nar-row, I can see a path-way thro';

Where the air is pure, e-the-real, La-den with the breath of flowers.
Bro-ken vows and dis-ap-point-ments Thick-ly sprin-kled all the way,
There's no thirst-ing for life's pleasures, Nor a-dorn-ing rich and gay,
And I love to fol-low Je-sus, Glad-ly count-ing all but dross,
And how sweet-ly Je-sus whis-pers: "Take the cross; thou need'st not fear,

They are bloom-ing by the foun-tain, 'Neath the am-a-ran-thine bow'rs.
But the Spir-it led, un-err-ing, To the land I hold to-day.
For I've found a rich-er treas-ure, One that fad-eth not a-way.
World-ly hon-ors all for-sak-ing For the glo-ry of the Cross.
For I've trod the way be-fore thee, And the glo-ry lin-gers near."

Is Not This the Land of Beulah?

CHORUS

Is not this the Land of Beu-lah? Bless-ed, bless-ed land of light,

Where the flow-ers bloom for-ev-er And the sun is al-ways bright!

121   Come, Thou Almighty King

ANONYMOUS   FELICE DE GIARDINI

1. Come, Thou Al - might-y King. Help us Thy name to sing.
2. Come, Thou In - car - nate Word, Gird on Thy might - y sword,
3. Come, Ho - ly Com - fort - er, Thy sa - cred wit - ness bear
4. To the great One in Three E - ter - nal prais - es be

Help us to praise. Fa - ther, all - glo - ri - ous, O'er all vic-
Our prayer at - tend. Come, and Thy peo - ple bless, And give Thy
In this glad hour. Thou who al - might - y art, Now rule in
Hence ev - er - more. His sov'reign maj - es - ty May we in

to - ri - ous, Come and reign o - ver us, An - cient of Days.
Word suc - cess. Spir - it of ho - li - ness, On us de - scend.
ev - 'ry heart; And ne'er from us de - part, Spir - it of pow'r.
glo - ry see, And to e - ter - ni - ty Love and a - dore.

122 Oh, Could I Speak

SAMUEL MEDLEY

LOWELL MASON

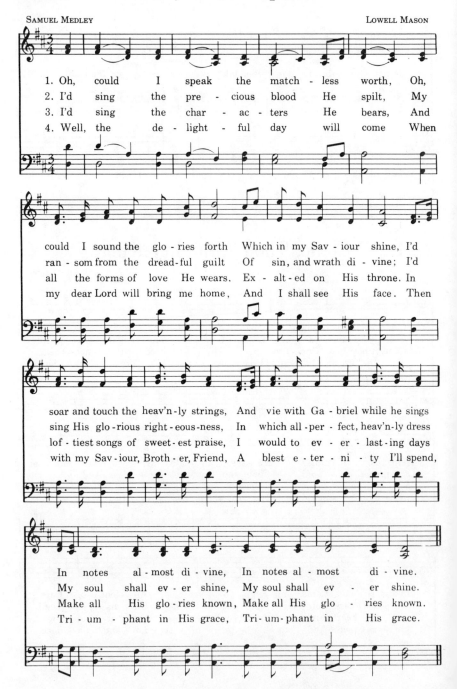

1. Oh, could I speak the match - less worth, Oh, could I sound the glo - ries forth Which in my Sav - iour shine, I'd soar and touch the heav'n - ly strings, And vie with Ga - briel while he sings In notes al - most di - vine, In notes al - most di - vine.

2. I'd sing the pre - cious blood He spilt, My ran - som from the dread - ful guilt Of sin, and wrath di - vine; I'd sing His glo - rious right - eous - ness, In which all - per - fect, heav'n - ly dress My soul shall ev - er shine, My soul shall ev - er shine.

3. I'd sing the char - ac - ters He bears, And all the forms of love He wears, Ex - alt - ed on His throne. In lof - tiest songs of sweet - est praise, I would to ev - er - last - ing days Make all His glo - ries known, Make all His glo - ries known.

4. Well, the de - light - ful day will come When my dear Lord will bring me home, And I shall see His face. Then with my Sav - iour, Broth - er, Friend, A blest e - ter - ni - ty I'll spend, Tri - um - phant in His grace, Tri - um - phant in His grace.

123 Look, Ye Saints, the Sight Is Glorious

Thomas Kelly

Henry Smart

1. Look, ye saints, the sight is glo - rious; See the Man of
2. Crown the Sav - iour, an - gels, crown Him. Rich the tro - phies
3. Hark, those bursts of ac - cla - ma - tion! Hark, those loud, tri -

Sor - rows now, From the fight re - turned vic - to - rious.
Je - sus brings. In the seat of pow'r en - throne Him,
um - phant chords! Je - sus takes the high - est sta - tion.

Ev - 'ry knee to Him shall bow. Crown Him, crown Him!
While the vault of heav - en rings. Crown Him, crown Him!
Oh, what joy the sight af - fords! Crown Him, crown Him!

Crown Him, crown Him! Crowns be - come the Vic - tor's brow.
Crown Him, crown Him! Crown the Sav - iour King of Kings.
Crown Him, crown Him! King of Kings, and Lord of Lords!

124   Thou Thinkest, Lord, of Me

E. D. MUND

E. S. LORENZ

1. A - mid the tri - als which I meet, A - mid the thorns that pierce my feet,
2. The cares of life come thronging fast, Up - on my soul their shadows cast;
3. Let shad-ows come, let shad-ows go; Let life be bright or dark with woe.

One tho't re - mains su - preme-ly sweet: Thou think-est, Lord, of me!
Their gloom re-minds my heart at last, Thou think-est, Lord, of me!
I am con - tent, for this I know: Thou think-est, Lord, of me!

CHORUS

Thou think-est, Lord, of me.   Thou think-est, Lord, of me.
of me.   of me.

What need I fear when Thou art near, And think - est, Lord, of me?

125   Dear Lord and Father of Mankind

JOHN G. WHITTIER

FREDERICK C. MAKER

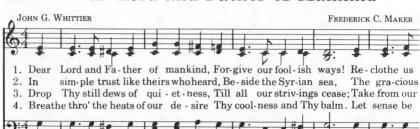

1. Dear Lord and Fa - ther of mankind, For-give our fool-ish ways! Re - clothe us
2. In sim - ple trust like theirs who heard, Be - side the Syr-ian sea, The gra-cious
3. Drop Thy still dews of qui - et - ness, Till all our striv-ings cease; Take from our
4. Breathe thro' the heats of our de - sire Thy cool-ness and Thy balm. Let sense be

Dear Lord and Father of Mankind

in our right-ful mind; In pur-er lives Thy service find; In deep - er rev'rence, praise.
call-ing of the Lord, Let us, like them, without a word, Rise up and fol-low Thee.
souls the strain and stress, And let our ordered lives confess The beauty of Thy peace.
dumb, let flesh retire; Speak thro' the earthquake, wind, and fire, O still small voice of calm!

126   Jewels

W. O. Cushing

Geo. F. Root

1. When He com - eth, when He com - eth, To make up His jew - els,
2. He will gath - er, He will gath - er The gems for His king-dom:
3. Lit - tle chil - dren, lit - tle chil - dren Who love their Re - deem - er

All His jew - els, pre - cious jew - els, His loved and His own.
All the pure ones, all the bright ones, His loved and His own.
Are the jew - els, pre - cious jew - els, His loved and His own.

Chorus

Like the stars of the morn - ing, His bright crown a - dorn - ing,

They shall shine in their beau - ty Bright gems for His crown.

127 Oh, That Will Be Glory

C. H. G.

CHAS. H. GABRIEL

1. When all my la-bors and tri-als are o'er, And I am safe on that
2. When, by the gift of His in-fi-nite grace, I am ac-cord-ed in
3. Friends will be there I have loved long a-go; Joy like a riv-er a-

beau-ti-ful shore, Just to be near the dear Lord I a-dore
heav-en a place, Just to be there and to look on His face
round me will flow; Yet, just a smile from my Sav-iour, I know,

rit.

CHORUS *faster*

Will thro' the a-ges be glo-ry for me. ___ Oh, that will be
Oh, ___ that will

glo-ry for me, Glo-ry for me, glo-ry for me. When by His grace
be glo-ry for me, glo-ry for me, glo-ry for me;

rit.

I shall look on His face, That will be glo-ry, be glo-ry for me.

128   My Saviour First of All

FANNY J. CROSBY

JNO. R. SWENEY

1. When my life-work is end-ed, and I cross the swell-ing tide, When the
2. Oh, the soul-thrill-ing rap-ture when I view His bless-ed face, And the
3. Oh, the dear ones in glo-ry, how they beck-on me to come, And our
4. Thro' the gates to the cit-y in a robe of spot-less white, He will

bright and glorious morning I shall see, I shall know my Redeem-er when I
lus-ter of His kind-ly beam-ing eye! How my full heart will praise Him for the
part-ing at the riv-er I re-call! To the sweet vales of Eden they will
lead me where no tears will ev-er fall; In the glad song of a-ges I shall

reach the oth-er side, And His smile will be the first to wel-come me.
mer-cy, love, and grace That pre-pare for me a man-sion in the sky!
sing my welcome home; But I long to meet my Sav-iour first of all.
min-gle with de-light. But I long to meet my Sav-iour first of all.

CHORUS

I shall know Him. I shall know Him, And redeem'd by His side I shall stand.
I shall know Him.

I shall know___ Him. I shall know Him By the print of the nails in His hand.
I shall know Him.

129   Sweet By and By

S. F. Bennett   J. P. Webster

1. There's a land that is fair-er than day, And by faith we can
2. We shall sing on that beau-ti-ful shore The me-lo-di-ous
3. To our boun-ti-ful Fa-ther a-bove We will of-fer our

see it a-far; For the Fa-ther waits o-ver the way, To pre-
songs of the blest, And our spir-its shall sor-row no more, Not a
trib-ute of praise, For the glo-ri-ous gift of His love And the

CHORUS

pare us a dwell-ing place there.
sigh for the bless-ing of rest.   In the sweet   by and
bless-ings that hal-low our days.   In the sweet

by,   We shall meet on that beau-ti-ful shore.   In the
by and by,
by and by.

sweet   by and by,   We shall meet on that beau-ti-ful shore.
In the sweet   by and by,

130 The Last Mile of the Way

JOHNSON OATMAN, JR.

WM. EDIE MARKS

1. If I walk in the path-way of du-ty, If I work till the close of the day, I shall see the great King in His beau-ty,
2. If for Christ I pro-claim the glad sto-ry, If I seek for His sheep gone a-stray, I am sure He will show me His glo-ry,
3. Here the dear-est of ties we must sev-er; Tears of sor-row are seen ev-'ry day; But no sick-ness, no sigh-ing for-ev-er,
4. And if here I have ear-nest-ly striv-en, And have tried all His will to o-bey, 'Twill en-hance all the rap-ture of heav-en,

CHORUS

When I've gone the last mile of the way. When I've gone the last mile of the way, the last mile of the way, I will rest at the close of the day; at the close of the day; And I know there are joys that a-wait me, When I've gone the last mile of the way.

131 The Eastern Gate

Copyright 1905. Renewed 1933 by I. G. Martin
Assigned to Nazarene Publishing House

I. G. M.   I. G. MARTIN

1. I   will meet you in the morn - ing,   Just in - side the East-ern Gate.
2. If   you has-ten off to   glo - ry,   Lin - ger near the East-ern Gate,
3. Keep your lamps all trimmed and burning; For the Bridegroom watch and wait.
4. Oh, the joys of that glad meet - ing With the saints who for us wait!

Then be read - y, faith-ful   pil - grim, Lest with you it be too late.
For   I'm com-ing in the morn - ing; So you'll not have long to wait.
He'll be with us at the meet - ing Just in - side the East-ern Gate.
What a bless-ed, hap - py meet - ing, Just in - side the East-ern Gate!

CHORUS

I will meet you,   I will meet you,   Just in -
      in the morn-ing,   in the morn-ing,

side the Eastern Gate over there.   I will meet you,
          o - ver there.   in the morn - ing,

I will meet you,   I will meet you in the morning o - ver there.
      in the morn-ing,

132 The Home Over There

D. W. C. Huntington

Tullius C. O'Kane

1. Oh, think of the home o - ver there, By the side of the riv - er of light,
2. Oh, think of the friends o - ver there, Who be - fore us the journey have trod;
3. My Sav-iour is now o - ver there; There my kindred and friends are at rest.
4. I'll soon be at home o - ver there, For the end of my jour-ney I see.

over there

Where the saints, all immortal and fair, Are robed in their garments of white.
Of the songs that they breathe on the air, In their home in the pal - ace of God.
Then a - way from my sor-row and care, Let me fly to the land of the blest.
Man - y dear to my heart o - ver there Are watch-ing and waiting for me.

over there

Refrain

O-ver there, o - ver there, Oh, think of the home o - ver there;
Oh, think of the friends o - ver there;
My Sav-iour is now o - ver there;
Over there, over there, I'll soon be at home o - ver there;

over there

O-ver there, o - ver there, o-ver there, Oh, think of the home o - ver there.
Oh, think of the friends o - ver there.
My Sav-iour is now o - ver there.
Over there, o - ver there, I'll soon be at home o - ver there.

133 In the New Jerusalem

C. B. W.

C. B. WIDMEYER

1. When the toils of life are o-ver And we lay our ar-mor down, And we
2. Tho' the way is some-times lone-ly, He will hold me with His hand. Thro' the
3. When the last good-by is spo-ken And the tear stains wiped a-way, And our
4. When we join the ran-somed ar-my In the sum-mer-land a-bove, And the

bid fare-well to earth with all its cares, We shall meet and greet our
test-ings and the tri - als I must go. But I'll trust and glad - ly
eyes shall catch a glimpse of glo - ry fair, Then with bound-ing hearts we'll
face of our dear Sav-iour we be - hold, We will sing and shout for-

loved ones, And our Christ we then shall crown In the new Je-ru-sa-lem.
fol - low, For some-time I'll un-der-stand, In the new Je-ru-sa-lem.
meet Him Who hath washed our sins a-way, In the new Je-ru-sa-lem.
ev - er And we'll grow in per-fect love, In the new Je-ru-sa-lem.

CHORUS

There'll be sing-ing, there'll be shout-ing When the saints come march-ing home,

In Je-ru-sa-lem, In Je-ru-sa-lem;
In the new Je-ru-sa-lem, In the new Je-ru-sa-lem;

In the New Jerusalem

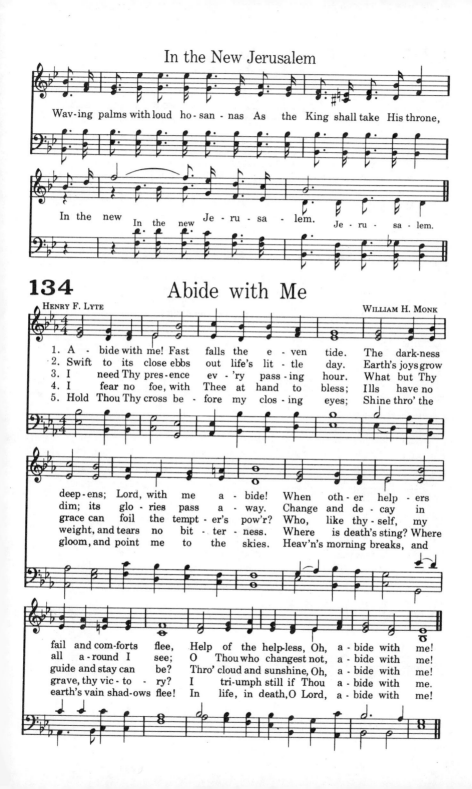

Wav-ing palms with loud ho-san-nas As the King shall take His throne,

In the new In the new Je-ru-sa-lem. Je-ru-sa-lem.

134 Abide with Me

Henry F. Lyte

William H. Monk

1. A - bide with me! Fast falls the e - ven tide. The dark-ness
2. Swift to its close ebbs out life's lit - tle day. Earth's joys grow
3. I need Thy pres-ence ev - 'ry pass - ing hour. What but Thy
4. I fear no foe, with Thee at hand to bless; Ills have no
5. Hold Thou Thy cross be - fore my clos - ing eyes; Shine thro' the

deep-ens; Lord, with me a - bide! When oth - er help - ers
dim; its glo - ries pass a - way. Change and de - cay in
grace can foil the tempt - er's pow'r? Who, like thy - self, my
weight, and tears no bit - ter - ness. Where is death's sting? Where
gloom, and point me to the skies. Heav'n's morning breaks, and

fail and com-forts flee, Help of the help-less, Oh, a - bide with me!
all a-round I see; O Thou who changest not, a - bide with me!
guide and stay can be? Thro' cloud and sunshine, Oh, a - bide with me!
grave, thy vic - to - ry? I tri-umph still if Thou a - bide with me.
earth's vain shad-ows flee! In life, in death, O Lord, a - bide with me!

135 The Pearly-white City

(The City That's Coming Down)

Copyright 1902. Renewed 1929 by Arthur F. Ingler Assigned to Nazarene Publishing House

A. F. I.

ARTHUR F. INGLER

1. There's a ho - ly and beau-ti - ful cit - y, Whose Builder and Ruler is God;
2. No sin is al-lowed in that cit - y, And nothing de - fil - ing nor mean;
3. No heart-aches are known in that city; No tears ev - er moisten the eye;
4. My loved ones are gath-er-ing yon-der; My friends are fast passing a - way;

John saw it de-scending from heav-en, When Patmos in ex - ile he trod.
No pain and no sick-ness can en - ter; No crape in that cit - y is seen;
There's no dis-ap-point-ment in heav-en, No en - vy and strife in the sky.
And soon I may join their bright number, And dwell in e - ter - ni - ty's day.

Its high, mas-sive wall is of jas-per; The cit - y it - self is pure gold.
Earth's sorrows and cares are for-got-ten; No tempt-er is there to an - noy;
The saints are all sanc-ti - fied whol-ly; They live in sweet har-mo-ny there.
They're safe now in glo - ry with Je - sus; Their tri - als and bat - tles are past;

rit. *ad lib.*

And when my frail tent here is fold-ed, Mine eyes shall its glo - ry be - hold.
No parting words ev - er are spo-ken; There's nothing to hurt and de - stroy.
My heart now is set on that cit - y, And some-day its blessings I'll share.
They o - ver-came sin and the tempter; They've reached that fair city at last.

CHORUS *Slow.*

In that bright cit - y,__ pearl - y - white cit - y,__ I have a

The Pearly-white City

man - sion, a harp, and a crown. Now I am watch-ing, wait-ing, and

rit. ad lib.

long - ing For the white cit - y.... John saw com - ing down.

136   Jesus Is Mine

CATHERINE J. BONAR   T. E. PERKINS

1. Fade, fade each earth - ly joy; Je - sus is mine! Break ev - 'ry
2. Tempt not my soul a - way; Je - sus is mine! Here would I
3. Fare - well, ye dreams of night; Je - sus is mine! Lost in this
4. Fare - well, mor - tal - i - ty; Je - sus is mine! Wel - come, e -

ten - der tie; Je - sus is mine! Dark is the wil - der - ness;
ev - er stay; Je - sus is mine! Per - ish - ing things of clay,
dawn - ing light, Je - sus is mine! All that my soul has tried
ter - ni - ty; Je - sus is mine! Wel - come, O loved and blest!

Earth has no rest - ing place. Je - sus a - lone can bless; Je - sus is mine!
Born for but one brief day, Pass from my heart a - way. Je - sus is mine!
Left but a dis - mal void. Je - sus has sat - is - fied; Je - sus is mine!
Wel - come, sweet scenes of rest! Wel - come, my Saviour's breast! Je - sus is mine!

137   We'll Understand It Better

C. A. T.

C. A. TINDLEY ARR. BY F. A. CLARK

1. We are of-ten tossed and driv'n on the rest-less sea of time.
2. We are of-ten des-ti-tute of the things that life de-mands—
3. Tri-als dark on ev-'ry hand, and we can-not un-der-stand
4. Temp - ta-tions, hid-den snares, of-ten take us un - a-wares,

Som-ber skies and howl-ing tem - pests oft suc-ceed a bright sunshine.
Want of food and want of shel - ter, thirst-y hills and bar-ren lands.
All the ways that God would lead us to that bless-ed Promised Land.
And our hearts are made to bleed for many a thought-less word or deed;

In that land of per-fect day, when the mists have rolled a-way, We will
We are trust-ing in the Lord and, ac - cord-ing to His Word, We will
But He guides us with His eye and we'll fol - low till we die, For we'll
And we won-der why the test when we try to do our best. But we'll

CHORUS

un-der-stand it bet-ter by and by (by and by). By and by when the morning comes,

When the saints of God are gathered home, We'll tell the sto-ry how we've o - ver-

We'll Understand It Better

come; For we'll un-der-stand it bet-ter by and by (by and by).

138   Saviour, More than Life

FANNY J. CROSBY

W. H. DOANE

1. Sav-iour, more than life to me, I am cling-ing, clinging close to Thee.
2. Thro' this changing world be - low Lead me gen-tly, gen-tly as I go.
3. Let me love Thee more and more Till this fleeting, fleeting life is o'er;

Let Thy pre-cious blood ap - plied Keep me ev - er, ev - er near Thy side.
Trusting Thee, I can - not stray; I can nev - er, nev - er lose my way.
Till my soul is lost in love In a brighter, brighter world a - bove.

REFRAIN

Ev-'ry day, ev'ry hour, Let me feel Thy cleansing pow'r.
Ev-'ry day and hour, ev - 'ry day and hour,

May Thy ten - der love to me Bind me clos-er, clos-er, Lord, to Thee.

139 Home of the Soul

ELLEN H. GATES

PHILIP PHILLIPS

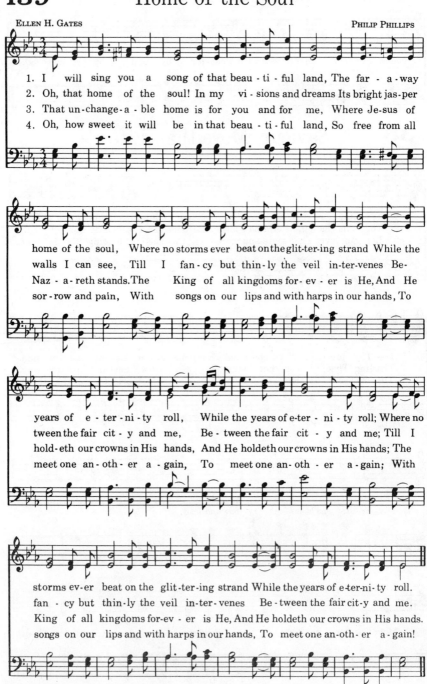

1. I will sing you a song of that beau-ti-ful land, The far-a-way
2. Oh, that home of the soul! In my vi-sions and dreams Its bright jas-per
3. That un-change-a-ble home is for you and for me, Where Je-sus of
4. Oh, how sweet it will be in that beau-ti-ful land, So free from all

home of the soul, Where no storms ever beat on the glit-ter-ing strand While the
walls I can see, Till I fan-cy but thin-ly the veil in-ter-venes Be-
Naz-a-reth stands. The King of all kingdoms for-ev-er is He, And He
sor-row and pain, With songs on our lips and with harps in our hands, To

years of e-ter-ni-ty roll, While the years of e-ter-ni-ty roll; Where no
tween the fair cit-y and me, Be-tween the fair cit-y and me; Till I
hold-eth our crowns in His hands, And He holdeth our crowns in His hands; The
meet one an-oth-er a-gain, To meet one an-oth-er a-gain; With

storms ev-er beat on the glit-ter-ing strand While the years of e-ter-ni-ty roll.
fan-cy but thin-ly the veil in-ter-venes Be-tween the fair cit-y and me.
King of all kingdoms for-ev-er is He, And He holdeth our crowns in His hands.
songs on our lips and with harps in our hands, To meet one an-oth-er a-gain!

140 The Unclouded Day

J. K. A.

J. K. ALWOOD

1. Oh, they tell me of a home far be - yond the skies; Oh, they
2. Oh, they tell me of a home where my friends have gone; Oh, they
3. Oh, they tell me of a King in His beau - ty there, And they
4. Oh, they tell me that He smiles on His chil - dren there, And His

tell me of a home far a - way; Oh, they tell me of a home
tell me of that land far a - way, Where the tree of life
tell me that mine eyes shall be - hold Where He sits on the throne
smile drives their sor - rows all a - way; And they tell me that no tears

where no storm-clouds rise; Oh, they tell me of an un - cloud-ed day!
in e - ter - nal bloom Sheds its fra-grance thro' the un - cloud-ed day!
that is whit-er than snow, In the cit - y that is made of gold!
ev - er come a - gain In that love - ly land of un - cloud-ed day.

CHORUS

Oh, the land of cloud-less day! Oh, the land of an un-clouded sky! Oh, they

tell me of a home where no storm-clouds rise! Oh, they tell me of an un-cloud-ed day!

141   There'll Be No Sorrow There

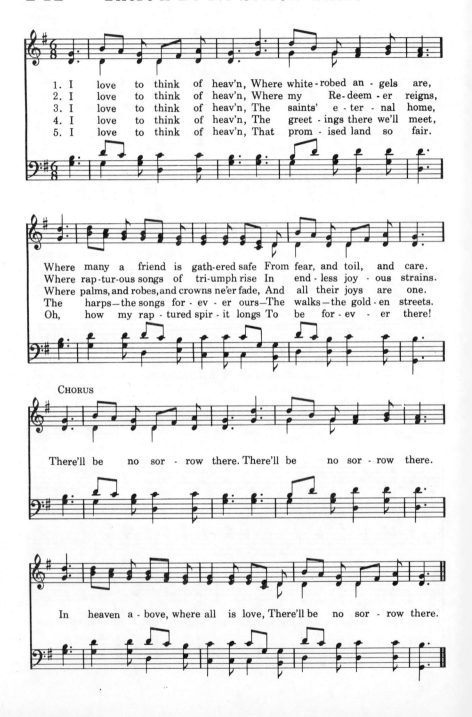

1. I love to think of heav'n, Where white-robed an - gels are,
2. I love to think of heav'n, Where my Re - deem - er reigns,
3. I love to think of heav'n, The saints' e - ter - nal home,
4. I love to think of heav'n, The greet - ings there we'll meet,
5. I love to think of heav'n, That prom - ised land so fair.

Where many a friend is gath-ered safe From fear, and toil, and care.
Where rap -tur-ous songs of tri-umph rise In end - less joy - ous strains.
Where palms, and robes, and crowns ne'er fade, And all their joys are one.
The harps—the songs for - ev - er ours—The walks—the gold - en streets.
Oh, how my rap - tured spir - it longs To be for - ev - er there!

CHORUS

There'll be no sor - row there. There'll be no sor - row there.

In heaven a - bove, where all is love, There'll be no sor - row there.

142 There'll Be No Shadows

EDGAR LEWIS

L. E. JONES

1. Tho' dark the path my feet may tread, it is but joy to know
2. Life's bright-est day may have its clouds, but still our hearts should sing,
3. We're marching home-ward to a land where wea-ry feet may rest.

There'll be no shad-ows on the oth-er side. We should not fear the
There'll be no shad-ows on the oth-er side. 'Twill not be long till
There'll be no shad-ows on the oth-er side. No pain nor sor-row

wild-est storm, but sing as on we go, There'll be no shad-ows
cares are o'er and we are with the King. There'll be no shad-ows
e'er can touch the re-gions of the blest. There'll be no shad-ows

CHORUS

on the other side. { There'll be no shadows, no shadows. Je-sus is the
{ There'll be no shadows, no shadows. Pain and death can

there'll be no more shadows.

1. sun-shine of that land so fair. nev-er en-ter there.
2. nev-er en-ter there.

143 Where They Need No Sun

Copyright 1912. Renewed 1939 by Chas. R. Scoville
Assigned to Nazarene Publishing House

H. L.

HALDOR LILLENAS

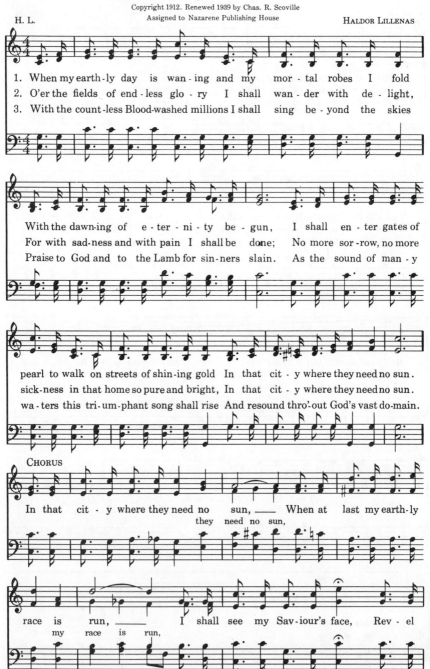

1. When my earth-ly day is wan-ing and my mor-tal robes I fold
2. O'er the fields of end-less glo-ry I shall wan-der with de-light,
3. With the count-less Blood-washed millions I shall sing be-yond the skies

With the dawn-ing of e-ter-ni-ty be-gun, I shall en-ter gates of
For with sad-ness and with pain I shall be done; No more sor-row, no more
Praise to God and to the Lamb for sin-ners slain. As the sound of man-y

pearl to walk on streets of shin-ing gold In that cit-y where they need no sun.
sick-ness in that home so pure and bright, In that cit-y where they need no sun.
wa-ters this tri-um-phant song shall rise And resound thro'-out God's vast do-main.

CHORUS

In that cit-y where they need no sun,—— When at last my earth-ly
they need no sun,

race is run,—— I shall see my Sav-iour's face, Rev-el
my race is run,

Where They Need No Sun

in His love and grace In that cit - y where they need no sun. no sun.

144   I Shall Be Like Him

W. A. S.

W. A. SPENCER

1. When I shall reach the more ex - cel-lent glo-ry, And all my tri-als are passed,
2. We shall not wait till the glo-ri-ous dawning Breaks on the vi-sion so fair.
3. More and more like Him, repeat the blest story O - ver and o - ver a - gain!

I shall be like Him, oh, won-der-ful sto-ry! I shall be like Him at last.
Now we may welcome the heav-en-ly morning; Now we His im-age may bear.
Changed by His Spirit from glo-ry to glo-ry, I shall be sat - is -fied then.

CHORUS

I shall be like Him, I shall be like Him, And in His beau-ty shall shine.

I shall be like Him, wondrously like Him, Je-sus, my Sav-iour di - vine.

145 When the Roll Is Called Up Yonder

J. M. B.

J. M. BLACK

1. When the trum-pet of the Lord shall sound, and time shall be no more, And the
2. On that bright and cloudless morning when the dead in Christ shall rise, And the
3. Let us la - bor for the Mas - ter from the dawn till set - ting sun; Let us

morning breaks, e - ter - nal, bright, and fair; When the saved of earth shall gath-er
glo - ry of His res - ur - rec -tion share; When His cho-sen ones shall gath-er
talk of all His wondrous love and care. Then when all of life is o - ver,

o - ver on the oth - er shore, And the roll is called up yon-der, I'll be there.
to their home beyond the skies, And the roll is called up yon-der, I'll be there.
and our work on earth is done, And the roll is called up yon-der, I'll be there.

CHORUS

When the roll _____ is called up yon - der, When the
When the roll is called up yon - der, I'll be there.

roll _____ is called up yon - der, When the roll _____ is called up
When the roll is called up yon-der, I'll be there.   When the roll is called up

When the Roll Is Called Up Yonder

yon - der, When the roll is called up yon - der, I'll be there.

146   Shall We Gather at the River?

R. L.

ROBERT LOWRY

1. Shall we gath - er at the riv - er, Where bright an-gel feet have trod,
2. On the mar-gin of the riv - er, Wash-ing up its sil - ver spray,
3. Ere we reach the shin-ing riv - er, Lay we ev - 'ry bur-den down;
4. Soon we'll reach the shin-ing riv - er; Soon our pil - grim-age will cease;

With its crys - tal tide for - ev - er Flow-ing by the throne of God?
We will walk and wor-ship ev - er, All the hap - py, gold - en day.
Grace our spir-its will de - liv - er And pro - vide a robe and crown.
Soon our hap - py hearts will quiv-er With the mel - o - dy of peace.

CHORUS   *p*

Yes, we'll gath-er at the riv - er, The beau - ti - ful, the beau - ti - ful riv - er;

Gath-er with the saints at the riv - er That flows by the throne of God.

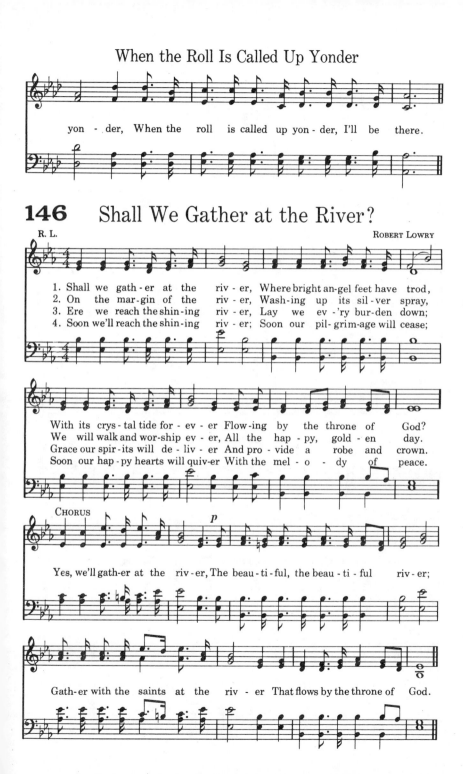

147 Zion's Hill

J. A. C.

JAMES ALLEN CRUTCHFIELD
ARR. BY H. L.

1. There waits for me a glad to-mor-row, Where gates of pearl swing open wide;
2. Some-day I'll hear the an-gels sing-ing, Be-yond the shadows of the tomb;
3. Some-day my la-bors will be end-ed, And all my wand'rings will be o'er,
4. Some-day the dark clouds will be rift-ed, And all the night of gloom be past,

And when I've passed this vale of sor-row, I'll dwell up-on the oth-er side.
And all the bells of heaven ringing, While saints are singing, "Home, sweet home."
And all earth's broken ties be mend-ed, And I shall sigh and weep no more.
And all life's burdens will be lift-ed; The day of rest shall dawn at last.

CHORUS

Some-day be-yond the reach of mor-tal ken; Some-day— God

on-ly knows just where and when—The wheels of mor-tal life shall

all stand still, And I shall go to dwell on Zi-on's hill.

148 He Never Has Failed Me Yet

W. J. H.   W. J. Henry

1. When I trav-el the path-way so rug-ged and steep, When I pass thro' the
2. So I walk by His side thro' the heat of the day. Where He leads me I
3. Then I'll dread not the fu-ture, and fear not the foe. I am safe in His

val-ley so dark and so deep, And when snares for my soul by my
fol-low; His will I o-bey. And He makes me to con-quer the
keep-ing wher-ev-er I go; For no soul that has trust-ed Him

Refrain

foes have been set, Je-sus nev-er has failed me yet.
ills that be-set, For He nev-er has failed me yet. He nev-er has
will He for-get, For He nev-er has failed me yet.

failed me yet. He nev-er has failed me yet. I have prov-en Him

true; what He says He will do. He nev-er has failed me yet.

149   Jesus Understands!

BIRDIE BELL   WM. J. KIRKPATRICK

1. Bowed be-neath your bur-den, is there none to share? Wea-ry with the
2. Ev - 'ry heav-y bur-den He will glad-ly share. Are you sad and
3. Tho' temp-ta-tion meet you, Je-sus can sus-tain. Life has vex-ing
4. Wea-ry heart, He calls you,"Come to Me and rest." Does the path grow

jour-ney, is there none to care? Cour-age, way-worn trav-'ler;
wea-ry? Je-sus has a care. Well He knows the path-way
prob-lems which He can ex-plain. Serve Him where He sends you,
rug-ged? Yet His way is best. Leave the un-known fu - ture

heed your Lord's commands. There's a tho't to cheer you: Je-sus un-der-stands.
o'er life's burning sands. Courage, fainting pil-grim; Je-sus un-der-stands.
though in dis-tant lands. Do not doubt or ques-tion; Je-sus un-der-stands.
in the Mas-ter's hands. Whether sad or joy-ful, Je-sus un-der-stands.

CHORUS

Yes, He un-der-stands. All His ways are best. Hear, He
oh, yes,   oh, hear,

calls to you,"Come to Me and rest." Leave the un-known fu - ture

Jesus Understands

in the Mas-ter's hands. Whether sad or joy - ful, Je - sus un - der-stands.

150 God Will Take Care of You

C. D. MARTIN

W. S. MARTIN

1. Be not dis-mayed what - e'er be-tide; God will take care of you.
2. Thro' days of toil when heart doth fail, God will take care of you;
3. All you may need He will pro-vide; God will take care of you.
4. No mat - ter what may be the test, God will take care of you.

Be - neath His wings of love a - bide; God will take care of you.
When dan - gers fierce your path as - sail, God will take care of you.
Noth-ing you ask will be de - nied; God will take care of you.
Lean, wea - ry one, up - on His breast; God will take care of you.

CHORUS

God will take care of you, Thro' ev -'ry day, O'er all the way.

He will take care of you; God will take care of you.
take care of you.

151 Never Alone

E. E. Hewitt

C. F. O. Arr. by W. J. K.

1. "Fear not, I am with thee"—Bless-ed gold-en ray, Like a
2. Ros-es fade a-round me, Lil-ies bloom and die, Earth-ly
3. Steps un-seen be-fore me, Hid-den dan-gers near; Near-er

star of glo-ry Light-ing up my way! Thro' the clouds of
sun-beams van-ish — Ra-diant still the sky! Je-sus, Rose of
still my Sav-iour, Whisp'ring, "Be of cheer!" Joys, like birds at

mid-night This bright prom-ise shone: "I will nev-er leave thee,
Shar-on, Bloom-ing for His own; Je-sus, heav-en's Sun-shine,
springtime, To my heart have flown, Sing-ing all so sweet-ly,

Chorus

Nev-er will leave thee a-lone." No, nev-er a-lone;
Nev-er will leave me a-lone.
"He will not leave me a-lone." Nev-er a-lone, nev-er a-lone,

No, nev-er a-lone; He prom-ised nev-er to leave me,

Never Alone

Nev - er to leave me a - lone. Nev - er to leave me a - lone.

152 I Must Tell Jesus

E. A. H.   E. A. HOFFMAN

1. I must tell Je-sus all of my tri-als; I cannot bear these burdens a-lone.
2. I must tell Je-sus all of my troubles; He is a kind, compassionate Friend.
3. Tempted and tried, I need a great Saviour, One who can help my burdens to bear.

In my dis - tress He kindly will help me; He ever loves and cares for His own.
If   I but   ask Him, He will de-liv- er, Make of my troub-les quickly an end.
I must tell Je-sus, I must tell Je-sus; He all my cares and sorrows will share.

REFRAIN

I must tell Je-sus! I must tell Je-sus! I can-not bear my burdens a - lone.

I must tell Je-sus! I must tell Je -sus! Je-sus can help me, Je-sus a - lone.

153 A Child of the King

HATTIE E. BUELL

JOHN R. SUMNER, ARR.

1. My Fa - ther is rich in hous - es and lands; He hold - eth the
2. My Fa - ther's own Son, the Sav - iour of men, Once wandered o'er
3. I once was an out - cast stran - ger on earth, A sin - ner by
4. A tent or a cot - tage, why should I care? They're building a

wealth of the world in His hands! Of ru - bies and dia-monds, of
earth as the poor - est of them; But now He is reign-ing for-
choice, an al - ien by birth! But I've been a - dopt-ed; my
pal - ace for me o - ver there! Tho' ex - iled from home, yet

sil - ver and gold, His cof - fers are full— He has rich-es un-told.
ev - er on high, And will give me a home in heav'n by and by.
name's written down; I'm heir to a man-sion, a robe, and a crown!
still I may sing: "All glo - ry to God, I'm a child of the King!"

CHORUS

I'm a child of the King! A child of the King!

With Je - sus, my Sav-iour, I'm a child of the King!

154 God Leads Us Along

G. A. Y.

G. A. Young

1. In shad-y green pas-tures so rich and so sweet, God leads His dear
2. Some-times on the mount where the sun shines so bright, God leads His dear
3. Tho' sor-rows be-fall us and Sa-tan op-pose, God leads His dear
4. A-way from the mire, and a-way from the clay, God leads His dear

chil-dren a-long. Where the wa-ter's cool flow bathes the wea-ry one's feet,
chil-dren a-long. Some-times in the val-ley in the dark-est of night,
chil-dren a-long. Through grace we can con-quer, de-feat all our foes.
chil-dren a-long. A-way up in glo-ry, e-ter-ni-ty's day,

CHORUS

God leads His dear children a-long. Some thro' the waters, some thro' the flood,

Some thro' the fire, but all thro' the Blood; Some thro' great sor-row, but

rit.

God gives a song In the night sea-son and all the day long.

155 How Can I Be Lonely?

H. L. *Legato*

HALDOR LILLENAS

1. One is walk-ing with me o - ver life's un - e - ven way, Con-stant-ly sup-
2. Days may bring their burdens and their trials as I go, But my Lord is
3. In the hour of sad be-reavement or of bit - ter loss, I can find sup-
4. In life's ros - y morning when the skies a - bove are clear, In its noon-tide

port-ing me each mo-ment of the day. How can I be lone-ly when such
near and helps to make them lighter grow. Life may have its cross-es or its
port and con - so - la - tion at the Cross. Want or woe or suf-f'ring, all seem
hours with man-y cares and problems near, Or when eve-ning shad-ows fall at

REFRAIN

fel-low-ship is mine, With my blessed Lord di - vine!
loss-es, or in-crease; Je-sus meets them all with peace.
glo-ri-fied when He Dai-ly walks and talks with me. How can I be lone-ly
clos-ing of my day, Je-sus will be there al - way.

When I've Je - sus on - ly To be my Com-pan-ion and un - fail-ing Guide?

rit.

Why should I be wea-ry, Or my path seem dreary, When He's walking by my side?

156 It Is Well with My Soul

H. G. SPAFFORD

P. P. BLISS

1. When peace like a riv - er at - tend-eth my way, When sor - rows like
2. Though Sa-tan should buf-fet, tho' trials should come, Let this blest as-
3. My sin—oh, the bliss of this glo - ri-ous tho't!—My sin — not in
4. And, Lord, haste the day when the faith shall be sight, The clouds be rolled

sea - bil-lows roll; What - ev - er my lot, Thou hast taught me to say,
sur - ance con - trol, That Christ hath re - gard - ed my help-less es - tate,
back as a scroll, The trump shall re-sound and the Lord shall de-scend.
back as a scroll, The trump shall re-sound and the Lord shall de-scend.

CHORUS

"It is well, it is well with my soul."
And hath shed His own blood for my soul. It is well ____
Praise the Lord, praise the Lord, O my soul!
"E - ven so"— it is well with my soul. It is well

with my soul. ____ It is well, it is well with my soul.
with my soul.

157   Jesus Is All I Need

JAMES ROWE

Arrangement copyright 1929 by Adger M. Pace

ADGER M. PACE

1. When I am bur-dened, or wea-ry and sad, Je-sus is
2. When I am tempt-ed and fear I may fall, Je-sus is
3. When I am swept by the tem-pests of life, Je-sus is
4. When thro' the val-ley He calls me to go, Je-sus is

all I need. Nev-er He fails to up-lift and make glad.
all I need. He nev-er fails to re-spond to my call.
all I need. Peace He im-parts, what-so-ev-er the strife.
all I'll need. He will be with me to cheer me, I know.

Je-sus is all I
Je-sus is all I
Je-sus is all I need. All that I need He will
Je-sus is all I'll

CHORUS

al-ways be, All that I need till His face I see. All that I

rit.

need thro' e-ter-ni-ty, Je-sus is all I need.

158 Jesus Will Walk with Me

H. L.

HALDOR LILLENAS

1. Je-sus will walk with me down thro' the val-ley. Je-sus will walk with me
2. Je-sus will walk with me when I am tempt-ed, Giv-ing me strength as my
3. Je-sus will walk with me, guarding me ev - er, Giv-ing me vic-t'ry thro'
4. Je-sus will walk with me in life's fair morning, And when the shadows of

o - ver the plain. When in the shad-ow or when in the sun-shine,
need may de - mand. When in af - flic-tion His pres-ence is near me,
storm and thro' strife. He is my Com-fort-er, Coun-sel - or, Lead-er,
eve - ning must come. Liv - ing or dy - ing, He will not for - sake me.

CHORUS

If He goes with me I shall not com-plain.
I am up-held by His al-might-y hand. Je———sus will
O - ver the un - e - ven jour-ney of life.
Je-sus will walk with me all the way home. Je - sus, my Sav-iour, will

walk with me. He will talk with me. He will walk with me. In joy or in

sor-row, to - day and to - mor-row, I know He will walk with me.
will walk with me.

159 The Cross Is Not Greater

B. B.

BALLINGTON BOOTH

1. The cross that He gave may be heav-y, But it ne'er out-weighs His grace.
2. The thorns in my path are not sharp-er Than composed His crown for me;
3. The light of His love shin-eth brighter As it falls on paths of woe.
4. His will I have joy in ful-fill-ing, As I'm walk-ing in His sight;

The storm that I feared may surround me, But it ne'er ex-cludes His face.
The cup that I drink not more bit-ter Than He drank in Geth-sem-a-ne.
The toil of my work groweth light-er As I stoop to raise the low.
My all to the Blood I am bring-ing. It a-lone can keep me right.

CHORUS

The cross is not great-er than His grace. The storm can-not

hide His bless-ed face. I am sat-is-fied to know

That, with Je-sus, here be-low I can con-quer ev-'ry foe.

160 Under His Wings

William O. Cushing

Ira D. Sankey

1. Un-der His wings I am safe-ly a-bid-ing. Tho' the night
2. Un-der His wings, what a ref-uge in sor-row! How the heart
3. Un-der His wings, oh, what pre-cious en-joy-ment! There will I

deep-ens and tem-pests are wild, Still I can trust Him; I
yearn-ing-ly turns to His rest! Of-ten when earth has no
hide till life's tri-als are o'er; Shel-tered, pro-tect-ed, no

know He will keep me. He has re-deemed me, and I am His child.
balm for my heal-ing, There I find com-fort, and there I am blest.
e - vil can harm me. Rest-ing in Je-sus, I'm safe ev-er-more.

CHORUS

Un-der His wings, un-der His wings, Who from His love can sev-er?

Un-der His wings my soul shall a-bide, Safe-ly a-bide for-ev-er.

161 Your Roses May Have Thorns

H. L.

HALDOR LILLENAS

1. Life's sunshine may be checkered with its shad-ows, The pleas-ant val-leys
2. The peace-ful day may change to rag-ing tem-pest, But know that af-ter
3. The with-ered flow-ers hold the seeds of prom-ise; The win-ter days are
4. The sor-rows that have come to you un-bid-den Have of-ten brought a

meet the rug-ged hills; The qui-et sea may change to rag-ing bil-lows; But
tem-pest comes the calm; And know that after night must come the morning, And
har-bin-gers of spring; The tri-als that may of-ten seem most bit-ter May
peace be-fore un-known. The Mak-er of your des-ti-ny is striv-ing To

CHORUS

all is well if so the Fa-ther wills.
af-ter sad bereavement heal-ing balm.
bring to you the joys that make you sing. Your roses may have thorns, but don't for-
fit your heart to be His roy-al throne.

get Your thorns may have some roses, too.___ The Lord of great com-
don't forget   ros-es, too.

pas-sion loves you yet, And He will nev-er fail to see you through.
loves you yet,

162 No, Not One!

JOHNSON OATMAN, JR.

GEO. C. HUGG

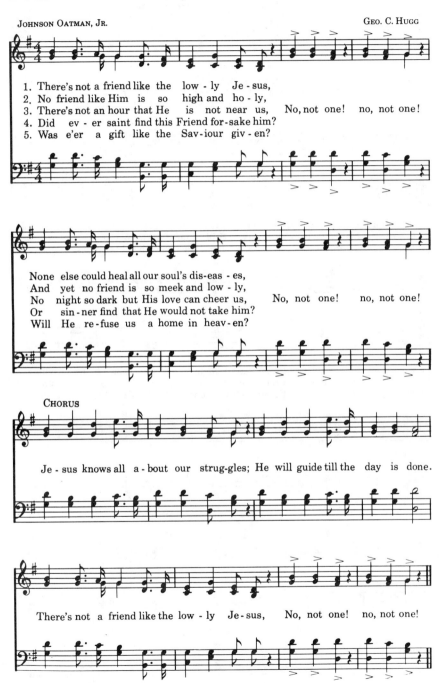

1. There's not a friend like the low-ly Je-sus,
2. No friend like Him is so high and ho-ly,
3. There's not an hour that He is not near us,   No, not one! no, not one!
4. Did ev-er saint find this Friend for-sake him?
5. Was e'er a gift like the Sav-iour giv-en?

None else could heal all our soul's dis-eas-es,
And yet no friend is so meek and low-ly,
No night so dark but His love can cheer us,   No, not one! no, not one!
Or sin-ner find that He would not take him?
Will He re-fuse us a home in heav-en?

CHORUS

Je-sus knows all a-bout our strug-gles; He will guide till the day is done.

There's not a friend like the low-ly Je-sus,   No, not one! no, not one!

163 'Tis Good to Live in Canaan

Mrs. C. H. M.

Mrs. C. H. Morris

1. I heard God's voice commanding, "Go up, the land pos-sess," And trust-ing
2. The land I'm now ex-plor-ing and get-ting far-ther in, And tent-ing
3. This land of peace and plen-ty is yours by faith to claim. There's perfect

in His grace I fol-lowed on. From E-gypt's cru-el bond-age and
tow'rds the highlands ev-'ry day; Still far-ther from the low-lands of
love and rest from in-bred sin. Its mountain heights possess-ing through

from the wil-der-ness, From Ka-desh in-to Ca-naan I have gone.
un-be-lief and sin, From glo-ry un-to glo-ry all the way.
faith in Je-sus' name, Cross o-ver and the vic-t'ry life be-gin.

CHORUS

'Tis good to live in Ca-naan, where grapes of Esh-col grow. 'Tis

good to live in Ca-naan, where milk and hon-ey flow. 'Tis good to live in

'Tis Good to Live in Canaan

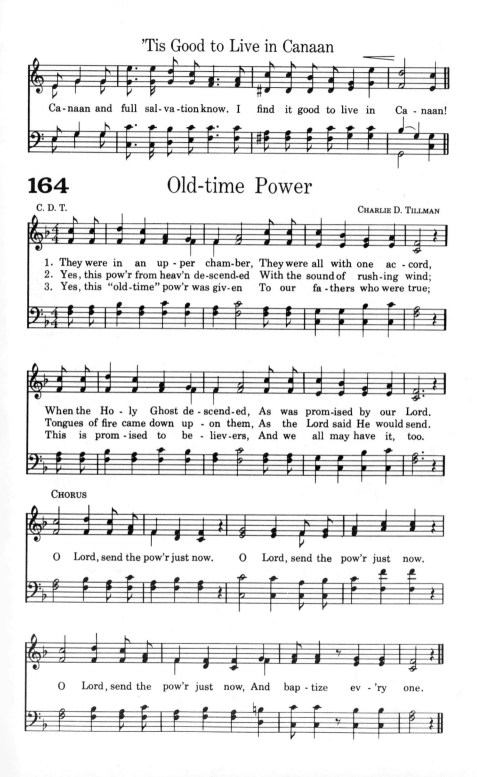

Ca-naan and full sal-va-tion know. I find it good to live in Ca - naan!

164   Old-time Power

C. D. T.   CHARLIE D. TILLMAN

1. They were in an up - per cham-ber, They were all with one ac - cord,
2. Yes, this pow'r from heav'n de-scend-ed With the sound of rush-ing wind;
3. Yes, this "old-time" pow'r was giv-en To our fa - thers who were true;

When the Ho - ly Ghost de - scend-ed, As was prom-ised by our Lord.
Tongues of fire came down up - on them, As the Lord said He would send.
This is prom -ised to be - liev-ers, And we all may have it, too.

CHORUS

O Lord, send the pow'r just now. O Lord, send the pow'r just now.

O Lord, send the pow'r just now, And bap - tize ev - 'ry one.

165 The Haven of Rest

H. L. GILMOUR

GEORGE D. MOORE

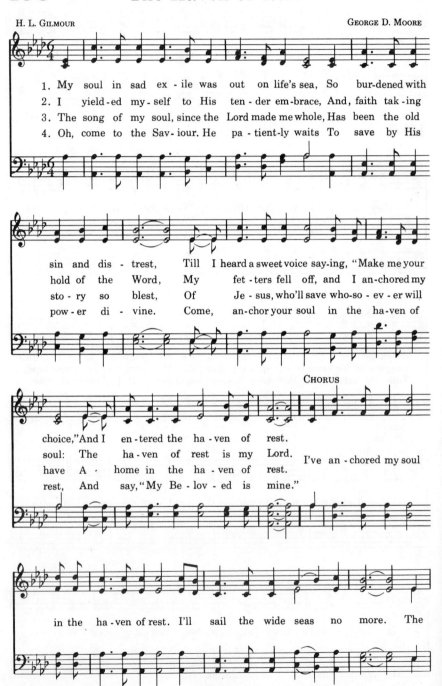

1. My soul in sad ex-ile was out on life's sea, So bur-dened with
2. I yield-ed my-self to His ten-der em-brace, And, faith tak-ing
3. The song of my soul, since the Lord made me whole, Has been the old
4. Oh, come to the Sav-iour. He pa-tient-ly waits To save by His

sin and dis-trest, Till I heard a sweet voice say-ing, "Make me your
hold of the Word, My fet-ters fell off, and I an-chored my
sto-ry so blest, Of Je-sus, who'll save who-so-ev-er will
pow-er di-vine. Come, an-chor your soul in the ha-ven of

CHORUS

choice,"And I en-tered the ha-ven of rest.
soul: The ha-ven of rest is my Lord.
have A home in the ha-ven of rest.
rest, And say, "My Be-lov-ed is mine."

I've an-chored my soul

in the ha-ven of rest. I'll sail the wide seas no more. The

The Haven of Rest

tem - pest may sweep o'er the wild, storm-y deep; In Je-sus I'm safe ev-er - more.

166 Wonderful Words of Life

P. P. B.

P. P. BLISS

1. Sing them o - ver a - gain to me, Won-der-ful words of Life!
2. Christ, the bless - ed One, gives to all Won-der-ful words of Life.
3. Sweet - ly ech - o the gos - pel call, Won-der-ful words of Life!

Let me more of their beau - ty see, Won-der-ful words of Life!
Sin - ner, list to the lov - ing call, Won-der-ful words of Life.
Of - fer par - don and peace to all, Won-der-ful words of Life!

Words of life and beau-ty, Teach me faith and du - ty:
All so free - ly giv - en, Woo - ing us to heav - en:
Je - sus, on - ly Sav-iour, Sanc - ti - fy for - ev - er.

REFRAIN

Beau-ti-ful words, wonder-ful words, Wonder-ful words of Life! Life!

167 Since the Holy Ghost Abides

Copyright 1905. Renewed 1933 by Mrs. F. E. Hill
Nazarene Publishing House, owner

F. E. H.

MRS. F. E. HILL

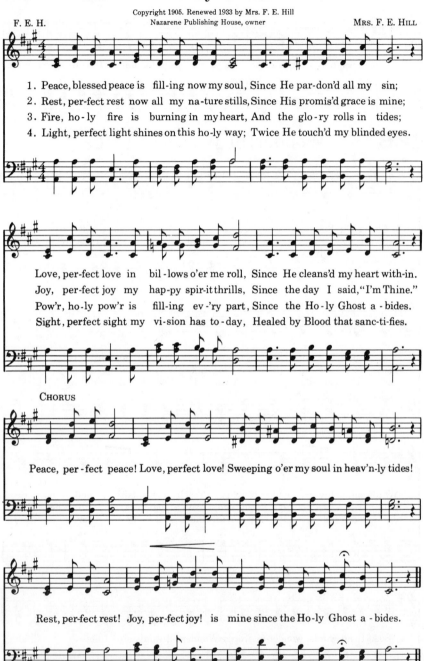

1. Peace, blessed peace is fill-ing now my soul, Since He par-don'd all my sin;
2. Rest, per-fect rest now all my na-ture stills, Since His promis'd grace is mine;
3. Fire, ho-ly fire is burning in my heart, And the glo-ry rolls in tides;
4. Light, perfect light shines on this ho-ly way; Twice He touch'd my blinded eyes.

Love, per-fect love in bil-lows o'er me roll, Since He cleans'd my heart with-in.
Joy, per-fect joy my hap-py spir-it thrills, Since the day I said, "I'm Thine."
Pow'r, ho-ly pow'r is fill-ing ev-'ry part, Since the Ho-ly Ghost a-bides.
Sight, perfect sight my vi-sion has to-day, Healed by Blood that sanc-ti-fies.

CHORUS

Peace, per-fect peace! Love, perfect love! Sweeping o'er my soul in heav'n-ly tides!

Rest, perfect rest! Joy, per-fect joy! is mine since the Ho-ly Ghost a-bides.

168 The Blood Will Never Lose Its Power

MRS. C. D. MARTIN

W. STILLMAN MARTIN

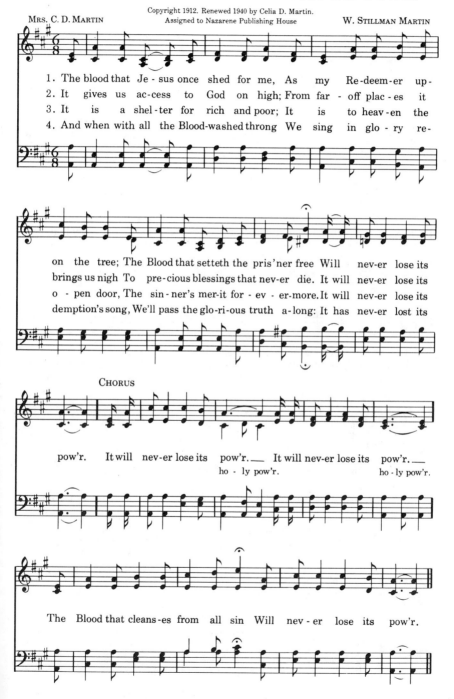

1. The blood that Je - sus once shed for me, As my Re-deem-er up-
2. It gives us ac-cess to God on high; From far - off plac-es it
3. It is a shel-ter for rich and poor; It is to heav-en the
4. And when with all the Blood-washed throng We sing in glo-ry re-

on the tree; The Blood that setteth the pris'ner free Will nev-er lose its
brings us nigh To pre-cious blessings that nev-er die. It will nev-er lose its
o - pen door, The sin-ner's mer-it for-ev-er-more. It will nev-er lose its
demption's song, We'll pass the glo-ri-ous truth a-long: It has nev-er lost its

CHORUS

pow'r. It will nev-er lose its pow'r. — It will nev-er lose its pow'r. —
ho - ly pow'r. ho - ly pow'r.

The Blood that cleans-es from all sin Will nev - er lose its pow'r.

169 'Tis Burning in My Soul

DELIA T. WHITE   WM. J. KIRKPATRICK

1. God sent His might-y pow'r To this poor, sin-ful heart, To
2. Be-fore the Cross I bow, Up-on the al-tar lay A
3. No good that I have done, His prom-ise I em-brace; Ac-

keep me ev-'ry hour And need-ful grace im-part; And since His Spir-it came
will-ing of-f'ring now, My all from day to day. My Sav-iour paid the price;
cept-ed in the Son, He saves me by His grace. All glo-ry be to God!

To take su-preme control, The love-en-kin-dled flame Is burn-ing in my soul.
My name He sweetly calls. Up-on the sac-ri-fice The fire from heav-en falls.
Let hal-le-lu-jahs roll! His love is shed a-broad; The fire is in my soul.

CHORUS

'Tis burn-ing in my soul. 'Tis burn-ing in my soul. The fire of heav'n-ly

love is burn-ing in my soul. The Ho-ly Spir-it came, All
burn-ing in my soul.

'Tis Burning in My Soul

glo-ry to His name! The fire of heav'nly love is burn-ing in my soul.

burn-ing in my soul.

170 At Calvary

WM. R. NEWELL

D. B. TOWNER

1. Years I spent in van-i-ty and pride, Car-ing not my Lord was
2. By God's Word at last my sin I learned; Then I trem-bled at the
3. Now I've giv'n to Je-sus ev-'ry-thing; Now I glad-ly own Him
4. Oh, the love that drew sal-va-tion's plan! Oh, the grace that bro't it

cru-ci-fied, Know-ing not it was for me He died On Cal-va-ry.
law I'd spurned, Till my guilt-y soul im-plor-ing turned To Cal-va-ry.
as my King; Now my raptured soul can on-ly sing Of Cal-va-ry.
down to man! Oh, the might-y gulf that God did span At Cal-va-ry!

CHORUS

Mer-cy there was great, and grace was free; Par-don there was mul-ti-

plied to me; There my burdened soul found lib-er-ty, At Cal-va-ry.

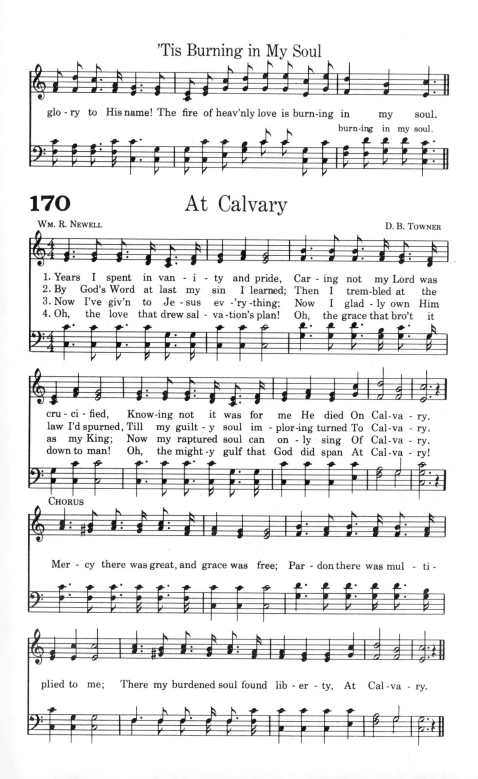

171 The Hallelujah Side

JOHNSON OATMAN, JR.

J. HOWARD ENTWISLE

1. Once a sin-ner far from Je-sus, I was per-ish-ing with cold; But the
2. Tho' the world may sweep a-round me with her daz-zle and her dreams, Yet I
3. Not for all earth's golden millions would I leave this pre-cious place, Tho' the
4. Here the sun is al-ways shining, here the sky is always bright; 'Tis no
5. And up-on the streets of glo-ry, when we reach the other shore, And have

bless-ed Sav-iour heard me when I cried. Then He threw His robe a-round me, and He
en-vy not her van-i-ties and pride; For my soul looks up to heaven, where the
tempt-er to per-suade me oft has tried; For I'm safe in God's pa-vil-ion, hap-py
place for gloomy Christians to a-bide. For my soul is filled with music and my
safe-ly crossed the Jordan's rolling tide, You will find me shouting "Glory" just out-

led me to His fold, And
gold-en sun-light gleams, And
in His love and grace, And I'm liv-ing on the hal-le-lu-jah side.
heart with great de-light, And
side my man-sion door, Where

CHORUS

Oh, glo-ry be to Je-sus! Let the hal-le-lu-jahs roll. Help me

ring the Saviour's praises far and wide. For I've o-pened up tow'rd heaven all the

The Hallelujah Side

win-dows of my soul, And I'm liv-ing on the hal-le-lu-jah side.

172 At the Cross

Isaac Watts

R. E. Hudson

1. A - las! and did my Sav-iour bleed, And did my Sov'reign die? Would
2. Was it for crimes that I have done He groaned up-on the tree? A -
3. Well might the sun in dark-ness hide, And shut his glo-ries in When
4. But drops of grief can ne'er re - pay The debt of love I owe. Here,

Chorus

He de-vote that sa-cred head For such a worm as I?
maz-ing pit - y, grace unknown, And love be-yond de-gree! At the Cross, at the
Christ, the mighty Mak - er, died For man, the creature's, sin.
Lord, I give my-self a-way; 'Tis all that I can do!

Cross, where I first saw the light, And the burden of my heart rolled a-way,

rolled a-way,

It was there by faith I re-ceived my sight, And now I am hap-py all the day!

173   The Solid Rock

EDWARD MOTE

WILLIAM B. BRADBURY

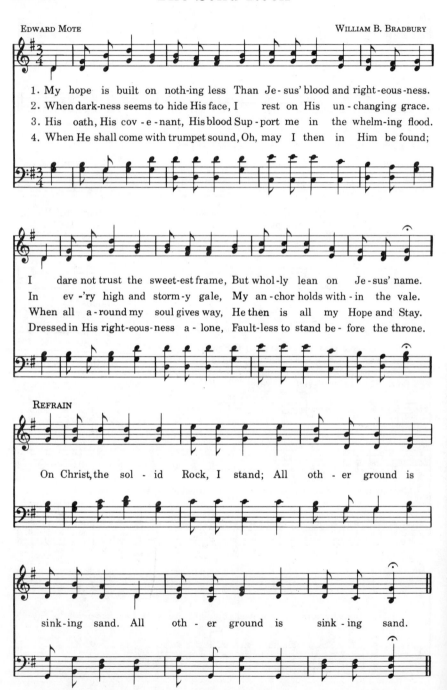

1. My hope is built on noth-ing less Than Je-sus' blood and right-eous-ness.
2. When dark-ness seems to hide His face, I rest on His un-changing grace.
3. His oath, His cov-e-nant, His blood Sup-port me in the whelm-ing flood.
4. When He shall come with trumpet sound, Oh, may I then in Him be found;

I dare not trust the sweet-est frame, But whol-ly lean on Je-sus' name.
In ev-'ry high and storm-y gale, My an-chor holds with-in the vale.
When all a-round my soul gives way, He then is all my Hope and Stay.
Dressed in His right-eous-ness a-lone, Fault-less to stand be-fore the throne.

REFRAIN

On Christ, the sol-id Rock, I stand; All oth-er ground is

sink-ing sand. All oth-er ground is sink-ing sand.

174 The Cleansing Wave

PHOEBE PALMER

MRS. J. F. KNAPP

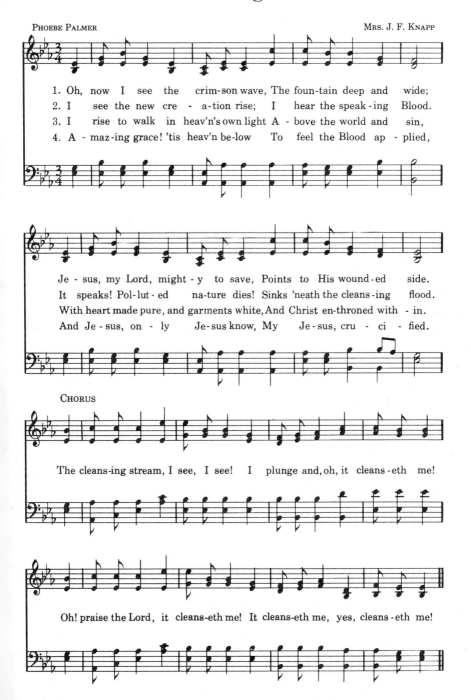

1. Oh, now I see the crim-son wave, The foun-tain deep and wide;
2. I see the new cre - a-tion rise; I hear the speak-ing Blood.
3. I rise to walk in heav'n's own light A - bove the world and sin,
4. A - maz-ing grace! 'tis heav'n be-low To feel the Blood ap - plied,

Je - sus, my Lord, might - y to save, Points to His wound-ed side.
It speaks! Pol-lut - ed na-ture dies! Sinks 'neath the cleans-ing flood.
With heart made pure, and garments white, And Christ en-throned with - in.
And Je - sus, on - ly Je-sus know, My Je-sus, cru - ci - fied.

CHORUS

The cleans-ing stream, I see, I see! I plunge and, oh, it cleans-eth me!

Oh! praise the Lord, it cleans-eth me! It cleans-eth me, yes, cleans-eth me!

175   The Comforter Has Come

F. Bottome   Wm. J. Kirkpatrick

1. Oh, spread the ti-dings 'round, wher-ev-er man is found, Wher-
2. The long, long night is past; the morn-ing breaks at last; And
3. Lo, the great King of Kings, with heal-ing in His wings, To
4. Oh, bound-less love di-vine! How shall this tongue of mine To

ev-er hu-man hearts and hu-man woes a-bound; Let ev-
hushed the dread-ful wail and fu-ry of the blast, As o'er
ev-'ry cap-tive soul a full de-liv'rance brings; And thro'
won-d'ring mor-tals tell the match-less grace di-vine— That I,

'ry Christian tongue pro-claim the joy-ful sound:
the gold-en hills the day ad-vanc-es fast!
the va-cant cells the song of tri-umph rings:
a child of hell, should in His im-age shine!

The Com-fort-er has

CHORUS

come! The Com-fort-er has come! The Com-fort-er has come! The

Ho-ly Ghost from heav'n, The Fa-ther's prom-ise giv'n! Oh, spread the ti-dings

The Comforter Has Come

'round, wher - ev - er man is found: The Com - fort - er has come!

176 Where Jesus Is, 'Tis Heaven

C. F. BUTLER

J. M. BLACK

1. Since Christ my soul from sin set free, This world has been a heav'n to me;
2. Once heav - en seemed a far - off place, Till Je - sus showed His smiling face.
3. What mat - ters where on earth we dwell? On moun-tain-top or in the dell,

And mid earth's sor - rows and its woe 'Tis heav'n my Je - sus here to know.
Now it's be - gun with - in my soul; 'Twill last while end-less a - ges roll.
In cot - tage or a man-sion fair, Where Je-sus is, 'tis heav - en there.

CHORUS

Oh, hal - le - lu - jah, yes, 'tis heav'n, 'Tis heav'n to know my sins for - giv'n!

On land or sea, what mat-ters where? Where Je-sus is, 'tis heav - en there.

177 Tell Me the Story of Jesus

FANNY J. CROSBY

JNO. R. SWENEY

1. Tell me the sto - ry of Je - sus; Write on my heart ev -'ry word.
2. Fast - ing a - lone in the des - ert, Tell of the days that are past:
3. Tell of the cross where they nailed Him, Writh - ing in an - guish and pain;

Tell me the sto - ry most pre - cious, Sweet - est that ev - er was heard.
How for our sins He was tempt - ed, Yet was tri - um - phant at last.
Tell of the grave where they laid Him; Tell how He liv - eth a - gain.

Tell how the an - gels, in cho - rus, Sang as they wel - comed His birth:
Tell of the years of His la - bor; Tell of the sor - row He bore.
Love in that sto - ry so ten - der Clear - er than ev - er I see.

"Glo - ry to God in the high - est! Peace and good ti - dings to earth."
He was de - spised and af - flict - ed, Home - less, re - ject - ed, and poor.
Stay, let me weep while you whis - per Love paid the ran - som for me.

CHORUS

Tell me the sto - ry of Je - sus; Write on my heart ev -'ry word.

Tell Me the Story of Jesus

Tell me the sto - ry most pre - cious, Sweet-est that ev - er was heard.

178 O Happy Day

PHILIP DODDRIDGE

E. F. RIMBAULT

1. O hap - py day that fixed my choice On Thee, my Sav-iour and my God!
2. 'Tis done, the great trans - ac-tion's done; I am my Lord's, and He is mine;
3. Now rest, my long di - vid - ed heart; Fixed on this bliss-ful cen-ter, rest;

Well may this glow-ing heart re - joice, And tell its rap-tures all a - broad.
He drew me, and I fol - lowed on, Charmed to confess the voice di - vine.
Nor ev - er from my Lord de - part, With Him of ev - 'ry good pos-sessed.

Fine

Hap - py day, hap - py day, When Je - sus washed my sins a - way!

D.S.

He taught me how to watch and pray, And live re - joic - ing ev - 'ry day.

179   I Am Resolved

PALMER HARTSOUGH

J. H. FILLMORE

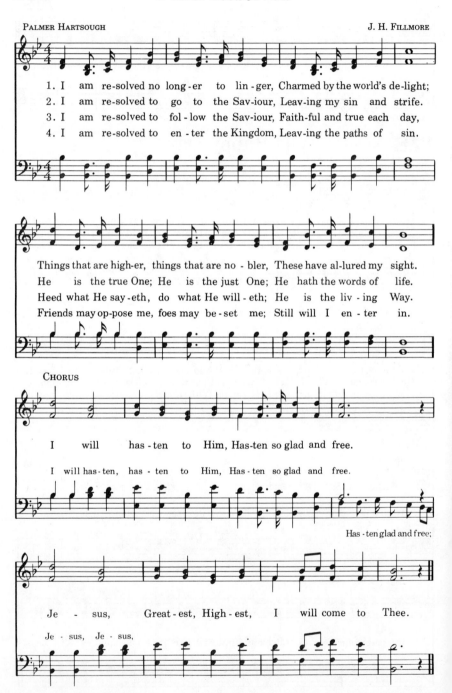

1. I am re-solved no long-er to lin-ger, Charmed by the world's de-light;
2. I am re-solved to go to the Sav-iour, Leav-ing my sin and strife.
3. I am re-solved to fol-low the Sav-iour, Faith-ful and true each day,
4. I am re-solved to en-ter the Kingdom, Leav-ing the paths of sin.

Things that are high-er, things that are no-bler, These have al-lured my sight.
He is the true One; He is the just One; He hath the words of life.
Heed what He say-eth, do what He will-eth; He is the liv-ing Way.
Friends may op-pose me, foes may be-set me; Still will I en-ter in.

CHORUS

I will has-ten to Him, Has-ten so glad and free.

I will has-ten, has-ten to Him, Has-ten so glad and free.

Has-ten glad and free;

Je-sus, Great-est, High-est, I will come to Thee.

Je-sus, Je-sus,

180 My Wonderful Lord

H. L.

Haldor Lillenas

1. I have found a deep peace that I nev-er had known And a joy this world
2. I de - sire that my life shall be or-dered by Thee, That my will be in
3. All the tal-ents I have I have laid at Thy feet; Thy ap-prov-al shall
4. Thou art fair - er to me than the fair-est of earth, Thou om-nip-o-tent,

could not af - ford ___ Since I yield - ed con -trol of my bod - y and soul
per - fect ac - cord ___ With Thine own sov'reign will, Thy de-sires to ful -fill,
be my re - ward. ___ Be my store great or small, I sur -ren - der it all
life - giv-ing Word. ___ O Thou An -cient of Days, Thou art worthy all praise,

CHORUS

To my won-der-ful, won-der-ful Lord.
My won-der-ful, won-der-ful Lord.
To my won-der-ful, won-der-ful Lord.
My won-der-ful, won-der-ful Lord!

My won - der - ful Lord, my

won - der-ful Lord, By an - gels and ser - aphs in heav - en a - dored! I

bow at Thy shrine, my Sav-iour di-vine, My won-der-ful, won - der-ful Lord.

181 On the Victory Side

JAMES L. BLACK

JNO. R. SWENEY

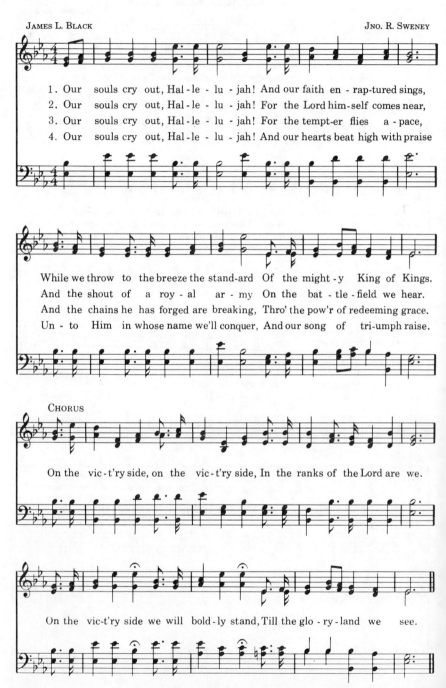

1. Our souls cry out, Hal-le-lu-jah! And our faith en-rap-tured sings,
2. Our souls cry out, Hal-le-lu-jah! For the Lord him-self comes near,
3. Our souls cry out, Hal-le-lu-jah! For the tempt-er flies a-pace,
4. Our souls cry out, Hal-le-lu-jah! And our hearts beat high with praise

While we throw to the breeze the stand-ard Of the might-y King of Kings.
And the shout of a roy-al ar-my On the bat-tle-field we hear.
And the chains he has forged are breaking, Thro' the pow'r of redeeming grace.
Un-to Him in whose name we'll conquer, And our song of tri-umph raise.

CHORUS

On the vic-t'ry side, on the vic-t'ry side, In the ranks of the Lord are we.

On the vic-t'ry side we will bold-ly stand, Till the glo-ry-land we see.

182 Look and Live

W. A. O.

W. A. OGDEN

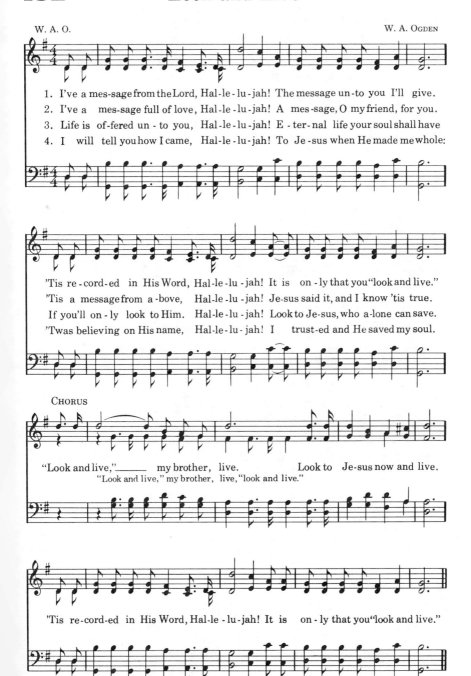

1. I've a mes-sage from the Lord, Hal-le-lu-jah! The message un-to you I'll give.
2. I've a mes-sage full of love, Hal-le-lu-jah! A mes-sage, O my friend, for you.
3. Life is of-fered un-to you, Hal-le-lu-jah! E-ter-nal life your soul shall have
4. I will tell you how I came, Hal-le-lu-jah! To Je-sus when He made me whole:

'Tis re-cord-ed in His Word, Hal-le-lu-jah! It is on-ly that you "look and live."
'Tis a message from a-bove, Hal-le-lu-jah! Je-sus said it, and I know 'tis true.
If you'll on-ly look to Him. Hal-le-lu-jah! Look to Je-sus, who a-lone can save.
'Twas believing on His name, Hal-le-lu-jah! I trust-ed and He saved my soul.

CHORUS

"Look and live," _____ my brother, live. Look to Je-sus now and live.
"Look and live," my brother, live, "look and live."

'Tis re-cord-ed in His Word, Hal-le-lu-jah! It is on-ly that you "look and live."

183 Sweeter as the Years Go By

MRS. C. H. M.

MRS. C. H. MORRIS

1. Of Je - sus' love that sought me, When I was lost in sin; Of won-drous
2. He trod in old Ju - de - a Life's pathway long a - go; The peo - ple
3. 'Twas wondrous love which led Him For us to suf -fer loss—To bear with-

grace that brought me Back to His fold a - gain; Of heights and depths of
thronged a - bout Him, His sav - ing grace to know. He healed the bro - ken-
out a mur -mur The an - guish of the Cross. With saints re-deemed in

mer - cy, Far deep - er than the sea, And high-er than the heav-ens,
heart-ed, And caused the blind to see; And still His great heart yearn-eth
glo - ry, Let us our voic - es raise, Till heav'n and earth re - ech - o

My theme shall ev - er be.
In love for e - ven me.
With our Re-deem-er's praise.

CHORUS

Sweet-er as the years go by, _____
Sweet - er as the years go by, 'Tis

Sweet-er as the years go by;
Sweet - er as the years go by;

Rich-er, full - er, deep - er,

Sweeter as the Years Go By

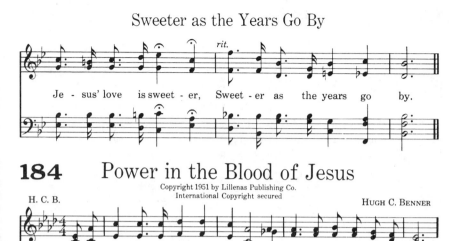

Je - sus' love is sweet - er, Sweet - er as the years go by.

184   Power in the Blood of Jesus

H. C. B.   HUGH C. BENNER

1. There is pow'r in the blood of Je - sus To make the vil - est sin - ner whole;
2. There is pow'r in the blood of Je - sus To cleanse the heart from ev'ry stain;
3. There is pow'r in the blood of Je - sus To keep me faith - ful day by day;

Pow'r to take the guilt and con - dem - na - tion From the wea - ry, sin - sick soul.
Pow'r to cause the Spir - it in His full - ness O - ver all to rule and reign.
Pow'r to make me hap - py in His serv - ice, Trav'ling on this ho - ly way.

CHORUS

There is pow'r in the blood of Je - sus: Pow'r to save, pow'r to cleanse from sin;

from sin;

And the crim - son tide from His wounded side Gives me joy and peace with - in.

185 Rescue the Perishing

Fanny J. Crosby

W. H. Doane

1. Res - cue the per-ish-ing; Care for the dy - ing; Snatch them in pit - y from
2. Tho' they are slighting Him, Still He is wait-ing, Wait - ing the pen - i - tent
3. Down in the human heart, Crushed by the tempter, Feel - ings lie bur-ied that
4. Res - cue the per-ish-ing; Du - ty de-mands it. Strength for thy la - bor the

sin and the grave. Weep o'er the err - ing one; Lift up the fall - en;
child to re-ceive. Plead with them ear-nest-ly, Plead with them gen - tly;
grace can re-store. Touched by a lov - ing heart, Wak - ened by kind-ness,
Lord will pro-vide. Back to the nar-row way Pa - tient-ly win them;

Chorus

Tell them of Je - sus, the Might - y to Save.
He will for-give if they on - ly be-lieve.
Chords that are bro-ken will vi - brate once more. Res - cue the per - ish - ing;
Tell the poor wand'rer a Sav - iour has died.

Care for the dy - ing. Je - sus is mer - ci - ful; Je-sus will save.

186 His Grace Aboundeth More

KATE ULMER

WM. J. KIRKPATRICK

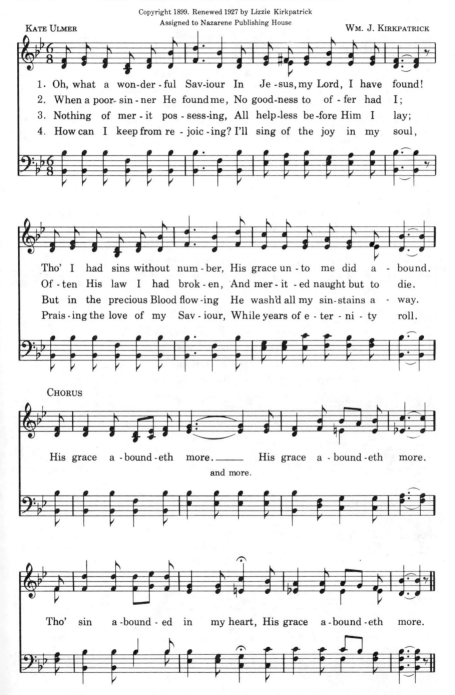

1. Oh, what a won-der-ful Sav-iour In Je-sus, my Lord, I have found!
2. When a poor sin-ner He found me, No good-ness to of-fer had I;
3. Nothing of mer-it pos-sess-ing, All help-less be-fore Him I lay;
4. How can I keep from re-joic-ing? I'll sing of the joy in my soul,

Tho' I had sins without num-ber, His grace un-to me did a-bound.
Of-ten His law I had brok-en, And mer-it-ed naught but to die.
But in the precious Blood flow-ing He wash'd all my sin-stains a-way.
Prais-ing the love of my Sav-iour, While years of e-ter-ni-ty roll.

CHORUS

His grace a-bound-eth more.___ His grace a-bound-eth more.
and more.

Tho' sin a-bound-ed in my heart, His grace a-bound-eth more.

187 Still Sweeter Every Day

W. C. MARTIN

C. AUSTIN MILES

1. To Je - sus ev - 'ry day I find my heart is clos - er drawn; He's
2. His glo - ry broke up - on me when I saw Him from a - far: He's
3. My heart is some - times heav - y, but He comes with sweet re - lief; He

fair - er than the glo - ry of the gold and pur - ple dawn; He's all my
fair - er than the lil - y, bright - er than the morn - ing star. He fills and
folds me to His bos - om when I droop with blighting grief. I love the

fan - cy pic - tures in its fair - est dreams, and more.
sat - is - fies my long - ing spir - it o'er and o'er. Each day He grows still
Christ, who all my bur - dens in His bod - y bore.

CHORUS

sweet - er than He was the day be - fore. The half_____ can - not be
The half can - not be fan - cied on this

fan - cied this side_____ the gold - en shore. Oh,
side the gold - en shore. The half can - not be fan - cied on this side the golden shore. Oh,

Still Sweeter Every Day

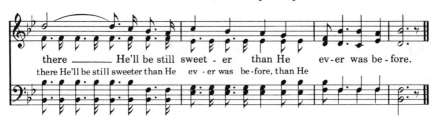

there _____ He'll be still sweet - er than He ev-er was be - fore.
there He'll be still sweeter than He ev - er was be -fore, than He

188 We'll Work till Jesus Comes

ELIZABETH MILLS

WILLIAM MILLER

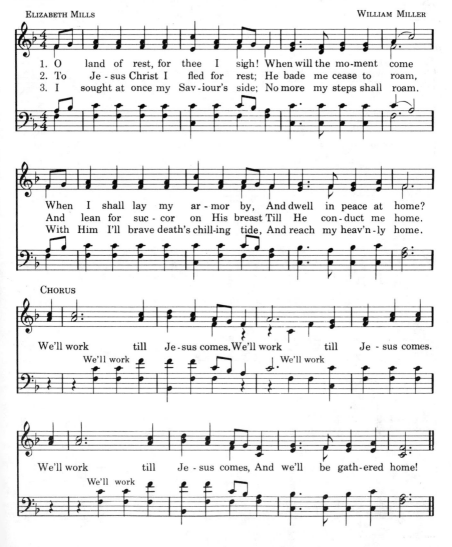

1. O land of rest, for thee I sigh! When will the mo-ment come
2. To Je - sus Christ I fled for rest; He bade me cease to roam,
3. I sought at once my Sav-iour's side; No more my steps shall roam.

When I shall lay my ar-mor by, And dwell in peace at home?
And lean for suc - cor on His breast Till He con-duct me home.
With Him I'll brave death's chill-ing tide, And reach my heav'n-ly home.

CHORUS

We'll work till Je-sus comes. We'll work till Je - sus comes.
We'll work   We'll work

We'll work till Je - sus comes, And we'll be gath-ered home!
We'll work

189 There Shall Be Showers of Blessing

D. W. WHITTLE

JAMES McGRANAHAN

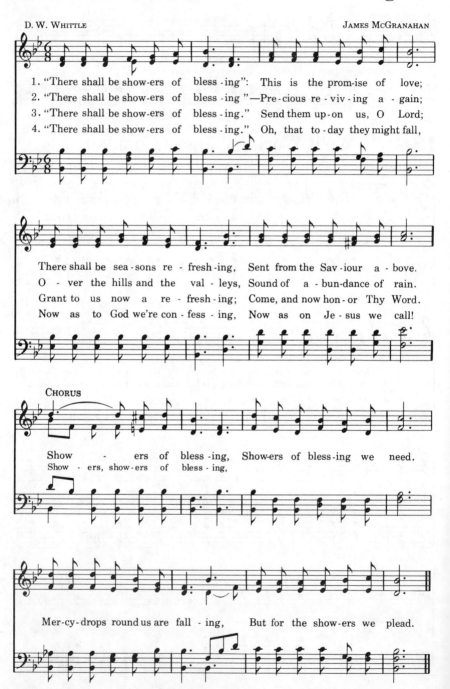

1. "There shall be show-ers of bless-ing": This is the prom-ise of love;
2. "There shall be show-ers of bless-ing"—Pre-cious re-viv-ing a-gain;
3. "There shall be show-ers of bless-ing." Send them up-on us, O Lord;
4. "There shall be show-ers of bless-ing." Oh, that to-day they might fall,

There shall be sea-sons re-fresh-ing, Sent from the Sav-iour a-bove.
O-ver the hills and the val-leys, Sound of a-bun-dance of rain.
Grant to us now a re-fresh-ing; Come, and now hon-or Thy Word.
Now as to God we're con-fess-ing, Now as on Je-sus we call!

CHORUS

Show - ers of bless-ing, Show-ers of bless-ing we need.
Show - ers, show-ers of bless-ing,

Mer-cy-drops round us are fall-ing, But for the show-ers we plead.

190   Trusting Jesus

E. PAGE

IRA D. SANKEY

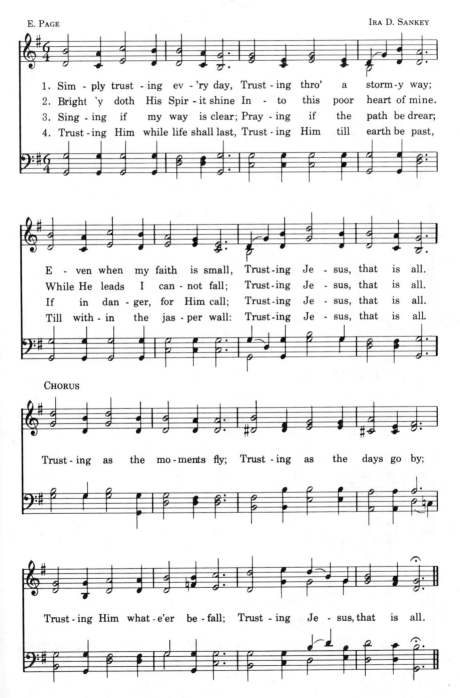

1. Sim - ply trust - ing ev - 'ry day, Trust - ing thro' a storm-y way;
2. Bright 'y doth His Spir - it shine In - to this poor heart of mine.
3. Sing - ing if my way is clear; Pray - ing if the path be drear;
4. Trust - ing Him while life shall last, Trust - ing Him till earth be past,

E - ven when my faith is small, Trust - ing Je - sus, that is all.
While He leads I can - not fall; Trust - ing Je - sus, that is all.
If in dan - ger, for Him call; Trust - ing Je - sus, that is all.
Till with - in the jas - per wall: Trust - ing Je - sus, that is all.

CHORUS

Trust - ing as the mo - ments fly; Trust - ing as the days go by;

Trust - ing Him what - e'er be - fall; Trust - ing Je - sus, that is all.

191 Wonderful

H. L.

HALDOR LILLENAS

1. Oh, my heart sings to-day, sings for joy and glad-ness. Je-sus saves,
2. Once a slave, now I'm free, free from con-dem-na-tion. Je-sus gives
3. Liv-ing here with my Lord in a ho-ly un-ion, Day by day,

sat-is-fies, takes a-way my sad-ness. Guilt is gone; peace is mine,
lib-er-ty and a full sal-va-tion. Now the sins of the past
all the way hold-ing sweet com-mun-ion; Oh, what change grace hath wrought

peace like to a riv-er. Je-sus is won-der-ful, might-y to de-liv-er.
have been all for-giv-en, And my name is inscribed in the book of heav-en.
in my low-ly sta-tion Since my soul has received full and free sal-va-tion!

CHORUS

Won-der-ful, won-der-ful, Je-sus is to me! Coun-sel-or,

Prince of Peace, Might-y God is He! Sav-ing me, keep-ing me

Wonderful

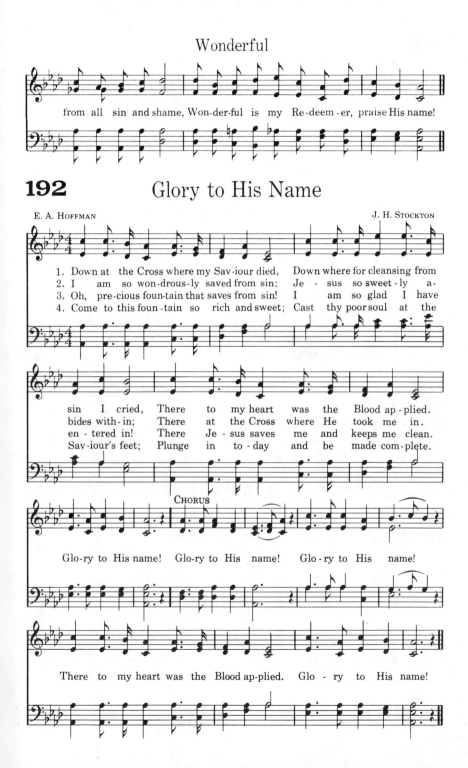

from all sin and shame, Won-der-ful is my Re-deem-er, praise His name!

192 Glory to His Name

E. A. HOFFMAN

J. H. STOCKTON

1. Down at the Cross where my Sav-iour died, Down where for cleansing from
2. I am so won-drous-ly saved from sin; Je - sus so sweet-ly a-
3. Oh, pre-cious foun-tain that saves from sin! I am so glad I have
4. Come to this foun-tain so rich and sweet; Cast thy poor soul at the

sin I cried, There to my heart was the Blood ap - plied.
bides with-in; There at the Cross where He took me in.
en - tered in! There Je - sus saves me and keeps me clean.
Sav-iour's feet; Plunge in to - day and be made com-plete.

CHORUS

Glo-ry to His name! Glo-ry to His name! Glo-ry to His name!

There to my heart was the Blood ap-plied. Glo - ry to His name!

193 Sanctifying Power

Mrs. C. H. M.

Mrs. C. H. Morris

1. There is sanc-ti-fy-ing pow'r, Like a sweet refreshing show'r, Wait-ing
2. I'm so glad it reach-es me, All un-wor-thy tho' I be, O - ver-
3. This God's will for you and me, That we sanc-ti-fied should be, Dwell-ing
4. Songs of prais-es let us sing To our bless-ed Lord and King For this

for each con - se - crat - ed heart: Pow'r to cleanse us from all sin, Pow'r to
com-ing grace made free - ly mine. Since the Com-fort-er a -bides, And with-
in this land of plen -teous-ness; Fling your doubts and fears aside, Bold - ly
great sal-va-tion rich and free; Ev -'ry need- ed grace sup-plied, Ev - 'ry

keep us pure with - in, Pow'r for ser - vice which He will im - part.
in my heart re - sides, I am walk-ing in the light di - vine.
cross the Jor-dan's tide, And your her - it - age in Christ pos - sess.
long-ing sat - is -fied, Saved for time and for e -ter - ni - ty.

CHORUS

I'm so glad, _____ I'm so glad, _____ For this
I'm so glad, hal - le - lu - jah, I'm so glad,

sav-ing, sanc-ti - fy - ing pow'r. Waves of glo - ry o'er me roll; Peace a-

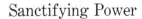

Sanctifying Power

bides with-in my soul. I'm so glad for this sanc-ti-fy-ing pow'r!

194 Leaning on the Everlasting Arms

E. A. HOFFMAN

A. J. SHOWALTER

1. What a fel-low-ship, what a joy di-vine, Leaning on the ev-er-last-ing arms!
2. Oh, how sweet to walk in this pilgrim way, Leaning on the ev-er-last-ing arms!
3. What have I to dread, what have I to fear, Leaning on the ev-er-last-ing arms?

What a bless-ed-ness, what a peace is mine, Leaning on the ev-er-last-ing arms!
Oh, how bright the path grows from day to day, Leaning on the ev-er-last-ing arms!
I have bless-ed peace with my Lord so near, Leaning on the ev-er-last-ing arms.

CHORUS

Lean - ing, lean - ing, Safe and se-cure from all a-larms;
Lean-ing on Je - sus, lean-ing on Je - sus,

Lean - ing, lean - ing, Lean-ing on the ev-er - last-ing arms.
Lean-ing on Je - sus, lean-ing on Je - sus,

195 Living by Faith

James Wells
4 v. R. E. W.

J. L. Heath

1. I care not to-day what the morrow may bring, If shadow or sun-shine or rain.
2. Tho' tempests may blow and storm-clouds a-rise, Obscuring the brightness of life,
3. I know that He safe-ly will car-ry me thro', No mat-ter what e-vils be-tide.
4. Our Lord will return to this earth some sweet day; Our troubles will then all be o'er.

The Lord, I know, rul-eth o'er ev-er-y-thing, And all of my wor-ry is vain.
I'm nev-er a-larmed at the over-cast skies; The Master looks on at the strife.
Why should I then care, tho' the tempest may blow, If Jesus walks close to my side?
The Mas-ter so gen-tly will lead us a-way, Beyond that blest heaven-ly shore.

REFRAIN

Liv-ing by faith _____ in Je-sus a-bove; _____
Yes, liv-ing by faith in Je-sus a-bove;

Trust-ing, con-fid - ing in His great love; _____
Trust-ing, con-fid - ing yes, in His great love;

Safe from all harm _____ in His shel-ter-ing arm, _____
I'm safe from all harm His shel-ter-ing arm,

Living by Faith

I'm liv-ing by faith _____ and feel no a - larm.

I'm liv - ing by faith   feel no a -larm.

196   He Loves Me

ISAAC WATTS

ARR.

1. A - las! and did my Sav - iour bleed? And did my Sov -'reign die?
2. Was it for crimes that I have done He groaned up - on the tree?
3. Well might the sun in dark - ness hide, And shut His glo - ries in,
4. But drops of grief can ne'er re - pay The debt of love I owe.

Would He de - vote that sa - cred head For such a worm as I?
A - maz -ing pit - y! grace un-known! And love be -yond de - gree!
When Christ, the might-y Mak - er, died For man, the crea-ture's, sin.
Here, Lord, I give my - self a - way; 'Tis all that I can do.

REFRAIN

He loves me; He loves me; He loves me, this I know.

I know.

He gave him - self to die for me Be - cause He loves me so!

197   Joy in My Soul

J. B. M.

J. B. MacKay

1. In the blood of Je-sus that was shed for me My trans-
2. When I came be-liev-ing, Je-sus took me in, And for-
3. I was filled with rap-ture as my heart be-lieved, As my
4. I will sing of Je-sus and His pow'r to save, I will

gressions have been washed a-way. Oh, my heart o'er-flow-eth with His
gave the debt I ne'er could pay. His re-deem-ing blood has can-celed
all up-on the al-tar lay. Oh, the won-drous bless-ing that I
shout His praise while here I stay; For the great sal-va-tion that to

love so free, And there's joy in my soul to-day.
all my sin, And there's joy in my soul to-day.
there re-ceived Lives a joy in my soul to-day.
me He gave Is the joy of my soul to-day.

Chorus

There is joy in my soul, Oh, glo-ry, hal-le-lu-jah! Je-sus'

blood makes me whole, Oh, glo-ry, hal-le-lu-jah! His love and pow'r di-

Joy in My Soul

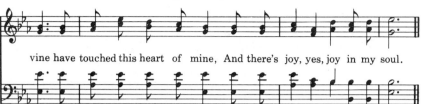

vine have touched this heart of mine, And there's joy, yes, joy in my soul.

198 'Tis So Sweet to Trust in Jesus

Louisa M. R. Stead

Wm. J. Kirkpatrick

1. 'Tis so sweet to trust in Je - sus, Just to take Him at His word;
2. Oh, how sweet to trust in Je - sus, Just to trust His cleansing blood;
3. Yes, 'tis sweet to trust in Je - sus, Just from sin and self to cease;
4. I'm so glad I learned to trust Thee, Pre - cious Je - sus, Sav-iour, Friend;

Just to rest up - on His prom-ise; Just to know, "Thus saith the Lord."
Just in sim - ple faith to plunge me 'Neath the heal-ing, cleans-ing flood!
Just from Je - sus sim - ply tak - ing Life and rest, and joy and peace.
And I know that Thou art with me, Wilt be with me to the end.

Chorus

Je - sus, Je - sus, how I trust Him! How I've proved Him o'er and o'er!

p

Je - sus, Je - sus, pre - cious Je - sus! Oh, for grace to trust Him more!

199 Holiness unto the Lord

Mrs. C. H. M.

Mrs. C. H. Morris

1. "Called un-to ho-li-ness," Church of our God, Pur-chase of
2. "Called un-to ho-li-ness," chil-dren of light, Walk-ing with
3. "Called un-to ho-li-ness," praise His dear name! This bless-ed
4. "Called un-to ho-li-ness," Bride of the Lamb, Wait-ing the

Je-sus, re-deemed by His blood; Called from the world and its
Je-sus in gar-ments of white; Rai-ment un-sul-lied, nor
se-cret to faith now made plain: Not our own right-eous-ness,
Bride-groom's re-turn-ing a-gain! Lift up your heads, for the

i-dols to flee, Called from the bond-age of sin to be free.
tar-nished with sin; God's Ho-ly Spir-it a-bid-ing with-in.
but Christ with-in, Liv-ing, and reign-ing, and sav-ing from sin.
day draw-eth near When in His beau-ty the King shall ap-pear.

Chorus

"Ho-li-ness unto the Lord" is our watch-word and song, "Ho-li-ness un-to the
Lord" as we're march-ing a-long. Sing it, shout it,
"Ho-li-ness un-to the Lord," Sing,

Holiness unto the Lord

loud and long. "Ho-li-ness un-to the Lord" now and for - ev - er!
"Ho - li-ness un - to the Lord,"

200 Nothing but the Blood

R. L.

ROBERT LOWRY

1. What can wash a - way my sin?
2. For my par - don this I see—
3. Noth - ing can for sin a - tone— Noth-ing but the blood of Je - sus.
4. This is all my hope and peace—

What can make me whole a - gain?
For my cleans-ing this my plea—
Naught of good that I have done— Noth-ing but the blood of Je - sus.
This is all my right - eous-ness—

REFRAIN

Oh, pre - cious is the flow That makes me white as snow.

No oth - er fount I know, Noth-ing but the blood of Je - sus.

201 I Know God's Promise Is True

Copyright 1899. Renewed 1927 by Lelia N. Morris
Assigned to Nazarene Publishing House

Mrs. C. H. M.

Mrs. C. H. Morris

1. For God so loved this sin - ful world, His Son He free - ly gave,
2. I was a way - ward, wand'ring child, A slave to sin and fear,
3. The "who - so - ev - er" of the Lord, I, trust - ed was for me.
4. E - ter - nal life, be - gun be - low, Now fills my heart and soul.

That who - so - ev - er would be - lieve E - ter - nal life should have.
Un - til this bless - ed prom - ise fell Like mu - sic on my ear.
I took Him at His gra - cious word; From sin He set me free.
I'll sing His praise for - ev - er - more Who has re-deemed my soul.

CHORUS

'Tis true, oh, yes, 'tis true.____ God's won-der-ful prom-ise is true;____
the prom-ise is true.   'tis true;

For I've trusted, and tested, and tried it, And I know God's promise is true.
                                                        'tis true.

202 A Holy Ghost Revival

MRS. C. H. M.

MRS. C. H. MORRIS

1. For a Ho - ly Ghost re - viv - al, bless-ed Lord, we pray. Send the
2. May the Church on earth be quickened and new life re-ceive. May lost
3. Send a great world-wide re - viv - al; may the peo - ple say That the

Pen - te - cos-tal bless-ing in our hearts to - day, Old-time Holy Ghost re-lig-ion
sin-ners be a - wakened and in Christ be-lieve; More of power and of bless-ing
mighty God of Pen-te-cost still lives to - day, Still convicting and converting

CHORUS

in the old-time way.
than we can conceive. Send a Holy Ghost re-viv-al, Lord. Send a Ho   ly
in the old-time way.
                                                              Send a blessed Ho-ly

Ghost re - viv- al, Lord. May the Spir   -   it on us be outpoured. Send a
Ghost re - viv - al, Lord.   May the Spir-it in His full-ness on us be outpoured;

Ho   -   ly Ghost re - viv - al, Lord, And be-gin it in my heart.
Send a bless-ed Ho - ly Ghost re - viv - al, now, O Lord,

203 Saved by the Blood

B. M. L.

BERTHA MAE LILLENAS

1. Saved by the blood of the Cru - ci -fied One, Washed and made whiter than snow:
2. Saved by the blood of the Cru - ci -fied One, I am a child of His love;
3. Saved by the blood of the Cru - ci -fied One, Heir to His rich-es of grace;
4. Saved by the blood of the Cru - ci -fied One, Soon I shall look on His face;

Life ev - er - last -ing with -in me be - gun,
Free -ly for - giv - en, my bur -den is gone!
Trust-ing in Him I find heav -en be - gun, Saved by the blood of the Lamb!
Meet Him in glo - ry when life's race is run,

CHORUS Saved,—— saved,——
Saved by the blood, saved by the blood, Saved by the blood of the Cru - ci -fied One;
Saved, saved, saved, saved,

Saved,—— saved,——
Saved by the blood, saved by the blood, Saved by the mer -it of God's on -ly Son.
Saved, saved, saved, saved,

Gone are my burdens and gone are my fears; Gone are the heartaches of many long years;

Saved by the Blood

poco rit.

Sim-ply be-liev-ing, I cast off my fears, Saved by the blood of the Lamb!

by the blood of the Lamb!

204   I'm Glad Salvation's Free

1. I'm glad sal - va - tion's free, And with - out price or cost;
2. Once I was blind and lost, Of sin and sor - row full.
3. And now I'm on the way To bright - er worlds a - bove.
4. O breth - ren, help me sing One song of vic - to - ry;

For had it been for me to buy, My soul must have been lost.
But now I'm saved thro' Je - sus' blood; I feel it in my soul.
I hope to tri - umph ev - er - more Thro' the Re - deem - er's love.
For with - out mon - ey, with - out price, I've found sal - va - tion free.

CHORUS

I'm glad sal - va - tion's free. I'm glad sal - va - tion's free.

Sal - va - tion's free for you and me. I'm glad sal - va - tion's free.

205 The Morning Light Is Breaking

S. F. SMITH

G. J. WEBB

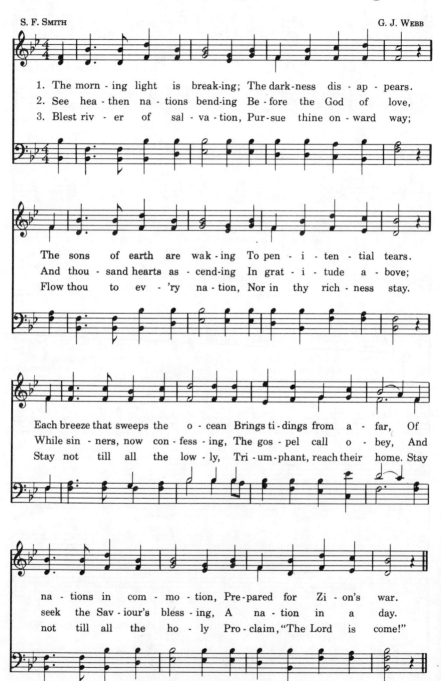

1. The morn-ing light is break-ing; The dark-ness dis-ap-pears.
2. See hea-then na-tions bend-ing Be-fore the God of love,
3. Blest riv-er of sal-va-tion, Pur-sue thine on-ward way;

The sons of earth are wak-ing To pen-i-ten-tial tears.
And thou-sand hearts as-cend-ing In grat-i-tude a-bove;
Flow thou to ev-'ry na-tion, Nor in thy rich-ness stay.

Each breeze that sweeps the o-cean Brings ti-dings from a-far, Of
While sin-ners, now con-fess-ing, The gos-pel call o-bey, And
Stay not till all the low-ly, Tri-um-phant, reach their home. Stay

na-tions in com-mo-tion, Pre-pared for Zi-on's war.
seek the Sav-iour's bless-ing, A na-tion in a day.
not till all the ho-ly Pro-claim, "The Lord is come!"

206 God Be with You

J. E. RANKIN

W. G. TOMER

1. God be with you till we meet a - gain; By His counsels guide, up-hold you;
2. God be with you 'till we meet a - gain; 'Neath His wings protecting hide you;
3. God be with you till we meet a - gain; When life's perils thick confound you,
4. God be with you till we meet a - gain; Keep love's banner floating o'er you;

With His sheep se -cure - ly fold you.
Dai - ly man-na still pro - vide you.
Put His arms un-fail-ing round you.   God be with you till we meet a-gain.
Smite death's threat'ning wave before you.

CHORUS

Till we meet,— till we meet, Till we meet at Je - sus' feet;
Till we meet,   till we meet,   till we meet;

Till we meet, —— till we meet, God be with you till we meet a - gain.
Till we meet,   till we meet,

207 I'll Go Where You Want Me to Go

MARY BROWN

CARRIE E. ROUNSEFELL

1. It may not be on the moun-tain height, Or o - ver the storm - y sea,
2. Per - haps to - day there are lov - ing words Which Jesus would have me speak;
3. There's surely somewhere a low - ly place In earth's harvest fields so wide

It may not be at the bat - tle's front My Lord will have need of me;
There may be now in the paths of sin Some wand'rer whom I should seek.
Where I may la - bor thro' life's short day For Je - sus, the Cru - ci - fied.

But if by a still, small voice He calls To paths that i do not know,
O Saviour, if Thou wilt be my Guide, Tho' dark and rug-ged the way,
So trust-ing my all to Thy ten - der care, And knowing Thou lov - est me,

I'll answer, dear Lord, with my hand in Thine, I'll go where You want me to go.
My voice shall ech - o the mes - sage sweet. I'll say what You want me to say.
I'll do Thy will with a heart sin-cere. I'll be what You want me to be.

REFRAIN

I'll go where You want me to go, dear Lord, Over mountain, or plain, or sea.

I'll Go Where You Want Me to Go

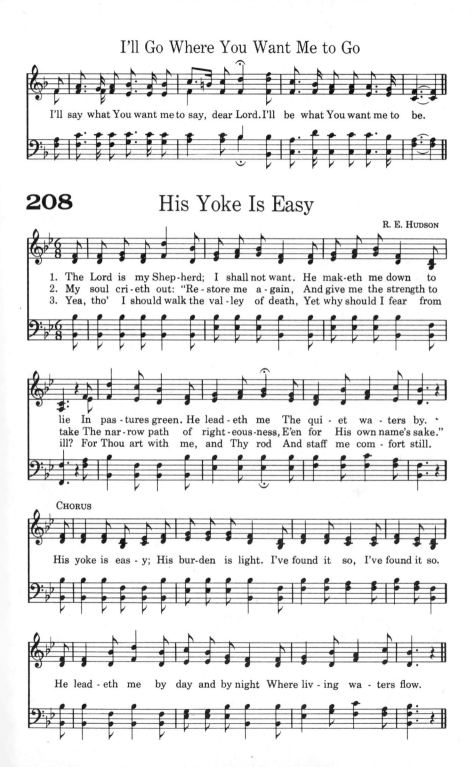

I'll say what You want me to say, dear Lord. I'll be what You want me to be.

208   His Yoke Is Easy

R. E. HUDSON

1. The Lord is my Shep-herd; I shall not want. He mak-eth me down to
2. My soul cri-eth out: "Re-store me a-gain, And give me the strength to
3. Yea, tho' I should walk the val-ley of death, Yet why should I fear from

lie In pas-tures green. He lead-eth me The qui-et wa-ters by.
take The nar-row path of right-eous-ness, E'en for His own name's sake."
ill? For Thou art with me, and Thy rod And staff me com-fort still.

CHORUS

His yoke is eas-y; His bur-den is light. I've found it so, I've found it so.

He lead-eth me by day and by night Where liv-ing wa-ters flow.

209 He Rolled the Sea Away

Rev. H. J. Zelley

H. L. Gilmour

1. When Is-rael out of bond-age came, A sea be-fore them lay;
2. Be - fore me was a sea of sin So great I feared to pray;
3. When sor - rows dark, like storm-y waves, Were dash-ing o'er my way,
4. And when I reach the sea of death, For need - ed grace I'll pray;

My Lord reached down His might-y hand, And rolled the sea a - way.
My heart's de - sire the Sav - iour read, And rolled the sea a - way.
A - gain the Lord in mer - cy came, And rolled the sea a - way.
I know the Lord will quick - ly come, And roll the sea a - way.

CHORUS

Then for-ward still, 'tis Je - ho - vah's will, Tho' the bil - lows dash and spray.

With a con-qu'ring tread we will push a-head; He'll roll the sea a - way.

210 A New Touch of Fire

MRS. C. H. M.

MRS. C. H. MORRIS

1. For a fresh a-noint-ing, Lord, for ser - vice Come we now in Je - sus'
2. Make us free to tell the gos - pel sto - ry; Lib - er - ty in ser - vice
3. Bring-ing all we have in con - se - cra - tion As a liv - ing sac - ri -
4. Let the great Re - fin - er throughly purge us, Pu - ri - fy our hearts like

pre - cious name; For the blessed Pen - te - cos - tal full - ness, Ev - 'ry heart with
may we have, Showing forth the Saviour's grace and glory, Tell - ing of His
fice for Thee; Trusting for an ut - ter-most sal - va - tion, Je - sus' pre-cious
as by fire; While for all the sanc - ti - fy - ing full - ness Here our wait-ing,

Chorus

heav'n-ly love a - flame.
won-drous pow'r to save. Send a new touch of fire on our souls, Lord.
blood our on - ly plea. on our wait - ing souls, O Lord.
long - ing hearts as - pire.

Send it now, Lord. Send it now, Lord. Touch our
Send it now, O Lord. Send it now, O bless-ed Lord.

lips to - day with the liv-ing coals. Send a new touch of fire on our souls.

211 He Will Carry You Through

A. A. J. AND HALDOR LILLENAS

A. A. JAMESON

1. If there's trouble an-y-where, And your soul is near de-spair, Just trust in the
2. Are your burdens hard to bear? Are you weighted down with care? Just trust in the
3. In temp-ta-tion's try-ing hour You will need His keeping pow'r. Just trust in the
4. When you reach the swelling tide Of death's river deep and wide, Just trust in the

Sav-iour and be true. His compassion nev-er doubt; He will al-ways help you
Sav-iour and be true. If you think you can-not stand, Let Him lead you by the
Sav-iour and be true. Tho' the shadows 'round you fall, He'll be with you thro' it
Sav-iour and be true. He will not for-sake your soul, Tho' the chill-y waves may

CHORUS

out, For He will car-ry you thro'. He will car-ry you thro', He will
hand, And He will car-ry you thro'.
all, And He will car-ry you thro'. (After last stanza)
roll, For He will car-ry you thro'. He will car-ry me thro', He will

car-ry you thro'. Just trust in the Sav-iour and be true; and be true; And when
car-ry me thro'. I'll trust in the Sav-iour and be true; And when

tri-als you re-ceive, Trust in God and still believe That He will car-ry you thro'.
tri-als I re-ceive, I will trust and still believe That He will car-ry me thro'.

212 Hallelujah! 'Tis Done!

P. P. B.

P. P. Bliss

1. 'Tis the prom-ise of God, full sal-va-tion to give
2. Tho' the path-way be lone-ly, and dan-ger-ous too,
3. Man-y loved ones have I in yon heav-en-ly throng;
4. Lit-tle chil-dren I see stand-ing close by their King,
5. There's a part in that cho-rus for you and for me,

Un-to him who on Je-sus, His Son, will be-lieve.
Sure-ly Je-sus is a-ble to car-ry me thro'.
They are safe now in glo-ry, and this is their song:
And He smiles as their song of sal-va-tion they sing.
And the theme of our prais-es for-ev-er will be:

Chorus

Hal-le-lu-jah, 'tis done! I be-lieve on the Son; I am

saved by the blood of the Cru-ci-fied One; fied One.

213 The Everlasting Arms

Mrs. C. H. M.   Mrs. C. H. Morris

1. I have found sweet rest for my wea - ry soul, Found a har - bor safe
2. When my way grows dark and no light I see, When my friends forsake
3. When my faith is weak He is near my side; When my heart grows faint
4. There is naught too hard for my Lord to do; I can safe - ly trust

tho' the bil - lows roll; Found a Might - y One who can storms con - trol,
and life's com - forts flee, Then I know His grace will suf - fi - cient be,
He will strength pro - vide; When the dan - gers press then will seas di - vide,
all life's jour - ney thro'. He will bear me up and my bur - dens too,

Chorus

Lean-ing on the ev - er - last - ing arms. Oh, the ev - er - last - ing arms

how they hold me! Ev - er hold me, and en - fold me! I am safe in life or

death, for a - round and un - der - neath Are the might - y, ev - er - last - ing arms.

214 I Will Make the Darkness Light

C. P. J

CHAS. P. JONES

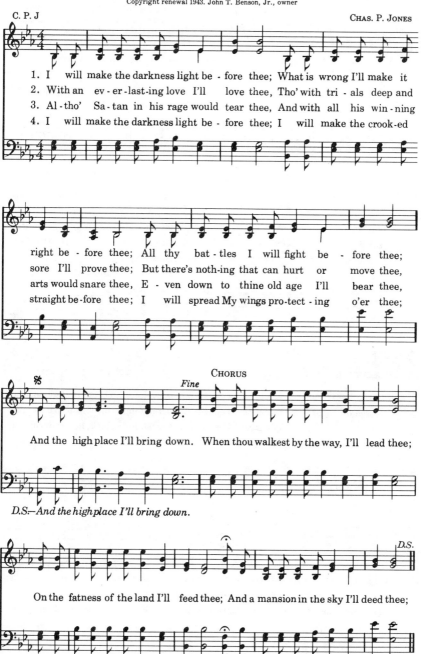

1. I will make the darkness light be - fore thee; What is wrong I'll make it
2. With an ev - er - last-ing love I'll love thee, Tho' with tri - als deep and
3. Al - tho' Sa - tan in his rage would tear thee, And with all his win - ning
4. I will make the darkness light be - fore thee; I will make the crook-ed

right be - fore thee; All thy bat - tles I will fight be - fore thee;
sore I'll prove thee; But there's noth-ing that can hurt or move thee,
arts would snare thee, E - ven down to thine old age I'll bear thee,
straight be-fore thee; I will spread My wings pro-tect - ing o'er thee;

CHORUS

Fine

And the high place I'll bring down. When thou walkest by the way, I'll lead thee;

D.S.—And the high place I'll bring down.

On the fatness of the land I'll feed thee; And a mansion in the sky I'll deed thee;

215 He Was Not Willing

L. R. M.

LUCY R. MEYER

1. He was not will-ing that an - y should per-ish; Je - sus, enthroned in the
2. He was not will-ing that an - y should per-ish; Clothed in our flesh with its
3. Plen-ty for pleas-ure, but lit -tle for Je - sus. Time for the world with its
4. He was not will-ing that an - y should per-ish. Am I His fol - low - er,

glo - ry a - bove, Looked on us ten - der - ly, pit - ied our sor-rows, Poured out His
sor-row and pain, Came He to seek the lost, com-fort the mourner, Heal the heart
troubles and toys; No time for Je - sus' work, feed-ing the hungry, Lift-ing lost
and can I live Long-er at ease with a soul go-ing downward, Lost for the

life for us— won-der-ful love! Per-ish-ing, per-ish-ing! Thronging our pathway,
bro-ken by sor-row and shame. Per-ish-ing, per-ish-ing! Har-vest is pass - ing,
souls to e - ter - ni - ty's joys. Per-ish-ing, per-ish-ing! Hark, how they call us,
lack of the help I might give? Per-ish-ing, per-ish-ing! Thou wast not will-ing.

Hearts break with bur-dens too heav - y to bear. Je - sus would save, but there's
Reap - ers are few, and the night draweth near. Je - sus is call-ing thee;
"Bring us your Sav-iour; oh, tell us of Him! We are so wea - ry, so
Mas - ter, for - give, and in - spire us a - new; Ban - ish our world - li - ness;

He Was Not Willing

no one to tell them, No one to lift them from sin and de-spair.
haste to the reap-ing. Thou shalt have souls, precious souls for thy hire.
heav-i-ly la-den, And with long weep-ing, our eyes have grown dim."
help us to ev-er Live with e-ter-ni-ty's val-ues in view.

216   Ready

S. E. L.

CHARLIE D. TILLMAN

1. Read-y to suf-fer grief or pain, Read-y to stand the test;
2. Read-y to go, read-y to bear, Read-y to watch and pray;
3. Read-y to speak, read-y to think, Read-y with heart and brain;
4. Read-y to speak, read-y to warn, Read-y o'er souls to yearn;

Read-y to stay at home and send Oth-ers if He sees best.
Read-y to stand a-side and give Till He shall clear the way.
Read-y to stand where He sees fit, Read-y to bear the strain.
Read-y in life, read-y in death, Read-y for His re-turn.

CHORUS

Read-y to go, read-y to stay, Read-y my place to fill;

Read-y for ser-vice, low-ly or great; Read-y to do His will.

217 He Ransomed Me

Julia H. Johnston

Copyright renewal 1943. John T. Benson, Jr., owner

J. W. Henderson

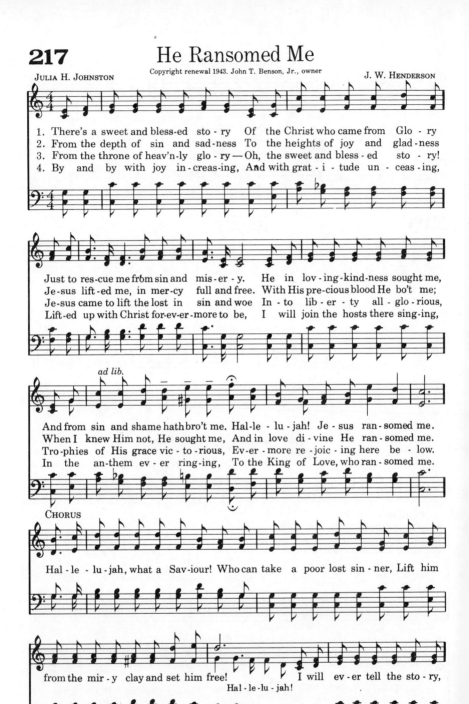

1. There's a sweet and bless-ed sto-ry Of the Christ who came from Glo-ry
2. From the depth of sin and sad-ness To the heights of joy and glad-ness
3. From the throne of heav'n-ly glo-ry—Oh, the sweet and bless-ed sto-ry!
4. By and by with joy in-creas-ing, And with grat-i-tude un-ceas-ing,

Just to res-cue me from sin and mis-er-y. He in lov-ing-kind-ness sought me,
Je-sus lift-ed me, in mer-cy full and free. With His pre-cious blood He bo't me;
Je-sus came to lift the lost in sin and woe In-to lib-er-ty all-glo-rious,
Lift-ed up with Christ for-ev-er-more to be, I will join the hosts there sing-ing,

ad lib.

And from sin and shame hath bro't me. Hal-le-lu-jah! Je-sus ran-somed me.
When I knew Him not, He sought me, And in love di-vine He ran-somed me.
Tro-phies of His grace vic-to-rious, Ev-er-more re-joic-ing here be-low.
In the an-them ev-er ring-ing, To the King of Love, who ran-somed me.

CHORUS

Hal-le-lu-jah, what a Sav-iour! Who can take a poor lost sin-ner, Lift him

from the mir-y clay and set him free! I will ev-er tell the sto-ry,
Hal-le-lu-jah!

He Ransomed Me

Shout-ing,"Glo-ry! Glo-ry! Glo-ry!" Hal-le-lu-jah! Je-sus ran-somed me.

218   I Feel Like Traveling On

WM. HUNTER

ARR. BY JAMES D. VAUGHAN

1. My heav'n-ly home is bright and fair.
2. Its glit-t'ring tow'rs the sun out-shine.
3. Let oth-ers seek a home be-low—   I feel like trav-el-ing on.
4. The Lord has been so good to me,

Nor pain, nor death can en-ter there.
That heav'n-ly man-sion shall be mine.
Which flames de-vour or waves o'er-flow.   I feel like trav-el-ing on.
Un-til that bless-ed home I see,

REFRAIN

Yes, I feel like trav-el-ing on.   I feel like trav-el-ing
trav-el-ing on.

on.   My heav'n-ly home is bright and fair. I feel like trav-el-ing on.
trav-el-ing on.

219   Bringing in the Sheaves

KNOWLES SHAW   GEORGE A. MINOR

1. Sow-ing in the morn-ing, sow-ing seeds of kind-ness, Sow-ing in the
2. Sow-ing in the sun-shine, sow-ing in the shad-ows, Fear-ing nei - ther
3. Go then, ev - er weep-ing, sow-ing for the Mas-ter, Tho' the loss sus-

noon-tide and the dew - y eve; Wait-ing for the har-vest and the
clouds nor win-ter's chill-ing breeze; By and by the har-vest and the
tained our spir - it of - ten grieves. When our weep-ing's o - ver, He will

time of reap-ing,
la - bor end - ed,   We shall come re - joic - ing, bring-ing in the sheaves.
bid us wel - come;

CHORUS

Bring-ing in the sheaves, bring-ing in the sheaves, We shall come re - joic - ing,

bring-ing in the sheaves.   We shall come re - joic - ing, bring-ing in the sheaves.

220 A Glorious Church

R. E. H.

R. E. HUDSON

1. Do you hear them com - ing, broth - er, Throng-ing up the
2. Do you hear the stir - ring an - thems Fill - ing all the
3. Nev - er fear the clouds of sor - row; Nev - er fear the
4. Wave the ban - ner, shout His prais - es, For our vic - to-

steeps of light, Clad in glo - rious shin - ing gar - ments —
earth and sky? 'Tis a grand, vic - to - rious ar - my.
storms of sin. We shall tri - umph on the mor - row;
ry is nigh! We shall join our con-qu'ring Sav - iour;

CHORUS

Blood-washed gar-ments pure and white?
Lift its ban - ner up on high!
E - ven now our joys be - gin.
We shall reign with Him on high!

'Tis a glo - rious Church with-

out spot or wrin-kle, Washed in the blood of the Lamb. 'Tis a

glo - rious Church, without spot or wrin-kle, Washed in the blood of the Lamb.

221 A Wonderful Fountain

HALDOR LILLENAS

ARR. BY HALDOR LILLENAS

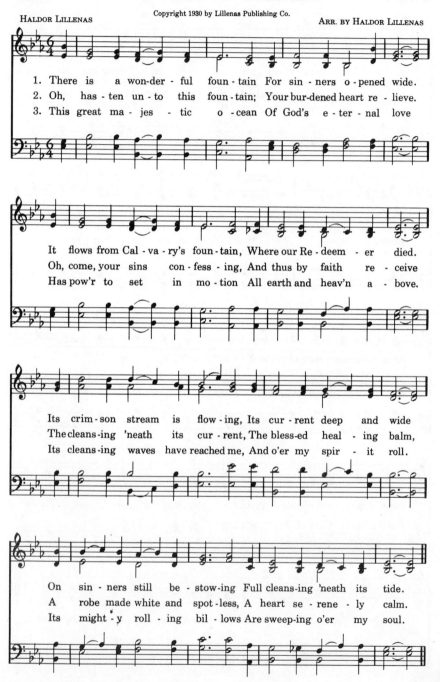

1. There is a won-der-ful foun-tain For sin-ners o-pened wide.
2. Oh, has-ten un-to this foun-tain; Your bur-dened heart re-lieve.
3. This great ma-jes-tic o-cean Of God's e-ter-nal love

It flows from Cal-va-ry's foun-tain, Where our Re-deem-er died.
Oh, come, your sins con-fess-ing, And thus by faith re-ceive
Has pow'r to set in mo-tion All earth and heav'n a-bove.

Its crim-son stream is flow-ing, Its cur-rent deep and wide
The cleans-ing 'neath its cur-rent, The bless-ed heal-ing balm,
Its cleans-ing waves have reached me, And o'er my spir-it roll.

On sin-ners still be-stow-ing Full cleans-ing 'neath its tide.
A robe made white and spot-less, A heart se-rene-ly calm.
Its might-y roll-ing bil-lows Are sweep-ing o'er my soul.

222 All in All

EDGAR LEWIS

L. E. JONES

1. Of Jesus' love I'm sing-ing; I praise Him ev-'ry day.
2. He's patient and so ten-der, so lov-ing and so kind. He is my all in
3. In time of need no oth-er to me can prove so dear.

all, all in all. An-oth-er Friend so faith-ful my soul will nev-er find.
He frees my soul from bond-age; He takes my guilt a-way.
He hears me tho' I whis-per; to help me He is near.

CHORUS

Je-sus is my all in all. All in all, all in all,
Je-sus is my all in all; Je-sus is my all in all,

A Strength in time of wea-ri-ness, a Light where shadows fall; All in
Je-sus is my

all, all in all, Je-sus is my all in all.
all in all; Je-sus is my all in all; all in all.

223 I Love to Tell the Story

KATHERINE HANKEY

WILLIAM G. FISCHER

1. I love to tell the sto-ry Of un-seen things a-bove, Of Je-sus
2. I love to tell the sto-ry; More won-der-ful it seems Than all the
3. I love to tell the sto-ry; 'Tis pleas-ant to re-peat What seems each
4. I love to tell the sto-ry, For those who know it best Seem hunger-

and His glo-ry, Of Je-sus and His love. I love to tell the sto-ry
gold-en fan-cies Of all our gold-en dreams. I love to tell the sto-ry,
time I tell it More won-der-ful-ly sweet. I love to tell the sto-ry,
ing and thirsting To hear it like the rest. And when in scenes of glo-ry

Be-cause I know 'tis true. It sat-is-fies my longings As nothing else can do.
It did so much for me; And that is just the rea-son I tell it now to thee.
For some have never heard The message of salvation From God's own holy Word.
I sing the new, new song, 'Twill be the old, old sto-ry That I have loved so long.

CHORUS

I love to tell the sto-ry! 'Twill be my theme in glo-ry

To tell the old, old sto-ry Of Je-sus and His love.

224 All the Way Along

ADA BLENKHORN

L. E. JONES

1. There is One who loves me, One who is my Friend
2. He doth still the tem-pest, bid its tu-mult cease,
3. In my Lord and Sav-iour I will joy-ful be
4. I will sing the prais-es of His won-drous love

All the way a-long,

all the way a-long.

He is ev-er near me, read-y to de-fend;
In the time of troub-le keeps in per-fect peace:
Speak-ing words of com-fort sweet and dear to me,
I will sing more sweet-ly in my home a-bove:

CHORUS

All the way a-long it is Je-sus. All the way a-long it is Je-sus; All the way a-long, bless-ed Je-sus. He's my joy and song, All the way a-long. All the way a-long it is Je-sus.

225 The Old Book and the Old Faith

G. H. C.

GEO. H. CARR

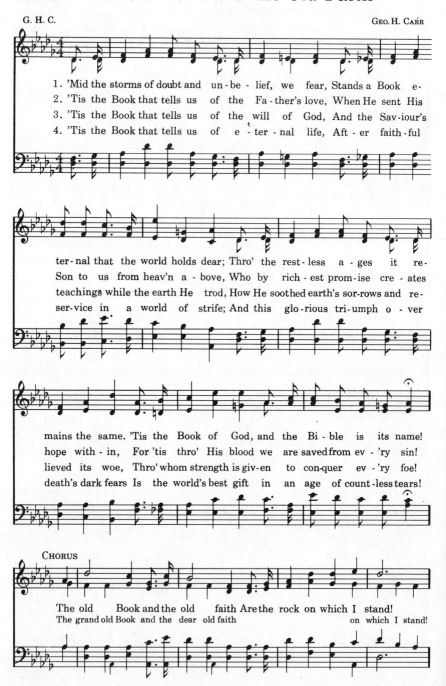

1. 'Mid the storms of doubt and un-be-lief, we fear, Stands a Book e-
2. 'Tis the Book that tells us of the Fa-ther's love, When He sent His
3. 'Tis the Book that tells us of the will of God, And the Sav-iour's
4. 'Tis the Book that tells us of e-ter-nal life, Aft-er faith-ful

ter-nal that the world holds dear; Thro' the rest-less a-ges it re-
Son to us from heav'n a-bove, Who by rich-est prom-ise cre-ates
teachings while the earth He trod, How He soothed earth's sor-rows and re-
ser-vice in a world of strife; And this glo-rious tri-umph o-ver

mains the same. 'Tis the Book of God, and the Bi-ble is its name!
hope with-in, For 'tis thro' His blood we are saved from ev-'ry sin!
lieved its woe, Thro' whom strength is giv-en to con-quer ev-'ry foe!
death's dark fears Is the world's best gift in an age of count-less tears!

CHORUS

The old Book and the old faith Are the rock on which I stand!
The grand old Book and the dear old faith on which I stand!

The Old Book and the Old Faith

The old Book and the old faith Are the bul-wark of the land!
The grand old Book and the dear old faith

Thro' storm and stress they stand the test, In ev-'ry clime and na-tion blest;

The old Book and the old faith Are the hope of ev-'ry land!
The grand old Book and the dear old faith

GRAND CHORUS AT CLOSE. (*May be omitted*)

Oh, the grand old Book and the dear old faith Are the rock on which I stand!

rit.

Oh, the grand old Book and the dear old faith Are the hope of ev - 'ry land!

226 Altogether Lovely

MARIE WOLF and
HALDOR LILLENAS

Copyright 1928 by Lillenas Publishing Co.

HALDOR LILLENAS

1. Since the wondrous grace of my lov - ing Lord Has redeemed and set me free,
2. He has made the des - ert a gar - den fair, Where the fragrant flow-ers grow.
3. He has come to dwell in my in - most self; He's the Bridegroom of my heart.
4. Now the night is gone and the ros - y dawn Of His love-light shines on me.

All my heart is filled and my soul is thrilled—He is all in all to me.
Ev - 'ry cross I bear He will glad - ly share, For I know He loves me so.
What communion sweet and what rest com-plete, Rest that nev-er shall de-part!
Earth has lost its charm; in His might-y arm Sat-is-fied my soul shall be.

CHORUS

He is al - to-geth-er love - ly, More than
He is al-to-geth-er, al-to-geth-er love-ly,

all _____ the world to me. _____ Fair - er than _____ the
More than all the world to me, to me. Fair - er than the

Rose of Shar - on Is Je-sus, my Sav-iour, to me.
Rose of Shar - on, Rose of Shar - on,

227 The Old Rugged Cross

G. B.   Copyright 1941, Renewal. The Rodeheaver Co., owner   GEORGE BENNARD

1. On a hill far a-way stood an old rug-ged Cross, The em-blem of suf-f'ring and shame; And I love that old Cross, where the dear-est and best For a world of lost sin-ners was slain.

2. Oh, the old rug-ged Cross, so de-spised by the world, Has a won-drous at-trac-tion for me; For the dear Lamb of God left His glo-ry a-bove To bear it to dark Cal-va-ry.

3. In the old rug-ged Cross, stained with Blood so di-vine, A won-drous beau-ty I see; For 'twas on that old Cross Je-sus suf-fered and died To par-don and sanc-ti-fy me.

4. To the old rug-ged Cross I will ev-er be true, Its shame and re-proach gladly bear; Then He'll call me someday to my home far a-way, Where His glo-ry for-ev-er I'll share.

CHORUS

So I'll cher-ish the old rug-ged Cross, the old rug-ged Cross, Cross, Till my tro-phies at last I lay down. I will cling to the old rug-ged Cross, the old rug-ged Cross, Cross, And ex-change it some-day for a crown.

228 I Will Sing the Wondrous Story

F. H. ROWLEY

PETER P. BILHORN

1. I will sing the won-drous sto - ry Of the Christ who died for me,
2. I was lost, but Je - sus found me, Found the sheep that went a - stray,
3. I was bruised, but Je - sus healed me; Faint was I from many a fall.
4. Days of dark-ness still come o'er me; Sor-row's paths I of - ten tread.
5. He will keep me till the riv - er Rolls its wa - ters at my feet;

How He left His home in glo - ry For the cross of Cal - va - ry.
Threw His lov - ing arms a - round me, Drew me back in - to His way.
Sight was gone, and fears pos-sessed me, But He freed me from them all.
But the Sav - iour still is with me; By His hand I'm safe - ly led.
Then He'll bear me safe - ly o - ver, Where the loved ones I shall meet.

CHORUS

Yes, I'll sing the won-drous sto - ry Of the
Yes, I'll sing the won-drous sto - ry

Christ who died for me, Sing it with the saints in
of the Christ who died for me, Sing it with

glo - ry, Gath-ered by the crys - tal sea.
the saints in glo - ry, Gath-ered by the crys - tal sea.

229 The Old-time Religion

Copyright 1908. Renewed 1935 by Mary Fuhrman
Assigned to Nazarene Publishing House

MRS. M. J. H.

MRS. M. J. HARRIS

1. I be-lieve in the old-time re-lig-ion, For it saves from all sin
2. I be-lieve in a heart-felt re-lig-ion, That brings joy to the soul
3. I be-lieve in a ho-ly re-lig-ion; For the saints of all a-
4. I be-lieve in the old-time re-lig-ion, For we know we are right

here be-low, Gives me peace pass-ing all un-der-stand-ing, While the
ev-'ry day; The as-sur-ance of sins all for-giv-en— Thro' the
ges have told How it saved them from sin and its bond-age, When they
with our God; And there's joy in our hearts as we're walk-ing In the

CHORUS

riv-er of pleas-ures doth flow.
Blood they are all washed a-way. Oh, give me the old-time re-lig-ion!
heard the sweet sto-ry of old. the old-time re-lig-ion!
paths which our fathers have trod.

Oh, give me the joy I can know! I be-lieve in the old-time re-
I can know! the

lig-ion As our fa-thers re-ceived long a-go.
old-time re-lig-ion,

230 Anywhere with Jesus

JESSIE H. BROWN AND MRS. C. M. ALEXANDER

D. B. TOWNER

1. An - y-where with Je-sus I can safe - ly go, An - y-where He
2. An - y-where with Je-sus I am not a - lone; Oth - er friends may
3. An - y-where with Je-sus o - ver land and sea, Tell - ing souls in
4. An - y-where with Je-sus I can go to sleep When the dark'ning

leads me in this world be - low. An - y-where with-out Him dear-est
fail me, He is still my own. Tho' His hand may lead me o - ver
dark-ness of sal - va - tion free; Read - y as He sum-mons me to
shad-ows round a - bout me creep, Know-ing I shall wak - en nev - er

joys would fade. An - y-where with Je - sus I am not a - fraid.
drear - y ways, An - y-where with Je - sus is a house of praise.
go or stay, An - y-where with Je - sus when He points the way.
more to roam. An - y-where with Je - sus will be home, sweet home.

CHORUS

An - y-where! an - y-where! Fear I can - not know.

An - y-where with Je - sus I can safe - ly go.

231 The Past Is All Under the Blood

MRS. C. H. M.

MRS. C. H. MORRIS

1. A pres-ent and per-fect sal-va-tion I have In Je-sus, my Sav-iour,
2. The blood of the Lamb cleanseth now from all sin, Than snow makes me whit-er;
3. The bur-den of guilt which so long I have borne, In weight like a moun-tain;
4. He leads me so gen-tly the way I should go, My won-der-ful Keep-er;
5. I'm lost and encompassed with won-der-ful love, Tho' noth-ing I mer-it;

For He is a-bun-dant-ly a-ble to save, Both now and for-ev-er.
The Com-fort-er prom-ised a-bid-eth with-in, My path grow-ing bright-er.
The sins which had caused me so of-ten to mourn, All lost in the foun-tain.
And gives sweetest com-fort the world cannot know, My peace growing deep-er.
A beau-ti-ful man-sion pre-par-ing a-bove I soon shall in-her-it.

CHORUS

He saves me just now, hal-le-lu-jah! The past is all

un-der the Blood,
un-der, yes, un-der the Blood,

And Cal-va-ry's flow makes me

whit-er than snow. The past is all un-der the Blood.

232 He Abides

HERBERT BUFFUM

D. M. SHANKS

1. I'm re-joic-ing night and day, As I walk the pil-grim way,
2. Once my heart was full of sin, Once I had no peace with-in,
3. He is with me ev-'ry-where, And He knows my ev-'ry care.
4. There's no thirst-ing for the things Of the world—they've tak-en wings;

For the hand of God in all my life I see. And the
Till I heard how Je-sus died up-on the tree. Then I
I'm as hap-py as a bird and just as free; For the
Long a-go I gave them up, and in-stant-ly All my

rea-son of my bliss, Yes, the se-cret all is this: That the
fell down at His feet, And there came a peace so sweet. Now the
Spir-it has con-trol, Je-sus sat-is-fies my soul, Since the
night was turned to day, All my bur-dens rolled a-way. Now the

CHORUS

Com-fort-er a-bides with me. He a-bides, He a-bides.
He a-bides, He a-bides.

Hal-le-lu-jah, He a-bides with me! I'm re-joic-ing night and day,

He Abides

As I walk the nar-row way, For the Com-fort-er a-bides with me.

233 **Satisfied**

CLARA TEARE

R. E. HUDSON

1. All my life-long I had pant-ed For a draught from some cool spring
2. Feed-ing on the husks a-round me Till my strength was al-most gone,
3. Poor I was, and sought for rich-es, Some-thing that would sat-is-fy;
4. Well of wa-ter, ev-er spring-ing, Bread of life, so rich and free,

That I hoped would quench the burn-ing Of the thirst I felt with-in.
Longed my soul for some-thing bet-ter, On-ly still to hun-ger on.
But the dust I gath-ered round me On-ly mocked my soul's sad cry.
Un-told wealth that nev-er fail-eth, My Re-deem-er is to me.

CHORUS

Hal-le-lu-jah! I have found Him—Whom my soul so long has craved!

Je-sus sat-is-fies my long-ings; Thro' His blood I now am saved.

234   What a Wonderful Saviour!

E. A. H.

ELISHA A. HOFFMAN

1. Christ has for sin a - tone -ment made.
2. I praise Him for the cleans - ing Blood.
3. He cleansed my heart from all its sin. What a won - der - ful Sav-iour!
4. He gives me o - ver - com - ing pow'r.
5. To Him I've giv - en all my heart.

We are re - deemed! the price is paid!
That rec - on - ciled my soul to God.
And now He reigns and rules there - in. What a won - der-ful Sav-iour!
And tri - umph in each try - ing hour.
The world shall nev - er share a part.

CHORUS

What a won - der - ful Sav - iour is Je - sus, my Je - sus!

What a won - der - ful Sav - iour is Je - sus, my Lord!

235 Dusky Hands

Copyright 1915. Renewed 1943 by Haldor Lillenas
Assigned to Nazarene Publishing House

H. L.

HALDOR LILLENAS

1. Dusk-y hands are reach-ing for the Bread of Life Far a-cross the
2. Dusk-y hands are bound in chains of want and woe In the far - off
3. We can-not be i-dle an-y lon-ger now, While the souls in
4. Dusk-y fac-es look to us for hope and peace. Shall they look to

roll-ing sea. Shall they per-ish in their mis-er-y and strife?
hea-then lands. Shall we not in haste un-to their bor-ders go,
dark-ness die. Gath-er them as jew-els for the Sav-iour's brow,
us in vain? Je-sus can re-deem them, cause their sighs to cease,

CHORUS

Shall they al-ways hun-gry be?
Set them free, as God com-mands?
While the days are pass-ing by.
Rend the chains of sin in twain.

Send the gos-pel ti-dings o-ver

land and sea. Let the hun-gry souls be sat-is-fied, Till the pow'r of

Je-sus sets the cap-tives free. Oh, lead them to the Mas-ter's side.

Blessed Assurance

FANNY J. CROSBY

MRS. JOS. F. KNAPP

1. Bless-ed as-sur-ance, Je-sus is mine! Oh, what a fore-taste of
2. Per-fect sub-mis-sion, per-fect de-light! Vi-sions of rap-ture now
3. Per-fect sub-mis-sion, all is at rest. I in my Sav-iour am

glo-ry di - vine! Heir of sal - va - tion, pur-chase of God, Born of His
burst on my sight! An-gels de-scend-ing, bring from a - bove Ech - oes of
hap-py and blest; Watching and wait-ing, look-ing a - bove, Filled with His

CHORUS

Spir - it, washed in His blood!
mer - cy, whis-pers of love. This is my sto - ry, this is my
good-ness, lost in His love.

song, Prais-ing my Sav - iour all the day long. This is my

sto - ry, this is my song, Prais-ing my Sav - iour all the day long.

237 The Sweet Beulah Land

H. J. ZELLEY

H. L. GILMOUR

1. I am walk-ing to-day in the sweet Beu-lah land. I have crossed to the glo-ry side. I am washed in the Blood and my soul is made white, And I know I am sanc-ti-fied.

2. I am now go-ing on to ex-plore Beu-lah land. 'Tis the gift of my Lord to me. I am tast-ing its joys, I am walk-ing in light, And the face of my Sav-iour see.

3. I have found a sweet peace that the world can-not know, As I walk by my Sav-iour's side. I am kept by His pow'r, I am led by His hand, And I'll ev-er with Him a-bide.

4. Oh, the sweet-ness of love that en-rap-tures my soul, For com-mun-ion with Christ I know! I am hap-py in Him and to-day thro' my soul Liv-ing streams of sal-va-tion flow.

CHORUS

Glo-ry, Glo-ry to God, oh, Glo-ry to God! My heart now is cleansed from sin. from sin. I've a-ban-doned my-self to the Ho-ly Ghost, And His full-ness a-bides with-in.

238   I Would Not Be Denied

C. P. J.

C. P. JONES

1. When pangs of fear seized on my soul, Un - to the
2. As Ja - cob in the days of old, I wres - tled
3. Old Sa - tan said my Lord was gone And would not

Lord I cried. Till Je - sus came and made me whole,
with the Lord; And in - stant - ly with cour - age bold
hear my prayer. But, praise the Lord! the work is done,

REFRAIN

I would not be de - nied.
I stood up - on His word. I would not be de - nied.
And Christ the Lord is here.

de - nied.

I would not be de - nied. Till Je - sus came and

de - nied.

made me whole, I would not be de - nied.

de - nied.

239 Blessed Redeemer

AVIS BURGESON CHRISTIANSEN   HARRY DIXON LOES

1. Up Calvary's mountain one dreadful morn Walked Christ, my Saviour, weary and worn;
2. "Fa-ther, forgive them!" thus did He pray, E'en while His lifeblood flowed fast a-way.
3. Oh, how I love Him, Saviour and Friend! How can my prais-es ev-er find end!

Fac-ing for sin-ners death on the cross, That He might save them from endless loss.
Pray-ing for sin-ners while in such woe — No one but Je-sus ev-er loved so.
Thro' years unnumbered on heaven's shore, My tongue shall praise Him for-ev-er-more.

CHORUS

Bless-ed Re-deem - er! Pre-cious Re-deem - er! Seems now I
Bless-ed Re-deem-er!   Bless-ed Re-deem-er!

see Him on Cal-va-ry's tree; Wound-ed and bleed - ing, for sin-ners
Wound-ed and bleed-ing,

plead - ing— Blind and un-heed - ing— dy-ing for me!
for sin-ners plead-ing—   Blind and un-heed-ing—

240   # Beulah Land

EDGAR PAGE STITES   JNO. R. SWENEY

1. I've reached the land of corn and wine, And all its rich - es free - ly mine;
2. My Sav-iour comes and walks with me, And sweet com-mun-ion here have we;
3. A sweet per-fume up - on the breeze Is borne from ev - er - ver-nal trees,
4. The zephyrs seem to float to me, Sweet sounds of heav-en's mel - o - dy,

Here shines undimmed one blissful day, For all my night has passed a - way.
He gen-tly leads me with the hand, For this is heav-en's bor-der-land.
And flow'rs that nev-er - fad-ing grow Where streams of life for - ev - er flow.
As angels with the white-robed throng Join in the sweet re - demp-tion song.

CHORUS

O Beu-lah Land, sweet Beu-lah Land, As on thy high - est mount I stand,

I look a-way a - cross the sea, Where mansions are pre-pared for me, And

view the shin - ing glo - ry-shore,—My heav'n, my home for - ev - er-more!

241 The Work Must Go On

LAURENE HIGHFIELD SAMUEL W. BEAZLEY

Unison

1. A glad mes-sage rings thro' the world to-day, It ech-oes thro' the
2. There are man-y souls that were dark as night, All shad-owed by the
3. There are hun-gry hearts that were starved for bread, But Je-sus has sup-
4. And the deaf shall hear, and the blind eyes see; The Word of God shall

coun-tries a-far, That the ris-ing Sun, with ce-les-tial ray,
black-ness of sin, That are glow-ing now with im-mor-tal light,
plied ev-'ry need; For on Him, the Bread of Life, they have fed
quick-en and glow; Christ the King of earth and heav-en still shall be

*REFRAIN Soprano and Tenor

Bass and Alto

Scat-ters heal-ing wher-e'er men are.
Since the glo-ry of God shone in. The good work must go on and on,
Till their spir-its are glad in-deed.
Till His glo-ry each heart shall know.

Till the world for our Lord is won. Great-er triumphs must be gained,

rit.

Great-er heights in love at-tained, Till the glo-rious day of God shall dawn.

*Melody in lower voice

242 Victory in Jesus

E. M. B.

E. M. BARTLETT

1. I heard an old, old sto - ry, how a Sav-iour came from glo-ry,
2. I heard a-bout His heal - ing, of His cleansing pow'r re - veal-ing,
3. I heard a-bout a man-sion He has built for me in glo-ry,

How He gave His life on Cal - va - ry to save a wretch like me.
How He made the lame to walk a - gain and caused the blind to see.
And I heard a - bout the streets of gold be - yond the crys - tal sea;

I heard a - bout His groan-ing, of His pre-cious blood's a - ton-ing.
And then I cried, "Dear Je - sus, come and heal my bro - ken spir-it";
A - bout the an - gels sing-ing, and the old re-demp-tion sto - ry,

Then I re - pent - ed of my sins and won the vic - to - ry.
And some-how Je - sus came and bro't to me the vic - to - ry.
And some sweet day I'll sing up there the song of vic - to - ry.

CHORUS

Oh, vic - to - ry in Je-sus, my Sav-iour, for - ev - er! He sought me and

Victory in Jesus

bought me with His re-deem-ing blood. He loved me ere I knew Him, and all my

love is due Him. He plunged me to vic-to-ry be-neath the cleansing flood.

243 Take Time to Be Holy

W. D. LONGSTAFF

GEO. C. STEBBINS

1. Take time to be ho - ly. Speak oft with thy Lord; A - bide in Him
2. Take time to be ho - ly. The world rush - es on; Spend much time in
3. Take time to be ho - ly. Let Him be thy Guide; And run not be-

al - ways, And feed on His Word. Make friends of God's children; Help
se - cret With Je - sus a - lone. By look - ing to Je - sus, Like
fore Him, What - ev - er be - tide. In joy or in sor - row, Still

those who are weak, For - get - ting in noth - ing His bless - ing to seek.
Him thou shalt be; Thy friends in thy con - duct His like - ness shall see.
fol - low thy Lord And, look - ing to Je - sus, Still trust in His Word.

244 Come Over into Canaan

H. L.

HALDOR LILLENAS

1. Why wan-der in the wil-der-ness, O faint-ing soul?
2. Its sun-kissed mountains rise a-bove the val-ley fair.
3. Sweet songs of tri-umph ring with-in its bor-ders bright.
4. This charm-ing land of Ca-naan is a land of love.

Come o-ver in-to

By faith cross o-ver Jor-dan, tho' the waves may roll.
And lus-cious fruits de-lec-ta-ble grow ev-'ry-where.
No burn-ing sands, but foun-tains spar-kling with de-light.
And thro' it we must pass to reach our home a-bove.

Ca-naan land.

CHORUS

Come o-ver in-to Ca-naan land. Come o-ver in-to Ca-naan

land. Come o-ver in-to Ca-naan land, Where the

in-to Ca-naan land. in-to Ca-naan land,

rit. ad lib.

grapes of Eshcol grow, Where the milk and honey flow. Come over in-to Ca-naan land.

245 I'm Pressing On

JOHNSON OATMAN, JR. HAMP SEWELL

1. Re-joic-ing on my way to the home a-bove,
2. Re-ject-ing ev-'ry-thing that would bid me stay,
3. Up tow'rd that blessed land where the an-gels sing, I'm press-ing,_____
4. Up where my Saviour's face I shall then be-hold,
5. The King re-quir-eth haste, so a-long life's way, I am press-ing on,

An-tic-i-pat-ing joys in that land of love,
De-pend-ing on God's help ev-'ry hour and day,
I'm press-ing;_____ As hap-py ev-'ry day as a bird on wing,
While faith e'er points the way to those streets of gold,
I am press-ing on; As-sured of find-ing rest at the close of day,

CHORUS

I'm pressing tow'rd the Glo-ry Land. I'm press-ing,_____ I'm press-ing _____
I am pressing on,   I am pressing on

Tow'rd the cit-y grand, led by Je-sus' hand. I'm press-ing,_____
I am press-ing on,

I am press-ing,_____ I am pressing tow'rd the Glo-ry Land.
I am press-ing on,

246 There Is Power in the Blood

L. E. J.   L. E. Jones

1. Would you be free from your bur-den of sin?
2. Would you be free from your pas-sion and pride?
3. Would you be whit-er, much whit-er than snow?
4. Would you do serv-ice for Je-sus, your King?

There's pow'r in the Blood, pow'r in the Blood.

Would you o'er e-vil a vic-to-ry win?
Come for a cleans-ing to Cal-va-ry's tide.
Sin stains are lost in its life-giv-ing flow.
Would you live dai-ly His prais-es to sing?

There's won-der-ful pow'r in the Blood.

CHORUS

There is pow'r, pow'r, won-der-working pow'r in the blood of the Lamb.

There is pow'r, In the blood of the Lamb.

There is pow'r, pow'r, won-der-work-ing pow'r In the pre-cious blood of the Lamb.

There is pow'r,

247 Redeemed

Fanny J. Crosby

Wm. J. Kirkpatrick

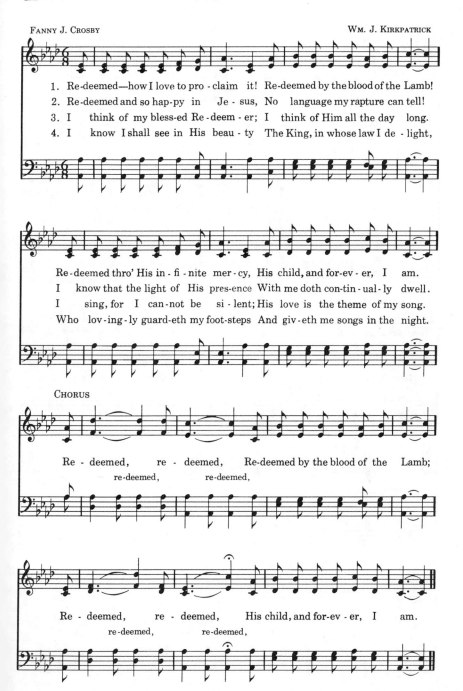

1. Re-deemed—how I love to pro-claim it! Re-deemed by the blood of the Lamb!
2. Re-deemed and so hap-py in Je-sus, No language my rapture can tell!
3. I think of my bless-ed Re-deem-er; I think of Him all the day long.
4. I know I shall see in His beau-ty The King, in whose law I de-light,

Re-deemed thro' His in-fi-nite mer-cy, His child, and for-ev-er, I am.
I know that the light of His pres-ence With me doth con-tin-ual-ly dwell.
I sing, for I can-not be si-lent; His love is the theme of my song.
Who lov-ing-ly guard-eth my foot-steps And giv-eth me songs in the night.

Chorus

Re-deemed, re-deemed, Re-deemed by the blood of the Lamb;
re-deemed, re-deemed,

Re-deemed, re-deemed, His child, and for-ev-er, I am.
re-deemed, re-deemed,

248 Come to the Feast

Charlotte G. Homer

W. A Ogden

1. "All things are ready," come to the feast! Come, for the ta-ble now is spread. Ye fam-ish-ing, ye wea-ry, come, And thou shalt be rich-ly fed.
2. "All things are ready," come to the feast! Come, for the door is o-pen wide. A place of hon-or is re-served For you at the Mas-ter's side.
3. "All things are ready," come to the feast! Come, while He waits to wel-come thee. De-lay not while this day is thine; To-mor-row may nev-er be.
4. "All things are ready," come to the feast! Leave ev-'ry care and world-ly strife. Come, feast up-on the love of God, And drink ev-er-last-ing life.

Chorus

Hear the in-vi-ta-tion. Come, "who-so-ev-er will." Praise God for full sal-va-tion For "who-so-ev-er will."

Hear the in-vi-ta-tion, "Who-so-ev-er will." Hear the in-vi-ta-tion, "Who-so-ev-er will." Praise God for full sal-va-tion For "who-so-ev-er will."

249 This Is Like Heaven to Me

Copyright 1903. Renewed 1931 by J. E. French
Assigned to Nazarene Publishing House

J. E. F.

J. E. FRENCH

1. We find man-y peo-ple who can't un-der-stand Why we are so
2. So when we are hap-py we sing and we shout. Some don't un-der-
3. We've heard the sweet mu-sic, the heav-en-ly chord, From glo-ry-land
4. We're look-ing for Je-sus with glo-ry to come; 'Tis Je-sus who

hap-py and free; We've crossed o-ver Jor-dan to Canaan's fair land,
stand us, I see. We're filled with the Spir-it, there is-n't a doubt,
o-ver the sea: A soul-thrill-ing mes-sage from Je-sus, our Lord,
died on the tree. A cloud of bright an-gels to car-ry me home—

CHORUS

1-3. And this is like heav-en to me. Oh, this is like heav-en to
4. Oh, that will be heav-en to me! Oh, that will be heav-en to

me. Yes, this is like heav-en to me. I've crossed o-ver
me. Yes, that will be heav-en to me. A cloud of bright
to me. to me.

Jor-dan to Canaan's fair land, And this is like heav-en to me.
an-gels to car-ry me home, Yes, that will be heav-en to me.
to me.

250 'Tis Marvelous and Wonderful

Mrs. C. H. M.

Mrs. C. H. Morris

1. The Sav-iour has come in His might-y pow'r, And spo-ken
2. 'Twas on-ly a fore-taste of joys di-vine In Ca-naan
3. From glo-ry to glo-ry He leads me on, From grace to
4. If fel-low-ship here with my Lord can be So in-ex-

peace to my soul; And all of my life from that ver-y hour I've
wait-ing for me, Where sweet-est of hon-ey and milk and wine Were
grace ev-'ry day; And bright-er and bright-er the glo-ry dawns, While
press-i-bly sweet, Oh, what will it be when His face we see, When

yield-ed to His con-trol, I've yield-ed to His con-trol.
drip-ping from ev-'ry tree, Were drip-ping from ev-'ry tree.
press-ing my home-ward way, While press-ing my home-ward way.
'round the white throne we meet? When 'round the white throne we meet?

Chorus

Won-der-ful, won-der-ful, Mar-vel-ous and won-der-ful, What

Oh, _____ it is won-der-ful! It is mar-vel-ous and won-der-ful, What

Male Voices Unison

He has done for my soul! The half has nev-er been told;

Je-sus has done for this soul of mine! The half has nev-er been told; _____

rit.

'Tis Marvelous and Wonderful

a tempo

Oh, _____ it is won-der-ful. It is mar-vel-ous and won-der-ful,

Won-der-ful,

What Je-sus has done for this soul of mine! The half has nev-er been told.

rit.

251 Revive Us Again

WM. P. MACKAY

J. J. HUSBAND

1. We praise Thee, O God, For the Son of Thy love, For Je - sus, who
2. We praise Thee, O God, For Thy Spir - it of Light, Who has shown us our
3. All glo - ry and praise To the Lamb that was slain, Who has borne all our
4. Re - vive us a - gain; Fill each heart with Thy love; May each soul be re -

died And is now gone a - bove.
Sav-iour And scat-tered our night.
sins And has cleansed ev 'ry stain.
kin - dled With fire from a - bove.

REFRAIN

Hal - le - lu - jah! Thine the glo - ry! Hal - le -

lu - jah! A - men! Hal - le - lu - jah! Thine the glo - ry! Re - vive us a - gain.

252 I'll Be a Soldier for Jesus

ISAAC WATTS
2ND VERSE AND CHO. BY MRS. C. H. M.

MRS. C. H. MORRIS

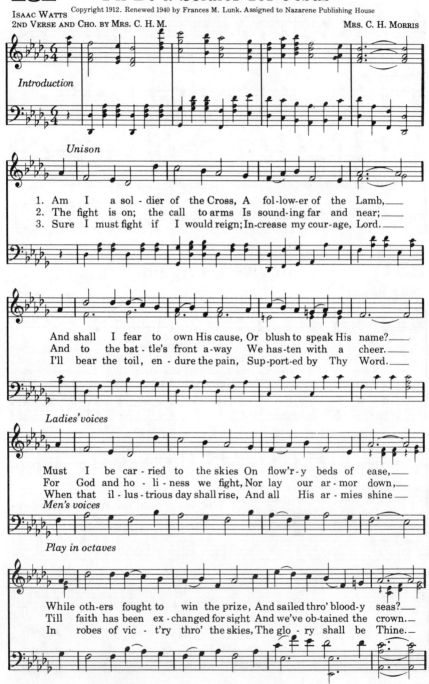

Introduction

Unison

1. Am I a sol - dier of the Cross, A fol-low-er of the Lamb,___
2. The fight is on; the call to arms Is sound-ing far and near;___
3. Sure I must fight if I would reign; In-crease my cour-age, Lord.___

And shall I fear to own His cause, Or blush to speak His name?___
And to the bat - tle's front a-way We has-ten with a cheer.___
I'll bear the toil, en - dure the pain, Sup-port-ed by Thy Word.___

Ladies' voices

Must I be car - ried to the skies On flow'r-y beds of ease,___
For God and ho - li - ness we fight, Nor lay our ar-mor down,___
When that il - lus-trious day shall rise, And all His ar - mies shine___

Men's voices

Play in octaves

While oth-ers fought to win the prize, And sailed thro' blood-y seas?___
Till faith has been ex - changed for sight And we've ob-tained the crown.___
In robes of vic - t'ry thro' the skies, The glo - ry shall be Thine.___

I'll Be a Soldier for Jesus

253 Throw Out the Lifeline

Edwin S. Ufford

Arr. by Geo. C. Stebbins

1. Throw out the life-line a-cross the dark wave. There is a
2. Throw out the life-line with hand quick and strong. Why do you
3. Throw out the life-line to dan-ger-fraught men, Sink-ing in
4. Soon will the sea-son of res-cue be o'er; Soon will they

broth-er whom some-one should save. Some-bod-y's broth-er! Oh,
tar-ry, why lin-ger so long? See! he is sink-ing. Oh,
an-guish where you've nev-er been. Winds of temp-ta-tion and
drift to e-ter-ni-ty's shore. Haste then, my broth-er, no

who then will dare To throw out the life-line, his per-il to share?
has-ten to-day— And out with the life-boat! A-way, then, a-way!
bil-lows of woe Will soon hurl them out where the dark wa-ters flow.
time for de-lay, But throw out the life-line and save them to-day.

CHORUS

Throw out the life-line! Throw out the life-line! Some-one is drift-ing a-way.

Throw out the life-line! Throw out the life-line! Some-one is sink-ing to-day.

254 Covered by the Blood

NELLIE EDWARDS

RAN C. STOREY

1. Once in sin's darkest night I was wand'ring alone; A stran-ger to mer-cy I
2. From the bur-den I car-ried now I am set free, For Je-sus has lift-ed my
3. I can ne'er understand why He sought even me, Why His life-blood on Cal-va-ry
4. Now He comes to my heart and removes ev'ry care; He bears all my cum-ber-ing

stood. But the Sav-iour came nigh When He heard my faint cry, And He put my sins
load. Oh, the love and the grace I re-ceived in its place When He put my sins
flowed. But suf-fi-cient for me, Since He died on the tree, He hath put my sins
load. In a path-way re-plete With His love are my feet, Since He put my sins

CHORUS

un-der the Blood. They are covered by the Blood, they are covered by the Blood,

My sins are all covered by the Blood.____ Mine in-iq-ui-ties so vast
pre-cious Blood.

Have been blot-ted out at last. My sins are all covered by the Blood.____
precious Blood.

255 Walking in the Beautiful Light of God

H. L.

HALDOR LILLENAS

1. What a bless - ed peace we know as we trav - el here be - low,
2. Like the sun - light from a - bove God re - veals His won - drous love,
3. Hold - ing sweet com - mun - ion here with our bless - ed Lord so dear,
4. O - ver moun - tains rough and steep, thro' the val - leys long and deep,

While we're
While we're
We are   walk - ing in the beau - ti - ful light of God!
We are   the beau - ti - ful light of God!

Bright - er, fair - er grows the way as we jour - ney day by day,
Here re - demp - tion's crim - son flow makes us whit - er than the snow,
From all con - dem - na - tion free, hav - ing per - fect vic - to - ry,
To the man - sions of de - light, to the land where comes no night,

While we're
While we're
We are   walk - ing in the beau - ti - ful light of God.
We are   the beau - ti - ful light of God.

CHORUS

Walk - ing in the beau - ti - ful light of God, Walk - ing
Walk - ing in the light,   Walk - ing in the light,

Walking in the Beautiful Light of God

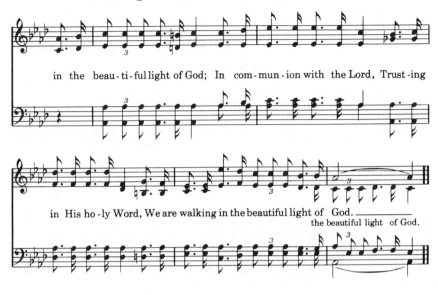

in the beau-ti-ful light of God; In com-mun-ion with the Lord, Trust-ing

in His ho-ly Word, We are walking in the beautiful light of God. _____

the beautiful light of God.

256   Soldiers of Christ, Arise

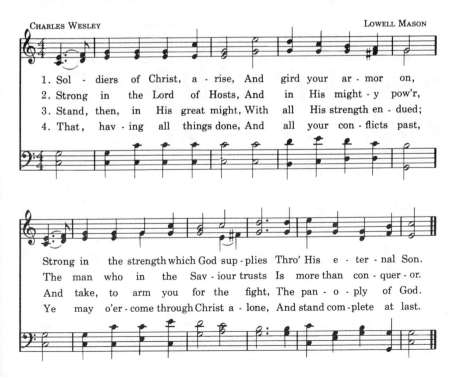

CHARLES WESLEY

LOWELL MASON

1. Sol - diers of Christ, a - rise, And gird your ar - mor on,
2. Strong in the Lord of Hosts, And in His might - y pow'r,
3. Stand, then, in His great might, With all His strength en - dued;
4. That, hav - ing all things done, And all your con - flicts past,

Strong in the strength which God sup - plies Thro' His e - ter - nal Son.
The man who in the Sav - iour trusts Is more than con - quer - or.
And take, to arm you for the fight, The pan - o - ply of God.
Ye may o'er - come through Christ a - lone, And stand com - plete at last.

257 To the Work

Fanny J. Crosby

W. H. Doane

1. To the work! to the work! We are serv-ants of God. Let us fol - low the path that our Mas - ter has trod. With the balm of His coun - sel our strength to re-new, Let us do with our might what our hands find to do.

2. To the work! to the work! Let the hun - gry be fed; To the foun-tain of life let the wea - ry be led. In the Cross and its ban - ner our glo - ry shall be, While we her - ald the ti - dings, "Sal-va - tion is free!"

3. To the work! to the work! There is la - bor for all; For the king-dom of dark - ness and er - ror shall fall; And the name of Je - ho - vah ex - alt - ed shall be, In the loud swell-ing cho - rus, "Sal-va - tion is free!"

4. To the work! to the work! in the strength of the Lord; And a robe and a crown shall our la - bor re-ward, When the home of the faith - ful our dwell - ing shall be, And we shout with the ran-somed, "Sal-va - tion is free!"

Chorus

Toil-ing on, toil-ing on, Toil-ing on, toil-ing on;
Toil-ing on, toil-ing on, Toil-ing on, toil-ing on;

Let us hope, let us watch, And la-bor till the Mas-ter comes.
and trust, and pray,

258 Deeper, Deeper

C. P. J.

C. P. Jones

1. Deep-er, deep-er in the love of Je - sus Dai - ly let me go;
2. Deep-er, deep-er! bless - ed Ho - ly Spir - it, Take me deep-er still,
3. Deep-er, deep-er! tho' it cost hard tri - als, Deep-er let me go!
4. Deep-er, high - er, ev - 'ry day in Je - sus, Till all con - flict past

High - er, high - er in the school of wis - dom, More of grace to know.
Till my life is whol - ly lost in Je - sus And His per - fect will.
Root - ed in the ho - ly love of Je - sus, Let me fruit - ful grow.
Finds me con - qu'ror, and in His own im - age Per - fect - ed at last.

Chorus

Oh, deep - er yet, I pray, _____ And
Oh, deep - er yet, I pray, deep - er yet, I pray, And

high - er ev - 'ry day, _____ And wis - er,
high - er ev - 'ry day, high - er ev - 'ry day, And wis - er, blessed Lord,

bless - ed Lord, _____ In Thy pre - cious, ho - ly Word.
wis - er, bless - ed Lord,

259 I've Anchored in Jesus

L. E. J.

L. E. JONES

1. Up - on life's bound-less o - cean where might-y bil - lows roll, I've
2. He keeps my soul from e - vil and gives me bless - ed peace; His
3. He is my Friend and Sav - iour; in Him my an - chor's cast. He

fixed my hope in Je - sus, blest An - chor of my soul. When tri - als fierce as-
voice hath stilled the wa - ters and bid their tu-mult cease. My Pi - lot and De-
drives a - way my sor - rows and shields me from the blast. By faith I'm look-ing

sail me, as storms are gath'ring o'er, I rest up - on His mer - cy and
liv - 'rer, to Him I all con - fide, For al - ways when I need Him He's
up - ward be - yond life's troubled sea; There I be - hold a ha - ven pre-

CHORUS

trust Him more.
at my side. I've an-chored in Je-sus; The storms of life I'll brave. I've
pared for me.

an-chored in Je-sus; I fear no wind or wave. I've an-chored in Je-sus, for

I've Anchored in Jesus

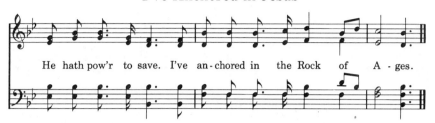

He hath pow'r to save. I've an-chored in the Rock of A - ges.

260 A Shelter in the Time of Storm

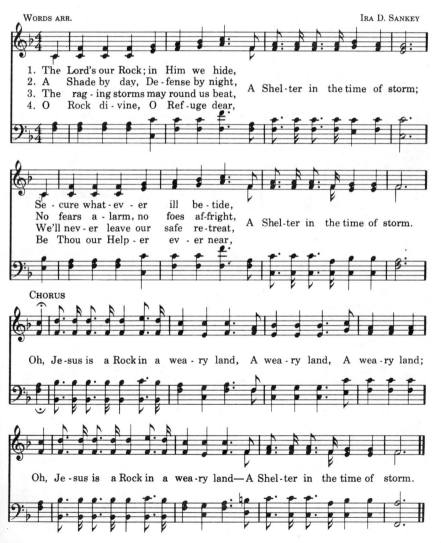

WORDS ARR.   IRA D. SANKEY

1. The Lord's our Rock; in Him we hide,
2. A Shade by day, De - fense by night,
3. The rag - ing storms may round us beat,
4. O Rock di - vine, O Ref - uge dear,

A Shel - ter in the time of storm;

Se - cure what - ev - er ill be - tide,
No fears a - larm, no foes af - fright,
We'll nev - er leave our safe re - treat,
Be Thou our Help - er ev - er near,

A Shel - ter in the time of storm.

CHORUS

Oh, Je - sus is a Rock in a wea - ry land, A wea - ry land, A wea - ry land;

Oh, Je - sus is a Rock in a wea - ry land—A Shel - ter in the time of storm.

261   The Old Account Settled

F. M. G.

F. M. GRAHAM

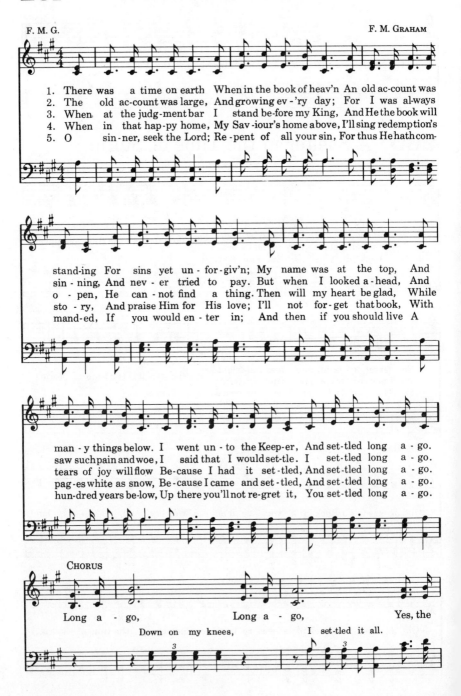

1. There was a time on earth When in the book of heav'n An old ac-count was
2. The old ac-count was large, And growing ev-'ry day; For I was al-ways
3. When at the judg-ment bar I stand be-fore my King, And He the book will
4. When in that hap-py home, My Sav-iour's home above, I'll sing redemption's
5. O sin-ner, seek the Lord; Re-pent of all your sin, For thus He hath com-

stand-ing For sins yet un-for-giv'n; My name was at the top, And
sin-ning, And nev-er tried to pay. But when I looked a-head, And
o-pen, He can-not find a thing. Then will my heart be glad, While
sto-ry, And praise Him for His love; I'll not for-get that book, With
mand-ed, If you would en-ter in; And then if you should live A

man-y things below. I went un-to the Keep-er, And set-tled long a-go.
saw such pain and woe, I said that I would set-tle. I set-tled long a-go.
tears of joy will flow Be-cause I had it set-tled, And set-tled long a-go.
pag-es white as snow, Be-cause I came and set-tled, And set-tled long a-go.
hun-dred years be-low, Up there you'll not re-gret it, You set-tled long a-go.

CHORUS

Long a-go, Long a-go, Yes, the

Down on my knees, I set-tled it all.

The Old Account Settled

old account was settled long a - go; And the record's clear to-day,

Hal - le - lu - jah!

For He washed my sins a-way, When the old account was settled long a - go.

262   Oh, How I Love Jesus!

1. There is a name I love to hear; I love to sing its worth. It sounds like
2. It tells me of a Saviour's love, Who died to set me free. It tells me
3. It tells me what my Fa-ther hath In store for ev-'ry day And, tho' I
4. It tells of One whose loving heart Can feel my deep-est woe, Who in each

CHORUS

mu - sic in mine ear, The sweetest name on earth.
of His precious blood, The sin - ner's per-fect plea.   Oh, how I love Je - sus!
tread a darksome path, Yields sunshine all the way.
sor - row bears a part That none can bear be - low.

Oh, how I love Je - sus! Oh, how I love Je - sus, Be-cause He first loved me!

263 Follow On

W. O. Cushing

Robert Lowry

1. Down in the val-ley with my Sav-iour I would go, Where the flow'rs are
2. Down in the val-ley with my Sav-iour I would go, Where the storms are
3. Down in the val-ley, or up-on the mountain steep, Close be-side my

bloom-ing and the sweet wa-ters flow. Ev-'ry-where He leads me I would
sweep-ing and the dark wa-ters flow. With His hand to lead me I will
Sav-iour would my soul ev-er keep. He will lead me safe-ly in the

fol-low, fol-low on, Walk-ing in His foot-steps till the crown be won.
nev-er, nev-er fear; Dan-ger can-not fright me if my Lord is near.
path that He has trod, Up to where they gath-er on the hills of God.

REFRAIN

Fol-low! fol-low! I will fol-low Je-sus! Anywhere, ev'rywhere, I will follow on!

Fol-low! fol-low! I will fol-low Je-sus! Ev'rywhere He leads me I will fol-low on!

264 Truehearted, Wholehearted

FRANCES R. HAVERGAL

GEO. C. STEBBINS

1. Truehearted, wholehearted, faith-ful and loy-al, King of our lives, by Thy grace we will be.
2. Truehearted, wholehearted, full-est al-le-giance Yield-ing henceforth to our glo-ri-ous King;
3. Truehearted, wholehearted, Sav-iour all-glo-rious! Take Thy great pow-er and reign there a-lone,

Under the standard ex-alt-ed and roy-al, Strong in Thy strength we will bat-tle for Thee.
Val-iant en-deav-or and lov-ing o-be-dience, Free-ly and joy-ous-ly now would we bring.
O-ver our wills and af-fec-tions vic-to-rious, Free-ly sur-ren-dered and whol-ly Thine own.

CHORUS

Peal out the watchword! Silence it nev-er! Peal out the watchword! Silence it nev-er!

Song of our spir-its, re-joic-ing and free! Peal out the watch-word!
Song of our spir-its, re-joic-ing and free! Peal out the watch-word!

Loy-al for-ev-er, King of our lives, by Thy grace we will be.
Loy-al for-ev-er, King of our lives, by Thy grace we will be.

265 The Fight Is On

MRS. C. H. M.

MRS. C. H. MORRIS

1. The fight is on! The trum-pet sound is ring-ing out; The cry "To
2. The fight is on! A - rouse, ye sol-diers brave and true! Je - ho - vah
3. The Lord is lead - ing on to cer-tain vic - to - ry; The bow of

arms!" is heard a-far and near. The Lord of Hosts is march-ing on to
leads, and vic - t'ry will as-sure. Go, buck - le on the ar - mor God has
prom-ise spans the east-ern sky. His glo-rious name in ev -'ry land shall

vic - to - ry; The tri - umph of the Christ will soon ap - pear.
giv - en you, And in His strength un - to the end en - dure.
hon - ored be. The morn will break; the dawn of peace is nigh.

CHORUS *Unison*

The fight is on, O Chris-tian sol - dier! And face to face in stern ar - ray,— With

ar-mor gleaming and col-ors streaming, The right and wrong engage to-day!

The Fight Is On

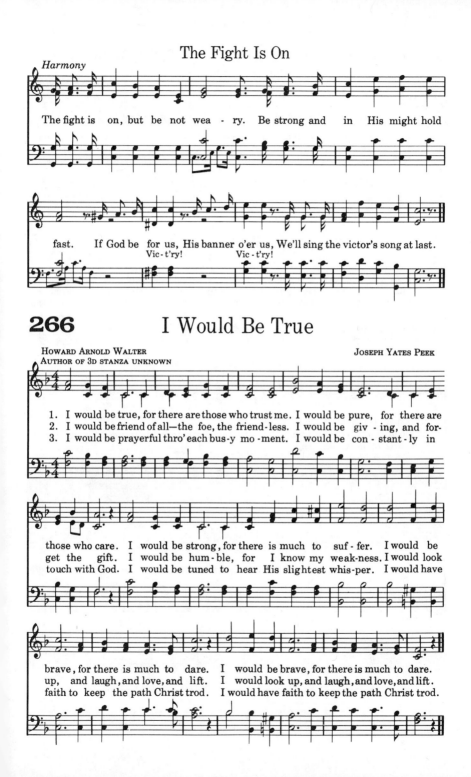

Harmony

The fight is on, but be not wea - ry. Be strong and in His might hold fast. If God be for us, His banner o'er us, We'll sing the victor's song at last.
Vic - t'ry!   Vic - t'ry!

266   I Would Be True

HOWARD ARNOLD WALTER
AUTHOR OF 3D STANZA UNKNOWN

JOSEPH YATES PEEK

1. I would be true, for there are those who trust me. I would be pure, for there are
2. I would be friend of all—the foe, the friend-less. I would be giv - ing, and for-
3. I would be prayerful thro' each bus-y mo -ment. I would be con - stant-ly in

those who care. I would be strong, for there is much to suf - fer. I would be
get the gift. I would be hum - ble, for I know my weak-ness. I would look
touch with God. I would be tuned to hear His slightest whis-per. I would have

brave, for there is much to dare. I would be brave, for there is much to dare.
up, and laugh, and love, and lift. I would look up, and laugh, and love, and lift.
faith to keep the path Christ trod. I would have faith to keep the path Christ trod.

267 In My Heart There Rings a Melody

E. M. R.

ELTON M. ROTH

1. I have a song that Je - sus gave me. It was sent from
2. I love the Christ who died on Cal - v'ry, For He washed my
3. 'Twill be my end - less theme in glo - ry; With the an - gels

heav'n a - bove. There nev-er was a sweet - er mel - o - dy; 'Tis a
sins a - way; He put with - in my heart a mel - o - dy, And I
I will sing; 'Twill be a song with glo - rious har - mo - ny When the

CHORUS

mel - o - dy of love.
know it's there to stay.
courts of heav - en ring.

In my heart there rings a mel - o - dy, There

rings a mel - o - dy with heav - en's har - mo - ny. In my heart there

rings a mel - o - dy, There rings a mel - o - dy of love.

268 From Greenland's Icy Mountains

REGINALD HEBER

LOWELL MASON

1. From Green-land's i - cy moun-tains, From In - dia's cor - al strand,
2. What though the spi - cy breez - es Blow soft o'er Cey - lon's isle,
3. Shall we, whose souls are light - ed With wis - dom from on high,
4. Waft, waft, ye winds, His sto - ry, And you, ye wa - ters, roll,

Where Af - ric's sun - ny foun - tains Roll down their gold - en sand—
Though ev - 'ry pros - pect pleas - es And on - ly man is vile?
Shall we to men be - night - ed The lamp of life de - ny?
Till, like a sea of glo - ry, It spreads from pole to pole—

From many an an - cient riv - er, From many a palm - y plain,
In vain with lav - ish kind - ness The gifts of God are strown;
Sal - va - tion! O sal - va - tion! The joy - ful sound pro - claim
Till o'er our ran - somed na - ture The Lamb for sin - ners slain,

They call us to de - liv - er Their land from er - ror's chain.
The hea - then in his blind-ness Bows down to wood and stone.
Till earth's re - mot - est na - tion Has learned Mes - si - ah's name.
Re - deem - er, King, Cre - a - tor, In bliss re - turns to reign.

269 Is My Name Written There?

MARY A. KIDDER

FRANK M. DAVIS

1. Lord, I care not for rich-es, Nei-ther sil-ver nor gold. I would
2. Lord, my sins they are man-y Like the sands of the sea; But Thy
3. Oh, that beau-ti-ful cit-y, With its man-sions of light, With its

make sure of heav-en; I would en-ter the fold. In the book of Thy
blood, O my Sav-iour, Is suf-fi-cient for me. For Thy prom-ise is
glo-ri-fied be-ings In pure gar-ments of white, Where no e-vil thing

king-dom, With its pa-ges so fair, Tell me, Je-sus, my Sav-iour, Is my
writ-ten, In bright let-ters that glow, "Tho' your sins be as scar-let, I will
com-eth To de-spoil what is fair, Where the an-gels are watch-ing—Yes, my

REFRAIN

name writ-ten there?
make them like snow." Is my name writ-ten there, On the page white and
name's writ-ten there. Yes, my name's, etc.

fair? In the book of Thy king-dom, Is my name writ-ten there?
Yes, my name's writ-ten there.

270 Under the Atoning Blood

H. L.

HALDOR LILLENAS

1. I have found a pre-cious rest-ing place, In the shel-ter
2. Where shall I the praise of Christ be-gin? Gone the heav-y
3. E-vil shall not here my soul en-snare; Ten-der-ly I'm
4. Now its heal-ing pow-er makes me whole, Thro' its mer-it

of re-deem-ing grace. Here with joy I see my Sav-iour's face,
bur-den of my sin! Grace has changed the world I'm liv-ing in,
kept with jeal-ous care; Je-sus walks be-side me ev-'ry-where,
Je-sus saves my soul. Sav-iour, keep me while the a-ges roll

CHORUS

Un-der the a-ton-ing Blood. Un-der the a-ton-ing blood of the Lamb,

Un-der the a-ton-ing blood of the Lamb; Safe-ly I am

hid-ing, Con-stant-ly a-bid-ing, Un-der the a-ton-ing Blood.

271 My Burden Is Gone

Copyright 1923. Renewed 1950 by Haldor Lillenas
Assigned to Lillenas Publishing Co.

H. L.

HALDOR LILLENAS

1. One day I trav-eled a toil-some road O-ver the
2. Gone is the night with its shad-ows drear; Morn-ing hath
3. No more the bur-den of guilt is mine; No more in

hills of de - spair; One day I car-ried a wea-ry load,
dawned up-on me. Gone is the bur-den of anx-ious fear;
bond-age I dwell. Un-to my glo-ri-ous King di-vine

CHORUS

Cum-bered with toil and with care.___
Free-dom my por-tion shall be.___ The bur-den that once I
Ju - bi - lant prais-es shall swell.___

car-ried Is gone,___ is gone.___ Of all of my sins there re-
Is gone, is gone.

main-eth Not one,___ not one.___ Je - sus, the Sav-iour, hath
Not one, not one.

My Burden Is Gone

ran - somed me, Bear-ing my sins up - on Cal - va - ry,

Giv-ing me glo - ri-ous lib - er-ty; My bur-den of sin is gone.

272 Jesus Never Fails

Copyright 1927 by Mrs. O. E. Williams
Used by permission

A. A. L.   A. A. LUTHER

1. Earth-ly friends may prove un-true, Doubts and fears as - sail;   One still
2. Tho' the sky be dark and drear, Fierce and strong the gale,   Just re-
3. In life's dark and bit - ter hour Love will still pre - vail.   Trust His

CHORUS

loves and cares for you,   One who will not fail.
mem-ber He is near,   And He will not fail.   Je-sus nev-er fails.
ev - er - last-ing pow'r; Je - sus will not fail.

Je - sus nev-er fails. Heav'n and earth may pass away, But Jesus nev-er fails.

273 Give Him the Glory

E. A. H.

ELISHA A. HOFFMAN

1. It was down at the feet of Je - sus, Oh, the hap - py,
2. It was down at the feet of Je - sus, Where I found such
3. It was down at the feet of Je - sus, Where I brought my

hap - py day! That my soul found peace in be - liev - ing,
per - fect rest, Where the light first dawned on my spir - it,
guilt and sin, That He can - celed all my trans - gres - sions,

CHORUS

And my sins were washed a - way.
And my soul was tru - ly blest. Let me tell the old, old
And sal - va - tion en - tered in.

sto - ry Of His grace so full and free; For I feel like

giv - ing Him the glo - ry For His won - drous love to me.

274 It Pays to Serve Jesus

F. C. H.

FRANK C. HUSTON

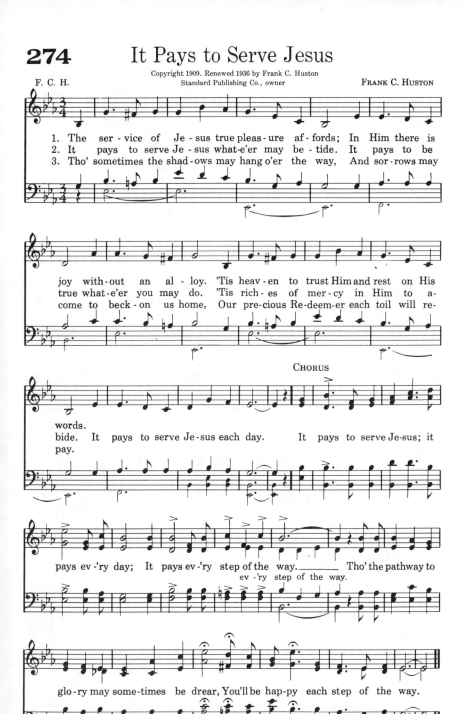

1. The ser-vice of Je-sus true pleas-ure af-fords; In Him there is
2. It pays to serve Je-sus what-e'er may be-tide. It pays to be
3. Tho' sometimes the shad-ows may hang o'er the way, And sor-rows may

joy with-out an al-loy. 'Tis heav-en to trust Him and rest on His
true what-e'er you may do. 'Tis rich-es of mer-cy in Him to a-
come to beck-on us home, Our pre-cious Re-deem-er each toil will re-

CHORUS

words.
bide. It pays to serve Je-sus each day. It pays to serve Je-sus; it
pay.

pays ev-'ry day; It pays ev-'ry step of the way._____ Tho' the pathway to
ev-'ry step of the way.

glo-ry may some-times be drear, You'll be hap-py each step of the way.

275 Give of Your Best to the Master

H. B. G.

MRS. CHARLES BARNARD

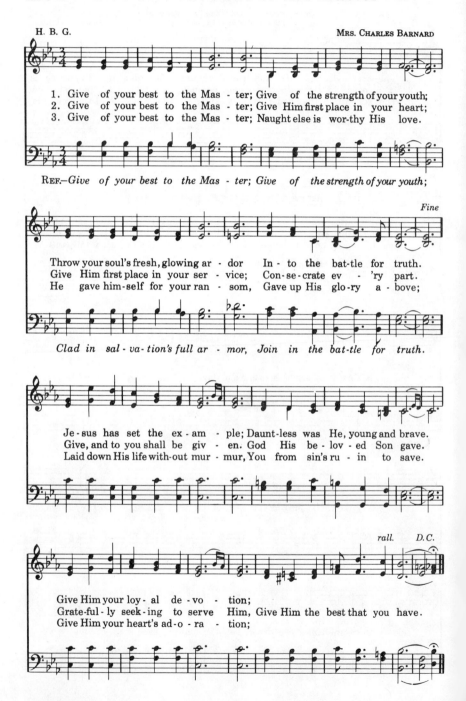

1. Give of your best to the Mas - ter; Give of the strength of your youth;
2. Give of your best to the Mas - ter; Give Him first place in your heart;
3. Give of your best to the Mas - ter; Naught else is wor-thy His love.

REF.—*Give of your best to the Mas - ter; Give of the strength of your youth;*

Throw your soul's fresh, glowing ar - dor In - to the bat-tle for truth.
Give Him first place in your ser - vice; Con-se-crate ev -'ry part.
He gave him-self for your ran - som, Gave up His glo-ry a - bove;

Clad in sal - va - tion's full ar - mor, Join in the bat-tle for truth.

Je-sus has set the ex - am - ple; Daunt-less was He, young and brave.
Give, and to you shall be giv - en. God His be - lov - ed Son gave.
Laid down His life with-out mur - mur, You from sin's ru - in to save.

Give Him your loy - al de - vo - tion;
Grate-ful - ly seek-ing to serve Him, Give Him the best that you have.
Give Him your heart's ad - o - ra - tion;

276 Glorious Freedom

HALDOR LILLENAS

ALFRED JUDSON

1. Once I was bound by sin's gall-ing fet-ters; Chained like a slave, I
2. Free-dom from all the car-nal af-fec-tions; Free-dom from en-vy,
3. Free-dom from pride and all sin-ful fol-lies; Free-dom from love and
4. Free-dom from fear with all of its tor-ments; Free-dom from care with

strug-gled in vain. But I re-ceived a glo-ri-ous free-dom
ha-tred, and strife; Free-dom from vain and world-ly am-bi-tions;
glit-ter of gold; Free-dom from e-vil tem-per and an-ger—
all of its pain; Free-dom in Christ, my bless-ed Re-deem-er,

CHORUS

When Je-sus broke my fet-ters in twain.
Free-dom from all that sad-dened my life. Glo-ri-ous free-dom!
Glo-ri-ous free-dom, rap-ture un-told!
He who has rent my fet-ters in twain.

Won-der-ful free-dom! No more in chains of sin I re-pine! Je-sus, the

glo-rious E-man-ci-pa-tor! Now and for-ev-er He shall be mine.

277 Victory All the Time

Mrs. C. H. M.   Mrs. C. H. Morris

1. They who know the Sav - iour shall in Him be strong, Might-y in the
2. In the midst of bat - tle be thou not dis-mayed, Tho' the pow'rs of
3. Brave to bear life's test - ing, strong the foe to meet, Walk-ing like a

conflict of the right 'gainst wrong; This the blessed prom-ise giv-en in God's Word,
darkness 'gainst thee are arrayed. God, thy Strength, is with thee, causing thee to stand;
he - ro midst the fur - nace heat, Do-ing won-drous exploits with the Spirit's Sword,

Chorus

Do - ing wondrous exploits, they who know the Lord. Vic - to - ry! vic - to - ry!
Heaven's al - lied ar - mies wait at thy com-mand.
Winning souls for Je - sus, praise, oh, praise the Lord! Vic - to - ry! yes, vic - to - ry!

blessed Blood-bo't vic-to-ry! Vic-to-ry! vic-to-ry! vict'ry all the time! As Jehovah
Vic-to-ry! yes, vic-to-ry!

liv-eth, strength divine He giveth Unto those who know Him, vict'ry all the time.

278 It Cleanseth Me

I John 1:9

REV. F. L. SNYDER

A. F. MYERS

1. There is a stream that flows from Cal-va-ry, A crim-son tide so
2. Its sav-ing vir-tues ev-er are the same. It cleans-eth still, and
3. No oth-er foun-tain can for sin a-tone But Je-sus' blood, O

deep and wide. It wash-es whit-er than the pur-est snow; It
al-ways will. Poor sin-ners who will seek the Sav-iour's face Shall
pre-cious flood! And who-so-ev-er will may plunge there-in, And

CHORUS

cleans-eth me, I know.
know His won-drous grace. Hal-le-lu-jah! 'tis His blood that cleanseth me,
be made free from sin.

'Tis His grace that makes me free, And, my brother, 'tis for thee. Oh, hal-le-lu-jah!

'tis sal-va-tion full and free; And it cleans-eth, yes, it cleans-eth me.

279 Great Is Immanuel

H. L.

HALDOR LILLENAS

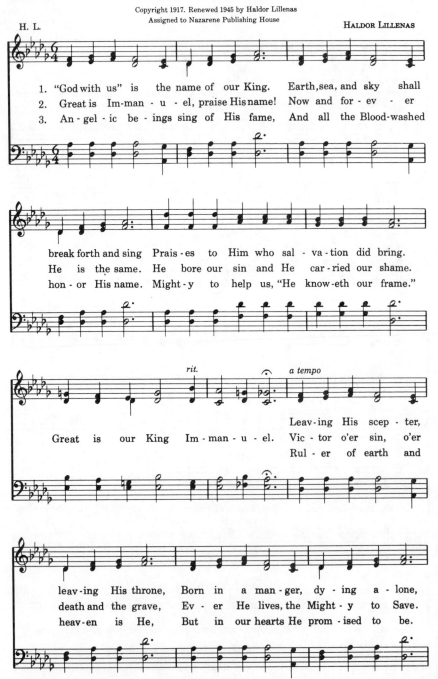

1. "God with us" is the name of our King. Earth, sea, and sky shall
2. Great is Im-man - u - el, praise His name! Now and for - ev - er
3. An - gel - ic be - ings sing of His fame, And all the Blood-washed

break forth and sing Prais - es to Him who sal - va - tion did bring.
He is the same. He bore our sin and He car - ried our shame.
hon - or His name. Might - y to help us, "He know-eth our frame."

rit.   *a tempo*

                                             Leav - ing His scep - ter,

Great is our King Im - man - u - el. Vic - tor o'er sin, o'er
                                        Rul - er of earth and

leav - ing His throne, Born in a man - ger, dy - ing a - lone,
death and the grave, Ev - er He lives, the Might - y to Save.
heav - en is He, But in our hearts He prom - ised to be.

Great Is Immanuel

280 Waiting on the Lord

C. F. W.

C. F. WEIGLE

1. Wait-ing on the Lord for the prom-ise giv-en; Wait-ing on the Lord
2. Wait-ing on the Lord, giv-ing all to Je-sus; Wait-ing on the Lord
3. Wait-ing on the Lord, long-ing to mount high-er; Wait-ing on the Lord,

to   send from heav-en; Wait-ing on the Lord, by our faith re-ceiv-ing;
till from sin He frees us; Wait-ing on the Lord for the heav'n-ly breez-es;
hav-ing great de-sire; Wait-ing on the Lord for the heav'n-ly fire;

CHORUS

Wait-ing in the Up-per Room. The pow - er! the
                              The Pen-te-cos-tal pow'r! the

pow - er! Gives vic-t'ry o-ver sin, and pu-ri-ty with-in. The
Pen-te-cos-tal pow'r

pow - er! the pow - er! The pow'r they had at Pen-te-cost!
Pen-te-cos-tal pow'r! the Pen-te-cos-tal pow'r!

281 The Garden of My Heart

H. L.

HALDOR LILLENAS

1. There's a sa - cred and hal - lowed re - treat, Where my soul finds a
2. There is naught can dis - turb or mo - lest; There my spir - it finds
3. Shut a - way from earth's strife and its din, And pro - tect-ed from
4. There the dove of sweet peace al - ways sings, And my faith ev - er

fel - low-ship sweet, Where the Lord of my life I may meet,
com-fort and rest; And my soul is no long - er dis - tressed
soul-stain-ing sin, For my Sav-iour is dwell-ing with - in,
trust-ing - ly clings; And the chime of sweet hap - pi - ness rings

CHORUS

In the gar-den of my heart. In the cool of the day He walks with me;

In the rose-bordered way He talks with me; In love's ho - ly un - ion,

And sa - cred com-mun-ion, In the gar - den of my heart.

282 The Healing Waters

H. H. Heimar

L. L. Pickett

1. Oh, the joy of sins for-giv'n! Oh, the bliss the Blood-washed know!
2. Now with Je-sus cru-ci-fied, At His feet I'm rest-ing low.
3. Oh, this pre-cious per-fect love! How it keeps the heart a-glow,
4. Oh, to lean on Je-sus' breast, While the tem-pests come and go!
5. Cleansed from ev'ry sin and stain, Whit-er than the driv-en snow,

Oh, the peace a-kin to heav'n, Where the heal-ing wa-ters flow!
Let me ev-er-more a-bide Where the heal-ing wa-ters flow.
Stream-ing from the fount a-bove, Where the heal-ing wa-ters flow!
Here is bless-ed peace and rest, Where the heal-ing wa-ters flow.
Now I sing my sweet re-frain, Where the heal-ing wa-ters flow.

CHORUS

Where the heal-ing wa-ters flow, Where the heal-ing wa-ters flow, Where the joys ce-les-tial glow, Where the joys celestial glow; Oh, there's peace and rest and love, Oh, there's peace and rest and love, Where the heal-ing wa-ters flow, Where the heal-ing wa-ters flow!

283 Walking in the King's Highway

Copyright 1906. Renewed 1933 by Florence Horton
Assigned to Nazarene Publishing House

F. H.

FLORENCE HORTON

1. We shall see the des-ert as the rose,
2. We shall see the glo-ry of the Lord,
3. There the rain shall come up-on the ground, Walk-ing in the
4. There no rav-'nous beast shall make a-fraid,
5. No un-clean thing shall pass o'er here,

There'll be sing-ing where sal-va-tion goes,
And be-hold the beau-ty of His Word,
King's high-way; And the springs of wa-ter will be found,
For the pu-ri-fied the way was made,
But the ran-somed ones with-out a fear,

CHORUS

Walk-ing in the King's high-way. There's a high-way there and a

way, Where sor-row shall flee a-way; And the
and a way, flee a-way;

light shines bright as the day, Walk-ing in the King's high-way.
as the day,

284 Hallelujah, I Am Free!

A. A. J.

A. A. JAMESON

1. I am re-deemed, all glo-ry to the Lamb! Saved from all sin and pu-ri-fied I am; Bought by the Blood that flowed from Cal-va-ry, For the Lord has made me free.

2. I am re-deemed, my ran-som has been paid. All of my guilt on Je-sus has been laid; From all my sins I now have lib-er-ty. Hal-le-lu-jah, I am free!

3. I am re-deemed, my bond-age now is past. I was a slave, but I am free at last. Once I was blind, but now the light I see. Hal-le-lu-jah, I am free!

4. "I am re-deemed," my song shall ev-er be, Both while on earth and for e-ter-ni-ty. Praise be to God for all He is to me. Hal-le-lu-jah, I am free!

CHORUS

Hal-le-lu-jah! I am free! Oh, what glo-rious lib-er-ty, Since the bless-ed Lord has cleansed and made me whole! made me whole! I am redeemed, all glo-ry to His name! He a-bides with-in my soul.

285 Hallelujah! We Shall Rise

J. E. T.

J. E. THOMAS

1. In the res - ur - rec -tion morn-ing, When the trump of God shall sound,
2. In the res - ur - rec -tion morn-ing, What a meet-ing it will be!
3. In the res - ur - rec -tion morn-ing, Blessed tho't it is to me,
4. In the res - ur - rec -tion morn-ing We shall meet Him in the air,

We shall rise, we shall rise! Then the saints will come re-joic-ing
When our fa-thers and our moth-ers
Hal-le-lu-jah! I shall see my bless-ed Sav-iour,
And be car-ried up to glo-ry,

And no tears will e'er be found. We shall rise, we shall rise.
And our loved ones we shall see!
Who so free-ly died for me.
To our home so bright and fair.

Hal-le-lu-jah! in that morn-ing we shall rise.

Fine

CHORUS

Hal-le-lu-jah! A-men! We shall rise!
We shall rise! We shall rise! Hal-le-lu-jah!

D. S.

In the res - ur - rec-tion morn-ing, When death's prison bars are brok-en,

He Brought Me Out

REV. H. J. ZELLEY
CHO. BY H. L. G.

H. L. GILMOUR

1. My heart was dis-tressed 'neath Je-ho-vah's dread frown; And low in the
2. He placed me up-on the strong Rock by His side. My steps were es-
3. He gave me a song; 'twas a new song of praise. By day and by
4. I'll sing of His won-der-ful mer-cy to me; I'll praise Him till

pit where my sins dragged me down I cried to the Lord from the
tab-lished, and here I'll a-bide. No dan-ger of fall-ing while
night its sweet notes I will raise. My heart's o-ver-flow-ing; I'm
all men His good-ness shall see; I'll sing of sal-va-tion at

deep, mir-y clay, Who ten-der-ly brought me out to gold-en day.
here I re-main, But stand by His grace un-til the crown I gain.
hap-py and free. I'll praise my Re-deem-er, who has res-cued me.
home and a-broad, Till man-y shall hear the truth and trust in God.

CHORUS

He brought me out of the mir-y clay; He set my feet on the Rock to stay;

He puts a song in my soul to-day, A song of praise, hal-le-lu-jah!

287 Hark! the Voice of Jesus Calling

DANIEL MARCH

LOUIS VON ESCH

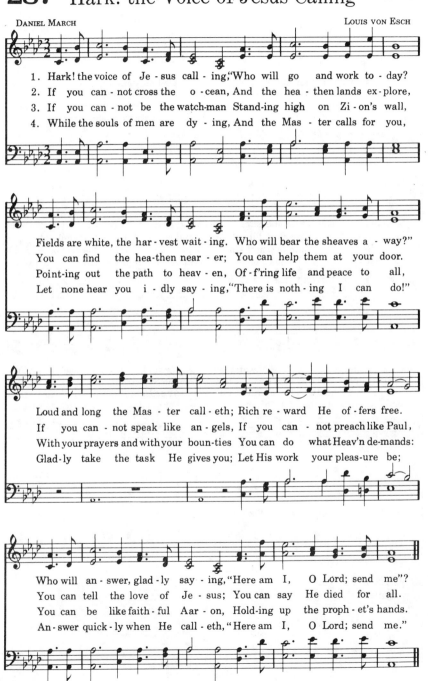

1. Hark! the voice of Je - sus call - ing, "Who will go   and work to - day?
2. If you can - not cross the   o - cean, And the hea - then lands ex - plore,
3. If you can - not be the watch-man Stand-ing high   on Zi - on's wall,
4. While the souls of men are   dy - ing, And the Mas - ter calls for you,

Fields are white, the har - vest wait - ing. Who will bear the sheaves a - way?"
You can find   the hea-then near - er; You can help them at your door.
Point-ing out   the path to heav - en, Of - f'ring life and peace to   all,
Let none hear you i - dly say - ing, "There is noth - ing I can   do!"

Loud and long the Mas - ter call - eth; Rich re - ward He of - fers free.
If   you can - not speak like an - gels, If you can - not preach like Paul,
With your prayers and with your boun-ties You can do   what Heav'n de-mands:
Glad - ly take   the task He gives you; Let His work   your pleas - ure be;

Who will an - swer, glad - ly say - ing, "Here am I,   O Lord; send me"?
You can tell   the love of Je - sus; You can say He died for   all.
You can be   like faith - ful Aar - on, Hold-ing up   the proph - et's hands.
An - swer quick - ly when He call - eth, "Here am I,   O Lord; send me."

288 Our Lord's Return to Earth Again

J. M. K.

J. M. KIRK

1. I am watching for the com-ing of the glad mil-len-nial day, When our
2. Je - sus' com-ing back will be the an-swer to earth's sorr'wing cry, For the
3. Yes, the ran-somed of the Lord shall come to Zi - on then with joy, And in
4. Then the sin and sor-row, pain and death of this dark world shall cease, In a

bless - ed Lord shall come and catch His wait-ing bride a - way. Oh! my heart is
knowledge of the Lord shall fill the earth and sea and sky. God shall take a-
all His ho - ly moun-tain noth-ing hurts or shall de - stroy. Per-fect peace shall
glo - rious reign with Je - sus of a thou-sand years of peace. All the earth is

filled with rapture as I la-bor, watch, and pray, For our Lord is coming back to earth a-
way all sickness and the suff'rer's tears will dry, When our Saviour shall come back to earth a-
reign in ev'ry heart, and love with-out al - loy, After Jesus shall come back to earth a-
groaning, crying for that day of sweet re-lease, For our Jesus to come back to earth a-

CHORUS

gain. Oh! our Lord is com-ing back to earth a - gain. Yes, our
is com-ing back to earth a - gain.

Lord is coming back to earth a - gain. Sa-tan will be bound a
is com-ing back to earth a-gain.

Our Lord's Return to Earth Again

thou-sand years; we'll have no tempter then, After Jesus shall come back to earth a-gain.

289 The Macedonian Cry

Mrs. Cecil F. Alexander

Thomas Hastings

1. Souls in hea-then dark-ness ly - ing, Where no light has bro - ken thro';
2. Christians, hearken! None has taught them Of His love so deep and dear;
3. Haste, oh, haste, and spread the ti - dings Wide to earth's re-mot - est strand.
4. Lo! the hills for har-vest whit - en, All a - long each dis - tant shore.

Souls that Je - sus bought by dy - ing, Whom His soul in trav - ail
Of the pre - cious price that bo't them; Of the nail, the thorn, the
Let no broth - er's bit - ter chid-ings Rise a-gainst us when we
Sea-ward far the is - lands bright - en, Light of na - tions, lead us

knew; Thou-sand voic - es Call us, o'er the wa - ters blue;
spear. Ye who know Him, Guide them from their dark - ness drear.
stand In the judg-ment, From some far, for - got - ten land;
o'er! When we seek them, Let Thy Spir - it go be - fore.

Thou - sand voic - es Call us, o'er the wa - ters blue.
Ye who know Him, Guide them from their dark - ness drear.
In the judg - ment, From some far, for - got - ten land.
When we seek them, Let Thy Spir - it go be - fore.

290 Washed in the Blood

C. P. J.   C. P. Jones

1. Washed in the Blood, by the Spir-it sealed, Christ in His Word is to
2. Once I was blind but, be-hold, I see; God from a-bove now hath
3. Oh, that the world might the Sav-iour see, That bless-ed Sav-iour who
4. Washed in the Blood! Sin-ner, come to-day; Je-sus so free-ly the

me re-vealed. Glo-ry to God! in my soul doth shine
shined in-to me. Cleansed from all sin, in His Word I be-hold
saved poor me! Oh, how the lost ones would come shout-ing home,
debt will pay. Come to His arms, to His arms of grace.

CHORUS

God, my Sal-va-tion, and His life is mine!
Wealth which can nev-er be com-pared to gold. Washed in the
Nev-er, nev-er, nev-er, nev-er-more to roam!
Come, now in meek-ness seek the Sav-iour's face.

Blood, washed in the Blood! Washed in the Blood, in the
Oh, glo-ry!   Hal-le-lu-jah!

1

soul-cleansing Blood! Sealed in the Spir-it true, and washed in the Blood!
Oh, glo-ry!

2

291   He Hideth My Soul

FANNY J. CROSBY   WM. J. KIRKPATRICK

1. A wonderful Saviour is Jesus, my Lord, A wonderful Saviour to me. He hideth my soul in the cleft of the rock, Where rivers of pleasure I see.

2. A wonderful Saviour is Jesus, my Lord. He taketh my burden away. He holdeth me up, and I shall not be moved. He giveth me strength as my day.

3. With numberless blessings each moment He crowns; And, filled with His fullness divine, I sing in my rapture, "Oh, glory to God For such a Redeemer as mine!"

4. When, clothed in His brightness, transported, I rise To meet Him in clouds of the sky, His perfect salvation, His wonderful love, I'll shout with the millions on high.

CHORUS

He hideth my soul in the cleft of the rock That shadows a dry, thirsty land. He hideth my life in the depths of His love, And covers me there with His hand, And covers me there with His hand.

292 The Way of the Cross Leads Home

JESSIE BROWN POUNDS

CHAS. H. GABRIEL

1. I must needs go home by the way of the Cross; There's no oth-er
2. I must needs go on in the Blood-sprinkled way, The path that the
3. Then I bid fare-well to the way of the world, To walk in it

way but this. I shall ne'er get sight of the Gates of Light
Sav-iour trod, If I ev-er climb to the heights sub-lime,
nev-er-more; For my Lord says, "Come," and I seek my home,

CHORUS

If the way of the Cross I miss.
Where the soul is at home with God. The way of the Cross leads
Where He waits at the o-pen door.

home. The way of the Cross leads home. It is

leads home.
leads home.

sweet to know, as I on-ward go, The way of the Cross leads home.

293 It Is Glory Just to Walk with Him

AVIS M. BURGESON

HALDOR LILLENAS

1. It is glo-ry just to walk with Him whose blood has ransomed me; It is
2. It is glo-ry when the shad-ows fall, to know that He is near. Oh, what
3. 'Twill be glo-ry when I walk with Him on heav-en's gold-en shore, Nev-er

rap-ture for my soul each day. It is joy di-vine to feel Him near wher-e'er my
joy to sim-ply trust and pray! It is glo-ry to a-bide in Him when skies a-
from His side a-gain to stray. 'Twill be glo-ry, wondrous glory with the Sav-iour

CHORUS

path may be. Bless the Lord, it's glo-ry all the way! It is glo-ry just to walk with
bove are clear. Yes, with Him, it's glo-ry all the way!
ev-er-more, Ev-er-last-ing glo-ry all the way!

Him. _____ It is glo-ry just to walk with Him. _____ He will guide my steps aright,
walk with Him.   walk with Him.

Thro' the vale and o'er the height. It is glo-ry just to walk with Him. _____
                                                        walk with Him.

294   We Have an Anchor

PRISCILLA J. OWENS

WM. J. KIRKPATRICK

1. Will your an - chor hold in the storms of life, When the
2. It is safe - ly moored, 'twill the storm with - stand, For 'tis
3. When our eyes be - hold through the gath - ering night The

clouds un - fold their wings of strife? When the strong tides lift, and the
well se - cured by the Sav - iour's hand. Though the tem-pest rage and the
cit - y of gold, our har - bor bright, We shall an - chor fast by the

ca - bles strain, Will your an - chor drift, or firm re - main?
wild winds blow, Not an an - gry wave shall our bark o'er - flow.
heav'n - ly shore, With the storms all past for - ev - er - more.

REFRAIN

We have an an-chor that keeps the soul Stead-fast and sure while the bil - lows roll,

Fastened to the Rock which can-not move, Grounded firm and deep in the Saviour's love.

295 It Is Jesus

W. POOLE

HALDOR LILLENAS

1. When the days are bright as some days will be; When the cause of
2. As we trav-el on to the great white throne, There is One who
3. When the shad-ows come, as some-times they will; When the days are
4. When we try so hard and we seem to fail, When our hopes are

right wins the vic-to-ry; When the sun-beams play o-ver
all of the way makes known; And the way He shows, for the
dark and the winds are chill, There is One whose light with a
lost in the storm-y gale, There is One who cares just how

life's glad day, There is One who can cheer us a-long our way.
way He knows, And He tem-pers for us each wind that blows.
glo-ry bright Will a-bove us shine thro' the dark-est night.
each one fares, And the wind and storms with His own He shares.

CHORUS

It is Je-sus, bless-ed Je-sus. He's the One who knows our ev-'ry need.

It is Je-sus, bless-ed Je-sus. He's a Sav-iour in-deed.

296 We Shall See the King Someday

L. E. J.   L. E. JONES

1. Tho' the way we jour-ney may be of-ten drear, We shall see the
2. Af-ter pain and an-guish, af-ter toil and care, We shall see the
3. Af-ter foes are con-quered, af-ter bat-tles won, We shall see the
4. There with all the loved ones who have gone be-fore, We shall see the

King some-day (some-day). On that bless-ed morn-ing clouds will dis-ap-pear.
King some-day (some-day); Thro' the end-less a-ges joy and blessings share.
King some-day (some-day). Af-ter strife is o-ver, af-ter set of sun,
King some-day (some-day). Sor-row past for-ev-er on that peace-ful shore,

CHORUS

We shall see the King some-day. We shall see the King some-day.
some-day.

We will shout and sing some-day. Gath-ered round the throne,
some-day.

When He shall call His own, We shall see the King some-day.

297   We Will Stand the Storm

Isaac Watts

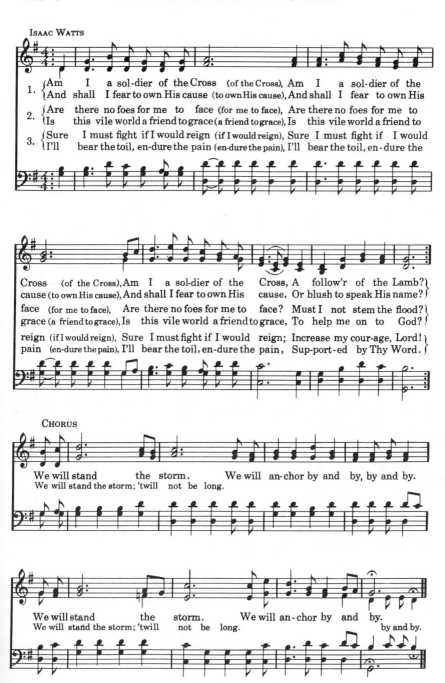

1. {Am I a sol-dier of the Cross (of the Cross), Am I a sol-dier of the
   {And shall I fear to own His cause (to own His cause), And shall I fear to own His

2. {Are there no foes for me to face (for me to face), Are there no foes for me to
   {Is this vile world a friend to grace (a friend to grace), Is this vile world a friend to

3. {Sure I must fight if I would reign (if I would reign), Sure I must fight if I would
   {I'll bear the toil, en-dure the pain (en-dure the pain), I'll bear the toil, en-dure the

Cross (of the Cross), Am I a sol-dier of the   Cross, A follow'r of the Lamb?)
cause (to own His cause), And shall I fear to own His   cause, Or blush to speak His name?/

face (for me to face), Are there no foes for me to   face? Must I not stem the flood?)
grace (a friend to grace), Is this vile world a friend to grace, To help me on to God?/

reign (if I would reign), Sure I must fight if I would   reign; Increase my cour-age, Lord!)
pain (en-dure the pain), I'll bear the toil, en-dure the pain, Sup-port-ed by Thy Word./

Chorus

We will stand   the storm.   We will an-chor by and by, by and by.
We will stand the storm; 'twill not be long.

We will stand   the storm.   We will an-chor by and by.
We will stand the storm; 'twill not be long.   by and by.

298 Living Forever

H. L.

HALDOR LILLENAS

1. Liv - ing for - ev - er, oh, mar - vel - ous thought! Je - sus to
2. Liv - ing for - ev - er where death is un - known, Dwell-ing where
3. Liv - ing for - ev - er where love nev - er dies, In that fair
4. Liv - ing for - ev - er, oh, des - ti - ny bright! In that bright

me im - mor - tal - i - ty brought: Liv - ing for - ev - er, though
sin nev - er reigned on the throne; Liv - ing for - ev - er where
land where are said no "good - bys"; Liv - ing for - ev - er where
E - den where com - eth no night; Liv - ing for - ev - er with

stars may de - cay, Suns cease to shine, and the worlds pass a - way.
sor - row - less days, Days nev - er end - ing are fra - grant with praise.
hope is ful - filled And all the voic - es of sor - row are stilled.
Je - sus will be Heav - en and glo - ry suf - fi - cient for me.

CHORUS

Liv - ing for - ev - er, Dy - ing, no, nev - er,
Liv-ing for - ev - er, yes, liv-ing for - ev - er, Dy-ing, no, nev - er, Dy-ing, no, nev - er,

Life _____ ev - er - last - ing My por - tion shall be. _____
Life nev - er end-ing, a life ev - er-last-ing My por-tion shall be, my por - tion shall be.

Living Forever

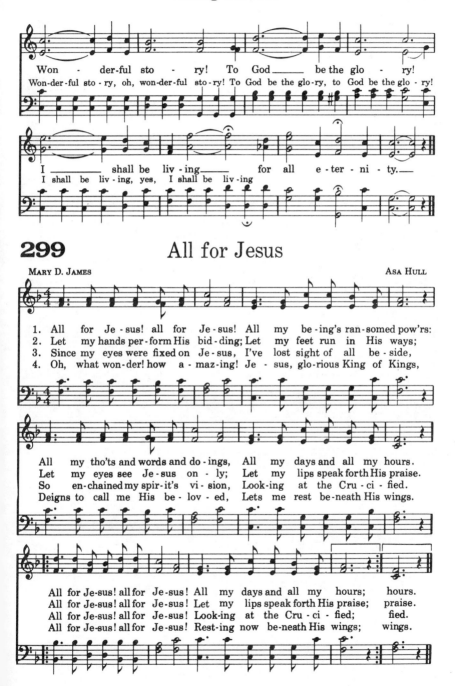

Won - der-ful sto - ry! To God___ be the glo - ry!
Won-der-ful sto - ry, oh, won-der-ful sto-ry! To God be the glo-ry, to God be the glo - ry!

I ___ shall be liv-ing___ for all e - ter - ni - ty. ___
I shall be liv - ing, yes, I shall be liv - ing

299 All for Jesus

MARY D. JAMES   ASA HULL

1. All for Je-sus! all for Je-sus! All my be-ing's ran-somed pow'rs:
2. Let my hands per-form His bid-ding; Let my feet run in His ways;
3. Since my eyes were fixed on Je-sus, I've lost sight of all be-side,
4. Oh, what won-der! how a-maz-ing! Je - sus, glo-rious King of Kings,

All my tho'ts and words and do-ings, All my days and all my hours.
Let my eyes see Je-sus on-ly; Let my lips speak forth His praise.
So en-chained my spir-it's vi-sion, Look-ing at the Cru-ci - fied.
Deigns to call me His be-lov-ed, Lets me rest be-neath His wings.

All for Je-sus! all for Je-sus! All my days and all my hours; hours.
All for Je-sus! all for Je-sus! Let my lips speak forth His praise; praise.
All for Je-sus! all for Je-sus! Look-ing at the Cru-ci - fied; fied.
All for Je-sus! all for Je-sus! Rest-ing now be-neath His wings; wings.

300 He Included Me

REV. J. OATMAN, JR.   HAMP SEWELL

1. I am so hap-py in Christ to-day That I go sing-ing a - long my way;
2. Glad-ly I read, "Who-so-ev - er may Come to the fountain of life to-day";
3. Ev-er God's Spir-it is saying, "Come!" Hear the Bride saying, "No longer roam."
4. "Freely come drink," words the soul to thrill! Oh, with what joy they my heart do fill!

Yes, I'm so hap-py to know and say, "Je-sus in-clud-ed me too."
But when I read it I al-ways say, "Je-sus in-clud-ed me too."
But I am sure while they're calling home, Je-sus in-clud-ed me too.
For when He said, "Who-so - ev - er will," Je-sus in-clud-ed me too.

CHORUS

Je - sus in - clud-ed me. Yes, He in-clud-ed me. When the Lord said,

"Who-so-ev - er," He in -clud-ed me. Je - sus in - clud-ed me. Yes, He in-

clud-ed me. When the Lord said, "Who-so-ev-er," He in-clud - ed me.

301 It Is Mine

ELISHA A. HOFFMAN   WM. EDIE MARKS

1. God's a - bid - ing peace is in my soul to - day. Yes, I feel it
2. He has wrought in me a sweet and per - fect rest. In my raptured
3. He has giv - en me a nev - er - fail - ing joy. Oh, I have it
4. Oh, the love of God is com - fort - ing my soul, For His love is

now; yes, I feel it now. He has tak - en all my doubts and fears a-
heart I can feel it now. He each pass - ing mo - ment keeps me saved and
now! oh, I have it now! To His praise I will my ransomed pow'rs em-
mine; yes, His love is mine! Waves of joy and glad - ness o'er my spir - it

CHORUS

way, Tho' I can - not tell you how.   It is mine,   mine,
blest, Floods with light my heart and brow.   It is mine, this priceless treasure, ev - er
ploy, And re - new my grate - ful vow.
roll, Thrill-ing me with life di - vine.

bless-ed be His name! He has giv - en peace, per - fect peace to me. It is

mine,   mine,   bless-ed be His name! Mine for all e - ter - ni - ty!
mine, this priceless treasure, ev - er

302 He Is Able to Deliver Thee

W. A. O.

W. A. OGDEN

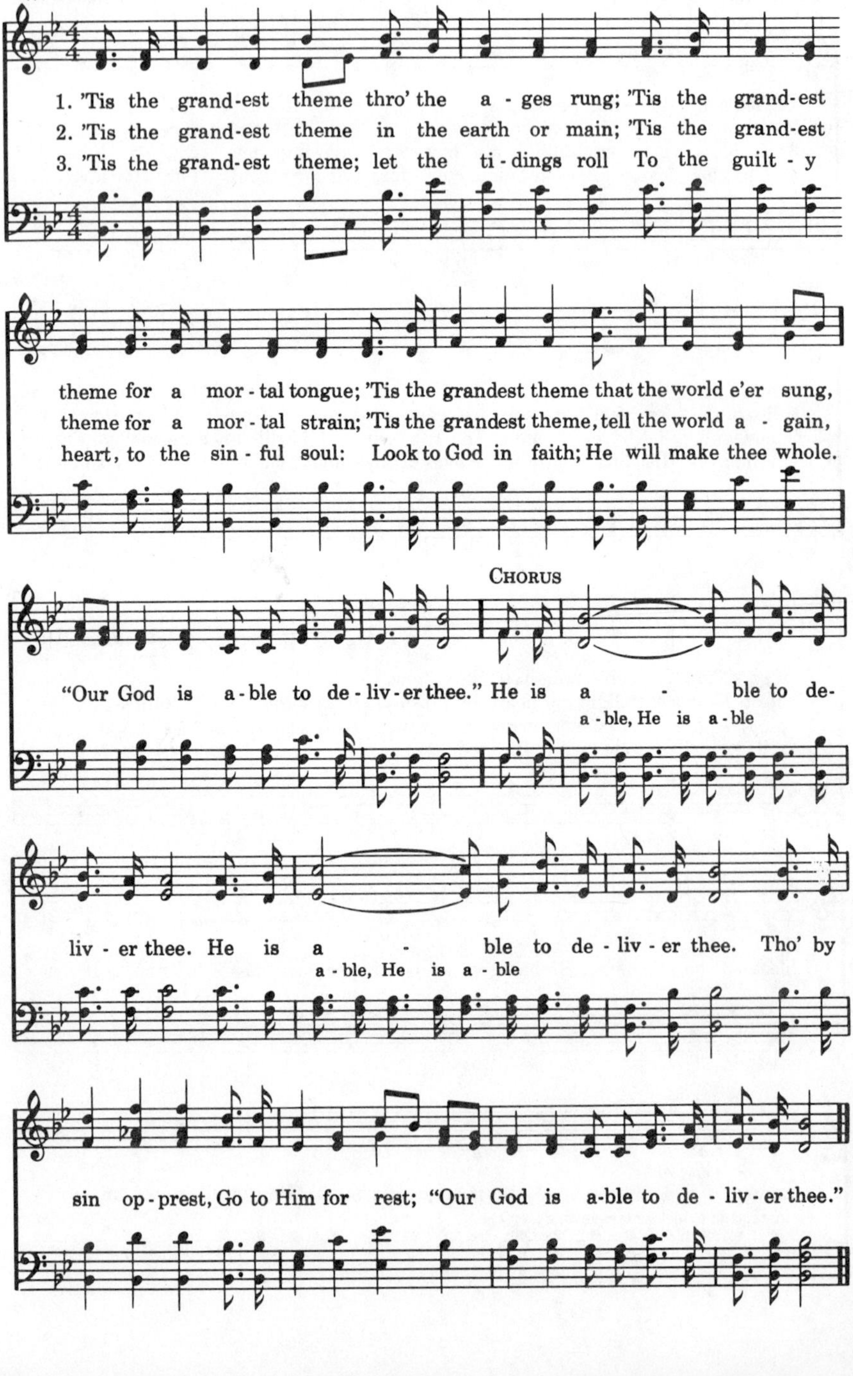

1. 'Tis the grand-est theme thro' the a - ges rung; 'Tis the grand-est
2. 'Tis the grand-est theme in the earth or main; 'Tis the grand-est
3. 'Tis the grand-est theme; let the ti - dings roll To the guilt - y

theme for a mor - tal tongue; 'Tis the grandest theme that the world e'er sung,
theme for a mor - tal strain; 'Tis the grandest theme, tell the world a - gain,
heart, to the sin - ful soul: Look to God in faith; He will make thee whole.

CHORUS

"Our God is a - ble to de - liv - er thee." He is a - ble to de-
a - ble, He is a - ble

liv - er thee. He is a - ble to de - liv - er thee. Tho' by
a - ble, He is a - ble

sin op - prest, Go to Him for rest; "Our God is a - ble to de - liv - er thee."

303 He Is So Precious to Me

C. H. G.

CHAS. H. GABRIEL

1. So pre-cious is Je - sus, my Sav - iour, my King, His praise all the
2. He stood at my heart's door 'mid sun-shine and rain, And pa - tient - ly
3. I stand on the moun-tain of bless - ing at last, No cloud in the
4. I praise Him be-cause He ap - point - ed a place Where, someday thro'

day long with rapture I sing; To Him in my weakness for strength I can cling,
wait-ed an en-trance to gain. What shame that so long He en-treat-ed in vain,
heav-ens a shad-ow to cast; His smile is up - on me, the val-ley is past,
faith in His won-der-ful grace, I know I shall see Him—shall look on His face,

CHORUS *faster*

For He is so pre-cious to me. For He is so pre-cious to

pre-cious to me, pre-cious to me;
me, _____ For He is so pre-cious to me; _____ 'Tis heav-en be-

rit.

low My Re-deem - er to know, For He is so pre-cious to me.

304 We'll Girdle the Globe

V. A. DAKE

IDA M. DAKE

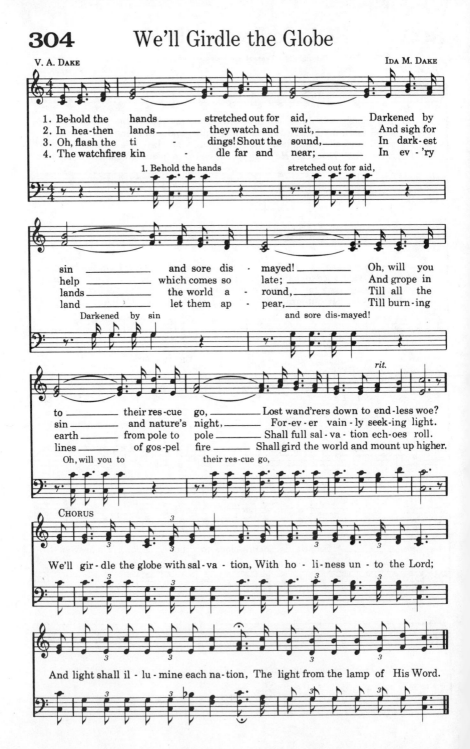

1. Be-hold the hands_____ stretched out for aid,_____ Darkened by
2. In hea-then lands_____ they watch and wait,_____ And sigh for
3. Oh, flash the ti - dings! Shout the sound,_____ In dark-est
4. The watchfires kin - dle far and near;_____ In ev - 'ry

sin_____ and sore dis - mayed!_____ Oh, will you
help_____ which comes so late;_____ And grope in
lands_____ the world a - round,_____ Till all the
land_____ let them ap - pear,_____ Till burn-ing

to_____ their res-cue go,_____ Lost wand'rers down to end-less woe?
sin_____ and nature's night,_____ For-ev-er vain-ly seek-ing light.
earth_____ from pole to pole_____ Shall full sal-va-tion ech-oes roll.
lines_____ of gos-pel fire_____ Shall gird the world and mount up higher.

CHORUS

We'll gir-dle the globe with sal-va-tion, With ho-li-ness un-to the Lord;

And light shall il-lu-mine each na-tion, The light from the lamp of His Word.

305 It Is Truly Wonderful

B. E. W.

B. E. WARREN

1. He par-doned my trans-gres-sions; He sanc-ti-fied my soul;
2. He keeps me ev-'ry mo-ment By trust-ing in His grace.
3. He brings me thro' af-flic-tion; He leaves me not a-lone;
4. He pros-pers and pro-tects me; His bless-ings ev-er flow;
5. There's not a sin-gle bless-ing Which we re-ceive on earth

He hon-ors my con-fes-sions Since by His blood I'm whole.
'Tis thro' His blest a-tone-ment That I may see His face.
He's with me in temp-ta-tion; He keeps me for His own.
He fills me with His glo-ry; He makes me white as snow.
That does not come from heav-en, The source of our new birth.

CHORUS

It is tru-ly won-der-ful What the Lord has done! It is

tru-ly won-der-ful! It is tru-ly won-der-ful! It is

tru-ly won-der-ful What the Lord has done! Glo-ry to His name!

306 Jesus Is All the World to Me

W. L. T.

WILL L. THOMPSON

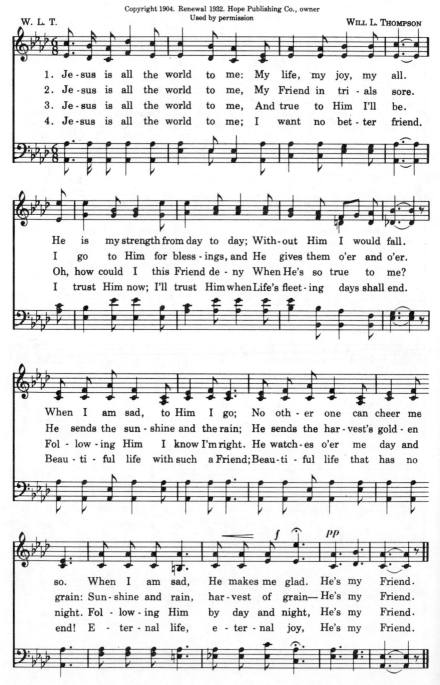

1. Je-sus is all the world to me: My life, my joy, my all.
2. Je-sus is all the world to me, My Friend in tri-als sore.
3. Je-sus is all the world to me, And true to Him I'll be.
4. Je-sus is all the world to me; I want no bet-ter friend.

He is my strength from day to day; With-out Him I would fall.
I go to Him for bless-ings, and He gives them o'er and o'er.
Oh, how could I this Friend de-ny When He's so true to me?
I trust Him now; I'll trust Him when Life's fleet-ing days shall end.

When I am sad, to Him I go; No oth-er one can cheer me
He sends the sun-shine and the rain; He sends the har-vest's gold-en
Fol-low-ing Him I know I'm right. He watch-es o'er me day and
Beau-ti-ful life with such a Friend; Beau-ti-ful life that has no

so. When I am sad, He makes me glad. He's my Friend.
grain: Sun-shine and rain, har-vest of grain— He's my Friend.
night. Fol-low-ing Him by day and night, He's my Friend.
end! E-ter-nal life, e-ter-nal joy, He's my Friend.

307 He Keeps Me Singing

Copyright 1938 by L. B. Bridgers, Renewal
The Broadman Press, owner

L. B. B.   L. B. BRIDGERS

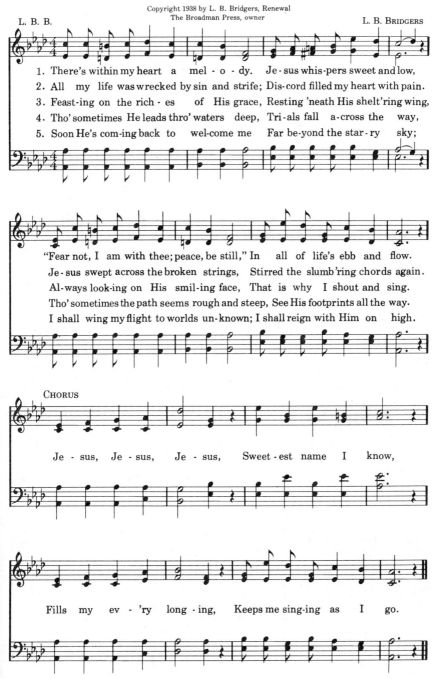

1. There's within my heart a mel - o - dy. Je - sus whis-pers sweet and low,
2. All my life was wrecked by sin and strife; Dis-cord filled my heart with pain.
3. Feast-ing on the rich - es of His grace, Resting 'neath His shelt'ring wing,
4. Tho' sometimes He leads thro' waters deep, Tri - als fall a-cross the way,
5. Soon He's com-ing back to wel-come me Far be-yond the star - ry sky;

"Fear not, I am with thee; peace, be still," In all of life's ebb and flow.
Je - sus swept across the broken strings, Stirred the slumb'ring chords again.
Al - ways look-ing on His smil-ing face, That is why I shout and sing.
Tho' sometimes the path seems rough and steep, See His footprints all the way.
I shall wing my flight to worlds un-known; I shall reign with Him on high.

CHORUS

Je - sus, Je - sus, Je - sus, Sweet - est name I know,

Fills my ev - 'ry long - ing, Keeps me sing-ing as I go.

308 We're Marching to Zion

Isaac Watts

Robert Lowry

1. Come, we that love the Lord, And let our joys be known. Join
2. Let those re - fuse to sing Who nev - er knew our God; But
3. The hill of Zi - on yields A thou - sand sa - cred sweets Be -
4. Then let our songs a - bound, And ev - 'ry tear be dry. We're

in a song with sweet ac - cord, Join in a song with sweet ac - cord, And
chil - dren of the heav'n - ly King, But chil - dren of the heav'n - ly King, May
fore we reach the heav'n - ly fields, Be - fore we reach the heav'n - ly fields, Or
marching thro' Immanuel's ground, We're marching thro' Immanuel's ground, To

thus sur - round the throne, And thus sur - round the throne.
speak their joys a - broad, May speak their joys a - broad.
walk the gold - en streets, Or walk the gold - en streets.
fair - er worlds on high, To fair - er worlds on high.

thus sur - round the throne, And thus sur - round the throne.

CHORUS

We're march - ing to Zi - on, Beau - ti - ful, beau - ti - ful Zi - on. We're
We're march - ing on to Zi - on,

march - ing up - ward to Zi - on, The beau - ti - ful cit - y of God.
Zi - on, Zi - on,

309 Jesus Is Mighty to Save

Copyright 1899. Renewed 1927 by Lelia N. Morris
Assigned to Nazarene Publishing House

Mrs. C. H. M.   Mrs. C. H. Morris

1. When the tempests rage and the storms beat high, There is ref-uge near and a
2. Not a cloud so dark but His love shines thro', Not a shade so deep but His
3. Not a tear-drop falls but the Saviour knows, And His great heart throbs with our
4. Nev-er yet in vain has a sin-ner cried; Nev-er yet in vain was the

shel-ter nigh. He who calmed the winds and the rolling wave Is Je - ho - vah
face we view; For His arm is strong and His heart is kind. All who in Him
bit - ter woes; For He knows our flesh and our fee-ble frame. Ev'ry pang we
Blood ap-plied. Who-so-ev - er will may in Him be blest; Who-so - ev - er

Chorus

still and is strong to save.
trust shall a Sav - iour find.
feel, He has known the same. Mighty to save and strong to de-liv-er,
will, find a per-fect rest.
                                                              Je-sus

Je-sus is might-y to save.   Might - y to save and
is might - y, yes, might - y to save. He is

strong to de - liv - er,   Je-sus is might-y to save.
                 Je - sus is might - y, yes, might-y to save.

310 When the Tithes Are Gathered In

MRS. C. H. M.

MRS. C. H. MORRIS

1. There'll be show'rs of blessing from our Fa-ther's hand; On His word of prom-ise we may firm-ly stand. There'll be rains re-fresh-ing on the thirst-y land.
2. There'll be shouts of triumph from the con-q'ring host; There'll be perfect freedom in the Ho-ly Ghost, Ev-'ry one em-pow-ered as at Pen-te-cost,
3. Then will come the dawn-ing of the reign of peace, When the wars and conflicts shall for-ev-er cease, And for strug-gling saints shall come a sweet re-lease,
4. We will rob no long-er, then, our Lord and King. What to Him be-longeth we will glad-ly bring. And we'll shout Ho-san-na, while the glad harps ring,

CHORUS

When the tithes are gath-ered in. When the tithes are gath-ered in. Tithes of love and will-ing ser-vice, Tithes of sil-ver and of gold, When the tithes are gathered in, When the tithes gath-ered in, When the tithes are gathered in; When the tithes gath-ered in, There'll be bless-ings

When the Tithes Are Gathered In

more than we can con-tain, When the tithes_____ are gath-ered in.

When the tithes are gath-ered in.

311

Dare to Be a Daniel

P. P. B.

P. P. BLISS

1. Stand-ing by a pur-pose true, Heed - ing God's com-mand,
2. Man - y might - y men are lost, Dar - ing not to stand,
3. Man - y gi - ants, great and tall, Stalk - ing thro' the land,
4. Hold the gos - pel ban-ner high! On to vic - t'ry grand!

Hon - or them, the faith - ful few! All hail to Dan - iel's Band!
Who for God had been a host By join - ing Dan - iel's Band!
Head-long to the earth would fall If met by Dan - iel's Band!
Sa - tan and his host de - fy, And shout for Dan - iel's Band!

CHORUS

Dare to be a Dan - iel! Dare to stand a - lone!

Dare to have a pur-pose firm! Dare to make it known!

312 He Shall Reign

Copyright 1925 by Haldor Lillenas
Assigned to Nazarene Publishing House International copyright secured

H. L.   HALDOR LILLENAS

1. Thrones may fall and crum-ble, Kingdoms may rise and fall; But the throne of Im-
2. He who bore our sor-row, Sorrows that weighed Him down; He who suffered up-

man-u-el Shall flour-ish a-bove them all. Hal-le-lu-jah! He is King for-
on a cross Now wears an e-ter-nal crown. He who was re-

ev-er O'er His vast do-main. Tho' the stars may fall, Far a-bove them all
ject-ed, And for sin-ners slain, Ev-er lives to save, Victor o'er the grave.

CHORUS

King Im-man-u-el shall reign. He shall reign, He shall
He shall reign, He shall reign, He shall reign, Oh,

reign, King of Kings and Lord of Lords, King of Kings and Lord of Lords.
He shall reign,

He Shall Reign

He shall reign for - ev - er-more; His reign shall ex-tend from shore to shore.

Hal - le - lu - jah! Hal - le - lu - jah! Hal - le - lu - jah!
Praise Him! Praise Him! Hal - le - lu - jah!

Hal - le - lu - jah, He shall reign! Hal - le - lu - jah, He shall reign! Hal - le-
shall reign! shall reign!

lu - jah, He shall reign for - ev - er and ev - er - more, For-ev-er-

more, _____ For-ev-er - more, _____ For-ev-er-more, for-ev - er - more!
For-ev - er-more, For-ev - er-more.

313　Trust and Obey

J. H. SAMMIS

D. B. TOWNER

1. When we walk with the Lord In the light of His Word, What a glo-ry He
2. Not a shad-ow can rise, Not a cloud in the skies, But His smile quickly
3. Not a bur-den we bear, Not a sor-row we share, But our toil He doth
4. But we nev-er can prove The de-lights of His love Un-til all on the
5. Then in fel-low-ship sweet We will sit at His feet, Or we'll walk by His

sheds on our way! While we do His good will, He a-bides with us still,
drives it a-way. Not a doubt nor a fear, Not a sigh nor a tear,
rich-ly re-pay. Not a grief nor a loss, Not a frown nor a cross,
al-tar we lay; For the fa-vor He shows, And the joy He be-stows,
side in the way. What He says we will do; Where He sends we will go;

CHORUS

And with all who will trust and o-bey.
Can a-bide while we trust and o-bey.
But is blest if we trust and o-bey.　Trust and o-bey, for there's
Are for them who will trust and o-bey.
Nev-er fear, on-ly trust and o-bey.

no oth-er way To be hap-py in Je-sus But to trust and o-bey.

314 He That Winneth Souls

E. E. Hewitt

J. M. Harris

1. Bless-ed is the ser-vice of our Lord and King; Pre-cious are the
2. In the qui-et home life, showing love's bright ray, More and more like
3. Out up-on the high-way, go-ing forth with prayer, For the lost and
4. Sow be-side all wa-ters; sow the gos-pel seed— Here a word in

jew-els we may help to bring. Down the pass-ing a-ges words of
Je-sus liv-ing ev-'ry day, We may guide a dear one to the
stray-ing seek-ing ev-'ry-where, Close be-side the Shep-herd, we His
sea-son, there a lov-ing deed. Sin-ners to the Sav-iour be it

rit.

CHORUS

coun-sel ring:
heav'n-ward way. He that win-neth souls is wise.
joy may share. He that win-neth,
ours to lead.

wise. ———— In the home be-yond the skies ————
win-neth souls is wise. In the home be-yond, be-yond the skies

rit.

There's a crown of glo-ry. Oh, the won-drous prize! He that winneth souls is wise.

315 Launch Out

A. B. Simpson
R. Kelso Carter

1. The mercy of God is an ocean divine, A
bound-less and fath-om-less flood. Launch out in the deep, cut a-
way the shore line, And be lost in the full-ness of God.

2. But many, a-las! only stand on the shore, And
gaze on the ocean so wide. They nev-er have ven-tured its
depths to ex-plore, Or to launch on the fath-om-less tide.

3. And oth-ers just ven-ture a-way from the land, And
lin-ger so near to the shore That the surf and the slime that beat
o-ver the strand Dash o'er them in floods ev-er-more.

4. Oh, let us launch out on this ocean so broad, Where
floods of sal-va-tion o'er-flow. Oh, let us be lost in the
mer-cy of God, Till the depths of His full-ness we know.

CHORUS

Launch out_____ in-to the deep. Oh, let the shore line go.
Oh, launch out   in the deep.

Launch out, launch out in the o-cean di-vine, Out where the full tides flow.

316 He Took My Sins Away

MRS. M. J. H.

MRS. M. J. HARRIS

1. I came to Je - sus, wea - ry, worn, and sad. He took my sins a - way,
2. The load of sin was more than I could bear. He took them all a - way,
3. No con - dem - na - tion have I in my heart. He took my sins a - way,
4. If you will come to Je - sus Christ to-day, He'll take your sins a - way,

He took my sins a - way. And now His love has made my heart so glad.
He took them all a - way. And now on Him I roll my ev - 'ry care.
He took my sins a - way. His per - fect peace He did to me im - part.
He'll take your sins a - way, And keep you hap - py in His love each day.

CHORUS

He took my sins a - way.
He took my sins a - way.
He took my sins a - way.
He'll take your sins a - way.

He took my sins a - way,

He took my sins a - way, And keeps me sing-ing ev - 'ry day!

I'm so glad He took my sins a - way. He took my sins a - way.

317 We've a Story to Tell to the Nations

COLIN STERNE

H. ERNEST NICHOL

1. We've a sto-ry to tell to the nations That shall turn their hearts
2. We've a song to be sung to the nations That shall lift their hearts
3. We've a mes-sage to give to the nations, That the Lord who reign-
4. We've a Sav-iour to show to the nations Who the path of sor-

to the right, A sto-ry of truth and mer - cy, A
to the Lord, A song that shall con - quer e - vil And
eth a-bove Hath sent us His Son to save us, And
row hath trod, That all of the world's great peo - ples Might

their hearts to the right,

sto-ry of peace and light, A sto-ry of peace and light.
shat-ter the spear and sword, And shat-ter the spear and sword.
show us that God is love, And show us that God is love.
come to the truth of God, Might come to the truth of God.

A sto - ry of peace and light.

CHORUS

For the darkness shall turn to dawn-ing, And the dawn-ing to noon-day bright,

rall.

And Christ's great kingdom shall come to earth, The King-dom of love and light.

318 He's a Wonderful Saviour to Me

VIRGIL P. BROCK

BLANCHE KERR BROCK

1. I was lost in sin but Je-sus res-cued me;
2. He's a Friend so true, so pa-tient, and so kind;
3. He is al-ways near to com-fort and to cheer;
4. Dear-er grows the love of Je-sus day by day;

He's a won-der-ful Sav-iour to me.

So won-der-ful!

I was bound by fear but Je-sus set me free;
Ev-'ry-thing I need in Him I al-ways find;
He for-gives my sins, He dries my ev-'ry tear;
Sweet-er is His grace while pressing on my way;

CHORUS

He's a won-der-ful Sav-iour to me._____ For He's a won-der-ful

So won-der-ful!

Sav-iour to me, He's a won-der-ful Sav-iour to me; I was

won-der-ful!

won-der-ful!

lost in sin, but Je-sus took me in; He's a won-der-ful Sav-iour to me.

319 When I See the Blood

320 He's Coming Again

ARR.

1. How sweet are the ti - dings that greet the pil-grim's ear, As he
2. The mos - sy old graves where the pil - grims sleep Shall be
3. There we'll meet all our loved ones in E - den, our home. Sweet
4. Hal - le - lu - jah! A - men, Hal - le - lu - jah! a - gain. In a

wan - ders in ex - ile from home! Soon, soon will the Sav - iour in
o - pened as wide as be - fore; And the mil - lions that sleep in the
songs of re - demp-tion we'll sing. From the north, from the south, all the
lit - tle while we shall be there. Oh, be faith - ful, be hope - ful, be

Chorus

glo - ry ap - pear, And soon will His king-dom come.
might - y deep Shall live on this earth once more.
ran-somed shall come, And wor - ship our Heav'n-ly King.
joy - ful till then, And a crown of bright glo - ry wear.

He's com - ing,

com - ing, com-ing soon I know, Com-ing back to this earth to reign;

And the wea - ry pil-grim will to glo - ry go When Je - sus comes a - gain.

321 Love Lifted Me

JAMES ROWE

HOWARD E. SMITH

1. I was sink-ing deep in sin, Far from the peaceful shore, Ver - y deep-ly
2. All my heart to Him I give; Ev - er to Him I'll cling, In His bless-ed
3. Souls in dan-ger, look a-bove; Je-sus com-plete-ly saves. He will lift you

stained with-in, Sink-ing to rise no more. But the Mas-ter of the sea
pres - ence live, Ev - er His prais-es sing. Love so might-y and so true
by His love Out of the an - gry waves. He's the Mas-ter of the sea;

Heard my de-spairing cry, From the wa - ters lift - ed me; Now safe am I.
Mer-its my soul's best songs; Faith-ful, lov - ing ser - vice, too, To Him be - longs.
Bil - lows His will o - bey. He your Sav-iour wants to be — Be saved to - day.

CHORUS

Love lift - ed me! Love lift - ed me! When noth - ing
e - ven me! e - ven me!

1
else could help, Love lift - ed me.

2
Love lift - ed me.

322 Heavenly Sunlight

REV. H. J. ZELLEY

G. H. COOK

1. Walk-ing in sun-light, all of my jour-ney, O - ver the moun-tains,
2. Shad-ows a - round me, shad-ows a - bove me, Nev-er con - ceal my
3. In the bright sun-light, ev - er re - joic - ing, Press-ing my way to

thro' the deep vale! Je -sus has said, "I'll nev - er for - sake thee." Promise di-
Sav-iour and Guide. He is the Light; in Him is no dark-ness. Ev- er I'm
man-sions a - bove; Sing-ing His prais-es, glad -ly I'm walk-ing. Walk-ing in

CHORUS

vine that nev - er can fail! Heav-en - ly sun-light, heav - en - ly
walk-ing close to His side.
sun - light, sun-light of love.

sun-light, Flooding my soul with glo - ry di - vine! Hal - le - lu - jah!

I am re - joic - ing, Sing-ing His prais - es. Je - sus is mine.

323 Hidden Peace

Copyright 1899. Renewed 1927 by L. O. Brown
Assigned to Nazarene Publishing House

John S. Brown

L. O. Brown

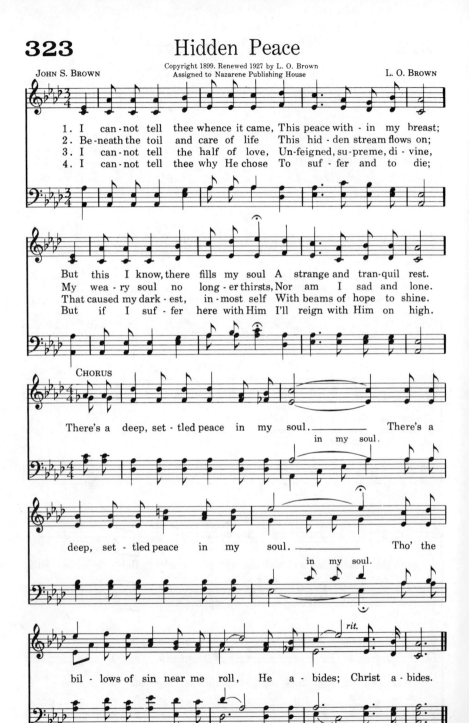

1. I can-not tell thee whence it came, This peace with-in my breast;
2. Be-neath the toil and care of life This hid-den stream flows on;
3. I can-not tell the half of love, Un-feigned, su-preme, di-vine,
4. I can-not tell thee why He chose To suf-fer and to die;

But this I know, there fills my soul A strange and tran-quil rest.
My wea-ry soul no long-er thirsts, Nor am I sad and lone.
That caused my dark-est, in-most self With beams of hope to shine.
But if I suf-fer here with Him I'll reign with Him on high.

CHORUS

There's a deep, set-tled peace in my soul. _____ There's a
in my soul.

deep, set-tled peace in my soul. _____ Tho' the
in my soul.

bil-lows of sin near me roll, He a-bides; Christ a-bides.

rit.

324 When We All Get to Heaven

E. E. HEWITT

MRS. J. G. WILSON

1. Sing the won-drous love of Je-sus; Sing His mer-cy and His grace.
2. While we walk the pil-grim path-way, Clouds will o-ver-spread the sky;
3. Let us then be true and faith-ful, Trust-ing, serv-ing ev-'ry day.
4. On-ward to the prize be-fore us! Soon His beau-ty we'll be-hold;

In the man-sions, bright and bless-ed, He'll pre-pare for us a place.
But when trav'ling days are o-ver, Not a shad-ow, not a sigh!
Just one glimpse of Him in glo-ry Will the toils of life re-pay.
Soon the pearl-y gates will o-pen, We shall tread the streets of gold.

for us a place.

CHORUS

When we all get to heav-en, What a day of re-
When we all   What a

joic-ing that will be! When we all see
day of re-joic-ing that will be! When we all

Je-sus, We'll sing and shout the vic-to-ry.
and shout the vic-to-ry.

325 Holiness Forevermore

H. L.   HALDOR LILLENAS

1. There's a bless-ed and tri-um-phant song: Ho-li-ness for-ev-er-more.
2. We will praise the Lord for vic-to-ry, Ho-li-ness for-ev-er-more;
3. From this stand-ard we will not de-part, Ho-li-ness for-ev-er-more;
4. We will shout our glo-rious lib-er-ty, Ho-li-ness for-ev-er-more;

It is sung by the might-y, Bloodwashed throng:
From the car-nal mind we now are free,
'Tis the song of the pu-ri-fied in heart,
We shall sing it by the crys-tal sea,
Ho-li-ness for-ev-er-more.

CHORUS mf

Ho-li-ness for-ev-er-more! _____ Ho-li-ness for-
Sing the hap-py song!

ev-er-more! _____ We will sing it! shout it!
As we march a-long, and and

Preach it and live it, Ho-li-ness for-ev-er-more!

326 Where He Leads I'll Follow

W. A. O.

W. A. OGDEN

1. Sweet are the prom-is-es; Kind is the Word, Dear-er far than
2. Sweet is the ten-der love Je - sus hath shown, Sweet-er far than
3. List to His lov-ing words, "Come un-to Me!" Wea-ry, heav-y-

an - y mes-sage man ev - er heard. Pure was the mind of Christ,
an - y love that mor - tals have known. Kind to the err-ing one,
la - den, there is sweet rest for thee. Trust in His prom-is - es,

Sin - less, I see. He the great Ex - am - ple is, and Pat - tern for me.
Faith-ful is He. He the great Ex - am - ple is, and Pat - tern for me.
Faith-ful and sure; Lean up - on the Sav-iour, and thy soul is se - cure.

CHORUS

Where _____ He leads I'll fol - low,
Where He leads I'll fol - low,   Where He leads I'll fol - low,

Fol - low all the way.   Fol-low Je-sus ev - 'ry day.
Fol-low all the way, yes,   fol-low all the way.

327 It's Real

H. L. C.   H. L. Cox

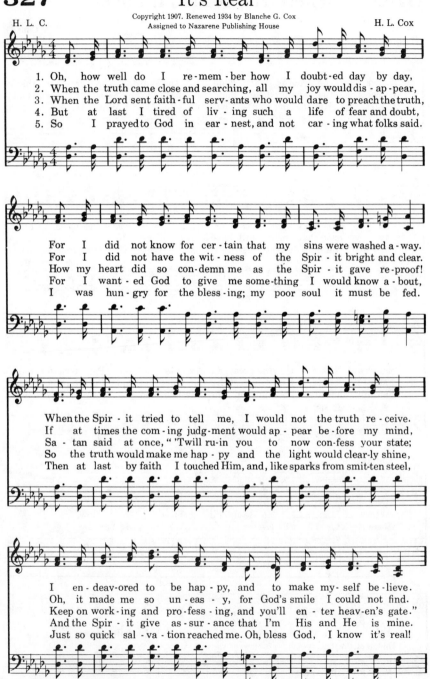

1. Oh, how well do I re-mem-ber how I doubt-ed day by day,
2. When the truth came close and searching, all my joy would dis-ap-pear,
3. When the Lord sent faith-ful serv-ants who would dare to preach the truth,
4. But at last I tired of liv-ing such a life of fear and doubt,
5. So I prayed to God in ear-nest, and not car-ing what folks said.

For I did not know for cer-tain that my sins were washed a-way.
For I did not have the wit-ness of the Spir-it bright and clear.
How my heart did so con-demn me as the Spir-it gave re-proof!
For I want-ed God to give me some-thing I would know a-bout,
I was hun-gry for the bless-ing; my poor soul it must be fed.

When the Spir-it tried to tell me, I would not the truth re-ceive.
If at times the com-ing judg-ment would ap-pear be-fore my mind,
Sa-tan said at once, "'Twill ru-in you to now con-fess your state;
So the truth would make me hap-py and the light would clear-ly shine,
Then at last by faith I touched Him, and, like sparks from smit-ten steel,

I en-deav-ored to be hap-py, and to make my-self be-lieve.
Oh, it made me so un-eas-y, for God's smile I could not find.
Keep on work-ing and pro-fess-ing, and you'll en-ter heav-en's gate."
And the Spir-it give as-sur-ance that I'm His and He is mine.
Just so quick sal-va-tion reached me. Oh, bless God, I know it's real!

It's Real

But it's real, it's real. Oh, I know it's real.
It's real, I know

Praise God, the doubts are set - tled, For I know, I know it's real!

328 Break Thou the Bread of Life

MARY A. LATHBURY   WILLIAM F. SHERWIN

1. Break Thou the bread of life, Dear Lord, to me, As Thou didst
2. Bless Thou the truth, dear Lord, To me, to me, As Thou didst
3. Teach me to live, dear Lord, On - ly for Thee, As Thy dis-

break the loaves Be - side the sea. Be - yond the sa - cred page
bless the bread By Gal - i - lee. Then shall all bond - age cease,
ci - ples lived In Gal - i - lee. Then, all my strug - gles o'er,

I seek Thee, Lord; My spir - it pants for Thee, O liv - ing Word!
All fet - ters fall, And I shall find my peace, My All in All
Then, vic - t'ry won, I shall be - hold Thee, Lord, The Liv - ing One.

329 Jesus Saves

PRISCILLA J. OWENS

WM. J. KIRKPATRICK

1. We have heard the joy - ful sound:
2. Waft it on the roll - ing tide:
3. Sing a - bove the bat - tle strife:
4. Give the winds a might - y voice.

Je - sus saves! Je - sus saves!

Spread the ti - dings all a - round:
Tell to sin - ners far and wide:
By His death and end - less life,
Let the na - tions now re - joice.

Je - sus saves! Je - sus saves!

Bear the news to ev - 'ry land; Climb the steeps and cross the waves.
Sing, ye is - lands of the sea; Ech - o back, ye o - cean caves.
Sing it soft - ly through the gloom, When the heart for mer - cy craves;
Shout sal - va - tion full and free, High - est hills and deep - est caves.

On - ward!—'tis our Lord's com - mand.
Earth shall keep her ju - bi - lee.
Sing in tri - umph o'er the tomb:
This our song of vic - to - ry:

Je - sus saves! Je - sus saves!

330 Whosoever Meaneth Me

J. E. M.

J. Edwin McConnell

1. I am hap-py to-day and the sun shines bright; The clouds have been rolled a-way; For the Sav-iour said Who-so-ev-er will May come with Him to stay (to stay).

2. All my hopes have been raised, Oh, His name be praised! His glo-ry has filled my soul. I've been lift-ed up, and from sin set free. His blood has made me whole (me whole).

3. Oh, what won-der-ful love! Oh, what grace di-vine, That Je-sus should die for me! I was lost in sin; for the world I pined. But now I am set free (set free).

Chorus

Who-so-ev-er sure-ly mean-eth me, Sure-ly mean-eth me, Oh, sure-ly mean-eth me! Who-so-ev-er sure-ly mean-eth me. Who-so-ev-er mean-eth me. mean-eth me.

331 "Whosoever Will"

P. P. B.

P. P. BLISS

1. "Who-so-ev-er hear-eth," shout, shout the sound! Spread the bless-ed ti-dings all the world a-round. Tell the joy-ful news wher-ev-er man is found,

2. Who-so-ev-er com-eth need not de-lay. Now the door is o-pen; en-ter while you may. Je-sus is the true, the on-ly Liv-ing Way.

3. "Who-so-ev-er will!" the prom-ise is se-cure; "Who-so-ev-er will" for-ev-er shall en-dure; "Who-so-ev-er will!" 'tis life for-ev-er-more.

CHORUS

"Who-so-ev-er will" may come. "Who-so-ev-er will, who-so-ev-er will!" Send the proc-la-ma-tion o-ver vale and hill. 'Tis a lov-ing Fa-ther calls the wan-d'rer home: "Who-so-ev-er will" may come.

332 Joy Unspeakable

B. E. W.

B. E. WARREN

1. I have found His grace in all com-plete; He sup-pli-eth ev-'ry need.
2. I have found the pleas-ure I once craved; It is joy and peace with-in.
3. I have found that hope so bright and clear, Liv-ing in the realm of grace.
4. I have found the joy no tongue can tell. How its waves of glo-ry roll!

While I sit and learn at Je-sus' feet, I am free, yes, free in-deed.
What a won-drous bless-ing! I am saved From the aw-ful gulf of sin.
Oh, the Sav-iour's pres-ence is so near, I can see His smil-ing face.
It is like a great o'er-flow-ing well, Springing up with-in my soul.

CHORUS

It is joy un-speak-a-ble and full of glo-ry, Full of glo-ry, full of glo-ry. It is joy un-speak-a-ble and full of glo-ry. Oh, the half has nev-er yet been told!

333 Wonderful Grace of Jesus

H. L.

HALDOR LILLENAS

1. Won-der-ful grace of Je - sus, Great - er than all my sin!
2. Won-der-ful grace of Je - sus, Reach-ing to all the lost!
3. Won-der-ful grace of Je - sus, Reach-ing the most de - filed,

How shall my tongue de-scribe it? Where shall its praise be - gin?
By it I have been par-doned, Saved to the ut - ter - most.
By its trans-form-ing pow - er Mak-ing him God's dear child,

Tak - ing a-way my bur-den, Set-ting my spir - it free;
Chains have been torn a - sun-der, Giv-ing me lib - er - ty;
Pur-chas-ing peace and heav-en, For all e - ter - ni - ty;

For the won - der - ful grace of Je - sus reach-es me.
For the won - der - ful grace of Je - sus reach-es me.
And the won - der - ful grace of Je - sus reach-es me.

CHORUS

the match-less grace of Je - sus,
Won - der - ful the match-less grace of Je - sus,

Wonderful Grace of Jesus

Deep-er than the might-y, roll-ing sea; the roll-ing sea!

Won - - - der-ful grace, all suf-fi-

High-er than the moun-tain, spar-kling like a foun - tain, All suf-fi-cient

cient for me, for e-ven me! Broad-er than the scope of my trans-

grace for e-ven me!

gres - sions, Great-er far than all my sin and shame!

gres-sions, sing it! my sin and shame!

Oh, mag-ni-fy the pre-cious name of Je-sus! Praise His name!

334 Wonderful Peace

W. D. CORNELL ALT.

W. G. COOPER

1. Far a-way in the depths of my spir-it to-night Rolls a
2. What a treas-ure I have in this won-der-ful peace, Bur-ied
3. I am rest-ing to-night in this won-der-ful peace, Rest-ing
4. And me-thinks when I rise to that cit-y of peace, Where the
5. Ah! soul, are you here with-out com-fort or rest, March-ing

mel - o-dy sweet-er than psalm; In ce-les-tial-like strains it un-
deep in the heart of my soul, So se-cure that no pow-er can
sweet-ly in Je-sus' con - trol; For I'm kept from all dan-ger by
Au - thor of peace I shall see, That one strain of the song which the
down the rough pathway of time? Make Je - sus your Friend ere the

ceas-ing - ly falls O'er my soul like an in - fi - nite calm.
mine it a - way While the years of e - ter - ni - ty roll.
night and by day, And His glo - ry is flood-ing my soul.
ran-somed will sing In that heav - en - ly king-dom shall be:
shad-ows grow dark. Oh, ac - cept this sweet peace so sub - lime.

CHORUS

Peace! peace! won-der-ful peace, Coming down from the Fa-ther a - bove! Sweep

o - ver my spir - it for - ev-er, I pray, In fath-om-less bil-lows of love.

335 Reach Your Arms Around the World

VIDA MUNDEN NIXON

HALDOR LILLENAS

1. Reach your arms a-round the world for Je-sus And win it in His name.
2. Spread a-broad the sto-ry of sal - va-tion, The whole wide world around;
3. Reach your arms, ex-tend a hand of heal-ing To dy-ing souls a - far;

Tell to all how His re-demp-tion frees us; The gos-pel news pro-claim.
To each kin-dred, ev-'ry tribe and na-tion, Wher-ev-er sin is found.
Send your light, the love of God re - veal-ing, To be their guid-ing star.

CHORUS

Reach your arms a-round the world, All a-round the world, With a

strong and firm em-brace. Ev-'ry na-tion, ev-'ry kin, For the

Sav-iour strive to win Through God's re-deem-ing grace.

336   Wonderful Story of Love

J. M. D.

REV. J. M. DRIVER

1. Won-der-ful sto-ry of love! Tell it to me a-gain. Won-der-ful story of love! Wake the im-mor-tal strain! An-gels with rapture announce it; Shepherds with wonder re-ceive it; Sin-ner, oh, won't you be-lieve it?

2. Won-der-ful sto-ry of love! Tho' you are far a-way— Won-der-ful story of love! Still He doth call to-day: Calling from Calvary's moun-tain, Down from the crys-tal-bright foun-tain, E'en from the dawn of cre-a-tion,

3. Won-der-ful sto-ry of love! Je-sus pro-vides a rest— Won-der-ful story of love! For all the pure and blest: Rest in those mansions a-bove us, With those who've gone on be-fore us, Sing-ing the rap-tur-ous cho-rus,

CHORUS

Won-der-ful sto-ry of love! Won - der - ful! Won - der - ful! Won - der - ful! Won-der-ful sto-ry of love!

Won-der-ful sto-ry of love! Won-der-ful sto-ry of love! Won-der-ful sto-ry of love!

337   Yield Not to Temptation

H. R. P.

H. R. PALMER

1. Yield not to temp-ta-tion, For yield-ing is sin. Each vic-t'ry will
2. Shun e-vil com-pan-ions; Bad lan-guage dis-dain. God's name hold in
3. To him that o'er-com-eth God giv-eth a crown. Thro' faith we shall

help you Some oth-er to win. Fight man-ful-ly on-ward;
rev-erence, Nor take it in vain. Be thought-ful and ear-nest,
con-quer, Though of-ten cast down; He who is our Sav-iour

Dark pas-sions sub-due.
Kind-heart-ed and true. Look ev-er to Je-sus; He'll car-ry you through.
Our strength will re-new.

Chorus

Ask the Sav-iour to help you, Com-fort, strengthen, and keep you.

He is will-ing to aid you; He will car-ry you through.

338 Lean on His Arms

EDGAR LEWIS

L. E. JONES

1. Just lean up-on the arms of Je - sus; He'll help you a - long,
2. Just lean up-on the arms of Je - sus; He'll bright-en the way,
3. Just lean up-on the arms of Je - sus. Oh, bring ev - 'ry care,
4. Just lean up-on the arms of Je - sus; Then leave all to Him,

help you a-long. If you will trust His love un - fail - ing, He'll
bright-en the way. Just fol - low glad - ly where He lead - eth, His
bring ev - 'ry care! The bur - den that has seemed so heav - y, Take
leave all to Him. His heart is full of love and mer - cy; His

CHORUS

fill your heart with song.
gen - tle voice o - bey. Lean on His arms, trust-ing in His love.
to the Lord in prayer. Lean up-on His arms, ful - ly
eyes are nev - er dim.

Lean on His arms, all His mer - cies prove. Lean on His
Lean up - on His arms, and Lean up - on His

arms, look-ing home a - bove. Just lean on the Sav - iour's arms!
arms, ev - er

339 Wonderful Peace

H. L.

New Arrangement Copyright 1929 by Lillenas Publishing Co.

HALDOR LILLENAS

1. Com - ing to Je - sus, my Sav - iour, I found
2. Peace like a riv - er so deep and so broad,
3. Peace like a ho - ly and in - fi - nite calm,
4. Gone is the bat - tle that once raged with - in.

Won - der - ful peace,

won - der - ful peace. Storms in their fu - ry may rage all a - round;
won - der - ful peace! Rest - ing my soul on the bos - om of God,
won - der - ful peace; Like to the strains of an eve - ning psalm,
won - der - ful peace! Je - sus has saved me and cleansed me from sin;

CHORUS

I have peace, sweet peace. Peace, peace,
Won - der - ful, won - der - ful, glo - ri - ous peace.

won - der - ful peace! Peace, peace, glo - ri - ous peace! Since my Re -

poco rit.

deem - er has ran - somed my soul I have peace, sweet peace.
won - der - ful peace.

340   Ring the Bells of Heaven

Rev. W. O. Cushing

G. F. Root

1. Ring the bells of heav-en! there is joy to-day   For a soul re-
2. Ring the bells of heav-en! there is joy to-day,   For the wand'rer
3. Ring the bells of heav-en! spread the feast to-day!   An-gels, swell the

turn-ing from the wild! See! the Fa-ther meets him out up-on the way,
now is rec-on-ciled. Yes, a soul is res-cued from his sin-ful way,
glad, tri-um-phant strain! Tell the joy-ful ti-dings, bear it far a-way!

CHORUS

Wel-com-ing His wea-ry, wan-d'ring child.
And is born a-new a ran-somed child.   Glo-ry! glo-ry! how the
For a pre-cious soul is born a-gain.

an-gels sing! Glo-ry! glo-ry! how the loud harps ring! 'Tis the ran-somed

ar-my, like a might-y sea, Peal-ing forth the an-them of the free.

341 Honey in the Rock

F. A. G.

F. A. GRAVES

1. O my broth-er, do you know the Sav - iour, Who is won - drous
2. Have you tast-ed that the Lord is gra - cious? Do you walk in the
3. Do you pray un - to God the Fa - ther, "What wilt Thou have
4. Then go out thro' the streets and by - ways; Preach the Word to the

kind and true? He's the Rock of your sal - va - tion!
way that's new? Have you drunk from the liv - ing foun - tain?
me to do?" Nev - er fear, He will sure - ly an - swer,
man - y or few; Say to ev - 'ry fall - en broth - er,

CHORUS

There's hon-ey in the Rock for you. Oh, there's hon-ey in the Rock, my

broth-er; _____ There's hon-ey in the Rock for you. Leave your
my broth-er;   for you.

rit.

sins for the Blood to cov-er. There's hon-ey in the Rock for you.
                                                        for you.

342 It's Just Like His Great Love

Copyright 1903. Renewed 1931 by Maccie Haas Strouse
Assigned to Lillenas Publishing Co.

EDNA R. WORRELL

CLARENCE B. STROUSE

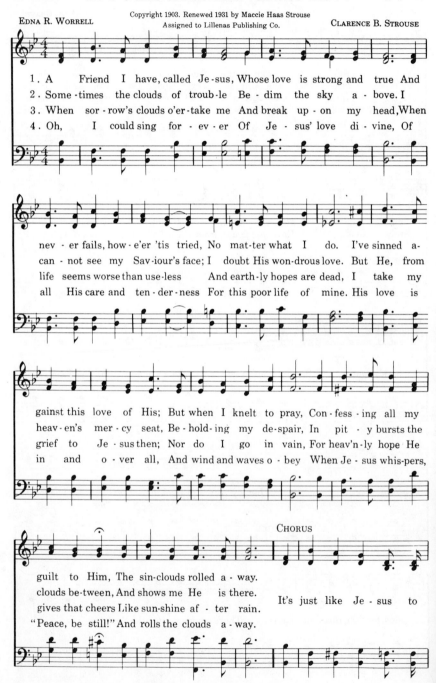

1. A Friend I have, called Je-sus, Whose love is strong and true And
2. Some-times the clouds of troub-le Be-dim the sky a-bove. I
3. When sor-row's clouds o'er-take me And break up-on my head, When
4. Oh, I could sing for-ev-er Of Je-sus' love di-vine, Of

nev-er fails, how-e'er 'tis tried, No mat-ter what I do. I've sinned a-
can-not see my Sav-iour's face; I doubt His won-drous love. But He, from
life seems worse than use-less And earth-ly hopes are dead, I take my
all His care and ten-der-ness For this poor life of mine. His love is

gainst this love of His; But when I knelt to pray, Con-fess-ing all my
heav-en's mer-cy seat, Be-hold-ing my de-spair, In pit-y bursts the
grief to Je-sus then; Nor do I go in vain, For heav'n-ly hope He
in and o-ver all, And wind and waves o-bey When Je-sus whis-pers,

CHORUS

guilt to Him, The sin-clouds rolled a-way.
clouds be-tween, And shows me He is there.
gives that cheers Like sun-shine af-ter rain.   It's just like Je-sus to
"Peace, be still!" And rolls the clouds a-way.

It's Just Like His Great Love

roll the clouds a-way. It's just like Je-sus to keep me day by day.

It's just like Je-sus all a-long the way. It's just like His great love.

343   Close to Thee

FANNY J. CROSBY   SILAS J. VAIL

1. Thou, my ev-er-last-ing por-tion, More than friend or life to me,
2. Not for ease or world-ly pleas-ure, Nor for fame my prayer shall be;
3. Lead me thro' the vale of shad-ows, Bear me o'er life's fit-ful sea;

Fine

D.S.– All a-long my pil-grim jour-ney, Sav-iour, let me walk with Thee.
D.S.– Glad-ly will I toil and suf-fer, On-ly let me walk with Thee.
D.S.– Then the gate of life e-ter-nal May I en-ter, Lord, with Thee.

REFRAIN   D.S.

Close to Thee, close to Thee, Close to Thee, close to Thee;

344 Rise and Shine

DELL AYCOCK

JARRETTE AYCOCK

1. When our Lord re-turns to take us To our man-sions in the sky, We shall
2. Pris - on bars of death can't hold us When our Sav-iour comes a-gain. We shall
3. With our loved ones gone be-fore us, We'll assemble 'round the throne, Where we'll

rise and shine.——We shall rise to life e-ter-nal, Nev-er-
rise and shine.——From the grave we'll rise tri-um-phant, And with
shine and shine.—— There we'll shout and praise our Saviour, Who re-

We shall rise and shine, we shall shine.

more to sin or die. We shall rise and shine.
Christ we'll live and reign. We shall rise and shine. We shall rise,—— we shall
deemed us for His own. We shall shine and shine.

We shall rise and shine.

CHORUS

We shall rise,

shine;—— We shall shine with Him in glo-ry by and by.———— When the
we shall shine;   by and by.

bonds of death are broken, We shall meet Him in the sky. We shall rise —— and shine.
We shall rise

345 How the Fire Fell

JOHNSON OATMAN, JR.

MIRIAM E. OATMAN

1. Oh, I love to tell the bless-ed sto-ry
2. All my doubts and fears are gone for-ev-er
3. To the world no more my heart is turn-ing
4. There's a crown a-wait-ing me in heav-en

Since the Lord

For my soul re-ceived a flood of glo-ry
For His peace flowed o'er me like a riv-er
For on me His Spir-it fell with burn-ing
For a heart made clean to me was giv-en

sanc-ti-fied me;

CHORUS

When the Lord sanc-ti-fied me. Oh, I nev-er shall for-get how the

fire fell, How the fire fell, how the fire fell. Oh, I

nev-er shall for-get how the fire fell When the Lord sanc-ti-fied me.

346 Saved, Saved!

J. P. S.   J. Scholfield

1. I've found a Friend who is all to me; His
2. He saves me from ev'ry sin and harm, Se-
3. When poor and need-y and all a-lone, In

love is ev-er true. I love to tell how He
cures my soul each day. I'm lean-ing strong on His
love He said to me, "Come un-to Me and I'll

lift-ed me, And what His grace can do for you.
might-y arm; I know He'll guide me all the way.
lead you home, To live with Me e-ter-nal-ly."

Chorus

Saved by His pow'r di-vine, Saved to new life sub-lime!
Saved by His pow'r, Saved to new life,

cresc.   *rit.*

Life now is sweet and my joy is com-plete, For I'm saved, saved, saved!

347 I Belong to the King

IDA L. REED

MAURICE A. CLIFTON

1. I be-long to the King, I'm a child of His love, I shall dwell in His
2. I be-long to the King, and He loves me I know, For His mer-cy and
3. I be-long to the King, and His prom-ise is sure, That we all shall be

pal - ace so fair; For He tells of its bliss in yon heav-en a-bove, And His
kind-ness so free Are un - ceas-ing-ly mine where-so-ev - er I go, And my
gath-ered at last In His king-dom a-bove, by life's wa-ters so pure, When this

chil-dren in splen - dor shall share.
Ref-uge un - fail - ing is He.
life with its tri - als is past.

CHORUS

I be - long to the King, I'm a child of His love, And He nev - er for - sak-eth His own. He will call me some-day to His pal - ace a - bove. I shall dwell by His glo - ri - fied throne.

348 Leaving All to Follow Jesus

IDA M. BUDD

CHAS. H. GABRIEL

1. Leav - ing all to fol-low Je - sus, Turn-ing from the world a - way,
2. Naught re-serv-ing, on the al - tar all I lay, and wait the hour
3. Tak - ing up the cross for Je - sus, Glad for Him to suf - fer shame,
4. Praise His pre-cious name for-ev - er That His blood hath made me free!

Step - ping out up - on His prom-ise, All I have is His to - day.
When the fire from heav'n de-scend-ing Shall at-test His glo - rious pow'r.
All my gain I count but loss - es, For the glo - ry of His name.
Now my soul shall joy to tell it Thro' the long e -ter - ni - ty.

CHORUS

Leav - ing all to fol - low Je - sus, Turn - ing
Leav - ing all to fol - low, fol - low Je - sus,

from the world a - way, Step - ping out up-
Turn-ing, turn - ing from the world a - way, Step - ping out up-

on His prom - ise, All I have is His to - day.
on His bless - ed prom - ise,

349 Saved to the Uttermost

W. J. K.

W. J. KIRKPATRICK

1. Saved to the ut - ter-most! I am the Lord's. Je - sus, my
2. Saved to the ut - ter-most! Je - sus is near; Keep-ing me
3. Saved to the ut - ter-most! This I can say, "Once all was
4. Saved to the ut - ter-most! Cheer-ful - ly sing Loud hal - le-

Sav - iour, sal - va - tion af - fords; Gives me His Spir - it, a
safe - ly, He cast - eth out fear. Trust - ing His prom - is - es,
dark - ness, but now it is day; Beau - ti - ful vis - ions of
lu - jahs to Je - sus, my King. Ran - somed and par - doned, re -

wit - ness with - in, Whis-p'ring of par - don and sav - ing from sin.
now I am blest. Lean - ing up - on Him, how sweet is my rest!
glo - ry I see, Je - sus in bright - ness re - vealed un - to me."
deemed by His blood, Cleansed from un - right - eous - ness—glo - ry to God!

REFRAIN

Saved, saved, saved to the ut - ter-most! Saved, saved by pow - er di - vine!

Saved, saved, saved to the ut - ter-most: Je - sus, the Sav - iour, is mine!

350 Let the Holy Ghost Come In

R. F. REYNOLDS

C. E. ROWLEY

1. Would you be re-deemed from ev - 'ry in-born sin, Have the Ho - ly Spir - it
2. Would you have the Spir - it in your heart to cheer? Would you be re-lieved from
3. Do you want the "fire of God" to fill your soul, Burn up all the dross, and
4. Do you want the "pow'r" to make you true and brave, So that you can res - cue

con - stant-ly with - in?
ev - 'ry doubt and fear?
sanc - ti - fy the whole? Make the con-se-cra - tion, trust in God, and then
those that Christ would save?

REFRAIN

Let the Ho - ly Ghost come in. Let the Ho - ly Ghost come
come in.

in. Let the Ho - ly Ghost come in. Make the con - se-
come in. come in.

cra - tion, trust in God, and then Let the Ho - ly Ghost come in.
come in.

351   Tell Me the Old, Old Story

KATE HANKEY

W. H. DOANE

1. Tell me the old, old story Of un-seen things a-bove, Of Je-sus
2. Tell me the sto-ry slow-ly, That I may take it in— That wonder-
3. Tell me the same old sto-ry When you have cause to fear That this world's

and His glo-ry, Of Je-sus and His love. Tell me the sto-ry
ful re-demp-tion, God's rem-e-dy for sin. Tell me the sto-ry
emp-ty glo-ry Is cost-ing me too dear. Yes, and when that world's

sim-ply, As to a lit-tle child; For I am weak and wea-ry,
of-ten, For I for-get so soon. The "ear-ly dew" of morn-ing
glo-ry is dawn-ing on my soul, Tell me the old, old sto-ry:

CHORUS

And help-less and de-filed.
Has passed a-way at noon. Tell me the old, old sto-ry. Tell me the
"Christ Je-sus makes thee whole."

old, old sto-ry. Tell me the old, old sto-ry, Of Je-sus and His love.

352 I Love to Walk with Jesus

C. F. W.

C. F. WEIGLE

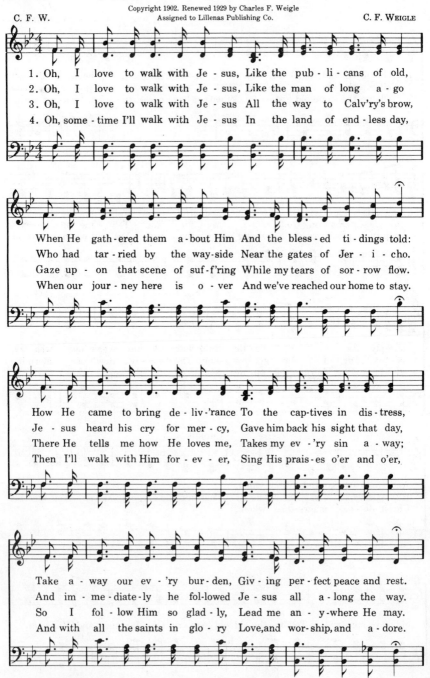

1. Oh, I love to walk with Je - sus, Like the pub - li - cans of old,
2. Oh, I love to walk with Je - sus, Like the man of long a - go
3. Oh, I love to walk with Je - sus All the way to Calv'ry's brow,
4. Oh, some - time I'll walk with Je - sus In the land of end - less day,

When He gath - ered them a - bout Him And the bless - ed ti - dings told:
Who had tar - ried by the way - side Near the gates of Jer - i - cho.
Gaze up - on that scene of suf - f'ring While my tears of sor - row flow.
When our jour - ney here is o - ver And we've reached our home to stay.

How He came to bring de - liv - 'rance To the cap - tives in dis - tress,
Je - sus heard his cry for mer - cy, Gave him back his sight that day,
There He tells me how He loves me, Takes my ev - 'ry sin a - way;
Then I'll walk with Him for - ev - er, Sing His prais - es o'er and o'er,

Take a - way our ev - 'ry bur - den, Giv - ing per - fect peace and rest.
And im - me - diate - ly he fol - lowed Je - sus all a - long the way.
So I fol - low Him so glad - ly, Lead me an - y - where He may.
And with all the saints in glo - ry Love, and wor - ship, and a - dore.

I Love to Walk with Jesus

CHORUS

I will fol-low where He lead-eth; I will pas-ture where He feed-eth;

I will fol-low all the way, Lord. I will fol-low Je-sus ev-'ry day.

353   Come, Ye Disconsolate

THOMAS MOORE AND THOMAS HASTINGS   SAMUEL WEBBE

1. Come, ye dis-con-so-late, wher-e'er ye lan-guish; Come to the
2. Joy of the des-o-late, Light of the stray-ing, Hope of the
3. Here see the Bread of Life; see wa-ters flow-ing Forth from the

mer-cy seat, fer-vent-ly kneel. Here bring your wounded hearts, here
pen-i-tent, fade-less and pure! Here speaks the Com-fort-er, ten-
throne of God, pure from a-bove. Come to the feast of love; come,

tell your an-guish; Earth has no sor-row that Heav'n can-not heal.
der-ly say-ing, "Earth has no sor-row that Heav'n can-not cure."
ev-er know-ing Earth has no sor-row but Heav'n can re-move.

354 Master, the Tempest Is Raging

Mary A. Baker

H. R. Palmer

1. Mas-ter, the tem-pest is rag-ing. The bil-lows are toss-ing high.
2. Mas-ter, with an-guish of spir-it I bow in my grief to-day;
3. Mas-ter, the ter-ror is o-ver; The el-e-ments sweet-ly rest;

The sky is o'er-shadowed with black-ness. No shel-ter or help is nigh.
The depths of my sad heart are troub-led. Oh, wak-en and save, I pray!
Earth's sun in the calm lake is mir-rored, And heaven's with-in my breast.

"Car-est thou not that we per-ish?" How canst Thou lie a-sleep
Tor-rents of sin and of an-guish Sweep o'er my sink-ing soul!
Lin-ger, O bless-ed Re-deem-er; Leave me a-lone no more;

When each moment so mad-ly is threatening A grave in the an-gry deep?
And I per-ish! I per-ish, dear Mas-ter! Oh, has-ten, and take con-trol!
And with joy I shall make the blest har-bor, And rest on the bliss-ful shore.

Master, the Tempest Is Raging

"The winds and the waves shall o - bey My will. Peace, be still!"
Peace, be still! peace, be still!

Wheth-er the wrath of the storm-tossed sea, Or de-mons, or men, or what-

ev - er it be, No wa-ter can swal-low the ship where lies The Mas-ter of

o - cean and earth and skies. "They all shall sweetly o - bey My will; Peace, be still!

Peace, be still! They all shall sweet-ly o - bey My will; Peace, peace, be still!"

355 Send the Light

C. H. G.

Chas. H. Gabriel

1. There's a call comes ring-ing o'er the rest-less wave, "Send the light!—
2. We have heard the Mac-e-do-nian call to-day,
3. Let us pray that grace may ev-'ry-where a-bound,
4. Let us not grow wea-ry in the work of love. "Send the light!

Send the light!" There are souls to res-cue, there are souls to save.
And a gold-en of-f'ring at the Cross we lay.
And a Christ-like spir-it ev-'ry-where be found.
Send the light!" Let us gath-er jew-els for a crown a-bove.

Send the light! Send the light!
Send the light! Send the light!

Chorus

Send the light, the bless-ed gos - pel light. Let it
Send the light, and let its ra - diant beams Light the
Send the light, the bless - ed gos - pel light.

shine from shore to shore!
world for-ev-er- (*Omit*) more.
Let it shine from shore to shore! for - ev - er-more.

356 I Know Whom I Have Believed

D. W. WHITTLE

JAMES McGRANAHAN

1. I know not why God's won-drous grace To me He hath made known;
2. I know not how this sav-ing faith To me He did im - part,
3. I know not how the Spir - it moves, Con-vinc-ing men of sin,
4. I know not what of good or ill May be re-served for me,
5. I know not when my Lord may come, At night or noon-day fair,

Nor why, un - wor - thy, Christ in love Re-deemed me for His own.
Nor how be - liev - ing in His Word Wrought peace within my heart.
Re - veal - ing Je - sus thro' the Word, Cre - at - ing faith in Him.
Of wea - ry ways or gold - en days, Be - fore His face I see.
Nor if I'll walk the vale with Him, Or meet Him in the air.

CHORUS

But "I know whom I have be - liev - ed, and am per - suad-ed that He is

a - ble To keep that which I've com-mit-ted Un - to Him a-gainst that day."

357 Since I Have Been Redeemed

E. O. E.

E. O. Excell

1. I have a song I love to sing, Since I have been re-deemed,
2. I have a Christ that sat-is-fies, Since I have been re-deemed.
3. I have a wit-ness bright and clear, Since I have been re-deemed,
4. I have a home pre-pared for me, Since I have been re-deemed,

Of my Re-deem-er, Sav-iour, King,
To do His will my high-est prize,
Dis-pel-ling ev-'ry doubt and fear, Since I have been re-deemed.
Where I shall dwell e-ter-nal-ly,

Chorus

Since I ———— have been re-deemed, Since I have been re-
Since I have been redeemed, Since I have been redeemed,

deemed, I will glo-ry in His name. Since I ———— have been re-
Since I have been redeemed, Since

deemed, I will glo-ry in my Sav-iour's name.
I have been re-deemed,

358 I Love Him Better Every Day

Copyright 1926 by Thoro Harris
Assigned to Nazarene Publishing House

T. H.

THORO HARRIS
CHORUS BY ADJT. SIDNEY COX

1. The bless-ed Je-sus loved me Be-fore I ev-er came And tas-ted His sal-
2. Each day the path grows brighter, And I can al-most see The mansions of the
3. O soul with-out this Saviour, Why will you long-er roam, When Je-sus still in-

va-tion, Or tho't up-on His name. He called me and He wooed me, And I am
faith-ful, Where I so soon shall be. In that ce-les-tial cit-y I'll sing un-
vites you, "Ye wea-ry ones, come home"? To-day, if you ac-cept Him, He of-fers

poco rit.

His to-day, As hand in hand we jour-ney A-long the heav'nward way.
end-ing praise To my di-vine Re-deem-er, Thro' ev-er-last-ing days.
you His grace; His providence shall guide you Un-til you see His face.

CHORUS   *a tempo*

I love Him bet-ter ev-'ry day.
ev-'ry day.

I love Him bet-ter ev-'ry

poco rit.

day.
ev-'ry day.

Close by His side I will a-bide. I love Him bet-ter ev-'ry day.

359 I Have Settled the Question

Copyright 1919. Renewed 1947 by Haldor Lillenas
Assigned to Nazarene Publishing House

H. L.

HALDOR LILLENAS

1. I re - mem - ber when the Lord spoke to my soul (to my soul).
2. I no long - er walk the ways of sin - ful - ness (sin-ful-ness),
3. I will choose the ho - ly joys that al - ways last (al-ways last),
4. Oth - ers may de - ny the Lord and live in sin (live in sin),

I could feel the heav - y bur - den from me roll (from me roll)
But I dai - ly tread the paths of right - eous - ness (right-eous-ness)
And re - ject sin's pleas - ures that will soon be past (soon be past).
But the race that I have en - tered I must win (I must win).

When He spoke the gra - cious words, "Wilt thou be whole?" (be whole?) Then I
Since the day the Lord has come my life to bless (to bless). I have
To the treas - ures of true worth I'm hold - ing fast (hold-ing fast). I have
Thro' the pearl - y gates I mean to en - ter in (en - ter in). I have

CHORUS

set - tled the question for - ev - er. I have set - tled the ques - tion, hal - le-

lu - jah! I will nev - er turn back from the nar - row way.
lu - jah! hal - le - lu - jah!

I Have Settled the Question

I am go-ing thro' with Je-sus, hal-le-lu jah!
hal-le-lu-jah! hal-le-lu-jah!

Till I reach the gates of glo-ry some sweet day (some sweet day).

360 Faith of Our Fathers

FREDERICK W. FABER

H. F. HEMY AND J. G. WALTON

1. Faith of our fa-thers, liv-ing still In spite of dun-geon, fire, and sword!
2. Our fa-thers, chained in pris-ons dark, Were still in heart and conscience free.
3. Faith of our fa-thers! we will love Both friend and foe in all our strife;

Oh, how our hearts beat high with joy Whene'er we hear that glo-rious word!
How sweet would be their children's fate If they, like them, could die for thee!
And preach thee, too, as love knows how, By kind-ly words and vir-tuous life.

Faith of our fa-thers! ho-ly faith! We will be true to thee till death!

361 Since Jesus Came into My Heart

R. H. McDaniel

Chas. H. Gabriel

1. What a won-der-ful change in my life has been wrought Since Je-sus came
2. I have ceased from my wand'ring and go-ing a-stray Since Je-sus came
3. I'm pos-sessed of a hope that is stead-fast and sure, Since Je-sus came
4. There's a light in the val-ley of death now for me, Since Je-sus came
5. I shall go there to dwell in that cit-y I know, Since Je-sus came

in-to my heart! I have light in my soul for which long I had sought,
in-to my heart; And my sins which were man-y are all washed a-way,
in-to my heart; And no dark clouds of doubt now my path-way ob-scure,
in-to my heart; And the gates of the cit-y be-yond I can see,
in-to my heart; And I'm hap-py, so hap-py, as on-ward I go,

Chorus

Since Je-sus came in-to my heart. Since Je-sus came in-to my
heart, Since Je-sus came in-to my heart, Floods of joy o'er my
soul like the sea bil-lows roll, Since Je-sus came in-to my heart.

362 The Light of the World Is Jesus

P. P. B.

PHILIP P. BLISS

1. The whole world was lost in the dark-ness of sin; The
2. No dark-ness have we who in Je-sus a-bide; The
3. Ye dwell-ers in dark-ness with sin-blind-ed eyes— The
4. No need of the sun-light in heav-en we're told; The

Light of the world is Je-sus. Like sun-shine at noon-day His
Light of the world is Je-sus. We walk in the Light when we
Light of the world is Je-sus— Go, wash at His bid-ding, and
Light of the world is Je-sus. The Lamb is the Light in the

glo-ry shone in;
fol-low our Guide;   The Light of the world is Je-sus.
light will a-rise.
cit-y of gold;

CHORUS

Come to the Light; 'tis shin-ing for thee. Sweet-ly the Light has dawned upon me.

Once I was blind, but now I can see. The Light of the world is Je-sus.

363 Soldiers of Immanuel

H. L.

HALDOR LILLENAS

1. Sol-diers of Im-man-u-el, go for-ward in His name, Ho-ly war-fare
2. Sol-diers of Im-man-u-el, go for-ward to the fray, Songs of triumph
3. Sol-diers of Im-man-u-el, the bat-tle soon shall cease. In a home of

wag-ing, pow'rs of sin en-gag-ing. Lift His roy-al stand-ard and His
sing-ing, shouts of vic-t'ry ring-ing. Fol-low your Com-man-der; He is
splen-dor we shall hom-age ren-der Un-to Je-sus, Him who is the

truth di-vine pro-claim, Till the world shall own Him King.
with you ev-'ry day. On-ward! is the bat-tle cry.
glo-rious Prince of Peace, When we lay our ar-mor down.

CHORUS

Go forth, go forth, and battle for the right. De-feat the foe and put his host to

flight. Ye sol-diers of Im-man-u-el, press on Un-til the vic-to-ry is won.

364 My Burdens Rolled Away

M. A. S.

Mrs. Minnie A. Steele

1. I re-mem-ber when my bur-dens rolled a-way; I had car-ried them for
2. I re-mem-ber when my bur-dens rolled a-way, 'That I feared would nev-er
3. I re-mem-ber when my bur-dens rolled a-way, That had hin-dered me for
4. I am sing-ing since my bur-dens rolled a-way; There's a song with-in my

years, night and day. When I sought the bless-ed Lord, and I took Him at His
leave night or day. Je-sus showed to me the loss, so I left them at the
years, night and day. As I sought the throne of grace, just a glimpse of Je-sus'
heart night and day. I am liv-ing for my King, and with joy I shout and

Chorus

word, Then at once all my bur-dens rolled a-way. Rolled a-way, rolled a-
Cross; I was glad when my bur-dens rolled a-way.
face, And I knew that my bur-dens could not stay.
sing. Hal-le-lu-jah! all my bur-dens rolled a-way! Rolled a-way,

way, I am hap-py since my bur-dens rolled a-way. Rolled a-
rolled a-way, since my bur-dens rolled a-way.

way, rolled a-way, I am hap-py since my bur-dens rolled a-way.
Rolled a-way, rolled a-way,

365 My Redeemer

P. P. Bliss

James McGranahan

1. I will sing of my Redeem-er And His won-drous love to me;
2. I will tell the won-drous sto-ry, How, my lost es-tate to save,
3. I will praise my dear Redeem-er; His tri-um-phant pow'r I'll tell,
4. I will sing of my Redeem-er, And His heav'n-ly love to me;

On the cru-el cross He suf-fered, From the curse to set me free.
In His bound-less love and mer-cy He the ran-som free-ly gave.
How the vic-to-ry He giv-eth O-ver sin, and death, and hell.
He from death to life hath bro't me, Son of God, with Him to be.

CHORUS

Sing, oh, sing of my Re-deem-er. With His

Sing, oh, sing of my Re-deem-er; Sing, oh, sing of my Re-deem-er. With His

blood He pur-chased me. On the cross He sealed my

blood He purchased me; With His blood He purchased me. On the cross He sealed my pardon, On the

par-don, Paid the debt and made me free.

cross He sealed my pardon, Paid the debt and made me free, and made me free.

366 Sound the Battle Cry

W. F. S.

WM. F. SHERWIN

1. Sound the bat-tle cry! See, the foe is nigh. Raise the standard high
2. Strong to meet the foe, Marching on we go, While our cause, we know,
3. O Thou God of all, Hear us when we call; Help us one and all

For the Lord. Gird your ar-mor on; Stand firm, ev-'ry one. Rest your
Must pre - vail. Shield and banner bright, Gleam-ing in the light; Bat - tling
By Thy grace. When the bat-tle's done, And the vic-t'ry's won, May we

CHORUS ff

cause up - on His ho - ly Word.
for the right, We ne'er can fail. Rouse, then, sol - diers; ral - ly round the
wear the crown Be - fore Thy face.

ban-ner. Read - y, stead - y, pass the word a-long.   On-ward, for -ward,

shout a - loud Ho - san - na! Christ is Cap - tain of the might- y throng.

367 Standing on the Promises

R. K. C.

R. KELSO CARTER

1. Stand-ing on the prom - is - es of Christ, my King! Thro' e - ter - nal
2. Stand-ing on the prom - is - es that can - not fail! When the howl-ing
3. Stand-ing on the prom - is - es, I now can see Per - fect, pres - ent
4. Stand-ing on the prom - is - es of Christ the Lord, Bound to Him e -
5. Stand-ing on the prom - is - es I can - not fall, Lis - t'ning ev - 'ry

a - ges let His prais-es ring. Glo - ry in the high-est I will shout and sing,
storms of doubt and fear as-sail, By the liv-ing Word of God I shall pre-vail,
cleansing in the Blood for me; Standing in the lib - erty where Christ makes free,
ter - nal-ly by love's strong cord, O - ver-com-ing dai - ly with the Spirit's Sword,
mo - ment to the Spir-it's call, Rest-ing in my Sav - iour as my all in all,

CHORUS

Standing on the prom-is-es of God. Stand - ing, stand -
Stand-ing on the prom-is - es, Stand - ing on the

ing, Stand-ing on the prom - is - es of God, my Sav-iour; Stand-
prom - is - es, Stand-ing on the

ing, stand - ing, I'm stand-ing on the prom-is - es of God.
prom - is - es, Stand-ing on the prom-is - es,

368 My Saviour's Love

C. H. G.

CHAS. H. GABRIEL

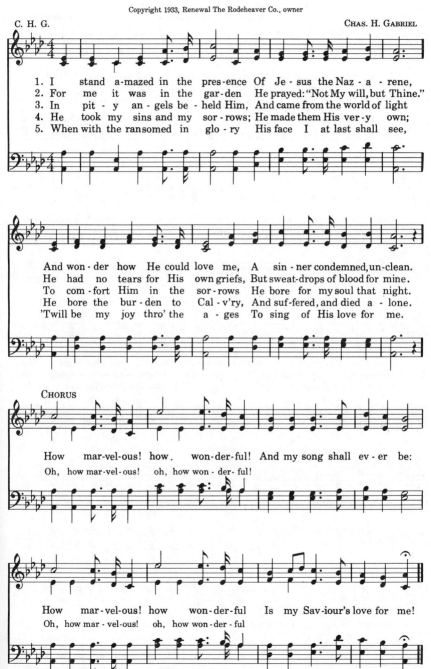

1. I stand a-mazed in the pres-ence Of Je - sus the Naz - a - rene,
2. For me it was in the gar-den He prayed: "Not My will, but Thine."
3. In pit - y an - gels be - held Him, And came from the world of light
4. He took my sins and my sor-rows; He made them His ver -y own;
5. When with the ransomed in glo - ry His face I at last shall see,

And won-der how He could love me, A sin - ner condemned, un-clean.
He had no tears for His own griefs, But sweat-drops of blood for mine.
To com-fort Him in the sor-rows He bore for my soul that night.
He bore the bur-den to Cal - v'ry, And suf-fered, and died a - lone.
'Twill be my joy thro' the a - ges To sing of His love for me.

CHORUS

How mar-vel-ous! how. won-der-ful! And my song shall ev - er be:
Oh, how mar-vel-ous! oh, how won - der-ful!

How mar-vel-ous! how won-der-ful Is my Sav-iour's love for me!
Oh, how mar - vel-ous! oh, how won-der-ful

369 He's Everything to Me

KATE BYRON

HAMP SEWELL

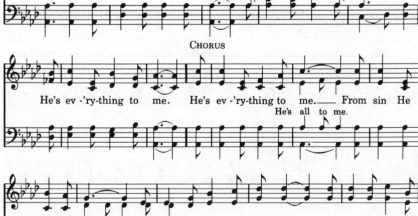

1. In sin I once had wan-dered, all wea - ry, sad, and lone, Till Je - sus
2. In sin no more I'll wan - der; He's Pilot, Friend, and Guide. He brings me
3. No long - er will I stray from His ten - der, lov-ing care; Like Him to

thro' His mer - cy - a-dopt-ed me His own. E'er since I learned to
joy and sing-ing. His Spir - it doth a - bide. A bless - ed, lov - ing
be my pur-pose, my aim, my con-stant prayer. And when He bids me

trust Him, His grace doth make me free, And now I feel His par - don.
Sav-iour, the Lamb of Cal - va - ry! He pur-chased my re - demp - tion.
wel-come thro'- out e - ter - ni - ty, I'll praise His name for - ev - er.

CHORUS

He's ev -'ry-thing to me. He's ev -'ry-thing to me.— From sin He
He's all to me.

sets me free;— His peace and love my por - tion thro' all e - ter - ni-
He sets me free; e-

He's Everything to Me

ty!__ He's ev-'ry-thing to me,__ More than I dreamed could
ter - ni - ty! He's all to me,

be.__ Oh, praise His name for - ev - er! He's ev - 'ry-thing to me.
could be.

370 From All That Dwell Below the Skies

Isaac Watts and John Wesley   John Hatton

1. From all that dwell be - low the skies Let the Cre-
2. In ev - 'ry land be - gin the song; To ev - 'ry
3. Your loft - y themes, ye mor - tals, bring; In songs of
4. E - ter - nal are Thy mer - cies, Lord; E - ter - nal

a - tor's praise a - rise. Let the Re - deem - er's name be
land the strains be - long; In cheer - ful sounds all voic - es
praise di - vine - ly sing. The great sal - va - tion loud pro-
truth at - tends Thy word. Thy praise shall sound from shore to

sung Thro' ev - 'ry land, by ev - 'ry tongue.
raise, And fill the world with loud - est praise.
claim, And shout for joy the Sav - iour's name.
shore, Till suns shall rise and set no more.

371 Standing on the Word

H. L.

HALDOR LILLENAS

1. Sure is my foundation, for I stand to-day On the living Word that faileth
2. Fearful are the storms that may around me beat; Man-y are the foes that would as-
3. Faith is rest-ing on the promise stong and sure; Hope is anchored safe and cannot
4. Like a bea-con star to lead me thro' the night, Like a light up-on my path-way

nev - er. Earth with all its glo-ry soon must pass a-way, But the Word of
sail me. I have found a nev-er-fail-ing, sure re-treat In the Word of
fal - ter; Peace has found a ha-ven from the storms se-cure In the Word of
streaming, Is the Word of God to guide my steps a-right To my homeland

CHORUS

God shall stand for-ev - er.
God that can-not fail me.
God that can-not al - ter.   Stand-ing on the Word, Stand-ing on the Word,
with its por-tals gleam-ing.

Stand-ing on the nev-er-fail-ing Word of God; Tho' man-y foes as-sail, His

prom-ise can-not fail, For I'm stand-ing on the nev-er-fail-ing Word.
of God.

372 My Soul Is Filled with Glory

J. M. H.

J. M. HARRIS

1. Je - sus found me when a - far I wandered; Bro't me par-don from the
2. Thro' His Word He taught me full sal - va - tion, How His blood could cleanse and
3. Tri - als man - y will be - set my path-way, And temp-ta-tions I shall

throne a - bove; Gave me peace that pass-eth un - der-stand-ing, Joy un-
sanc - ti - fy; Then by faith I plunged in - to the foun-tain. Now I'm
sure - ly meet; But my Sav-iour prom-ised grace to help me Till I

CHORUS

speak-a-ble and full of love.
look-ing for that home on high. Praise the Lord! my soul is filled with glo-ry!
lay my tro-phies at His feet.

Praise the Lord! I love to tell the sto - ry Of His grace that

jus - ti - fies me free - ly,
sanc-ti - fies me whol - ly, And I'm shout-ing glo - ry! till I get home.
keeps and gives me vic - t'ry,

373   Hallelujah, Praise Jehovah!

PSALM 16

WM. J. KIRKPATRICK

1. Hal - le - lu - jah, praise Je - ho - vah! From the heav - ens praise His name.
2. Let them prais - es give Je - ho - vah; They were made at His com - mand.
3. All ye fruit - ful trees and ce - dars, All ye hills and mountains high,

Praise Je - ho - vah in the high - est; All His an - gels, praise pro - claim.
Them for - ev - er He es - tab - lished; His de - cree shall ev - er stand.
Creep - ing things and beasts and cat - tle, Birds that in the heav - ens fly;

All His hosts, to - geth - er praise Him—Sun, and moon, and stars on high.
From the earth, oh, praise Je - ho - vah, All ye floods, ye drag - ons all;
Kings of earth and all ye peo - ple, Princ - es great, earth's judg - es all;

Praise Him, O ye heav'n of heav - ens, And ye floods a - bove the sky.
Fire, and hail, and snow, and va - pors, Storm - y winds that hear Him call.
Praise His name, young men and maid - ens, A - ged men, and chil - dren small.

CHORUS

Let them prais - es give Je - ho - vah, For His name a - lone is high,

Let them prais - es

Hallelujah, Praise Jehovah!

And His glo - ry is ex - alt - ed, And His glo - ry is ex - alt - ed,
And His glo - ry
And His glo - ry

And His glo - ry is ex - alt - ed Far a - bove the earth and sky.
And His glo - ry

374 Guide Me, O Thou Great Jehovah

W. WILLIAMS

THOMAS HASTINGS

1. Guide me, O Thou great Je - ho - vah, Pil - grim thro' this bar - ren land. I am
2. O - pen now the crys - tal foun - tain, Whence the healing waters flow; Let the
3. When I tread the verge of Jor - dan, Bid my anx - ious fears sub - side. Bear me

weak, but Thou art might - y. Hold me with Thy pow'r - ful hand. Bread of Heav - en,
fi - er - y, cloud - y pil - lar Lead me all my jour - ney thro'. Strong De - liv - 'rer,
thro' the swelling cur - rent; Land me safe on Ca - naan's side. Songs of prais - es

Feed me till I want no more. Bread of Heaven, Feed me till I want no more.
Be Thou still my Strength and Shield. Strong Deliv'rer, Be Thou still my Strength and Shield.
I will ev - er give to Thee. Songs of praises I will ev - er give to Thee.

375 My Wonderful Friend

H. L.

HALDOR LILLENAS

1. I found such a won-der-ful Sav-iour In Je-sus, my Lord and my King!
2. Sur - pass-ing the love that a moth - er May have for the child of her care;
3. The pleasures the world could af-ford me Are naught to compare with His joy;
4. When sor-row and pain are my por - tion, When tears of bereavement must fall,
5. When tempests around me are sweeping, My Pi-lot and Guide He will be;

Un - dy - ing and true His de - vo - tion. My heart shall His glad praises sing.
The love of a sis-ter or broth - er With His we can nev-er com - pare.
The rapture and peace that He gives me, Earth's sorrows can nev-er de - stroy.
My Sav-iour, my Friend, and Companion Will com-fort and keep thro' it all.
And safe is my soul in His keep-ing. My might-y De - liv -'rer is He.

CHORUS

Oh, what a won-der-ful Sav-iour is He! Con - stant and true is Je - sus.

More than I fan-cied He ev - er could be Is Je-sus, my won-der-ful Friend.

376 One More Day's Work for Jesus

ANNA B. WARNER

ROBERT LOWRY

1. One more day's work for Je - sus, One less of life for
me! But heav'n is near - er, And Christ is dear - er, Than yes-
ter - day to me. His love and light Fill all my soul to-night.

2. One more day's work for Je - sus! How sweet the work has
been, To tell the sto - ry, To show the glo - ry, When Christ's
flock en - ter in! How it did shine In this poor heart of mine!

3. One more day's work for Je - sus! Oh, yes, a wea - ry
day; But heav'n shines clearer, And rest comes near - er, At each
step of the way; And, Christ in all, Be - fore His face I fall.

4. Oh, bless - ed work for Je - sus! Oh, rest, at Je - sus'
feet! There toil seems pleasure, My wants are treas-ure, And pain
for Him is sweet. Lord, if I may, I'll serve an - oth - er day.

CHORUS

One more day's work for Je - sus, One more day's work for Je - sus,

One more day's work for Je - sus, One less of life for me!

377 Sunshine in the Soul

E. E. HEWITT

JNO. R. SWENEY

1. There's sun-shine in my soul to-day, More glo-ri-ous and bright
2. There's mu-sic in my soul to-day, A car-ol to my King;
3. There's springtime in my soul to-day; For when the Lord is near
4. There's glad-ness in my soul to-day, And hope and praise and love,

Than glows in an-y earth-ly sky, For Je-sus is my Light.
And Je-sus, lis-ten-ing, can hear The songs I can-not sing.
The dove of peace sings in my heart, The flow'rs of grace ap-pear.
For bless-ings which He gives me now, For joys "laid up" a-bove.

REFRAIN

Oh, there's sun - shine, bless-ed sun - shine,
sun-shine in the soul,
sun-shine in the soul,

While the peace-ful, hap-py mo-ments roll.
hap-py mo-ments roll.

When Je-sus shows His smil-ing face, There is sun-shine in my soul.

378 Tell the Blessed Story

H. L.

HALDOR LILLENAS

1. Church of God, a - wak - en; heed the Lord's com-mand.
2. Has He not com-mis-sioned you the news to bear?
3. Stand no long - er i - dle while the mo-ments fly.
4. Pub - lish un - to all the world re - deem-ing grace.

Tell the bless - ed sto - ry of the Cross.

Fields are white for har-vest-ing on ev - ry hand.
"Go ye in - to all the world," and ev -'ry-where
Mul - ti-tudes in hea-then dark-ness live and die.
Un - til in the home of rest you find your place,

CHORUS

Tell the bless-ed sto - ry of the Cross. Tell the bless-ed sto - ry of the cross of Je-sus. Tell the bless-ed sto - ry of the hal-lowed Cross. Un-til ev -'ry na-tion learns of full sal - va-tion, Tell the bless-ed sto - ry of the Cross.

379 Stepping in the Light

E. E. HEWITT

WM. J. KIRKPATRICK

1. Try-ing to walk in the steps of the Sav-iour, Try - ing to fol - low our
2. Pressing more closely to Him who is lead-ing, When we are tempt- ed to
3. Walking in foot-steps of gen -tle for-bearance, Foot-steps of faith - ful-ness,
4. Try-ing to walk in the steps of the Sav-iour, Up - ward, still up-ward we'll

Sav -iour and King; Shap - ing our lives by His bless - ed ex - am - ple,
turn from the way; Trust - ing the arm that is strong to de -fend us,
mer - cy, and love; Look - ing to Him for the grace free - ly prom -ised,
fol - low our Guide. When we shall see Him, "the king in his beau - ty,"

CHORUS

Hap-py, how hap-py, the songs that we bring!
Hap-py, how hap-py, our prais-es each day!
Hap-py, how hap-py, our jour -ney a -bove! How beau-ti-ful to walk in the
Hap-py, how hap-py, our place at His side!

steps of the Sav-iour, Step-ping in the light, Step-ping in the light! How

beau-ti-ful to walk in the steps of the Sav-iour, Led in paths of light!

380   Onward, Christian Soldiers

SABINE BARING-GOULD

ARTHUR SULLIVAN

1. On-ward, Christian sol - diers! Marching as to war, With the
2. Like a might-y ar - my Moves the Church of God; Broth-ers,
3. Crowns and thrones may per - ish, King-doms rise and wane; But the
4. On-ward, then, ye peo - ple! Join our hap - py throng; Blend with

cross of Je - sus Go-ing on be - fore. Christ, the roy - al Mas-ter,
we are treading Where the saints have trod. We are not di - vid - ed;
Church of Je - sus Con-stant will re - main. Gates of hell can nev - er
ours your voic - es In the tri-umph song. Glo - ry, laud, and hon - or

Leads a-gainst the foe; For-ward in - to bat-tle, See, His ban-ners go!
All one bod - y we: One in hope and doc-trine, One in char - i - ty.
'Gainst that Church prevail; We have Christ's own promise, Which can never fail.
Un - to Christ, the King; This thro' countless a - ges Men and an-gels sing.

CHORUS

On-ward, Chris-tian sol - diers! March-ing as to war,

With the cross of Je - sus Go - ing on be - fore.

381 Such Love

C. Bishop

Robert Harkness

1. That God should love a sinner such as I, Should yearn to change my
2. That Christ should join so free-ly in the scheme, Al-though it meant His
3. That for a will-ful out-cast such as I The Fa-ther planned, the
4. And now He takes me to His heart—a son; He asks me not to

sor-row in-to bliss, Nor rest till He had planned to bring me nigh,
death on Cal-va-ry— Did ev-er hu-man tongue find no-bler theme
Sav-iour bled and died, Re-demp-tion for a worth-less slave to buy,
fill a servant's place. The "far-off coun-try" wan-d'rings all are done;

Chorus

How won-der-ful is love like this!
Than love di-vine that ran-somed me?
Who long had law and grace de-fied!   Such love,———— such
Wide-o-pen are His arms of grace.   Such love,

won-drous love! Such love,   such won-drous love! That God should
Such love,

love a sin-ner such as I, How won-der-ful is love like this!

382 Pentecostal Power

CHARLOTTE G. HOMER

CHAS. H. GABRIEL

1. Lord, as of old at Pen - te - cost Thou didst Thy pow'r dis - play,
2. For might - y works for Thee, pre - pare And strengthen ev - 'ry heart;
3. All self con - sume, all sin de - stroy! With ear - nest zeal en - due
4. Speak, Lord. Be - fore Thy throne we wait; Thy prom - ise we be - lieve,

With cleans-ing, pu - ri - fy - ing flame De - scend on us to - day.
Come, take pos - ses - sion of Thine own, And nev - er - more de - part.
Each wait - ing heart to work for Thee; O Lord, our faith re - new!
And will not let Thee go un - til The bless-ing we re - ceive.

CHORUS

Lord, send the old-time pow'r, The Pen - te - cos - tal pow'r! Thy floodgates of

bless-ing on us throw o - pen wide! Lord, send the old - time pow'r, the

Pen-te-cos-tal pow'r, That sinners be con-vert-ed and Thy name glo-ri-fied!

383 My Mother's Old Bible Is True

D. M. S.

D. M. SHANKS

1. My moth-er's old Bi - ble, her treas-ure di-vine, So dear to her heart
2. My moth-er's old Bi - ble, God's mes-sage of love, That guid-ed her safe-
3. It tells of a Sav-iour who suf-fered for me, Who for my trans-gres-
4. "This pre-cious old Bi - ble," she told me one day, "Is God's ho - ly Word

and so pre-cious to mine, Each day growing sweeter, more fade-less and new—
ly to heav-en a-bove, Is lead-ing me on-ward and up-ward to God,
sions was nailed to a tree. It tells how He conquered death, hell, and the grave,
and will not pass a-way. 'Twill comfort, sustain you, and shield from the blast;

CHORUS

My mother's old Bi-ble so precious and true.
In paths that my Saviour be - fore me has trod.
And now at God's right hand has power to save.
This pre-cious old Bi-ble will tri-umph at last."

My mother's old Bi-ble is

true. My mother's old Bi - ble is true. My guide to that

'tis true. 'tis true.

shore where I'll meet her once more, My mother's old Bi - ble is true.

'tis true.

384 Sunlight, Sunlight

J. W. Van De Venter

W. S. Weeden

1. I wan-dered in the shades of night, Till Je - sus came to me,
2. Tho' clouds may gath - er in the sky, And bil - lows 'round me roll,
3. While walk-ing in the light of God, I sweet com-mun - ion find;
4. I cross the wide-ex - tend - ed fields, I jour - ney o'er the plain,
5. Soon I shall see Him as He is, The Light that came to me;

And with the sun - light of His love Bid all my dark-ness flee.
How - ev - er dark the world may be, I've sun-light in my soul.
I press with ho - ly vig - or on, And leave the world be-hind.
And in the sun - light of His love I reap the gold - en grain.
Be - hold the bright-ness of His face Thro'-out e - ter - ni - ty.

CHORUS

Sun-light, sun - light in my soul to - day!
to - day, yes,
Sun-light, sun-light

all a-long the way!
nar-row way!
Since the Sav-iour found me, took a-way my

sin,
load of sin,
I have had the sun - light of His love with - in.

385 Faith Is the Victory

JOHN H. YATES

IRA D. SANKEY

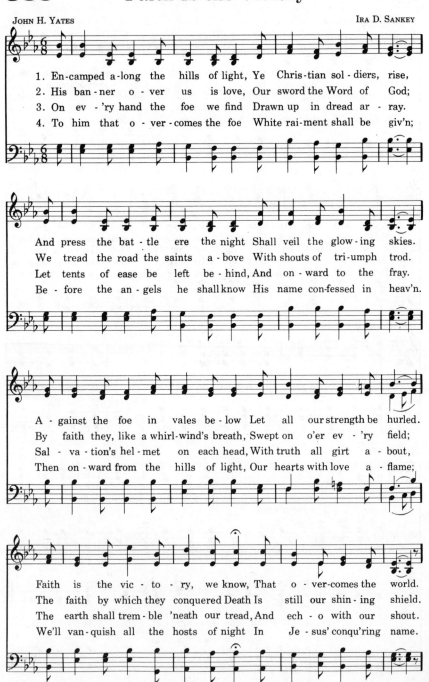

1. En-camped a-long the hills of light, Ye Chris-tian sol-diers, rise,
2. His ban-ner o-ver us is love, Our sword the Word of God;
3. On ev-'ry hand the foe we find Drawn up in dread ar-ray.
4. To him that o-ver-comes the foe White rai-ment shall be giv'n;

And press the bat-tle ere the night Shall veil the glow-ing skies.
We tread the road the saints a-bove With shouts of tri-umph trod.
Let tents of ease be left be-hind, And on-ward to the fray.
Be-fore the an-gels he shall know His name con-fessed in heav'n.

A-gainst the foe in vales be-low Let all our strength be hurled.
By faith they, like a whirl-wind's breath, Swept on o'er ev-'ry field;
Sal-va-tion's hel-met on each head, With truth all girt a-bout,
Then on-ward from the hills of light, Our hearts with love a-flame;

Faith is the vic-to-ry, we know, That o-ver-comes the world.
The faith by which they conquered Death Is still our shin-ing shield.
The earth shall trem-ble 'neath our tread, And ech-o with our shout.
We'll van-quish all the hosts of night In Je-sus' conqu'ring name.

Faith Is the Victory

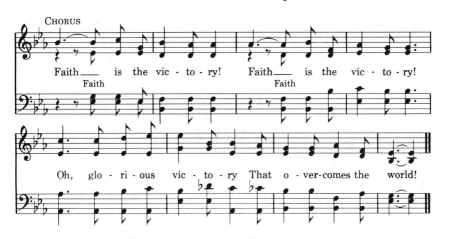

CHORUS

Faith___ is the vic - to - ry! Faith___ is the vic - to - ry!
Faith   Faith

Oh, glo - ri - ous vic - to - ry That o - ver-comes the world!

386 Holy, Holy, Holy, Lord God Almighty

REGINALD HEBER   JOHN B. DYKES

1. Ho - ly, Ho - ly, Ho - ly, Lord God Al - might - y! Ear - ly in the
2. Ho - ly, Ho - ly, Ho - ly! All the saints adore Thee, Casting down their
3. Ho - ly, Ho - ly, Ho - ly! Tho' the darkness hide Thee, Tho' the eye of
4. Ho - ly, Ho - ly, Ho - ly! Lord God Al - might - y! All Thy works shall

morn - ing our song shall rise to Thee. Ho - ly, Ho - ly, Ho - ly!
gold - en crowns a - round the glass - y sea; Cher - u - bim and ser - a - phim
sin - ful man Thy glo - ry may not see, On - ly Thou art ho - ly;
praise Thy name in earth, and sky, and sea. Ho - ly, Ho - ly, Ho - ly!

Mer - ci-ful and Might - y! God in Three Per - sons, bless-ed Trin - i - ty!
fall-ing down be-fore Thee, Which wert, and art, and ev - er-more shalt be.
there is none be-side Thee Per - fect in pow'r, in love, in pu - ri - ty.
Mer - ci-ful and Might - y! God in Three Per - sons, bless-ed Trin - i - ty!

387 Sweeping This Way

Mrs. C. H. Good
AUTHOR OF CHORUS UNKNOWN

J. W. Van De Venter
ARR. BY HALDOR LILLENAS

1. O - ver the hill - tops, down from the skies, Com-ing from glo - ry—lift up your
2. As He has prom-ised so shall it be: Blessings from glo-ry on you and
3. Prophets have told it: in the last days Hearts shall be filled with glo - ri - ous
4. Tar - ry for pow - er; this is our need. Pa - tient-ly la-bor, sow-ing the

eyes! While we are watch -ing and while we pray, A might - y re-
me; Wa - ters a - bun - dant, floods to o'er - flow. A might - y re-
praise; Our sons and daugh-ters both shall pro - claim The news of re-
seed; Soon comes the har - vest, glo - ri - ous day! A might - y re-

CHORUS

viv - al is sweep-ing this way.
viv - al is com - ing, I know.
demp-tion thro' His great name. Sweep-ing this way, yes, sweep-ing this
viv - al is sweep-ing this way.

way, A might-y re - viv - al is sweep-ing this way. Keep on be-

liev-ing; trust and o - bey. A might-y re - viv - al is sweep-ing this way.

The Blood-washed Pilgrim

ANON.

1. I saw a Blood-washed pil-grim, A sin - ner saved by grace,
2. I saw him in the fur-nace. He doubt - ed not nor feared,
3. 'Mid storms, and clouds, and tri - als, In pris - on, at the stake,
4. I saw him o - ver - com - ing, Thro' all the swell - ing strife,

Up - on the King's great high-way With peace - ful, shin - ing face.
And in the flames be - side him The Son of God ap -peared.
He leaped for joy, re - joic - ing 'Twas all for Je - sus' sake.
Un - til he crossed the thresh-old Of God's e - ter - nal life.

Temp - ta - tions sore be - set him, But noth - ing could af - fright.
Tho' sev - en times 'twas heat - ed With all the tempt - er's might,
That God should count him wor - thy Was such su - preme de - light,
The crown, the throne, the scep - ter, The name, the stone so white

He said: "The yoke is eas - y; The bur - den, it is light."
He said: "The yoke is eas - y; The bur - den, it is light."
He cried: "The yoke is eas - y; The bur - den is so light."
Were his who found in Je - sus The yoke and bur - den light.

CHORUS

Then palms of vic - to - ry, crowns of glo - ry, Palms of vic - to - ry I shall wear.

389 Constantly Abiding

Mrs. W. L. M.

MRS. WILL L. MURPHY

1. There's a peace in my heart that the world nev-er gave, A peace it can-
2. All the world seemed to sing of a Sav-iour and King When peace sweet-ly
3. This treas-ure I have in a tem-ple of clay, While here on His

not take a - way. Tho' the tri - als of life may sur-round like a cloud,
came to my heart. Trou-bles all fled a - way and my night turned to day.
foot-stool I roam; But He's com-ing to take me some glo - ri - ous day

CHORUS

I've a peace that has come there to stay! Con - stant-ly a-
Bless-ed Je - sus, how glo-rious Thou art! Constantly a-bid-ing,
O - ver there to my heav-en - ly home! Constantly a-bid-ing,

bid - ing, Je - sus is mine;
con-stant-ly a - bid-ing, Je-sus is mine, yes, Je - sus is mine;

Con - stant-ly a - bid - ing, rap - ture di-
Constant-ly a-bid - ing, con-stant-ly a-bid-ing, rap-ture di-vine, oh,

Constantly Abiding

vine! He nev-er leaves me lone - ly; whis-pers,
rap-ture di-vine! He nev-er leaves me, nev-er leaves me lonely; whis-pers,

oh, so kind: "I will nev-er leave thee." Je - sus is mine.
whis-pers, oh, so kind: nev-er leave thee." Je-sus, Je-sus is mine.

390 How Sweet the Name of Jesus Sounds!

JOHN NEWTON   THOMAS HASTINGS

1. How sweet the name of Je - sus sounds In a be - liev - er's
2. It makes the wound-ed spir - it whole, And calms the trou - bled
3. Dear name! the Rock on which I build, My Shield and Hid - ing
4. Je - sus, my Shep-herd, Broth-er, Friend, My Proph-et, Priest, and

ear! It soothes his sor - rows, heals his wounds, And
breast. 'Tis man - na to the hun - gry soul, And
Place; My nev - er - fail - ing Treas - ury, filled With
King, My Lord, my Life, my Way, my End, Ac-

drives a - way his fear, And drives a - way his fear.
to the wea - ry, rest, And to the wea - ry, rest.
bound - less stores of grace, With bound-less stores of grace!
cept the praise I bring, Ac - cept the praise I bring.

391 Sweet Peace, the Gift of God's Love

P. P. B.

P. P. BILHORN

1. There comes to my heart one sweet strain (sweet strain), A glad and a joy-ous re-frain (re-frain); I sing it a-gain and a-gain: Sweet peace,

2. Thro' Christ on the cross peace was made (was made); My debt by His death was all paid (all paid). No oth-er foun-da-tion is laid For peace,

3. When Je-sus as Lord I had crowned (had crowned), My heart with this peace did a-bound (a-bound). In Him the rich bless-ing I found, Sweet peace,

4. In Je-sus for peace I a-bide (a-bide); And as I keep close to His side (His side), There's noth-ing but peace doth be-tide, Sweet peace, the gift of God's love.

CHORUS

Peace, peace, sweet peace! Won-der-ful gift from a-bove (a-bove)! Oh, won-der-ful, won-der-ful peace! Sweet peace, the gift of God's love!

392 The Closer I Walk

Copyright 1931 by Lillenas Publishing Co.

H. L.

HALDOR LILLENAS

1. A Sav - iour have I more pre - cious to me Than all of earth's
2. If rug - ged the way that I must pur - sue, If dark be the
3. My heart sings a glad and ju - bi - lant song, As on - ward we
4. I feast on His truth, His rich - es of grace; And dai - ly His

friend-ships ev - er could be. His rich - es of grace more clear-ly I see
night that I jour - ney thro', My fears all de -part, my tears are but few
go life's path-way a-long. My hope is renewed, my faith becomes strong,
count-less mer - cies I trace, Be - hold-ing the glo - ry light of His face,

CHORUS

The clos - er I walk to Him. The clos - er I walk the

sweet - er He seems. Much fair - er is He than all of my dreams. His

love lights my way when path-ways are dim, The clos - er I walk to Him.

393 Tell It to Jesus

J. E. RANKIN

E. S. LORENZ

1. Are you wea - ry, are you heav - y - heart - ed?
2. Do the tears flow down your cheeks unbidden?
3. Do you fear the gath - 'ring clouds of sor - row?
4. Are you trou - bled at the tho't of dy - ing?

Tell it to Je - sus,

Tell it to Je - sus.

Are you griev - ing o - ver joys de - part - ed?
Have you sins that to men's eyes are hid - den?
Are you anx - ious what shall be to - mor - row?
For Christ's com - ing king - dom are you sigh - ing?

CHORUS

Tell it to Je - sus a - lone. Tell it to Je - sus, Tell it to Je - sus.

He is a Friend that's well known. You've no oth - er

such a friend or broth - er. Tell it to Je - sus a - lone.

394 The Comforter Has Come to Abide

H. L.

HALDOR LILLENAS

1. Gra - cious is the prom-ise of our liv - ing Lord: "I will not leave you
2. Cleans-ing, pu - ri - fy - ing like a liv - ing flame, He comes the heart to
3. This God's bless-ed will that we should ho - ly be, And to His ser-vice
4. Com - ing like the rain up - on the thirst - y ground, Re - viv-ing like a

com - fort - less." That prom-ise is ful-filled, ac-cord-ing to His word; He
bless and fill; To make us more than con - quer-ors thro' Je-sus' name, Ac-
set a - part; From sin and its pol - lu - tion set at lib - er - ty, A
sum - mer show'r; The Com - fort-er will come, where yielded hearts are found, In

CHORUS

comes our wait-ing souls to bless.
cord - ing to His ho - ly will.
pu - ri - fied and per - fect heart.   He has come, He has come.
might - y Pen - te - cos - tal pow'r.

The Com - fort - er has come to a - bide. _____ He has
                                            a - bide.

made my heart His home. The Com-fort-er has come to a - bide.

395 Conquerors Through the Blood

Mrs. C. H. M.

Mrs. C. H. Morris

1. Con-quer-ors and o-ver-com-ers now are we; Thro' the pre-cious blood of
2. In the name of Israel's God we'll on-ward press, O - ver-com-ing sin and
3. Un - to him that o - ver-com-eth shall be giv'n Here to eat of hid-den

Christ we've vic - to - ry. If the Lord be for us, we can nev - er fail;
all un - right-eous-ness. Not to us but un - to Him the praise shall be
man - na sent from heav'n; O - ver yon-der he the vic-tor's palm shall bear,

Chorus

Nothing 'gainst His mighty pow - er can pre - vail. Con - quer-ors are
For sal - va - tion and for Blood-bought vic-to - ry.
And a robe of white and golden crown shall wear. Conquerors are we,

we, Thro' the Blood, thro' the Blood. God will
con-quer-ors are we, Thro' the Blood, thro' the Blood.

give _____ us vic - to - ry, Thro' the Blood, thro' the
God will give vic - to - ry, Thro' the Blood,

Conquerors Through the Blood

Blood.
thro' the Blood.

Thro' the Lamb for sin-ners slain, Yet who lives and reigns a-gain,

More than con - quer-ors are we, More than con - quer-ors are we.

396 I Need Thee Every Hour

ANNIE S. HAWKS

ROBERT LOWRY

1. I need Thee ev -'ry hour, Most gra - cious Lord; No ten - der voice like
2. I need Thee ev -'ry hour; Stay Thou near - by. Temptations lose their
3. I need Thee ev -'ry hour, In joy or pain; Come quick-ly and a-
4. I need Thee ev -'ry hour, Most Ho - ly One. Oh, make me Thine in-

CHORUS

Thine Can peace af - ford.
pow'r When Thou art nigh.
bide, Or life is vain.
deed, Thou bless - ed Son!

I need Thee, oh, I need Thee; Ev -'ry hour I

need Thee! Oh, bless me now, my Sav-iour; I come to Thee!

397 Come and Dine

C. B. W.

C. B. WIDMEYER

1. Je - sus has a ta - ble spread Where the saints of God are fed.
2. The dis - ci - ples came to land, Thus o - bey - ing Christ's com - mand,
3. Soon the Lamb will take His bride To be ev - er at His side.

He in - vites His cho - sen peo - ple, "Come and dine." With His man - na He doth
For the Mas - ter called to them, "Oh, come and dine." There they found their hearts' de-
All the host of heav - en will as - sem - bled be. Oh, 'twill be a glo - rious

feed And supplies our ev 'ry need. Oh, 'tis sweet to sup with Je - sus all the time!
sire, Bread and fish up - on the fire. Thus He sat - is - fies the hun - gry ev - 'ry time.
sight, All the saints in spotless white; And with Je - sus they will feast e - ter - nal - ly.

CHORUS

"Come and dine," the Master calleth; "Come and dine (Oh, come and dine)." You may feast at

Je - sus' ta - ble all the time. (Oh, come and dine!) He who fed the mul - ti - tude,

Come and Dine

Turned the wa - ter in - to wine, To the hun-gry call-eth now,"Come and dine."

398 Hallelujah! Amen!

HENRIETTA E. BLAIR

ARR. BY WM. J. KIRKPATRICK

1. How oft in ho - ly con - verse With Christ, my Lord, a - lone,
2. They passed thro' toils and tri - als And, though the strife was long,
3. My soul takes up the cho - rus And, press - ing on my way,
4. Thro' grace I soon shall con - quer, And reach my home on high;

I seem to hear the mil - lions That sing a - round His throne:
They share the vic - tor's con - quest, And sing the vic - tor's song:
Com - mun - ing still with Je - sus, I sing from day to day:
And thro' e - ter - nal a - ges I'll shout be - yond the sky:

CHORUS

Hal - le - lu - jah! A - men! Hal - le - lu - jah! A - men!

poco rit.

Hal - le - lu - jah! A - men! A - men! A - men!

399   Blessed Be the Fountain

E. R. Latta

H. S. Perkins

1. Bless-ed be the foun-tain of Blood, To a world of sin-ners re-vealed.
2. Thorn-y was the crown that He wore, And the cross His bod-y o'er-came;
3. Fa-ther, I have wandered from Thee; Of-ten has my heart gone a-stray;

Bless-ed be the dear Son of God—On-ly by His stripes we are healed.
Griev-ous were the sor-rows He bore, But He suf-fered thus not in vain.
Crim-son do my sins seem to me—Wa-ter can-not wash them a-way.

Tho' I've wandered far from His fold, Bringing to my heart pain and woe,
May I to that foun-tain be led, Made to cleanse my sins here be-low;
Je-sus, to that foun-tain of Thine, Lean-ing on Thy prom-ise I go;

Wash me in the blood of the Lamb,
Wash me in the blood that He shed, And I shall be whit-er than snow.
Cleanse me by Thy wash-ing di-vine,

Chorus

Whit - er than the snow,   Whit - er
Whit-er than the snow, whit-er than the snow, Whit-er than the snow,

Blessed Be the Fountain

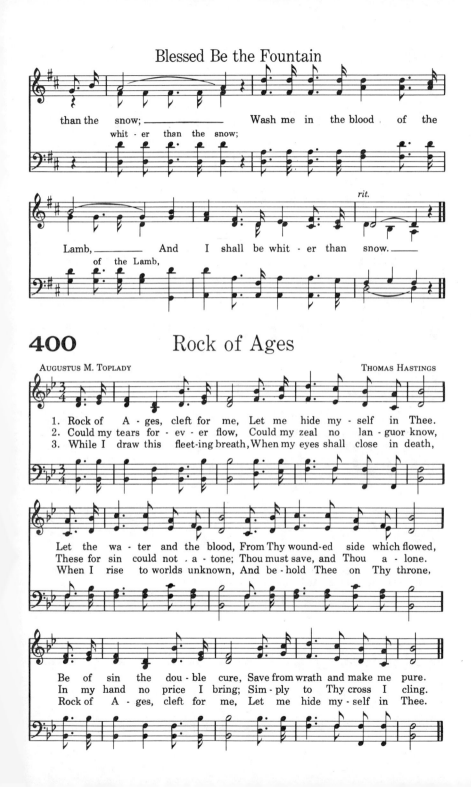

than the snow; _____ Wash me in the blood of the
whit - er than the snow;

Lamb, _____ And I shall be whit - er than snow. ____
of the Lamb,

rit.

400   Rock of Ages

AUGUSTUS M. TOPLADY   THOMAS HASTINGS

1. Rock of A - ges, cleft for me, Let me hide my - self in Thee.
2. Could my tears for - ev - er flow, Could my zeal no lan - guor know,
3. While I draw this fleet-ing breath, When my eyes shall close in death,

Let the wa - ter and the blood, From Thy wound-ed side which flowed,
These for sin could not . a - tone; Thou must save, and Thou a - lone.
When I rise to worlds unknown, And be - hold Thee on Thy throne,

Be of sin the dou - ble cure, Save from wrath and make me pure.
In my hand no price I bring; Sim - ply to Thy cross I cling.
Rock of A - ges, cleft for me, Let me hide my - self in Thee.

401 A World-wide Revival

Mrs. C. H. M.　　　　　　　　　　　　　　　　　　　Mrs. C. H. Morris

1. For a world-wide re-viv-al, Bless-ed Mas-ter, we pray.
2. Send the "show-ers of bless-ing," As de-clared in Thy Word.
3. There's a "sound of a go-ing In the mul-ber-ry trees,"

Let the pow'r of the high-est Be up-on us to-day;
Let the "Spir-it of prom-ise" On all flesh be out-poured;
News of na-tions a-wak-ing Borne up-on ev-'ry breeze;

For this world, dear-ly pur-chased By the blood of God's Son, Back from
Send the "lat-ter rain" on us, Till the land o-ver-flows, Till the
For the pray'rs of His chil-dren, God in mer-cy doth own. The re-

Sa-tan's do-min-ion And from sin must be won.
des-ert, re-joic-ing, Blos-soms forth as the rose. Send the pow'r, O Lord.
viv-al's be-gin-ning, And the power's coming down.

Chorus

Send the pow'r, O Lord. Send the Ho-ly Ghost pow-er; let it

A World-wide Revival

now be out-poured. Send it surg-ing and sweep-ing like the waves of the

sea. Send a world-wide re-viv-al, and be-gin it in me.

402 Jesus, Saviour, Pilot Me

EDWARD HOPPER

J. E. GOULD

1. Je-sus, Sav-iour, pi-lot me O-ver life's tem-pes-tuous sea.
2. As a moth-er stills her child, Thou canst hush the o-cean wild;
3. When at last I near the shore, And the fear-ful break-ers roar

Un-known waves be-fore me roll, Hid-ing rocks and treach-'rous shoal.
Bois-t'rous waves o-bey Thy will When Thou say'st to them, "Be still!"
'Twixt me and the peace-ful rest, Then, while lean-ing on Thy breast,

Chart and com-pass came from Thee; Je-sus, Sav-iour, pi-lot me.
Won-drous Sov-'reign of the sea, Je-sus, Sav-iour, pi-lot me.
May I hear Thee say to me, "Fear not, I will pi-lot thee."

403 It Never Runs Dry

MRS. C. H. M.

MRS. C. H. MORRIS

1. Heark-en to-day to the blest in-vi-ta-tion Giv-en in love by our Fa-ther on
2. Look! for its source is in Calvary's mountain, Where the dear Saviour was lifted on
3. Saints of all a-ges its vir-tue have tested; No oth-er hope of sal-va-tion is

high. Come to the won-der-ful stream of sal-va-tion; Drink of the fountain that
high; Pure and exhaustless it springs from the fountain, Life-giv-ing cur-rent that
nigh. Here where our fa-thers and mothers have feasted We too may drink, for it

CHORUS

It nev-er_____ runs dry._____ It
nev-er runs dry.
It nev-er, no nev-er runs dry.

nev-er_____ runs dry._____ This won-der-ful stream of sal-
It nev-er, nev-er runs dry.

va-tion,_____ It nev-er_____ runs dry._____ Tho'
sal-va-tion, It nev-er runs dry, nev-er runs dry.

It Never Runs Dry

mil-lions their thirst are now slaking,__ It nev-er runs dry;__ And
now slak-ing, It nev-er, nev-er runs dry;

millions may still come par-tak-ing. It nev-er__ runs dry.__
par-tak-ing. nev-er runs dry. It nev-er runs dry.

404   Have Thine Own Way, Lord

Copyright 1907. Renewal 1935. Hope Publishing Co., Owner
Used by permission

ADELAIDE A. POLLARD   GEO. C. STEBBINS

1. Have Thine own way, Lord! Have Thine own way! Thou art the
2. Have Thine own way, Lord! Have Thine own way! Search me and
3. Have Thine own way, Lord! Have Thine own way! Wound-ed and
4. Have Thine own way, Lord! Have Thine own way! Hold o'er my

Pot - ter; I am the clay. Mold me and make me Af - ter Thy
try me, Mas - ter, to - day! Whit - er than snow, Lord, Wash me just
wea - ry, Help me, I pray! Pow - er—all pow - er — Sure - ly is
be - ing Ab - so - lute sway! Fill with Thy Spir - it Till all shall

will, While I am wait - ing, Yield - ed and still.
now, As in Thy pres - ence Hum - bly I bow.
Thine! Touch me and heal me, Sav - iour di - vine!
see Christ on - ly, al - ways, Liv - ing in me!

405 Hallelujah for the Blood

Mrs. C. H. M.

Mrs. C. H. Morris

1. Hal-le-lu-jah for the Blood, for the sin-cleans-ing foun-tain! For the
2. Hal-le-lu-jah for the Blood! Sing for joy, all ye na-tions, And re-
3. Hal-le-lu-jah for the Blood! Hal-le-lu-jah for - ev - er! We shall

Lamb has been slain, and the ran-som price paid. Ful-ly can-celed was the
joice that the work of re-demp-tion is done. Here is par-don free for
sing it a-new in the king-dom of God, Where the anthems of de-

debt when on Cal-va-ry's moun-tain All the sins of this world up-on
all, and a per-fect sal-va-tion Thro' the sin-cleans-ing blood of the
light shall be si-lent, no, nev-er. Ev-er-more hal-le-lu-jah for

p Chorus

Je-sus were laid.
Cru-ci-fied One. There was no arm to save, there was no eye to pit-y,
Christ and the Blood!

cresc.

mf

Un-til Je-sus, our Sav-iour, from glo-ry came down. He was might-y to

Hallelujah for the Blood

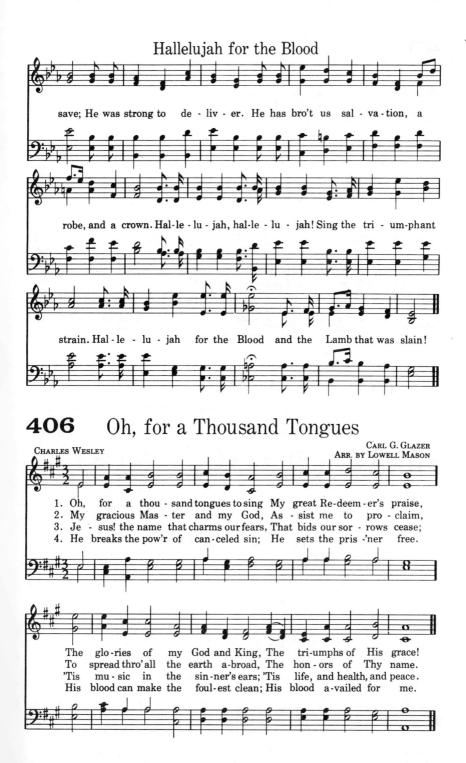

save; He was strong to de - liv - er. He has bro't us sal - va - tion, a
robe, and a crown. Hal - le - lu - jah, hal - le - lu - jah! Sing the tri - um - phant
strain. Hal - le - lu - jah for the Blood and the Lamb that was slain!

406   Oh, for a Thousand Tongues

CHARLES WESLEY

CARL G. GLAZER
ARR. BY LOWELL MASON

1. Oh, for a thou - sand tongues to sing My great Re - deem - er's praise,
2. My gracious Mas - ter and my God, As - sist me to pro - claim,
3. Je - sus! the name that charms our fears, That bids our sor - rows cease;
4. He breaks the pow'r of can - celed sin; He sets the pris -'ner free.

The glo - ries of my God and King, The tri - umphs of His grace!
To spread thro' all the earth a - broad, The hon - ors of Thy name.
'Tis mu - sic in the sin - ner's ears; 'Tis life, and health, and peace.
His blood can make the foul - est clean; His blood a - vailed for me.

407 The Lily of the Valley

C. W. Fry

ENGLISH MELODY

1. I've found a Friend in Je-sus. He's ev-'ry-thing to me. He's the
2. He all my griefs has tak-en, and all my sor-rows borne. In tempt-
3. He'll nev-er, nev-er leave me, nor yet for-sake me here, While I

fair-est of ten thou-sand to my soul. The Lil-y of the Val-ley, in
ta-tion He's my strong and might-y Tow'r. I've all for Him for-sak-en; I've
live by faith and do His bless-ed will. A wall of fire a-bout me, I've

Him a-lone I see All I need to cleanse and make me fully whole. In sorrow He's my
all my idols torn From my heart, and now He keeps me by His pow'r. Tho' all the world for-
nothing now to fear. With His manna He my hungry soul shall fill. Then sweeping up to

Com-fort; in trou-ble He's my Stay. He tells me ev-'ry care on Him to
sake me, and Sa-tan tempt me sore, Thro' Je-sus I shall safe-ly reach the
glo-ry, I'll see His bless-ed face, Where riv-ers of de-light shall ev-er

roll. (Hal-le-lu-jah!)
goal. He's the Lil-y of the Val-ley, the bright and Morning Star. He's the
roll.

The Lily of the Valley

CHORUS

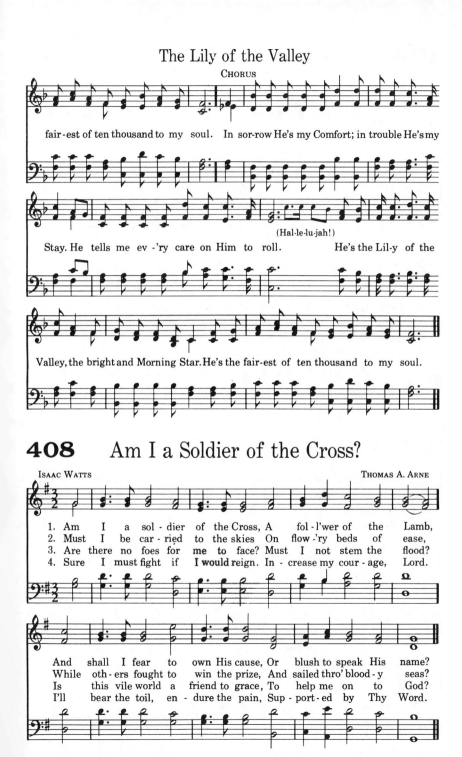

fair-est of ten thousand to my soul. In sor-row He's my Comfort; in trouble He's my

Stay. He tells me ev-'ry care on Him to roll. He's the Lil-y of the

(Hal-le-lu-jah!)

Valley, the bright and Morning Star. He's the fair-est of ten thousand to my soul.

408 Am I a Soldier of the Cross?

ISAAC WATTS   THOMAS A. ARNE

1. Am I a sol-dier of the Cross, A fol-l'wer of the Lamb,
2. Must I be car-ried to the skies On flow-'ry beds of ease,
3. Are there no foes for me to face? Must I not stem the flood?
4. Sure I must fight if I would reign. In-crease my cour-age, Lord.

And shall I fear to own His cause, Or blush to speak His name?
While oth-ers fought to win the prize, And sailed thro' blood-y seas?
Is this vile world a friend to grace, To help me on to God?
I'll bear the toil, en-dure the pain, Sup-port-ed by Thy Word.

409 It Is for Us All Today

L. L. P.

REV. L. L. PICKETT

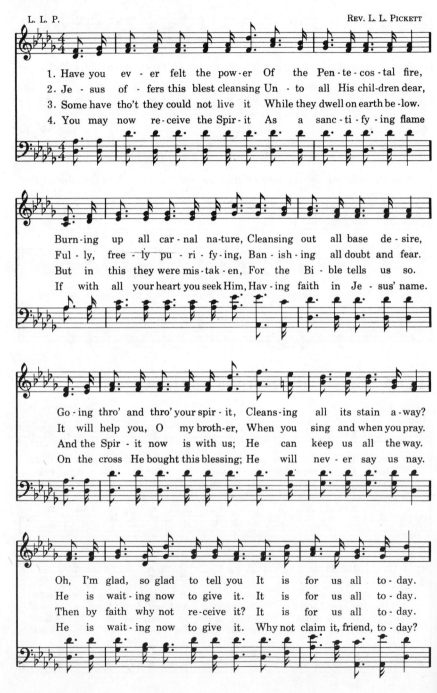

1. Have you ev-er felt the pow-er Of the Pen-te-cos-tal fire,
2. Je-sus of-fers this blest cleansing Un-to all His chil-dren dear,
3. Some have tho't they could not live it While they dwell on earth be-low.
4. You may now re-ceive the Spir-it As a sanc-ti-fy-ing flame

Burn-ing up all car-nal na-ture, Cleansing out all base de-sire,
Ful-ly, free-ly pu-ri-fy-ing, Ban-ish-ing all doubt and fear.
But in this they were mis-tak-en, For the Bi-ble tells us so.
If with all your heart you seek Him, Hav-ing faith in Je-sus' name.

Go-ing thro' and thro' your spir-it, Cleans-ing all its stain a-way?
It will help you, O my broth-er, When you sing and when you pray.
And the Spir-it now is with us; He can keep us all the way.
On the cross He bought this blessing; He will nev-er say us nay.

Oh, I'm glad, so glad to tell you It is for us all to-day.
He is wait-ing now to give it. It is for us all to-day.
Then by faith why not re-ceive it? It is for us all to-day.
He is wait-ing now to give it. Why not claim it, friend, to-day?

It Is for Us All Today

It- is for _____ us all to-day _____ If we
It is for us all for us all to-day

trust _____ and tru - ly pray. Consecrate to Christ your all,
If we trust and pray, if we tru - ly trust and pray.

And up - on the Sav-iour call. Bless God, it is for us all to - day (to-day)!

410 Blest Feast of Love Divine

Sir Edward Denney   H. G. Nageli

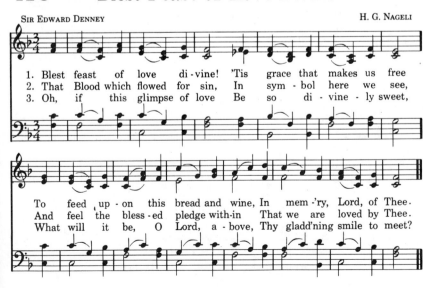

1. Blest feast of love di - vine! 'Tis grace that makes us free
2. That Blood which flowed for sin, In sym - bol here we see,
3. Oh, if this glimpse of love Be so di - vine - ly sweet,

To feed up - on this bread and wine, In mem - 'ry, Lord, of Thee.
And feel the bless - ed pledge with-in That we are loved by Thee.
What will it be, O Lord, a - bove, Thy gladd'ning smile to meet?

411 Seeking the Lost

W. A. O.

W. A. OGDEN

1. Seek-ing the lost, yes, kind-ly en-treat-ing Wan-der-ers on the moun-tain a-stray; "Come un-to Me," His mes-sage re-peat-ing, Words of the Mas-ter speak-ing to-day.

2. Seek-ing the lost, and point-ing to Je-sus Souls that are weak and hearts that are sore; Lead-ing them forth in ways of sal-va-tion, Show-ing the path to life ev-er-more.

3. Thus I would go on mis-sions of mer-cy, Fol-low-ing Christ from day un-to day; Cheer-ing the faint, and rais-ing the fall-en; Point-ing the lost to Je-sus, the Way.

CHORUS

Go-ing a-far up-on the moun-tain, Bring-ing the wan-d'rer back a-gain, back a-gain, In-to the fold

Go-ing a-far up-on the moun-tain, Bring-ing the wan d'rer back a-gain, In-to the fold

Seeking the Lost

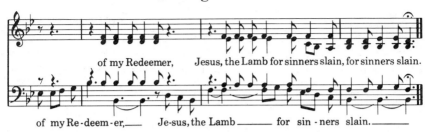

of my Redeemer, Jesus, the Lamb for sinners slain, for sinners slain.

of my Re-deem-er,— Je-sus, the Lamb —— for sin-ners slain.——

412 Let the Lower Lights Be Burning

P. P. B.

P. P. Bliss

1. Bright-ly beams our Fa-ther's mer-cy From His light-house ev-er-more;
2. Dark the night of sin has set-tled, Loud the an-gry bil-lows roar;
3. Trim your fee-ble lamp, my broth-er! Some poor sail-or, tem-pest-tossed,

But to us He gives the keep-ing Of the lights a-long the shore.
Ea-ger eyes are watch-ing, long-ing For the lights a-long the shore.
Try-ing now to make the har-bor, In the dark-ness may be lost.

CHORUS

Let the low-er lights be burn-ing! Send a gleam a-cross the wave!

Some poor faint-ing, strug-gling sea-man You may res-cue, you may save.

413 There Is a Fountain

WILLIAM COWPER
CHORUS BY MRS. J. T. B.

ARR. BY MRS. JOHN T. BENSON

1. There is a foun - tain filled with blood Drawn from Im-man-uel's veins; And sin-ners, plunged be-neath that flood, Lose all their guilt-y stains.
2. The dy - ing thief re-joiced to see That foun - tain in his day; And there may I, tho' vile as he, Wash all my sins a - way.
3. E'er since by faith I saw the stream Thy flow - ing wounds supply, Re-deem-ing love has been my theme And shall be till I die.
4. Then in a no - bler, sweet-er song I'll sing Thy pow'r to save, When this poor lisp - ing, stamm'ring tongue Lies si - lent in the grave.

1. There is a foun-tain filled with blood Drawn from Im-man-uel's veins; And sin-ners, plunged be-neath that flood,

CHORUS

I've been re - deemed. I've been re - deemed. I've been re - deemed. I've been re - deemed. I've been washed in the blood of the

and so have I. and so have I. and so have I. and so have I.

There Is a Fountain

Lamb. I've been washed in the blood of the Lamb. I've been
Hal - le - lu - jah!
Praise the Lord!

washed in the blood of the Lamb that flows from Cal-va-ry.
Hal - le - lu - jah!
from Cal - va - ry.

414 Bring Them In

ALEXCENAH THOMAS

W. A. OGDEN

1. Hark, 'tis the Shepherd's voice I hear, Out in the des-ert dark and drear,
2. Who'll go and help this Shepherd kind, Help Him the wand'ring ones to find?
3. Out in the des-ert hear their cry, Out on the mountains wild and high.

Call - ing the sheep who've gone a-stray, Far from the Shepherd's fold a-way.
Who'll bring the lost ones to the fold, Where they'll be sheltered from the cold?
Hark! 'tis the Mas-ter speaks to thee, "Go, find My sheep wher-e'er they be."

CHORUS

Bring them in, Bring them in, Bring them in from the fields of sin;
Bring them in, Bring them in, Bring the wand'ring ones to Je-sus.

415 Make His Praise Glorious

Copyright 1903. Renewed 1930 by William R. Lunk
Assigned to Nazarene Publishing House

Mrs. C. H. M.   Mrs. C. H. Morris

1. Prais - es, sing praises to Je - sus, our bless-ed Re-deem-er. Let ev 'ry
2. Prais - es, sing praises! our won-der-ing eyes shall be -hold Him When in His
3. Praise for the grace which is a - ble to keep us from fall - ing, And to pre-

voice to Him now a sweet mel-o - dy raise. Come ye be - fore Him; oh,
beau-ty King Je - sus de-scendeth to reign; Com - ing in glo - ry, oh,
sent us all fault-less be-fore the white throne, 'Mid joys su - per - nal to

wor-ship and laud and a - dore Him. Lo, He is wor - thy our high-est as-
tell out the won-der-ful sto - ry! Sing, "Hal - le - lu - jah! the Sav-iour is
praise Him thro' a-ges e - ter - nal, All the redeem'd ones, the Blood-wash'd, His

CHORUS

crip-tions of praise. Make His praise glo - ri - ous, Sav - iour vic-
com-ing a - gain." Praise! sing prais - es un - to
lov'd and His own.

to - ri - ous, Through-out the world be His great name a - dored;
Je - sus, Be His ho - ly name a - dored; Oh,

Make His Praise Glorious

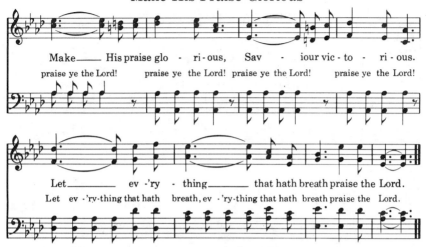

Make____ His praise glo - ri - ous, Sav - iour vic - to - ri - ous.

praise ye the Lord! praise ye the Lord! praise ye the Lord! praise ye the Lord!

Let____ ev -'ry - thing____ that hath breath praise the Lord.

Let ev -'ry-thing that hath breath, ev -'ry-thing that hath breath praise the Lord.

416 Work, for the Night Is Coming

ANNIE L. COGHILL

LOWELL MASON

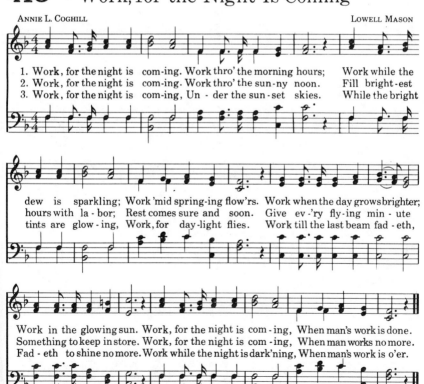

1. Work, for the night is com-ing. Work thro' the morning hours; Work while the
2. Work, for the night is com-ing. Work thro' the sun-ny noon. Fill bright-est
3. Work, for the night is com-ing, Un - der the sun-set skies. While the bright

dew is sparkling; Work 'mid spring-ing flow'rs. Work when the day grows brighter;
hours with la - bor; Rest comes sure and soon. Give ev -'ry fly-ing min - ute
tints are glow - ing, Work, for day-light flies. Work till the last beam fad - eth,

Work in the glowing sun. Work, for the night is com - ing, When man's work is done.
Something to keep in store. Work, for the night is com - ing, When man works no more.
Fad - eth to shine no more. Work while the night is dark'ning, When man's work is o'er.

417 "God's Kingdom Is at Hand"

Mrs. C. H. M.   Mrs. C. H. Morris

1. Com - mis-sioned by the Lord are we The glo-rious news to tell
2. Why will you long-er jeop-ard-ize Your nev-er-dy-ing soul,
3. With just a few more fleet-ing days, And life's work will be done.

Play in Octaves

Of God's sal-va-tion full and free, Which saves from sin and hell.
When Je-sus paid your ran-som price, And waits to make you whole?
E-ter-ni-ty draws on a-pace; Your race is al-most run.

Up - on His busi-ness here in-tent, We haste at His com-mand,
It is the Lord from heav'n who speaks In thun-der tones to-day,
The fi-nal con-sum-ma-tion nears, When time shall be no more.

Pro-claim-ing ev-'ry-where, "Re-pent; God's king-dom is at hand."
And bids you now sal-va-tion seek And turn from sin a-way.
We soon the warn-ing cry shall hear, "The Judge is at the door."

CHORUS UNISON   PARTS

We'll tell it out, ___ "God's king-dom is at hand"; ___

"God's Kingdom Is at Hand"

UNISON   PARTS

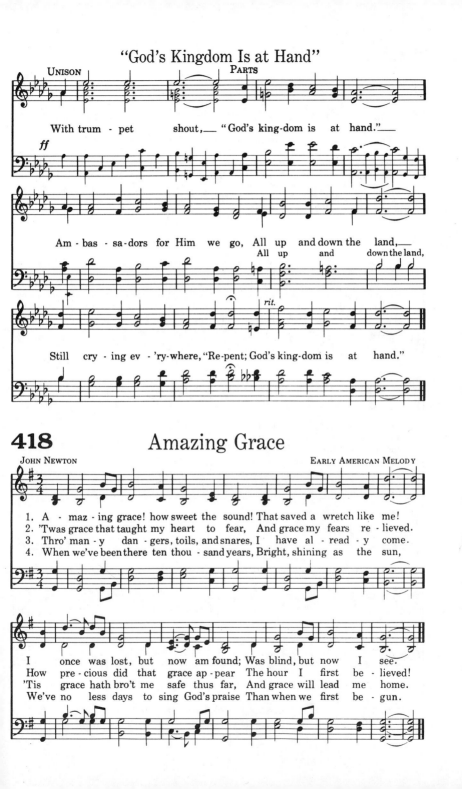

With trum - pet shout,___ "God's king-dom is at hand."___

ff

Am - bas - sa -dors for Him we go, All up and down the land,___
All up and down the land,

Still cry - ing ev - 'ry-where, "Re-pent; God's king-dom is at hand."

418   Amazing Grace

JOHN NEWTON   EARLY AMERICAN MELODY

1. A - maz - ing grace! how sweet the sound! That saved a wretch like me!
2. 'Twas grace that taught my heart to fear, And grace my fears re - lieved.
3. Thro' man - y dan - gers, toils, and snares, I have al - read - y come.
4. When we've been there ten thou - sand years, Bright, shining as the sun,

I once was lost, but now am found; Was blind, but now I see.
How pre - cious did that grace ap - pear The hour I first be - lieved!
'Tis grace hath bro't me safe thus far, And grace will lead me home.
We've no less days to sing God's praise Than when we first be - gun.

419   Moment by Moment

D. W. WHITTLE

MAY WHITTLE MOODY

1. Dy - ing with Je - sus, by death reckoned mine;   Liv - ing with Je - sus a
2. Nev - er a tri - al that He is not there,   Nev - er a bur-den that
3. Nev - er a heart-ache and nev - er a groan,   Nev - er a tear-drop and
4. Nev - er a weak-ness that He doth not feel,   Nev - er a sick-ness that

new life di - vine; Look-ing to Je - sus till glo - ry doth shine, Mo - ment by
He doth not bear, Nev - er a sor-row that He doth not share; Mo - ment by
nev - er a moan, Nev - er a dan-ger but there on the throne, Mo - ment by
He can-not heal; Mo - ment by mo-ment, in woe or in weal, Je - sus, my

CHORUS

mo-ment, O Lord, I am Thine.
mo-ment, I'm un-der His care.
mo-ment, He thinks of His own.
Sav-iour, a-bides with me still.

Mo-ment by mo-ment I'm kept in His love;

Mo-ment by mo-ment I've life from a - bove. Look-ing to Je - sus till

glo - ry doth shine, Mo-ment by mo - ment, O Lord, I am Thine.

420 Tell Me the Stories of Jesus

W. H. PARKER

F. A. CHALLINOR

1. Tell me the sto-ries of Je-sus I love to hear,
Things I would ask Him to tell me If He were here:
Scenes by the way-side, Tales of the sea—
Sto-ries of Je-sus, Tell them to me.

2. First let me hear how the chil-dren Stood round His knee;
And I shall fan-cy His bless-ing Rest-ing on me:
Words full of kind-ness, Deeds full of grace,
All in the love-light Of Je-sus' face.

3. In-to the cit-y I'd fol-low The chil-dren's band,
Wav-ing a branch of the palm tree High in my hand.
One of His her-alds, Yes, I would sing
Loud-est ho-san-nas! Je-sus is King!

4. Tell me, in ac-cents of won-der, How rolled the sea,
Toss-ing the boat in a tem-pest On Gal-i-lee!
And how the Mas-ter, Read-y and kind,
Chid-ed the bil-lows, And hushed the wind.

421 Praise Him, All Ye Little Children

ANON.   ANON.

1. Praise Him, praise Him,
2. Love Him, love Him, all ye lit - tle chil - dren. God is love, God is love.
3. Thank Him, thank Him,

Praise Him, praise Him,
Love Him, love Him, all ye lit - tle chil - dren. God is love, God is love.
Thank Him, thank Him,

422 Jesus Loves Me

ANNA B. WARNER   WM. G. BRADBURY

1. Je - sus loves me! this I know, For the Bi - ble tells me so.
2. Je - sus loves me! He who died Heav - en's gates to o - pen wide.
3. Je - sus, take this heart of mine; Make it pure, and whol - ly Thine.

CHORUS

Lit - tle ones to Him be - long, They are weak but He is strong.
He will wash a - way my sin, Let His lit - tle child come in. Yes, Je - sus
Thou hast bled and died for me; I will henceforth live for Thee.

loves me. Yes, Jesus loves me. Yes, Je - sus loves me. The Bi - ble tells me so.

423 Jesus Loves Even Me

P. P. B.

P. P. Bliss

1. I am so glad that our Fa-ther in heav'n Tells of His love in the
2. Tho' I for-get Him and wan-der a-way, Still He doth love me wher-
3. Oh, if there's on-ly one song I can sing When in His beau-ty I

Book He has giv'n. Won-der-ful things in the Bi-ble I see;
ev-er I stray. Back to His dear, lov-ing arms would I flee
see the great King, This shall my song in e-ter-ni-ty be:

Chorus

This is the dear-est, that Je-sus loves me.
When I re-mem-ber that Je-sus loves me. I am so glad that
"Oh, what a won-der that Je-sus loves me!"

Je-sus loves me, Je-sus loves me, Je-sus loves me!

I am so glad that Je-sus loves me, Je-sus loves e-ven me!

424 Saviour, While My Heart Is Tender

JOHN BURTON

GEO. C. STEBBINS

1. Sav - iour, while my heart is ten - der I would
   yield that heart to Thee; All my pow'rs to
   Thee sur - ren - der, Thine and on - ly Thine to be.

2. Take me now, Lord Je - sus, take me; Let my
   youth - ful heart be Thine. Thy de - vot - ed
   serv - ant make me; Fill my soul with love di - vine.

3. Send me, Lord, where Thou wilt send me; On - ly
   do Thou guide my way. May Thy grace thro'
   life at - tend me; Glad - ly then shall I o - bey.

4. Thine I am, O Lord, for - ev - er, To Thy
   serv - ice set a - part. Suf - fer me to
   leave Thee nev - er; Seal Thine im - age on my heart.

425 Our Friendly Church

Copyright 1945 by Nazarene Publishing House

ELIZABETH B. JONES

HUGH C. BENNER

1. Our church is such a friend - ly place; It's where I
2. Our church is such a hap - py place In ev - 'ry-
3. Our church is such a qui - et place When heads are

Our Friendly Church

love to be. I smile at all the friends I meet; I
thing we do. We sing our love and thanks to God; We
bowed for prayer. We whis-per lov-ing words to God; We

smile at all the friends I meet, And they smile back at me.
sing our love and thanks to God, And know He loves us too.
whis-per lov-ing words to God, And thank Him for His care.

426 Fairest Lord Jesus

CRUSADERS' HYMN

ARR. BY RICHARD S. WILLIS

1. Fair - est Lord Je - sus! Rul - er of all na - ture!
2. Fair are the mead - ows; Fair - er still the wood - lands,
3. Fair is the sun - shine, Fair - er still the moon - light,
4. Beau - ti - ful Sav - iour! Lord of all the na - tions!

O Thou of God and man the Son! Thee will I cher - ish,
Robed in the bloom-ing garb of spring. Je - sus is fair - er,
And all the twin - kling star - ry host. Je - sus shines bright-er,
The Son of God and Son of Man! Glo - ry and hon - or,

Thee will I hon - or, Thou, my soul's glo - ry, joy, and crown!
Je - sus is pur - er, Who makes the woe - ful heart to sing!
Je - sus shines pur - er, Than all the an - gels heav'n can boast!
Praise, ad - o - ra - tion, Now and for - ev - er - more be Thine!

427   We Gather Together

FOLKSONG OF THE NETHERLANDS
ARR. BY E. KREMSER

1. We gath - er to - geth - er to ask the Lord's bless - ing.
2. Be - side us to guide us, our God with us join - ing,
3. We all do ex - tol Thee, Thou Lead - er tri - um - phant,

He chas - tens and has - tens His will to make known.
Or - dain - ing, main - tain - ing His king - dom di - vine;
And pray that Thou still our De - fend - er wilt be.

The wick - ed op - press - ing now cease from dis - tress - ing.
So from the be - gin - ning the fight we were win - ning.
Let Thy con - gre - ga - tion es - cape trib - u - la - tion.

Sing prais - es to His name; He for - gets not His own.
Thou, Lord, wast at our side— all glo - ry be Thine!
Thy name be ev - er praised. O Lord, make us free!

428   Come, Ye Thankful People

HENRY ALFORD   GEORGE J. ELVEY

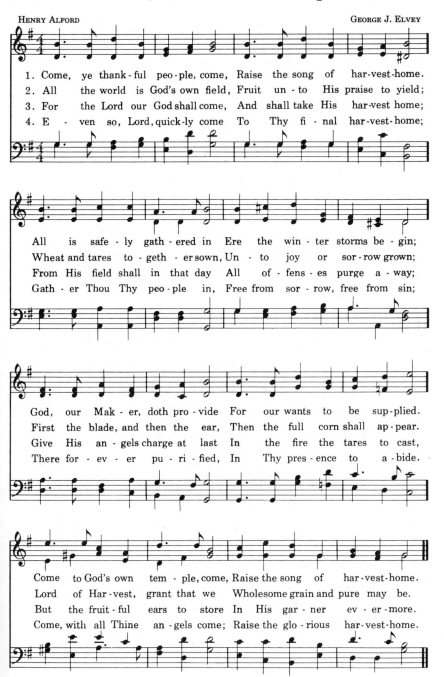

1. Come, ye thank-ful peo-ple, come, Raise the song of har-vest-home.
2. All the world is God's own field, Fruit un-to His praise to yield;
3. For the Lord our God shall come, And shall take His har-vest home;
4. E-ven so, Lord, quick-ly come To Thy fi-nal har-vest-home;

All is safe-ly gath-ered in Ere the win-ter storms be-gin;
Wheat and tares to-geth-er sown, Un-to joy or sor-row grown;
From His field shall in that day All of-fens-es purge a-way;
Gath-er Thou Thy peo-ple in, Free from sor-row, free from sin;

God, our Mak-er, doth pro-vide For our wants to be sup-plied.
First the blade, and then the ear, Then the full corn shall ap-pear.
Give His an-gels charge at last In the fire the tares to cast,
There for-ev-er pu-ri-fied, In Thy pres-ence to a-bide.

Come to God's own tem-ple, come, Raise the song of har-vest-home.
Lord of Har-vest, grant that we Wholesome grain and pure may be.
But the fruit-ful ears to store In His gar-ner ev-er-more.
Come, with all Thine an-gels come; Raise the glo-rious har-vest-home.

429 Battle Hymn of the Republic

JULIA WARD HOWE

JOHN WILLIAM STEFFE

1. Mine eyes have seen the glo - ry of the com-ing of the Lord. He is
2. I have seen Him in the watch-fires of a hundred circling camps; They have
3. He has sound-ed forth the trumpet that shall nev - er call re-treat; He is
4. In the beau-ty of the lil-ies Christ was born a-cross the sea, With a

tram-pling out the vin-tage where the grapes of wrath are stored; He hath
build-ed Him an al-tar in the eve-ning dews and damps; I can
sift-ing out the hearts of men be - fore His judg-ment seat. Oh, be
glo - ry in His bos-om that trans - fig-ures you and me. As He

loosed the fate-ful light-ning of His ter - ri - ble swift sword. His truth is
read His righteous sen-tence by the dim and flar-ing lamps. His day is
swift, my soul, to an - swer Him! be ju - bi - lant, my feet! Our God is
died to make men ho - ly, let us die to make men free, While God is

CHORUS

march-ing on. Glo - ry! glo - ry! Hal - le - lu - jah! Glo - ry! glo - ry! Hal - le -

lu - jah! Glo - ry! glo - ry! Hal - le - lu - jah! His truth is march-ing on.

430 God of Our Fathers

DANIEL C. ROBERTS

GEORGE W. WARREN

Trumpets, before each stanza.

1. God of our fa-thers, whose al-might-y
2. Thy love di-vine hath led us in the
3. From war's a-larms, from dead-ly pes-ti-
4. Re-fresh Thy peo-ple on their toil-some

hand / past. / lence, / way.

Leads forth in beau-ty all the star-ry
In this free land by Thee our lot is
Be Thy strong arm our ev-er sure de-
Lead us from night to nev-er-end-ing

band / cast. / fense. / day.

Of shin-ing worlds in splen-dor thro' the
Be Thou our Rul-er, Guard-ian, Guide, and
Thy true re-lig-ion in our hearts in-
Fill all our lives with love and grace di-

skies, / Stay, / crease; / vine;

Our grate-ful songs be-fore Thy throne a-rise.
Thy Word our law, Thy paths our cho-sen way.
Thy bounteous good-ness nour-ish us in peace.
And glo-ry, laud, and praise be ev-er Thine.

431 Doxology

THOS. KEN   LOUIS BOURGEOIS

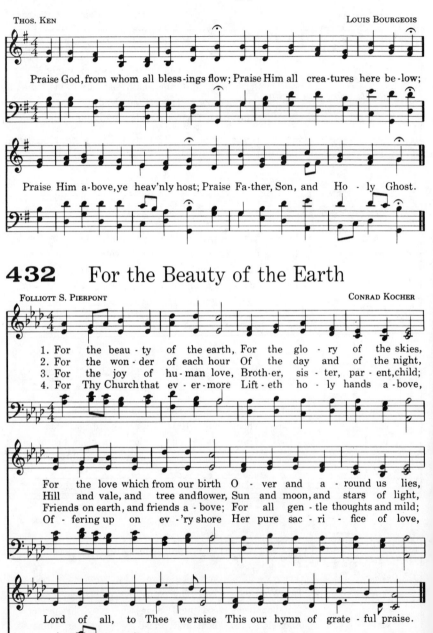

Praise God, from whom all bless-ings flow; Praise Him all crea-tures here be-low;

Praise Him a-bove, ye heav'nly host; Praise Fa-ther, Son, and Ho - ly Ghost.

432 For the Beauty of the Earth

FOLLIOTT S. PIERPONT   CONRAD KOCHER

1. For the beau - ty of the earth, For the glo - ry of the skies,
2. For the won - der of each hour Of the day and of the night,
3. For the joy of hu - man love, Broth-er, sis - ter, par - ent, child;
4. For Thy Church that ev - er-more Lift - eth ho - ly hands a - bove,

For the love which from our birth O - ver and a - round us lies,
Hill and vale, and tree and flower, Sun and moon, and stars of light,
Friends on earth, and friends a - bove; For all gen - tle thoughts and mild;
Of - fering up on ev - 'ry shore Her pure sac - ri - fice of love,

Lord of all, to Thee we raise This our hymn of grate - ful praise.

433 America the Beautiful

KATHARINE LEE BATES

SAMUEL A. WARD

1. O beau - ti - ful for spa - cious skies, For am - ber waves of grain,
2. O beau - ti - ful for pil - grim feet, Whose stern, im - pas - sioned stress
3. O beau - ti - ful for he - roes proved In lib - er - at - ing strife,
4. O beau - ti - ful for pa - triot dream That sees be - yond the years

For pur - ple moun - tain maj - es - ties A - bove the fruit - ed plain!
A thor - ough - fare for free - dom beat A - cross the wil - der - ness!
Who more than self their coun - try loved, And mer - cy more than life!
Thine al - a - bas - ter cit - ies gleam, Un - dimmed by hu - man tears!

A - mer - i - ca! A - mer - i - ca! God shed His grace on thee,
A - mer - i - ca! A - mer - i - ca! God mend thine ev - 'ry flaw,
A - mer - i - ca! A - mer - i - ca! May God thy gold re - fine
A - mer - i - ca! A - mer - i - ca! God shed His grace on thee,

And crown thy good with broth - er - hood From sea to shin - ing sea!
Con - firm thy soul in self - con - trol, Thy lib - er - ty in law!
Till all suc - cess be no - ble - ness, And ev - 'ry gain di - vine!
And crown thy good with broth - er - hood From sea to shin - ing sea!

434   The Star-spangled Banner

FRANCIS SCOTT KEY

JOHN STAFFORD SMITH

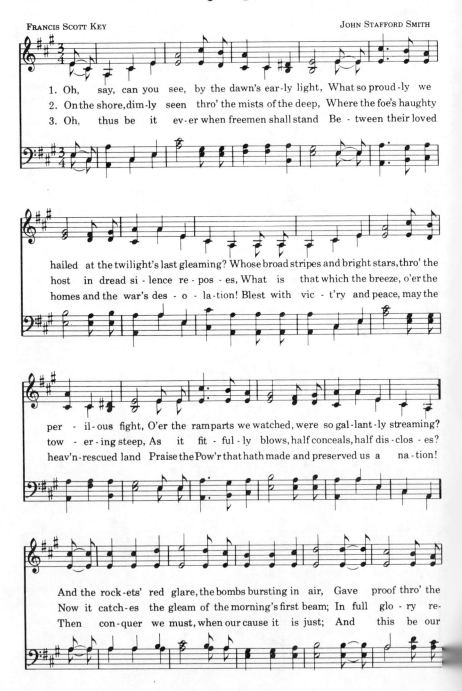

1. Oh, say, can you see, by the dawn's ear-ly light, What so proud-ly we
2. On the shore, dim-ly seen thro' the mists of the deep, Where the foe's haughty
3. Oh, thus be it ev-er when freemen shall stand Be-tween their loved

hailed at the twilight's last gleaming? Whose broad stripes and bright stars, thro' the
host in dread si-lence re-pos-es, What is that which the breeze, o'er the
homes and the war's des-o-la-tion! Blest with vic-t'ry and peace, may the

per-il-ous fight, O'er the ram-parts we watched, were so gal-lant-ly streaming?
tow-er-ing steep, As it fit-ful-ly blows, half conceals, half dis-clos-es?
heav'n-rescued land Praise the Pow'r that hath made and preserved us a na-tion!

And the rock-ets' red glare, the bombs bursting in air, Gave proof thro' the
Now it catch-es the gleam of the morning's first beam; In full glo-ry re-
Then con-quer we must, when our cause it is just; And this be our

The Star-spangled Banner

CHORUS ff

night that our flag was still there. Oh, say, does that star-span-gled
flect - ed, now shines on the stream. 'Tis the star-span-gled ban-ner; oh,
mot - to: "In God is our trust!" And the star-span-gled ban-ner in

ban - ner yet wave O'er the land of the free and the home of the brave?
long may it wave O'er the land of the free and the home of the brave!
tri - umph shall wave O'er the land of the free and the home of the brave.

435 My Country, 'Tis of Thee

S. F. SMITH

HENRY CAREY

1. My coun - try, 'tis of thee, Sweet land of lib - er - ty,
2. My na - tive coun - try, thee, Land of the no - ble, free,
3. Let mu - sic swell the breeze, And ring from all the trees
4. Our fa - thers' God, to Thee, Au - thor of lib - er - ty,

Of thee I sing: Land where my fa - thers died, Land of the
Thy name I love. I love thy rocks and rills, Thy woods and
Sweet free - dom's song; Let mor - tal tongues a - wake; Let all that
To Thee we sing. Long may our land be bright With free-dom's

Pil - grims' pride. From ev - 'ry moun - tain-side Let free - dom ring!
tem - pled hills; My heart with rap - ture thrills Like that a - bove.
breathe par - take; Let rocks their si - lence break, The sound pro - long.
ho - ly light; Pro - tect us by Thy might, Great God, our King!

436

O Canada!

National Song of Canada

ROUTHIER — WEIR

CALIXA LAVALLEE

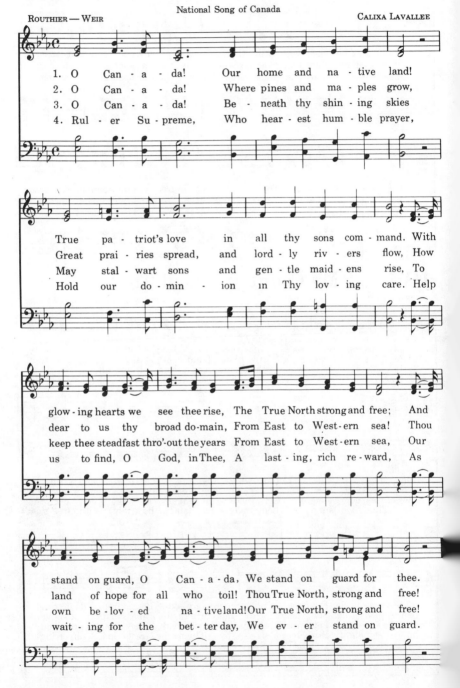

1. O Can - a - da! Our home and na - tive land!
2. O Can - a - da! Where pines and ma - ples grow,
3. O Can - a - da! Be - neath thy shin - ing skies
4. Rul - er Su - preme, Who hear - est hum - ble prayer,

True pa - triot's love in all thy sons com - mand. With
Great prai - ries spread, and lord - ly riv - ers flow, How
May stal - wart sons and gen - tle maid - ens rise, To
Hold our do - min - ion in Thy lov - ing care. Help

glow - ing hearts we see thee rise, The True North strong and free; And
dear to us thy broad do-main, From East to West-ern sea! Thou
keep thee steadfast thro'-out the years From East to West-ern sea, Our
us to find, O God, in Thee, A last - ing, rich re - ward, As

stand on guard, O Can - a - da, We stand on guard for thee.
land of hope for all who toil! Thou True North, strong and free!
own be - lov - ed na - tive land! Our True North, strong and free!
wait - ing for the bet - ter day, We ev - er stand on guard.

O Canada!

O Can - a - da! Glorious and free! We stand on guard, we stand on guard for thee. O Can - a - da! We stand on guard for thee.

437 God Save the Queen

National Song of the British Commonwealth

1. God save our gra - cious Queen! Long live our no - ble Queen!
2. Thy choic - est gifts in store, On her be pleased to pour;

God save the Queen! Send her vic - to - ri - ous, Hap - py and
Long may she reign. May she de - fend our laws And ev - er

glo - ri - ous, Long to reign o - ver us. God save the Queen!
give us cause To sing with heart and voice: "God save the Queen!"

438 On This Stone Now Laid with Prayer

JOHN PIERPONT

JOHANN R. AHLE

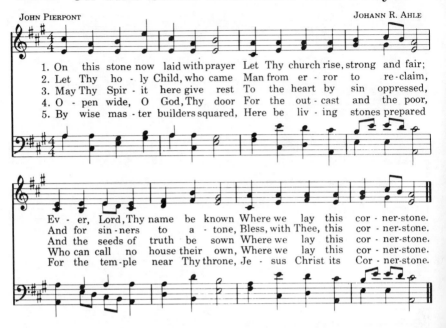

1. On this stone now laid with prayer Let Thy church rise, strong and fair;
2. Let Thy ho - ly Child, who came Man from er - ror to re - claim,
3. May Thy Spir - it here give rest To the heart by sin oppressed,
4. O - pen wide, O God, Thy door For the out - cast and the poor,
5. By wise mas - ter builders squared, Here be liv - ing stones prepared

Ev - er, Lord, Thy name be known Where we lay this cor - ner-stone.
And for sin - ners to a - tone, Bless, with Thee, this cor - ner-stone.
And the seeds of truth be sown Where we lay this cor - ner-stone.
Who can call no house their own, Where we lay this cor - ner-stone.
For the tem - ple near Thy throne, Je - sus Christ its Cor - ner-stone.

439 All Things Are Thine

Music copyright 1953 by Lillenas Publishing Co.

JOHN G. WHITTIER

HUGH C. BENNER

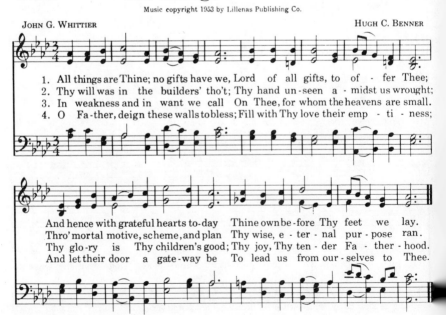

1. All things are Thine; no gifts have we, Lord of all gifts, to of - fer Thee;
2. Thy will was in the builders' tho't; Thy hand un - seen a - midst us wrought;
3. In weakness and in want we call On Thee, for whom the heavens are small.
4. O Fa - ther, deign these walls to bless; Fill with Thy love their emp - ti - ness;

And hence with grateful hearts to-day Thine own be - fore Thy feet we lay.
Thro' mortal motive, scheme, and plan Thy wise, e - ter - nal pur - pose ran.
Thy glo - ry is Thy children's good; Thy joy, Thy ten - der Fa - ther - hood.
And let their door a gate - way be To lead us from our - selves to Thee.

440 O Thou Whose Hand Hath Brought Us

Frederick W. Goadby

Samuel S. Wesley

1. O Thou whose hand hath brought us Un - to this joy - ful day,
2. For this new house we praise Thee, Reared at Thine own com-mand;
3. And oft as here we gath - er, And hearts in wor - ship blend,
4. And as the years roll on - ward, And strong af - fec - tions twine,
5. Lord God, our fa - thers' Help - er, Our Joy, and Hope, and Stay,

Ac - cept our glad thanks-giv - ing, And lis - ten as we pray;
For ev - 'ry gen -'rous spir - it, And ev - 'ry will - ing hand.
May truth re - veal its pow - er, And fer - vent prayer as - cend.
And ten - der mem -'ries gath - er A - bout this sa - cred shrine,
Grant now a gra - cious ear - nest Of man - y a com - ing day.

And may our prep - a - ra - tion For this day's ser - vice be
And now with - in Thy tem - ple Thy glo - ry let us see,
Here may the bus - y toil - er Rise to the things a - bove;
May this its chief - est hon - or, Its glo - ry ev - er be,
Our yearn - ing hearts Thou know - est; We wait be - fore Thy throne.

With one ac - cord to of - fer Our - selves, O Lord, to Thee.
For all its strength and beau - ty Are noth - ing with - out Thee.
The young, the old, be strength-ened, And all men learn Thy love.
That mul - ti - tudes with - in it Have found their way to Thee.
Oh, come, and by Thy pres - ence Make this new house Thine own.

441 The Church's One Foundation

Samuel J. Stone

Samuel S. Wesley

1. The Church's one foun-da-tion Is Je-sus Christ, her Lord.
2. E-lect from ev-'ry na-tion, Yet one o'er all the earth;
3. 'Mid toil and trib-u-la-tion, And tu-mult of her war,
4. Yet she on earth hath un-ion With God, the Three in One,

She is His new cre-a-tion By wa-ter and the word.
Her char-ter of sal-va-tion, One Lord, one faith, one birth;
She waits the con-sum-ma-tion Of peace for-ev-er-more;
And mys-tic, sweet com-mun-ion With those whose rest is won.

From heav'n He came and sought her To be His ho-ly bride; With
One ho-ly name she bless-es; Par-takes one ho-ly food; And
Till, with the vi-sion glo-rious, Her long-ing eyes are blest, And
Oh, hap-py ones and ho-ly! Lord, give us grace that we, Like

His own blood He bought her, And for her life He died.
to one hope she press-es, With ev-'ry grace en-dued.
the great Church vic-to-rious Shall be the Church at rest.
them, the meek and low-ly, On high may dwell with Thee.

442 Angels, from the Realms of Glory

JAMES MONTGOMERY

HENRY SMART

1. An - gels, from the realms of glo - ry, Wing your flight o'er all the earth. Ye who sang cre - a - tion's sto - ry, now pro - claim Mes - si - ah's birth.

2. Shep - herds, in the field a - bid - ing, Watch - ing o'er your flocks by night, God with man is now re - sid - ing; Yon - der shines the In - fant Light.

3. Sa - ges, leave your con - tem - pla - tions; Bright - er vi - sions beam a - far. Seek the great De - sire of Na - tions; Ye have seen His na - tal star.

4. Saints be - fore the al - tar bend - ing, Watch - ing long in hope and fear, Sud - den - ly the Lord, de - scend - ing, In His tem - ple shall ap - pear.

REFRAIN

Come and wor - ship. Come and wor - ship. Wor - ship Christ, the new - born King.

443 Hallelujah! Christ Is Born!

F. C. W. *With spirit*

FAITH CHAMBERS WILSON

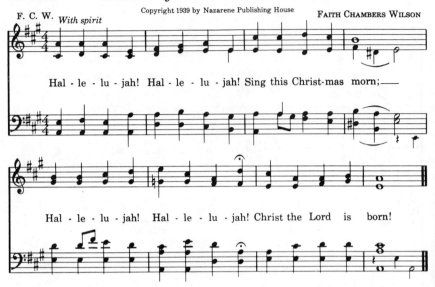

Hal - le - lu - jah! Hal - le - lu - jah! Sing this Christ-mas morn;——

Hal - le - lu - jah! Hal - le - lu - jah! Christ the Lord is born!

444 While Shepherds Watched Their Flocks

NAHUM TATE

GEORGE F. HANDEL

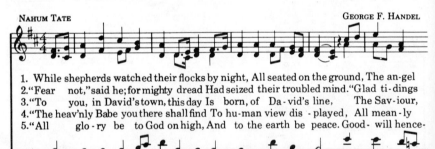

1. While shepherds watched their flocks by night, All seated on the ground, The an-gel
2. "Fear not," said he; for mighty dread Had seized their troubled mind. "Glad ti-dings
3. "To you, in David's town, this day Is born, of Da-vid's line, The Sav-iour,
4. "The heav'nly Babe you there shall find To hu-man view dis - played, All mean-ly
5. "All glo-ry be to God on high, And to the earth be peace. Good- will hence-

of the Lord came down, And glo-ry shone a - round, And glo-ry shone a - round.
of great joy I bring To you and all man - kind, To you and all man-kind.
who is Christ the Lord; And this shall be the sign, And this shall be the sign:
wrapped in swathing bands, And in a man - ger laid, And in a man-ger laid."
forth from heav'n to men Be - gin and nev - er cease, Be - gin and nev-er cease!"

445 It Came upon the Midnight Clear

EDMUND H. SEARS

RICHARD S. WILLIS

1. It came up-on the mid-night clear, That glo-rious song of old,
2. Still thro' the clo-ven skies they come, With peace-ful wings un-furled,
3. And ye, be-neath life's crush-ing load, Whose forms are bend-ing low,
4. For, lo, the days are hast'n-ing on, By proph-et bards fore-told,

From an-gels bend-ing near the earth To touch their harps of gold:
And still their heav'n-ly mu-sic floats O'er all the wea-ry world.
Who toil a-long the climb-ing way With pain-ful step and slow,
When with the ev-er-cir-cling years Comes round the age of gold;

"Peace on the earth, good will to men, From heav'n's all-gra-cious King."
A-bove its sad and low-ly plains They bend on hov-'ring wing,
Look up! For glad and gold-en hours Come swift-ly on the wing.
When peace shall o-ver all the earth Its an-cient splen-dors fling,

The world in sol-emn still-ness lay To hear the an-gels sing.
And ev-er o'er its ba-bel sounds The bless-ed an-gels sing.
Oh, rest be-side the wea-ry road And hear the an-gels sing.
And the whole world give back the song Which now the an-gels sing.

446 Hark! The Herald Angels Sing

CHARLES WESLEY

FELIX MENDELSSOHN

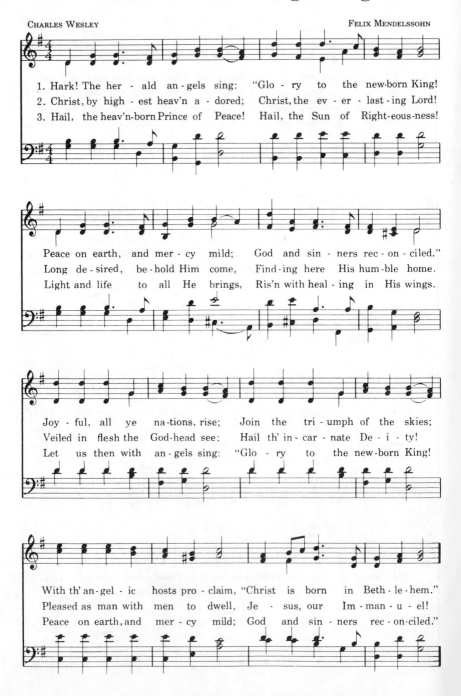

1. Hark! The her - ald an - gels sing: "Glo - ry to the new-born King!
2. Christ, by high - est heav'n a - dored; Christ, the ev - er - last-ing Lord!
3. Hail, the heav'n-born Prince of Peace! Hail, the Sun of Right-eous-ness!

Peace on earth, and mer - cy mild; God and sin - ners rec - on - ciled."
Long de - sired, be - hold Him come, Find-ing here His hum -ble home.
Light and life to all He brings, Ris'n with heal - ing in His wings.

Joy - ful, all ye na-tions, rise; Join the tri - umph of the skies;
Veiled in flesh the God-head see; Hail th' in - car - nate De - i - ty!
Let us then with an - gels sing: "Glo - ry to the new-born King!

With th' an-gel - ic hosts pro - claim, "Christ is born in Beth - le - hem."
Pleased as man with men to dwell, Je - sus, our Im - man - u - el!
Peace on earth, and mer - cy mild; God and sin - ners rec - on - ciled."

Hark! The Herald Angels Sing

REFRAIN

Hark! The her-ald an-gels sing, "Glo-ry to the new-born King."

447   Joy to the World

ISAAC WATTS   ARR. FROM GEO. F. HANDEL

1. Joy to the world! the Lord is come; Let earth re-ceive her King; Let
2. Joy to the world! the Sav-iour reigns; Let men their songs em-ploy; While
3. No more let sin and sor-row grow, Nor thorns in-fest the ground; He
4. He rules the world with truth and grace, And makes the na-tions prove The

ev-'ry heart pre-pare Him room, And heav'n and nature sing, And
fields and floods, rocks, hills, and plains Re-peat the sounding joy, Re-
comes to make His bless-ings flow Far as the curse is found, Far
glo-ries of His right-eous-ness And wonders of His love, And

And heav'n, And heav'n and na-ture

heav'n and na-ture sing, And heav'n, And heav'n and na-ture sing.
peat the sound-ing joy, Re-peat, Re-peat the sound-ing joy.
as the curse is found, Far as, Far as the curse is found.
won-ders of His love, And wonders, And won-ders of His love.

sing, And heav'n and na-ture sing,

448 O Little Town of Bethlehem

PHILLIPS BROOKS

LEWIS H. REDNER

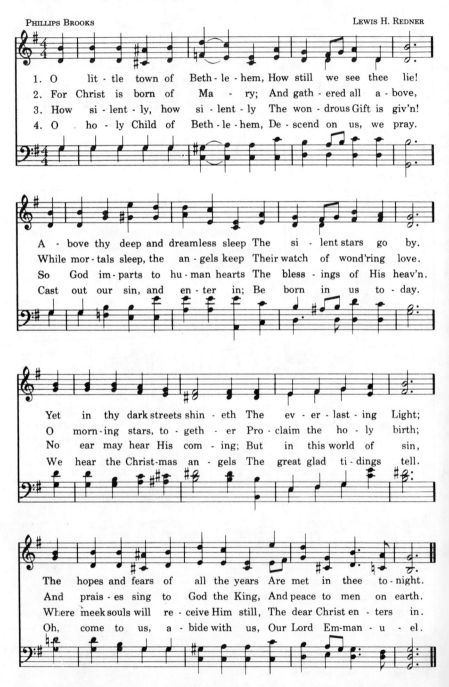

1. O lit - tle town of Beth - le - hem, How still we see thee lie!
2. For Christ is born of Ma - ry; And gath - ered all a - bove,
3. How si - lent - ly, how si - lent - ly The won - drous Gift is giv'n!
4. O ho - ly Child of Beth - le - hem, De - scend on us, we pray.

A - bove thy deep and dreamless sleep The si - lent stars go by.
While mor - tals sleep, the an - gels keep Their watch of wond'ring love.
So God im - parts to hu - man hearts The bless - ings of His heav'n.
Cast out our sin, and en - ter in; Be born in us to - day.

Yet in thy dark streets shin - eth The ev - er - last - ing Light;
O morn - ing stars, to - geth - er Pro - claim the ho - ly birth;
No ear may hear His com - ing; But in this world of sin,
We hear the Christ - mas an - gels The great glad ti - dings tell.

The hopes and fears of all the years Are met in thee to - night.
And prais - es sing to God the King, And peace to men on earth.
Where meek souls will re - ceive Him still, The dear Christ en - ters in.
Oh, come to us, a - bide with us, Our Lord Em - man - u - el.

449 The First Noel

TRADITIONAL
TRADITIONAL MELODY

1. The first No - el the an-gels did say Was to cer-tain poor
2. They look - ed up and saw a star Bright in the
3. And by the light of that same star Three Wise Men
4. Then en - tered in those Wise Men three, Full rev - 'rent-

shep-herds in fields as they lay; In fields where they lay
east be - yond them far, And to the earth it
came from coun - try far; To seek for a King was
ly up - on the knee, And of - fered there, in

keep-ing their sheep, On a cold win-ter's night that was so deep.
gave great light, And so it con - tin-ued both day and night.
their in - tent, And to fol-low the star wher - e'er it went.
His pres - ence, Their gold and myrrh and frank - in-cense.

REFRAIN

No - el, No - el, No - el, No - el, Born is the King of Is - ra-el.

450 Away in a Manger

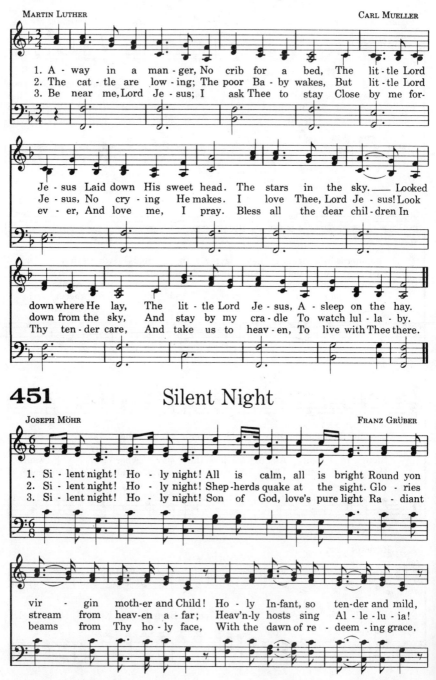

MARTIN LUTHER

CARL MUELLER

1. A - way in a man - ger, No crib for a bed, The lit - tle Lord
2. The cat - tle are low - ing; The poor Ba - by wakes, But lit - tle Lord
3. Be near me, Lord Je - sus; I ask Thee to stay Close by me for-

Je - sus Laid down His sweet head. The stars in the sky. __ Looked
Je - sus, No cry - ing He makes. I love Thee, Lord Je - sus! Look
ev - er, And love me, I pray. Bless all the dear chil - dren In

down where He lay, The lit - tle Lord Je - sus, A - sleep on the hay.
down from the sky, And stay by my cra - dle To watch lul - la - by.
Thy ten - der care, And take us to heav - en, To live with Thee there.

451 Silent Night

JOSEPH MÖHR

FRANZ GRÜBER

1. Si - lent night! Ho - ly night! All is calm, all is bright Round yon
2. Si - lent night! Ho - ly night! Shep -herds quake at the sight. Glo - ries
3. Si - lent night! Ho - ly night! Son of God, love's pure light Ra - diant

vir - gin moth-er and Child! Ho - ly In-fant, so ten-der and mild,
stream from heav-en a - far; Heav'n-ly hosts sing Al - le - lu - ia!
beams from Thy ho - ly face, With the dawn of re - deem - ing grace,

Silent Night

Sleep in heav-en-ly peace.   Sleep in heav-en-ly peace.
Christ, the Sav-iour, is born!   Christ, the Sav-iour, is born!
Je - sus, Lord, at Thy birth!   Je - sus, Lord, at Thy birth!

452   Oh, Come, All Ye Faithful

TR. BY FREDERICK OAKELEY   WADE'S CANTUS DIVERSI

1. Oh, come, all ye faith - ful, joy - ful and tri - um-phant. Oh,
2. — Sing, choirs of • an - gels, sing in ex - ul - ta - tion. Oh,
3. — Yea, Lord, we greet Thee, born this hap - py morn-ing. O

come ye, oh, come ye to Beth - le - hem. Come and be-
sing, all ye bright hosts of heav'n a - bove. Glo - ry to
Je - sus, to Thee be all glo - ry giv'n: Word of the

REFRAIN

hold Him, born the King of an - gels.   come
God, all glo - ry in the high - est!   Oh, come, let us a - dore Him. Oh,
Fa - ther, now in flesh ap - pear - ing.

come, let us a - dore Him. Oh, come, let us a - dore Him, Christ the Lord.

453 He Lives

A. H. A.

REV. A. H. ACKLEY

1. I serve a ris-en Sav-iour; He's in the world to-day. I know that He is
2. In all the world a-round me I see His loving care; And tho' my heart grows
3. Re-joice, re-joice, O Christian; lift up your voice and sing. E-ter-nal hal-le-

liv-ing, what-ev-er men may say. I see His hand of mer-cy; I
wea-ry I nev-er will de-spair. I know that He is lead-ing thro'
lu-jahs to Je-sus Christ, the King! The Hope of all who seek Him, the

hear His voice of cheer; And just the time I need Him He's al-ways near.
all the storm-y blast. The day of His ap-pear-ing will come at last.
Help of all who find, None oth-er is so lov-ing, so good and kind.

REFRAIN *Spirited*

He lives, He lives, Christ Je-sus lives to-day! He walks with me and
He lives, He lives,

talks with me a-long life's nar-row way. He lives, He lives, sal-
He lives, He lives,

He Lives

va-tion to im - part! You ask me how I know He lives? He lives within my heart.

Copyright 1952 by Lillenas Publishing Co.
International Copyright Secured

454   Oh, Shout the News!

H. C. B.

Hugh C. Benner

1. Oh, shout the news to all the earth, The joy - ous news the an - gel gives;
2. Oh, sing the glad, tri - umphant strain, The song of vic - t'ry o'er the grave;
3. Oh, tell the sto - ry o'er and o'er, The sto - ry of the Liv - ing Word,
4. Oh, praise the might - y Con-quer-or, Vic - to - rious o - ver death and hell,

Let all pro-claim the matchless worth Of Christ the Lord, for now He lives.
Let all re-joice with loud re - frain That Je - sus lives with pow'r to save.
That men may wor-ship and a - dore The Christ, the ev - er - liv - ing Lord.
The King of Life for - ev - er-more; Let heav'n and earth His glo-ries tell.

CHORUS

Christ is ris - en! Swell the strain! Christ is ris - en, ev - er - more to reign.

455 Crown Him

Mrs. C. H. M. Mrs. C. H. Morris

1. Be - hold one day a won-drous scene: There rode a Man of low - ly mien
2. He's pass-ing by, just as of yore, And great and small and rich and poor
3. Soon He is com-ing back a - gain, A thousand years on earth to reign.

A - long the dust - y way, A - long the dust - y way. The
To - day their Lord de - ny, To - day their Lord de - ny. Oh,
We'll see Him by and by; We'll see Him by and by. All

peo - ple thronged Him as He passed; Palm branches in His way they cast,
make of Him su - prem-est choice, And with up - lift - ed heart and voice,
the re-deemed with Him He'll bring Who in their hearts have crowned Him King,

CHORUS

And cried, "Ho-san-na to the King, to-day (to - day)!"
"Ho-san - na to the King of Kings," still cry (still cry). Crown Him! Crown
And they shall live and reign with Him on high (on high).

Him! Crown the Sav-iour King of Kings. In your hearts en-throne Him;

Crown Him

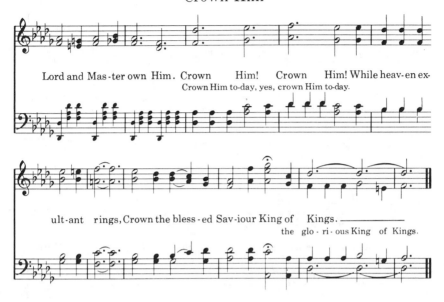

Lord and Mas-ter own Him. Crown Him! Crown Him! While heav-en ex-
Crown Him to-day, yes, crown Him to-day.

ult-ant rings, Crown the bless-ed Sav-iour King of Kings. —————
the glo - ri - ous King of Kings.

456   Hallelujah! What a Saviour!

P. P. B.   P. P. Bliss

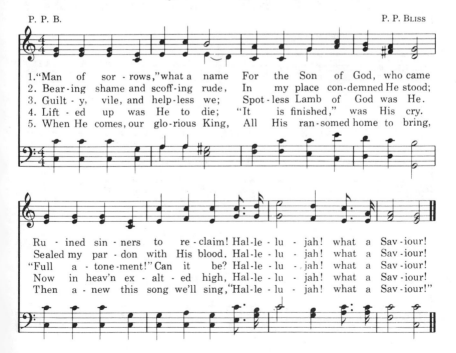

1. "Man of sor - rows," what a name   For the Son of God, who came
2. Bear-ing shame and scoff-ing rude,   In my place con-demned He stood;
3. Guilt - y, vile, and help-less we;   Spot-less Lamb of God was He.
4. Lift - ed up was He to die;   "It is finished," was His cry.
5. When He comes, our glo-rious King,   All His ran-somed home to bring,

Ru - ined sin - ners to re - claim! Hal-le - lu - jah! what a Sav-iour!
Sealed my par - don with His blood. Hal-le - lu - jah! what a Sav-iour!
"Full a - tone-ment!" Can it be? Hal-le - lu - jah! what a Sav-iour!
Now in heav'n ex - alt - ed high, Hal-le - lu - jah! what a Sav-iour!
Then a - new this song we'll sing, "Hal-le - lu - jah! what a Sav-iour!"

457 Christ Arose

R. L.

ROBERT LOWRY

1. Low in the grave He lay—Je-sus, my Sav-iour! Wait-ing the com-ing day—
2. Vain-ly they watch His bed—Je-sus, my Sav-iour! Vain-ly they seal the dead—
3. Death can-not keep his prey—Je-sus, my Sav-iour! He tore the bars a-way—

REFRAIN *faster*

Je-sus, my Lord! Up from the grave He a-rose, With a
He a-rose,

might-y tri-umph o'er His foes. He a-rose a Vic-tor from the
He a-rose!

dark do-main, And He lives for-ev-er with His saints to reign. He a-

rose! He a-rose! Hal-le-lu-jah! Christ a-rose!
He a-rose! He a-rose!

458 Crown Him with Many Crowns

MATTHEW BRIDGES

GEORGE J. ELVEY

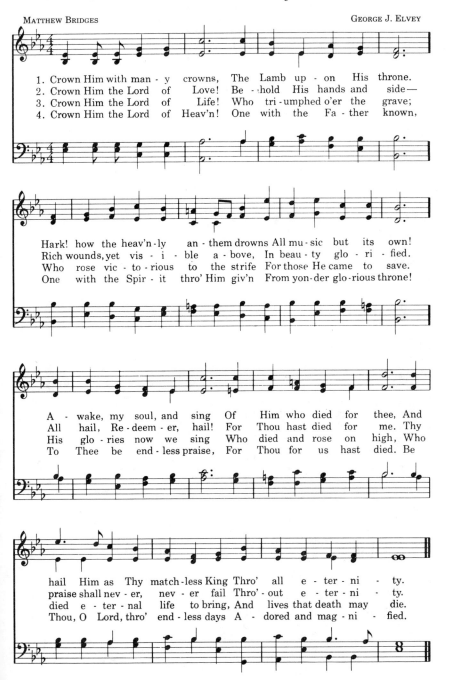

1. Crown Him with man - y crowns, The Lamb up - on His throne.
2. Crown Him the Lord of Love! Be - hold His hands and side—
3. Crown Him the Lord of Life! Who tri - umphed o'er the grave;
4. Crown Him the Lord of Heav'n! One with the Fa - ther known,

Hark! how the heav'n-ly an - them drowns All mu - sic but its own!
Rich wounds, yet vis - i - ble a - bove, In beau - ty glo - ri - fied.
Who rose vic - to - rious to the strife For those He came to save.
One with the Spir - it thro' Him giv'n From yon - der glo - rious throne!

A - wake, my soul, and sing Of Him who died for thee, And
All hail, Re - deem - er, hail! For Thou hast died for me. Thy
His glo - ries now we sing Who died and rose on high, Who
To Thee be end - less praise, For Thou for us hast died. Be

hail Him as Thy match - less King Thro' all e - ter - ni - ty.
praise shall nev - er, nev - er fail Thro' - out e - ter - ni - ty.
died e - ter - nal life to bring, And lives that death may die.
Thou, O Lord, thro' end - less days A - dored and mag - ni - fied.

459 Christ, the Lord, Is Risen Today

CHARLES WESLEY

FROM "LYRA DAVIDICA"

1. Christ, the Lord, is risen to - day,
2. Lives a - gain our glo - rious King:
3. Love's re - deem - ing work is done,
4. Soar we now, where Christ has led,

Al - le - lu - ia!

Sons of men and an - gels say:
Where, O death, is now thy sting?
Fought the fight, the bat - tle won;
Fol - lowing our ex - alt - ed Head;

Al - le - lu - ia!

Raise your joys and tri - umphs high,
Dy - ing once, He all doth save:
Death in vain for - bids Him rise;
Made like Him, like Him we rise;

Al - le - lu - ia!

Sing, ye heavens, and earth, re - ply,
Where thy vic - to - ry, O grave?
Christ has o - pened Par - a - dise.
Ours the cross, the grave, the skies;

Al - le - lu - ia!

460 Whiter than Snow

JAMES NICHOLSON

WM. G. FISCHER

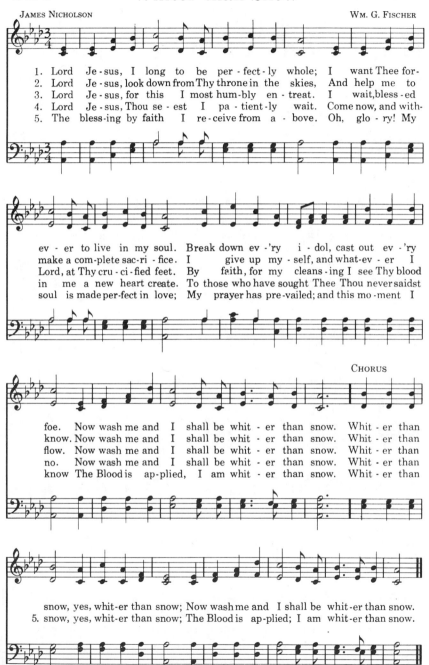

1. Lord Je-sus, I long to be per-fect-ly whole; I want Thee for-
2. Lord Je-sus, look down from Thy throne in the skies, And help me to
3. Lord Je-sus, for this I most hum-bly en-treat. I wait, bless-ed
4. Lord Je-sus, Thou se-est I pa-tient-ly wait. Come now, and with-
5. The bless-ing by faith I re-ceive from a-bove. Oh, glo-ry! My

ev-er to live in my soul. Break down ev-'ry i-dol, cast out ev-'ry
make a com-plete sac-ri-fice. I give up my-self, and what-ev-er I
Lord, at Thy cru-ci-fied feet. By faith, for my cleans-ing I see Thy blood
in me a new heart create. To those who have sought Thee Thou never saidst
soul is made per-fect in love; My prayer has pre-vailed; and this mo-ment I

CHORUS

foe. Now wash me and I shall be whit-er than snow. Whit-er than
know. Now wash me and I shall be whit-er than snow. Whit-er than
flow. Now wash me and I shall be whit-er than snow. Whit-er than
no. Now wash me and I shall be whit-er than snow. Whit-er than
know The Blood is ap-plied, I am whit-er than snow. Whit-er than

snow, yes, whit-er than snow; Now wash me and I shall be whit-er than snow.
5. snow, yes, whit-er than snow; The Blood is ap-plied; I am whit-er than snow.

461 Oh, to Be Like Thee

T. O. CHISHOLM

WM. J. KIRKPATRICK

1. Oh, to be like Thee! bless-ed Re-deem-er, This is my con-stant
2. Oh, to be like Thee! full of com-pas-sion, Lov-ing, for-giv-ing,
3. Oh, to be like Thee! low-ly in spir-it, Ho-ly and harm-less,
4. Oh, to be like Thee! while I am plead-ing, Pour out Thy Spir-it,

long-ing and prayer. Glad-ly I'll for-feit all of earth's treas-ures,
ten-der and kind, Help-ing the help-less, cheer-ing the faint-ing,
pa-tient and brave; Meek-ly en-dur-ing cru-el re-proach-es,
fill with Thy love; Make me a tem-ple meet for Thy dwell-ing,

CHORUS

Je-sus, Thy per-fect like-ness to wear.
Seek-ing the wan-d'ring sin-ner to find.
Will-ing to suf-fer oth-ers to save.
Fit me for life and heav-en a-bove.

Oh, to be like Thee!

Oh, to be like Thee, bless-ed Re-deem-er, pure as Thou art! Come in Thy

sweet-ness, come in Thy full-ness; Stamp Thine own im-age deep on my heart.

462   I Am Coming, Lord

L. H.

L. HARTSOUGH

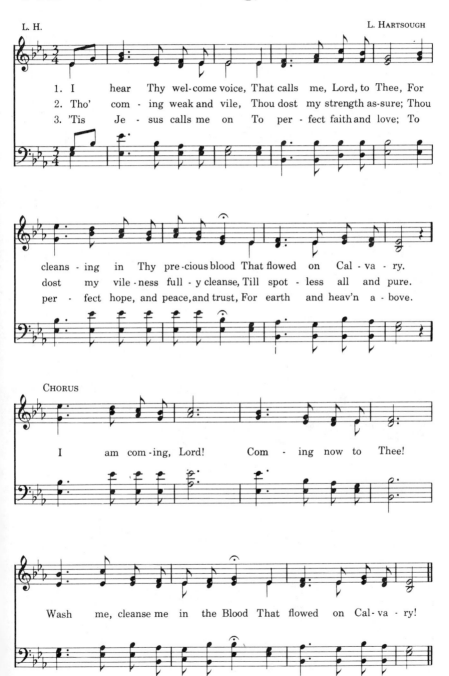

1. I hear Thy wel-come voice, That calls me, Lord, to Thee, For
2. Tho' com - ing weak and vile, Thou dost my strength as-sure; Thou
3. 'Tis Je - sus calls me on To per - fect faith and love; To

cleans - ing in Thy pre-cious blood That flowed on Cal - va - ry.
dost my vile -ness full - y cleanse, Till spot - less all and pure.
per - fect hope, and peace, and trust, For earth and heav'n a - bove.

CHORUS

I am com -ing, Lord! Com - ing now to Thee!

Wash me, cleanse me in the Blood That flowed on Cal - va - ry!

463 Almost Persuaded

P. P. B.   P. P. Bliss

1. "Al - most per - suad - ed" now to be - lieve; "Al - most per - suad - ed"
2. "Al - most per - suad - ed," come, come to - day. "Al - most per - suad - ed,"
3. "Al - most per - suad - ed," har - vest is past! "Al - most per - suad - ed,"

Christ to re - ceive;   Seems now some soul to say, "Go, Spir - it,
turn not a - way.   Je - sus in - vites you here, An - gels are
doom comes at last!   "Al - most" can - not a - vail; "Al - most" is

go Thy way. Some more con - ven - ient day On Thee I'll call."
lin - g'ring near, Prayers rise from hearts so dear. O wan - d'rer, come!
but to fail! Sad, sad, that bit - ter wail, "Al - most," but lost!

464 Just as I Am

Charlotte Elliott   William B. Bradbury

1. Just as I am, with - out one plea But that Thy blood was shed for me,
2. Just as I am, and wait - ing not To rid my soul of one dark blot,
3. Just as I am, tho' tossed a - bout With many a con - flict, many a doubt,
4. Just as I am—Thou wilt re - ceive, Wilt wel - come, par - don, cleanse, re - lieve;
5. Just as I am! Thy love unknown Hath bro - ken ev - 'ry bar - rier down;

Just as I Am

And that Thou bidd'st me come to Thee,
To Thee whose blood can cleanse each spot,
Fight-ings and fears with-in, with-out, O Lamb of God, I come! I come!
Be - cause Thy prom - ise I be - lieve,
Now to be Thine, yea, Thine a - lone,

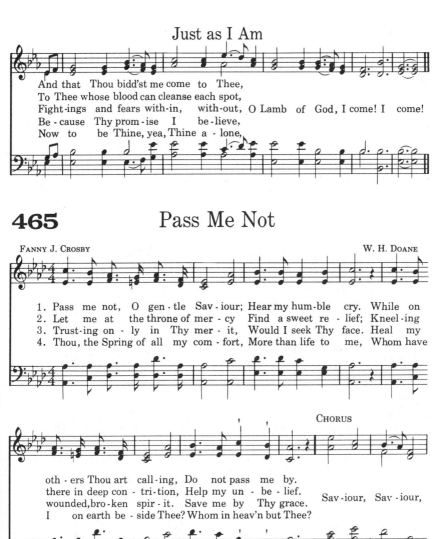

465 Pass Me Not

FANNY J. CROSBY

W. H. DOANE

1. Pass me not, O gen - tle Sav - iour; Hear my hum - ble cry. While on
2. Let me at the throne of mer - cy Find a sweet re - lief; Kneel-ing
3. Trust-ing on - ly in Thy mer - it, Would I seek Thy face. Heal my
4. Thou, the Spring of all my com - fort, More than life to me, Whom have

CHORUS

oth - ers Thou art call - ing, Do not pass me by.
there in deep con - tri - tion, Help my un - be - lief.
wounded, bro - ken spir - it. Save me by Thy grace. Sav - iour, Sav - iour,
I on earth be - side Thee? Whom in heav'n but Thee?

Hear my hum - ble cry. While on oth - ers Thou art call-ing, Do not pass me by.

466 Jesus, I Come

W. T. SLEEPER

GEO. C. STEBBINS

1. Out of my bond - age, sor - row, and night, Je-sus, I come; Je-sus, I come.
2. Out of my shame - ful fail-ure and loss, Je-sus, I come; Je-sus, I come.
3. Out of un - rest and ar - ro-gant pride, Je-sus, I come; Je-sus, I come.
4. Out of the fear and dread of the tomb, Je-sus, I come; Je-sus, I come.

In - to Thy free-dom, gladness, and light,
In - to the glo-rious gain of Thy cross,
In - to Thy bless-ed will to a-bide,   Je - sus, I come to   Thee.
In - to the joy and light of Thy home,

Out of my sick-ness in - to Thy health, Out of my want and in - to Thy wealth,
Out of earth's sorrows in - to Thy balm, Out of life's storms and in - to Thy calm,
Out of my-self to dwell in Thy love, Out of de-spair in-to rap-tures a - bove,
Out of the depths of ru - in un-told, In - to the peace of Thy sheltering fold,

Out of my sin and in - to thy-self,
Out of dis-tress to ju - bi-lant psalm,   Je - sus, I come to   Thee.
Up - ward for aye on wings like a dove,
Ev - er Thy glo-rious face to be-hold,

467 Lord, I'm Coming Home

W. J. K.

WM. J. KIRKPATRICK

1. I've wan-dered far a-way from God;
2. I've wast-ed man-y pre-cious years;
3. I'm tired of sin and stray-ing, Lord;
4. My soul is sick, my heart is sore;

Now I'm com-ing home.

The paths of sin too long I've trod;
I now re-pent with bit-ter tears;
I'll trust Thy love, be-lieve Thy Word;
My strength re-new, my hope re-store;

Lord, I'm com-ing home.

CHORUS

Com-ing home, com-ing home, Nev-er more to roam!

O-pen wide Thine arms of love; Lord, I'm com-ing home.

468 Where He Leads Me

E. W. BLANDLY

J. S. NORRIS

1. I can hear my Sav-iour call-ing, I can hear my Sav-iour call-ing,
2. I'll go with Him thro' the gar-den, I'll go with Him thro' the gar-den,
3. I'll go with Him thro' the judg-ment, I'll go with Him thro' the judg-ment,
4. He will give me grace and glo-ry, He will give me grace and glo-ry,

I can hear my Sav-iour call-ing, "Take thy cross and follow, fol-low Me."
I'll go with Him thro' the gar-den; I'll go with Him, with Him all the way.
I'll go with Him thro' the judg-ment; I'll go with Him, with Him all the way.
He will give me grace and glo-ry, And go with me, with me all the way.

REFRAIN

Where He leads me I will fol-low. Where He leads me I will fol-low.

Where He leads me I will fol-low. I'll go with Him, with Him all the way.

469 There's a Great Day Coming

W. L. T.   W. L. THOMPSON

1. There's a great day com-ing, A great day com-ing; There's a great day com-ing by and by, When the saints and the sin-ners shall be part-ed right and left.
2. There's a bright day com-ing, A bright day com-ing; There's a bright day com-ing by and by. But its bright-ness shall on-ly come to them that love the Lord. Are you read-y for that day to come?
3. There's a sad day com-ing, A sad day com-ing; There's a sad day com-ing by and by, When the sin-ner shall hear his doom, "De-part, I know ye not!"

CHORUS

Are you read-y? Are you read-y? Are you read-y for the judg-ment day? Are you read-y? Are you read-y for the judg-ment day?

470 Will Jesus Find Us Watching?

FANNY J. CROSBY

W. H. DOANE

1. When Je-sus comes to re-ward His ser-vants, Wheth-er it be
2. If at the dawn of the ear-ly morn-ing, He shall call us
3. Have we been true to the trust He left us? Do we seek to
4. Bless-ed are those whom the Lord finds watch-ing; In His glo-ry

noon or night, Faith-ful to Him, will He find us watch-ing,
one by one, When to the Lord we re-store our tal-ents,
do our best? If in our hearts there is naught con-demns us,
they shall share. If He shall come at the dawn or mid-night,

CHORUS

With our lamps all trimmed and bright?
Will He an-swer thee, Well done?
We shall have a glo-rious rest.   Oh, can we say we are
Will He find us watch-ing there?

read-y, broth-er, Read-y for the soul's bright home? Say, will He

find you and me still watch-ing, Wait-ing, waiting, when the Lord shall come?

471 For You I Am Praying

S. O'MALEY CLUFF

IRA D. SANKEY

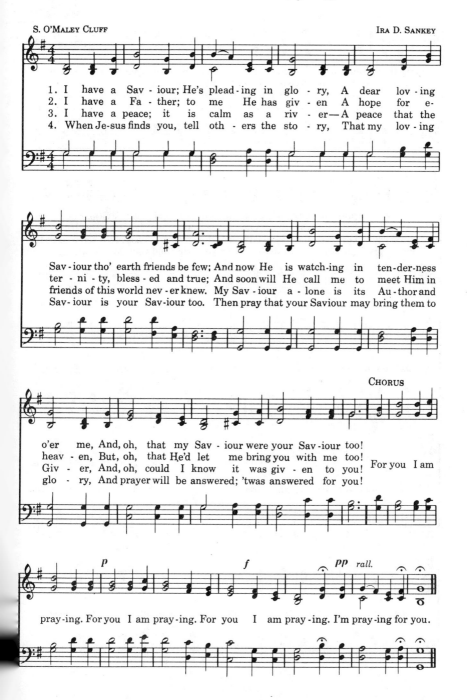

1. I have a Sav - iour; He's plead - ing in glo - ry, A dear lov - ing
2. I have a Fa - ther; to me He has giv - en A hope for e -
3. I have a peace; it is calm as a riv - er— A peace that the
4. When Je-sus finds you, tell oth - ers the sto - ry, That my lov - ing

Sav-iour tho' earth friends be few; And now He is watch-ing in ten-der-ness
ter - ni - ty, bless - ed and true; And soon will He call me to meet Him in
friends of this world nev - er knew. My Sav - iour a - lone is its Au-thor and
Sav-iour is your Sav-iour too. Then pray that your Saviour may bring them to

CHORUS

o'er me, And, oh, that my Sav - iour were your Sav-iour too!
heav - en, But, oh, that He'd let me bring you with me too! For you I am
Giv - er, And, oh, could I know it was giv - en to you!
glo - ry, And prayer will be answered; 'twas answered for you!

p *f* *pp* rall.

pray-ing. For you I am pray-ing. For you I am pray-ing. I'm pray-ing for you.

472 Jesus Will Give You Rest

FANNY J. CROSBY

JNO. R. SWENEY

1. Will you come, will you come, with your poor, bro-ken heart, Bur-dened and
2. Will you come, will you come? There is mer-cy for you, Balm for your
3. Will you come, will you come? You have noth-ing to pay; Je-sus, who
4. Will you come, will you come? How He pleads with you now! Fly to His

sin - op - pressed? Lay it down at the feet of your Sav-iour and Lord.
ach-ing breast. On-ly come as you are, and be-lieve on His name.
loves you best, By His death on the cross pur-chased life for your soul.
lov-ing breast; And what-ev - er your sin and your sor - row may be,

CHORUS

Je - sus will give you rest. Oh, hap-py rest; sweet, hap-py rest!

Je - sus will give you rest. Oh, why won't you
hap - py rest.

come in sim-ple, trust-ing faith? Je - sus will give you rest.

473 His Way with Thee

C. S. N.

CYRUS S. NUSBAUM

1. Would you live for Je-sus, and be always pure and good? Would you walk with
2. Would you have Him make you free, and fol-low at His call? Would you know the
3. Would you in His king-dom find a place of constant rest? Would you prove Him

Him with-in the nar-row road? Would you have Him bear your bur-den, car-ry
peace that comes by giving all? Would you have Him save you, so that you need
true in prov-i-den-tial test? Would you in His ser-vice la-bor al-ways

CHORUS

all your load?
nev-er fall? Let Him have His way with thee. His pow'r can make you what you
at your best?

ought to be. His blood can cleanse your heart and make you free. His love can

rit.

fill your soul, and you will see 'Twas best for Him to have His way with thee.

474 Jesus Is Calling

J. M. H.

J. M. HARRIS
CHO. ARR.

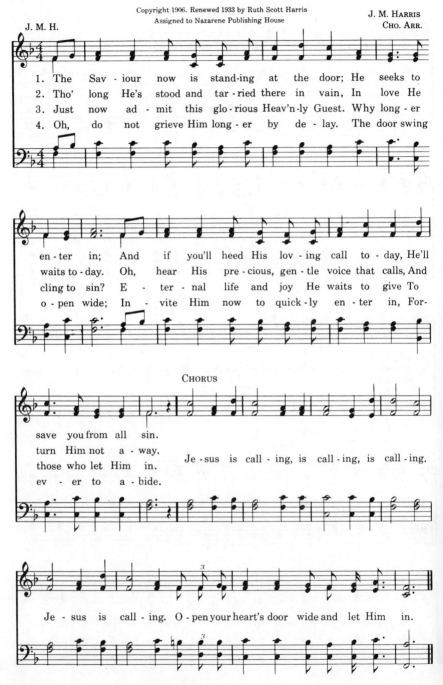

1. The Sav-iour now is stand-ing at the door; He seeks to
   en-ter in; And if you'll heed His lov-ing call to-day, He'll
   save you from all sin.

2. Tho' long He's stood and tar-ried there in vain, In love He
   waits to-day. Oh, hear His pre-cious, gen-tle voice that calls, And
   turn Him not a-way.

3. Just now ad-mit this glo-rious Heav'n-ly Guest. Why long-er
   cling to sin? E-ter-nal life and joy He waits to give To
   those who let Him in.

4. Oh, do not grieve Him long-er by de-lay. The door swing
   o-pen wide; In-vite Him now to quick-ly en-ter in, For-
   ev-er to a-bide.

CHORUS

Je-sus is call-ing, is call-ing, is call-ing,

Je-sus is call-ing. O-pen your heart's door wide and let Him in.

475 Is Your All on the Altar?

E. A. H.

ELISHA A. HOFFMAN

1. You have longed for sweet peace, and for faith to in-crease, And have ear-nest-ly,
2. Would you walk with the Lord, in the light of His Word, And have peace and con-
3. Oh, we nev-er can know what the Lord will be-stow Of the bless-ings for
4. Who can tell all the love He will send from a-bove, And how hap-py our

fer-vent-ly prayed; But you can-not have rest or be per-fect-ly blest
tent-ment al-way? You must do His sweet will; to be free from all ill,
which we have prayed Till our bod-y and soul He doth ful-ly con-trol,
hearts will be made; Of the fel-low-ship sweet we shall share at His feet,

CHORUS

Un-til all on the al-tar is laid.
On the al-tar your all you must lay.
And our all on the al-tar is laid.
When our all on the al-tar is laid!

Is your all on the al-tar of

sac-ri-fice laid? Your heart does the Spir-it con-trol?___ You can on-ly be

blest and have peace and sweet rest As you yield Him your bod-y and soul.

476 Come Just as You Are

Copyright 1928 by Lillenas Publishing Co.

H. L.

HALDOR LILLENAS

1. Ye who are troub-led and burdened by sin,
2. Deep in your heart sin has writ-ten its scar;
3. Sin - ful and guilt -y, heart-bro-ken and lost, Come just as you are.
4. Naught of your goodness for sin can a -tone;
5. Come with your heartache, your sorrow and pain;

Come to the Sav-iour, a new life be-gin. Oh, come just as you are!
Tho' from your Fa - ther you've wandered a - far, Oh, come just as you are!
Think what your ransom on Cal - va - ry cost! Oh, come just as you are!
Trust in the mer - it of Je - sus a -lone, And come just as you are.
No one has come to the Sav-iour in vain. Oh, come just as you are!

CHORUS

Come just as you are. Oh, come just as you are!__

Turn from your sin, let the Sav-iour come in, And come just as you are.

477 Is Thy Heart Right with God?

E. A. H.   ELISHA A. HOFFMAN

1. Have thy af-fec-tions been nailed to the Cross?
2. Hast thou do-min-ion o'er self and o'er sin?
3. Is there no more con-dem-na-tion for sin?
4. Are all thy pow'rs un-der Je-sus' con-trol?

Is thy heart right with God?

Dost thou count all things for Je-sus but loss?
O-ver all e-vil with-out and with-in?
Does Je-sus rule in the tem-ple with-in?
Does He each mo-ment a-bide in thy soul?

Is thy heart right with God?

CHORUS

Is thy heart right with God? Wash'd in the crim-son flood, Cleansed and made

ho-ly, hum-ble and low-ly, Right in the sight of God?___

of God?

478 Have Ye Received the Holy Ghost?

Mrs. C. H. M.

Mrs. C. H. Morris

1. Ye are the tem-ples, Je-sus hath spo-ken, Tem-ples of
2. He who has par-doned sure-ly will cleanse thee, All of the
3. Show-ers of mer-cy, full-ness of bless-ing Ev-er the
4. Wea-ry of wan-d'ring, come in-to Ca-naan; Feast on the

God's Ho-ly Spir-it di-vine. Have ye re-ceived Him, bid-den Him
dross of thy na-ture re-fine. Cleansed from all sin, His pow-er will
Spir-it's in-dwell-ing at-tend. 'Tis this en-due-ment, pow-er for
full-ness and fat of the land; Feed on the man-na; dwell in the

en-ter, Make His a-bode in that poor heart of thine?
en-ter, Fill you and thrill you with pow-er di-vine.
ser-vice; Fruits for your la-bor He sure-ly will send.
sun-shine, Led by His Spir-it and kept by His hand.

Chorus

Have ye re-ceived, since ye be-
Have ye re-ceived, have ye re-ceived, since ye be-lieved,

lieved, The bless-ed Ho-ly Ghost?
since ye be-lieved, The bless-ed, bless-ed Ho-ly, bless-ed Ho-ly Ghost?

Have Ye Received the Holy Ghost?

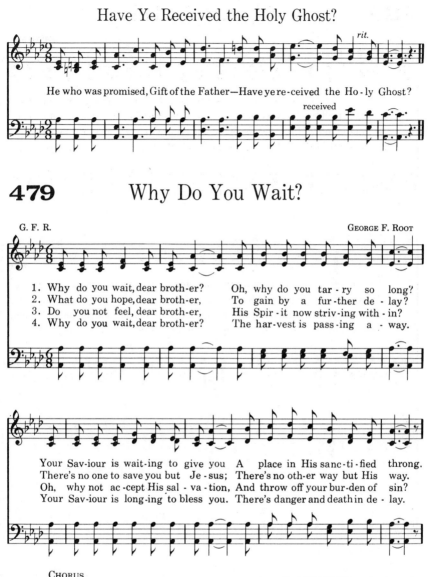

He who was promised, Gift of the Father—Have ye re-ceived the Ho-ly Ghost?

received

479 Why Do You Wait?

G. F. R.

GEORGE F. ROOT

1. Why do you wait, dear broth-er? Oh, why do you tar-ry so long?
2. What do you hope, dear broth-er, To gain by a fur-ther de-lay?
3. Do you not feel, dear broth-er, His Spir-it now striv-ing with-in?
4. Why do you wait, dear broth-er? The har-vest is pass-ing a-way.

Your Sav-iour is wait-ing to give you A place in His sanc-ti-fied throng.
There's no one to save you but Je-sus; There's no oth-er way but His way.
Oh, why not ac-cept His sal-va-tion, And throw off your bur-den of sin?
Your Sav-iour is long-ing to bless you. There's dan-ger and death in de-lay.

CHORUS

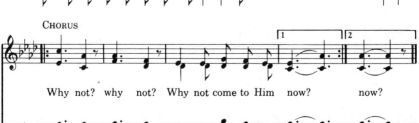

Why not? why not? Why not come to Him now? now?

480 Softly and Tenderly

W. L. T.

WILL L. THOMPSON

1. Soft-ly and ten-der-ly Je-sus is call-ing, Call-ing for you and for me.
2. Why should we tarry when Jesus is pleading, Pleading for you and for me?
3. Time is now fleeting; the moments are passing, Passing from you and from me;
4. Oh! for the wonder-ful love He has promised, Promised for you and for me!

See, on the portals He's waiting and watching, Watching for you and for me.
Why should we linger and heed not His mercies, Mer-cies for you and for me?
Shadows are gathering; death's night is coming, Com-ing for you and for me.
Tho' we have sinned, He has mercy and pardon, Par-don for you and for me.

CHORUS

Come home,___ come home.___ Ye who are wear-y, come home.___
Come home, come home.

Ear-nest-ly, ten-der-ly Je-sus is call-ing, Call-ing, "O sin-ner, come home!"

481 Don't Turn Him Away

H. L.

HALDOR LILLENAS
CHORUS ARRANGED

1. Pa-tient-ly, ten-der-ly plead-ing, Je-sus is stand-ing to-day;
2. Gracious, com-pas-sion-ate mer-cy Bro't Him from mansions a-bove;
3. Can you not now hear Him call-ing? Do not ill-treat such a Friend.
4. Now is the time to re-ceive Him; Grant Him ad-mis-sion to-day.

At your heart's door He knocks as be-fore. Oh, turn Him no long-er a-way!
Caused Him to wait Just out-side your gate. Oh, yield to His won-der-ful love!
Give up your sin. Oh, let Him come in! Lo! He will be true to the end.
Grieve Him no more, But o-pen your door, And turn Him no long-er a-way.

CHORUS

Don't turn Him a-way, don't turn Him a-way. He has come back to your heart again,

Al-tho' you've gone a-stray. Oh, how you'll need Him to plead your cause On that e-

ter-nal day! Don't turn the Saviour away from your heart; Don't turn Him a-way.

482   The Sheltering Rock

W. E. P.

W. E. PENN

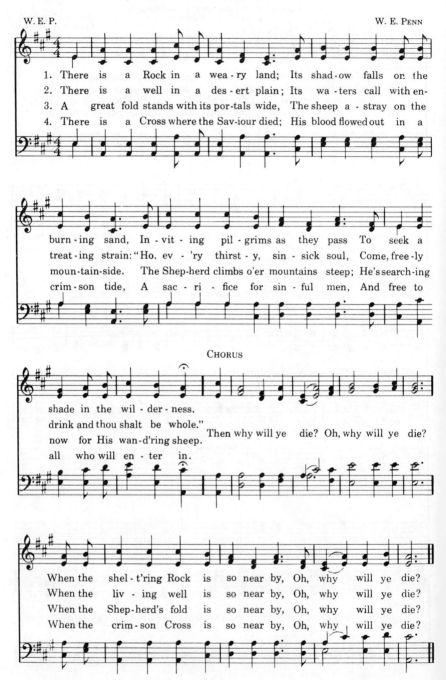

1. There is a Rock in a wea-ry land; Its shad-ow falls on the
2. There is a well in a des-ert plain; Its wa-ters call with en-
3. A great fold stands with its por-tals wide, The sheep a-stray on the
4. There is a Cross where the Sav-iour died; His blood flowed out in a

burn-ing sand, In-vit-ing pil-grims as they pass To seek a
treat-ing strain:"Ho, ev-'ry thirst-y, sin-sick soul, Come, free-ly
moun-tain-side. The Shep-herd climbs o'er mountains steep; He's search-ing
crim-son tide, A sac-ri-fice for sin-ful men, And free to

CHORUS

shade in the wil-der-ness.
drink and thou shalt be whole."   Then why will ye die? Oh, why will ye die?
now for His wan-d'ring sheep.
all who will en-ter in.

When the shel-t'ring Rock is so near by, Oh, why will ye die?
When the liv-ing well is so near by, Oh, why will ye die?
When the Shep-herd's fold is so near by, Oh, why will ye die?
When the crim-son Cross is so near by, Oh, why will ye die?

483 Are You Washed in the Blood?

E. A. H.

ELISHA A. HOFFMAN

1. Have you been to Je-sus for the cleans-ing pow'r?
2. Are you walk-ing dai-ly by the Sav-iour's side?
3. When the Bridegroom cometh will your robes be white?
4. Lay a-side the gar-ments that are stained with sin.

Are you washed in the

Are you ful-ly trust-ing in His grace this hour? Are you
blood of the Lamb? Do you rest each mo-ment in the Cru-ci-fied? Are you
Will your soul be read-y for the man-sions bright, And be
There's a fountain flow-ing for the soul un-clean. Oh, be

CHORUS

washed in the blood of the Lamb? Are you washed in the blood,

Are you washed in the blood,

In the soul-cleans-ing blood of the Lamb? Are your gar-ments

of the Lamb?

spot-less? Are they white as snow? Are you washed in the blood of the Lamb?

484 Oh, Why Not Tonight?

Elizabeth Reed

J. Calvin Bushey

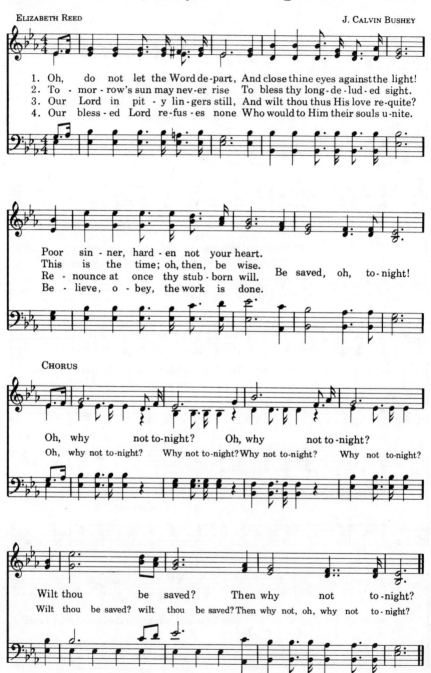

1. Oh, do not let the Word de-part, And close thine eyes against the light!
2. To - mor - row's sun may nev-er rise To bless thy long-de-lud-ed sight.
3. Our Lord in pit - y lin-gers still, And wilt thou thus His love re-quite?
4. Our bless - ed Lord re-fus - es none Who would to Him their souls u-nite.

Poor sin - ner, hard - en not your heart.
This is the time; oh, then, be wise.
Re - nounce at once thy stub - born will. Be saved, oh, to - night!
Be - lieve, o - bey, the work is done.

Chorus

Oh, why not to-night? Oh, why not to-night?
Oh, why not to-night? Why not to-night? Why not to-night? Why not to-night?

Wilt thou be saved? Then why not to-night?
Wilt thou be saved? wilt thou be saved? Then why not, oh, why not to-night?

485 Jesus Is Calling

FANNY J. CROSBY

GEO. C. STEBBINS

1. Je-sus is ten-der-ly call-ing thee home— Call-ing to-day,
2. Je-sus is call-ing the wea-ry to rest— Call-ing to-day,
3. Je-sus is wait-ing; oh, come to Him now— Wait-ing to-day,
4. Je-sus is plead-ing; oh, list to His voice— Hear Him to-day,

call-ing to-day. Why from the sun-shine of love wilt thou roam
call-ing to-day. Bring Him thy bur-den and thou shalt be blest;
wait-ing to-day. Come with thy sins; at His feet low-ly bow.
hear Him to-day. They who be-lieve on His name shall re-joice.

REFRAIN

Far-ther and far-ther a-way?
He will not turn thee a-way.   Call - ing to day,___
Come, and no long-er de-lay.
Quick-ly a-rise and a-way.   Call-ing, call-ing to-day, to-day,

Call - ing to day,___   Je - sus is
Call-ing, call-ing to-day, to-day; Je-sus is ten-der-ly

call - ing, Is ten-der-ly call-ing to-day.
call-ing to-day,

486 Only Trust Him

J. H. S.   J. H. Stockton

1. Come, ev - 'ry soul by sin op-pressed, There's mer-cy with the Lord;
2. For Je - sus shed His pre - cious blood Rich bless-ings to be - stow.
3. Yes, Je - sus is the Truth, the Way, That leads you in - to rest.

And He will sure - ly give you rest By trust - ing in His Word.
Plunge now in - to the crim - son flood That wash-es white as snow.
Be - lieve in Him with - out de - lay, And you are ful - ly blest.

REFRAIN

On - ly trust Him, on - ly trust Him, On - ly trust Him now;

He will save you, He will save you, He will save you now.

487 I Am Trusting, Lord, in Thee

WM. McDONALD

WM. G. FISCHER

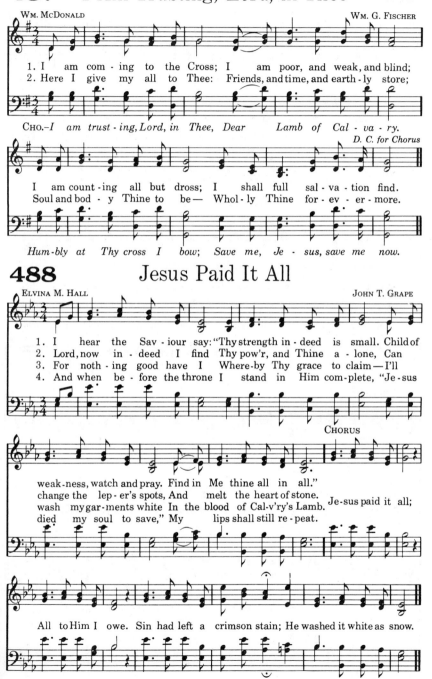

1. I am com - ing to the Cross; I am poor, and weak, and blind;
2. Here I give my all to Thee: Friends, and time, and earth - ly store;

CHO.–I am trust - ing, Lord, in Thee, Dear Lamb of Cal - va - ry.

D. C. for Chorus

I am count - ing all but dross; I shall full sal - va - tion find.
Soul and bod - y Thine to be — Whol - ly Thine for - ev - er - more.

Hum - bly at Thy cross I bow; Save me, Je - sus, save me now.

488 Jesus Paid It All

ELVINA M. HALL

JOHN T. GRAPE

1. I hear the Sav - iour say: "Thy strength in - deed is small. Child of
2. Lord, now in - deed I find Thy pow'r, and Thine a - lone, Can
3. For noth - ing good have I Where-by Thy grace to claim — I'll
4. And when be - fore the throne I stand in Him com - plete, "Je - sus

CHORUS

weak-ness, watch and pray. Find in Me thine all in all."
change the lep - er's spots, And melt the heart of stone.
wash my gar-ments white In the blood of Cal-v'ry's Lamb.   Je-sus paid it all;
died my soul to save," My lips shall still re - peat.

All to Him I owe. Sin had left a crimson stain; He washed it white as snow.

489 Room at the Fountain

M. J. H.

Mrs. M. J. Harris

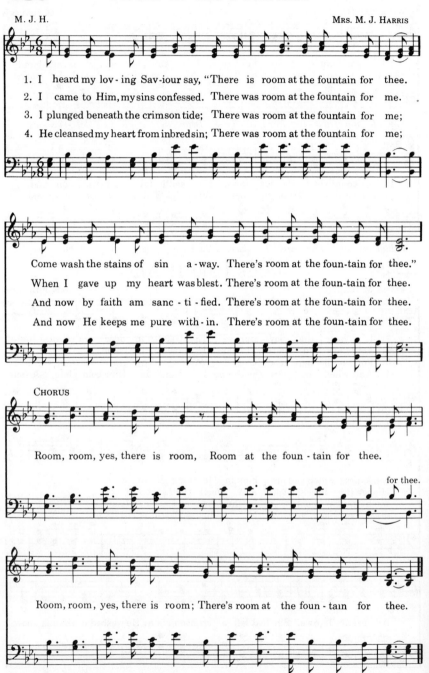

1. I heard my lov-ing Sav-iour say, "There is room at the fountain for thee.
2. I came to Him, my sins confessed. There was room at the fountain for me.
3. I plunged beneath the crimson tide; There was room at the fountain for me;
4. He cleansed my heart from inbred sin; There was room at the fountain for me;

Come wash the stains of sin a-way. There's room at the foun-tain for thee."
When I gave up my heart was blest. There's room at the foun-tain for thee.
And now by faith am sanc-ti-fied. There's room at the foun-tain for thee.
And now He keeps me pure with-in. There's room at the foun-tain for thee.

CHORUS

Room, room, yes, there is room, Room at the foun-tain for thee.

for thee.

Room, room, yes, there is room; There's room at the foun-tain for thee.

490 Jesus Breaks Every Fetter

OLD MELODY

1. I am all on the al - tar, I am all on the al - tar,
2. I will nev - er - more doubt Him, I will nev - er - more doubt Him,
3. I will rest on His prom - ise, I will rest on His prom - ise,

CHO.—Je - sus breaks ev - 'ry fet - ter. Je - sus breaks ev - 'ry fet - ter.

D. C. for Chorus

I am all on the al - tar, Which was made for me.
I will nev - er - more doubt Him, For He cleans - es me.
I will rest on His prom - ise, Which was made for me.

Je - sus breaks ev - 'ry fet - ter. Je - sus sets me free.

491 I'm Believing and Receiving

ARR. BY W. J. K.

1. Sins of years are washed a - way, Black-est stains be - come as snow,
2. Doubts and fears are borne a - long On the cur-rent's cease-less flow;
3. Ease and wealth be - come as dross; Worthless, earth's de-light and show;
4. Self-ish - ness is lost in love, Love for Him whose love you know;

CHO.—I'm be - liev - ing and re - ceiv - ing, While I to the foun-tain go;

D. C. for Chorus

Dark-est night is changed to day,
Sor-row chang - es in - to song
All my boast is in the Cross
All my treas - ure is a - bove

When I to the foun - tain go.

And my heart the waves are cleans-ing Whit-er than the driv - en snow.

492 Fill Me Now

E. H. STOKES

JNO. R. SWENEY

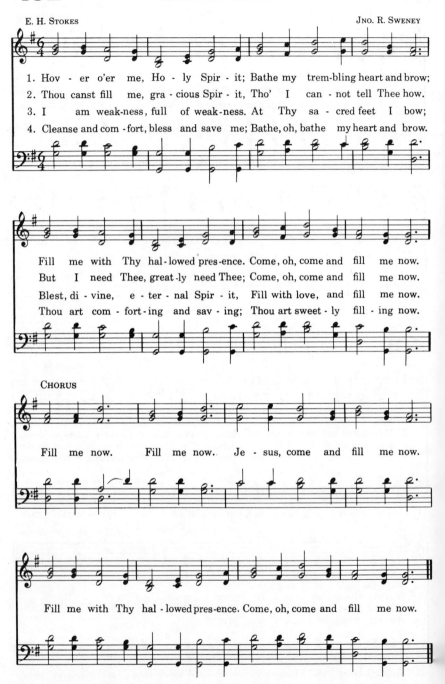

1. Hov - er o'er me, Ho - ly Spir - it; Bathe my trem-bling heart and brow;
2. Thou canst fill me, gra - cious Spir - it, Tho' I can - not tell Thee how.
3. I am weak-ness, full of weak-ness. At Thy sa - cred feet I bow;
4. Cleanse and com - fort, bless and save me; Bathe, oh, bathe my heart and brow.

Fill me with Thy hal - lowed pres-ence. Come, oh, come and fill me now.
But I need Thee, great -ly need Thee; Come, oh, come and fill me now.
Blest, di - vine, e - ter - nal Spir - it, Fill with love, and fill me now.
Thou art com - fort-ing and sav - ing; Thou art sweet - ly fill - ing now.

CHORUS

Fill me now. Fill me now. Je - sus, come and fill me now.

Fill me with Thy hal - lowed pres-ence. Come, oh, come and fill me now.

493   I Can, I Will, I Do Believe

1. I'm kneel-ing at the mer-cy seat, I'm kneel-ing at the mer-cy seat,
2. Re-fin-ing fire go thro' my heart, Re-fin-ing fire go thro' my heart,
3. Oh, that it now from heav'n might fall, Oh, that it now from heav'n might fall,

CHO.—I can, I will, I do be-lieve; I can, I will, I do be-lieve;

D. C. for Chorus

I'm kneel-ing at the mer-cy seat, Where Je-sus an-swers pray'r.
Re-fin-ing fire go thro' my heart, Il-lu-mi-nate my soul.
Oh, that it now from heav'n might fall, And all my sins con-sume.

I can, I will, I do be-lieve That Je-sus saves me now.

494   Take Me as I Am

ELIZA H. HAMILTON

J. H. STOCKTON

1. Je-sus, my Lord, to Thee I cry. Un-less Thou help me I must die.
2. Help-less I am, and full of guilt, But yet for me Thy blood was spilt;
3. I thirst, I long to know Thy love; Thy full sal-va-tion I would prove.
4. If Thou hast work for me to do, In-spire my will, my heart re-new,

Fine

Oh, bring Thy free sal-va-tion nigh, And take me as I am!
And Thou canst make me what Thou wilt, But take me as I am!
But since to Thee I can-not move, Oh, take me as I am!
And work both in and by me too; But take me as I am!

D.S.—bring Thy free sal-va-tion nigh, And take me as I am!

REFRAIN

D. S.

Take me as I am. Take me as I am. Oh,

495 I Surrender All

J. W. Van Deventer

W. S. Weeden

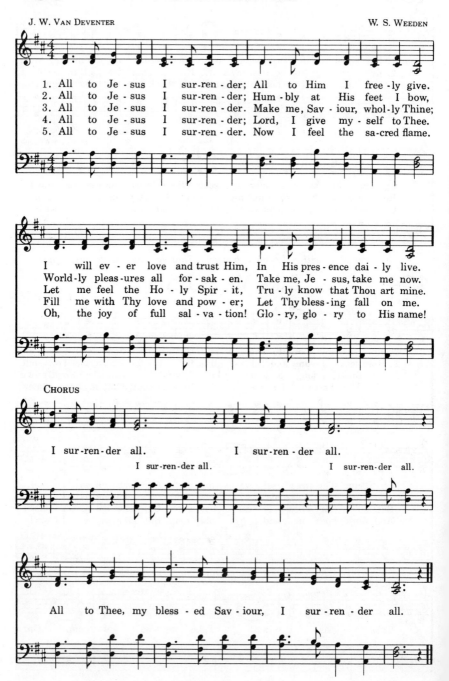

496 I Receive Him

D. G. B.

ARR. BY REV. D. G. BACON

1. He is cleans-ing, He is cleans-ing, The bless-ed Ho-ly Ghost;
2. He will teach me, He will teach me, The bless-ed Ho-ly Ghost;
3. He will guide me, He will guide me, The bless-ed Ho-ly Ghost;
4. He will keep me, He will keep me, The bless-ed Ho-ly Ghost;

CHO.—I re-ceive Him, I re-ceive Him, The bless-ed Ho-ly Ghost;

D. C. for Chorus

He is cleans-ing, He is cleans-ing, The bless-ed Ho-ly Ghost.
He will teach me, He will teach me, The bless-ed Ho-ly Ghost.
He will guide me, He will guide me, The bless-ed Ho-ly Ghost.
He will keep me, He will keep me, The bless-ed Ho-ly Ghost.

I re-ceive Him, I re-ceive Him, The bless-ed Ho-ly Ghost.

497 I'll Live for Him

R. E. HUDSON

C. R. DUNBAR

1. My life, my love, I give to Thee, Thou Lamb of God, who died for me.
2. I now be-lieve Thou dost re-ceive, For Thou hast died that I might live;
3. O Thou who died on Cal-va-ry, To save my soul and make me free,

CHO.—I'll live for Him who died for me. How hap-py then my life shall be!

D. C. for Chorus

Oh, may I ev-er faith-ful be,
And now hence-forth I'll trust in Thee, My Sav-iour and my God!
I'll con-se-crate my life to Thee,

I'll live for Him who died for me, My Sav-iour and my God!

RESPONSIVE READINGS

1 The Ten Commandments

1. Thou shalt have no other gods before me.

2. Thou shalt not make unto thee any graven image, or any likeness of any thing that is in heaven above, or that is in the earth beneath, or that is in the water under the earth: thou shalt not bow down thyself to them, nor serve them: for I the Lord thy God am a jealous God, visiting the iniquity of the fathers upon the children unto the third and fourth generation of them that hate me; and shewing mercy unto thousands of them that love me, and keep my commandments.

3. Thou shalt not take the name of the Lord thy God in vain; for the Lord will not hold him guiltless that taketh his name in vain.

4. Remember the sabbath day, to keep it holy. Six days shalt thou labour, and do all thy work: but the seventh day is the sabbath of the Lord thy God: in it thou shalt not do any work, thou, nor thy son, nor thy daughter, thy manservant, nor thy maidservant, nor thy cattle, nor thy stranger that is within thy gates: for in six days the Lord made heaven and earth, the sea, and all that in them is, and rested the seventh day: wherefore the Lord blessed the sabbath day, and hallowed it.

5. Honour thy father and thy mother: that thy days may be long upon the land which the Lord thy God giveth thee.

6. Thou shalt not kill.

7. Thou shalt not commit adultery.

8. Thou shalt not steal.

9. Thou shalt not bear false witness against thy neighbour.

Unison

10. Thou shalt not covet thy neighbour's house, thou shalt not covet thy neighbour's wife, nor his manservant, nor his maidservant, nor his ox, nor his ass, nor any thing that is thy neighbour's.

—*Exodus 20:3-17*

2   The Lord's Prayer

Unison

Our Father which art in heaven, Hallowed be thy name. Thy kingdom come. Thy will be done in earth, as it is in heaven. Give us this day our daily bread. And forgive us our debts, as we forgive our debtors. And lead us not into temptation, but deliver us from evil: for thine is the kingdom, and the power, and the glory, for ever. Amen.

—*Matthew 6:9b-13*

3 The Apostles' Creed

Unison

I believe in God the Father Almighty, Maker of heaven and earth;

And in Jesus Christ, His only Son, our Lord; who was conceived by the Holy Ghost, born of the Virgin Mary, suffered under Pontius Pilate, was crucified, dead, and buried; He descended into hell; the third day He arose again from the dead; He ascended into heaven, and sitteth at the right hand of God the Father Almighty; from thence He shall come to judge the quick and the dead.

I believe in the Holy Ghost, the Holy Church of Jesus Christ, the communion of saints, the forgiveness of sins, the resurrection of the body, and the life everlasting. Amen.

4   Resurrection

Now if Christ be preached that he rose from the dead, how say some among you that there is no resurrection of the dead?

But if there be no resurrection of the dead, then is Christ not risen:

And if Christ be not risen, then is our preaching vain, and your faith is also vain.

Yea, and we are found false witnesses of God; because we have testified of God that he raised up Christ: whom he raised not up, if so be that the dead rise not.

For if the dead rise not, then is not Christ raised:

And if Christ be not raised, your faith is vain; ye are yet in your sins.

Then they also which are fallen asleep in Christ are perished.

If in this life only we have hope in Christ, we are of all men most miserable.

But now is Christ risen from the dead, and become the firstfruits of them that slept.

Unison

For since by man came death, by man came also the resurrection of the dead. For as in Adam all die, even so in Christ shall all be made alive.

—*1 Corinthians 15:12-22*

5   God's Care

The Lord is my shepherd; I shall not want.

He maketh me to lie down in green pastures: he leadeth me beside the still waters.

He restoreth my soul: he leadeth me in the paths of righteousness for his name's sake.

Yea, though I walk through the valley of the shadow of death, I will fear no evil: for thou art with me; thy rod and thy staff they comfort me.

Thou preparest a table before me in the presence of mine enemies: thou anointest my head with oil; my cup runneth over.

Unison

Surely goodness and mercy shall follow me all the days of my life: and I will dwell in the house of the Lord for ever.

—*Psalms 23*

6   Redemption

O magnify the Lord with me, and let us exalt his name together.

I sought the Lord, and he heard me, and delivered me from all my fears.

They looked unto him, and were lightened: and their faces were not ashamed.

This poor man cried, and the Lord heard him, and saved him out of all his troubles.

The angel of the Lord encampeth round about them that fear him, and delivereth them.

O taste and see that the Lord is good: blessed is the man that trusteth in him.

O fear the Lord, ye his saints: for there is no want to them that fear him.

The Lord is nigh unto them that are of a broken heart; and saveth such as be of a contrite spirit.

Many are the afflictions of the righteous: but the Lord delivereth him out of them all.

Unison

The Lord redeemeth the soul of his servants: and none of them that trust in him shall be desolate.

—Psalms 34:3-9, 18-19, 22

7   Revivals

Wilt thou not revive us again: that thy people may rejoice in thee?

Shew us thy mercy, O Lord, and grant us thy salvation.

If my people, which are called by my name, shall humble themselves, and pray, and seek my face, and turn from their wicked ways; then will I hear from heaven, and will forgive their sin, and will heal their land.

For thus saith the high and lofty One that inhabiteth eternity, whose name is Holy; I dwell in the high and holy place, with him also that is of a contrite and humble spirit, to revive the spirit of the humble, and to revive the heart of the contrite ones.

O Lord, revive thy work in the midst of the years, in the midst of the years make known; in wrath remember mercy.

Now be ye not stiffnecked, as your fathers were, but yield yourselves unto the Lord, and enter into his sanctuary, which he hath sanctified for ever: and serve the Lord your God, that the fierceness of his wrath may turn away from you.

For if ye turn again unto the Lord, your brethren and your children shall find compassion before them that lead them captive, so that they shall come again into this land: for the Lord your God is gracious and merciful, and will not turn away his face from you, if ye return unto him.

Unison

Return, O Lord, how long? and let it repent thee concerning thy servants. O satisfy us early with thy mercy; that we may rejoice and be glad all our days.

—Psalms 85:6, 7; II Chronicles 7:14;
Isaiah 57:15; Habakkuk 3:2b;
II Chronicles 30:8, 9; Psalms 90:13, 14

8   Eternal Life

And as Moses lifted up the serpent in the wilderness, even so must the Son of man be lifted up:

That whosoever believeth in him should not perish, but have eternal life.

For God so loved the world, that he gave his only begotten Son, that whosoever believeth in him should not perish, but have everlasting life.

For God sent not his Son into the world to condemn the world; but that the world through him might be saved.

He that believeth on the Son hath everlasting life: and he that believeth not the Son shall not see life; but the wrath of God abideth on him.

Jesus saith unto her, Thy brother shall rise again.

Martha saith unto him, I know that he shall rise again in the resurrection at the last day.

Unison

Jesus saith unto her, I am the resurrection, and the life: he that believeth in me, though he were dead, yet shall he live: and whosoever liveth and believeth in me shall never die.

—*John 3:14-17, 36; 11:23-26a*

9   Temptation

Blessed is the man that endureth temptation:

For when he is tried, he shall receive the crown of life, which the Lord hath promised to them that love him.

Let no man say when he is tempted, I am tempted of God:

For God cannot be tempted with evil, neither tempteth he any man:

But every man is tempted, when he is drawn away of his own lust, and enticed.

Then when lust hath conceived, it bringeth forth sin: and sin, when it is finished, bringeth forth death.

Neither let us tempt Christ, as some of them also tempted, and were destroyed of serpents.

Neither murmur ye, as some of them also murmured, and were destroyed of the destroyer.

Wherefore let him that thinketh he standeth take heed lest he fall.

Unison

There hath no temptation taken you but such as is common to man: but God is faithful, who will not suffer you to be tempted above that ye are able; but will with the temptation also make a way to escape, that ye may be able to bear it.

—*James 1:12-15; I Corinthians 10:9-10, 12-13*

10   Invitation

Come unto me, all ye that labour and are heavy laden, and I will give you rest.

Take my yoke upon you, and learn of me; for I am meek and lowly in heart; and ye shall find rest unto your souls. For my yoke is easy, and my burden is light.

Ho, every one that thirsteth, come ye to the waters, and he that hath no money; come ye, buy, and eat; yea, come, buy wine and milk without money and without price.

Incline your ear, and come unto me: hear, and your soul shall live; and I will make an everlasting covenant with you, even the sure mercies of David.

Seek ye the Lord while he may be found, call ye upon him while he is near:

Let the wicked forsake his way, and the unrighteous man his thoughts: and let him return unto the Lord, and he will have mercy upon him; and to our God, for he will abundantly pardon.

And the Spirit and the bride say, Come. And let him that heareth say, Come. And let him that is athirst come.

Unison
And whosoever will, let him take the water of life freely.
—*Matthew 11:28-30; Isaiah 55:1, 3, 6, 7; Revelation 22:17*

11 Christmas

Now when Jesus was born in Bethlehem of Judaea in the days of Herod the king, behold, there came wise men from the east to Jerusalem,

Saying, Where is he that is born King of the Jews? for we have seen his star in the east, and are come to worship him.

When Herod the king had heard these things, he was troubled, and all Jerusalem with him.

And when he had gathered all the chief priests and scribes of the people together, he demanded of them where Christ should be born.

And they said unto him, In Bethlehem of Judaea: for thus it is written by the prophet,

And thou Bethlehem, in the land of Juda, art not the least among the princes of Juda: for out of thee shall come a Governor, that shall rule my people Israel.

Then Herod, when he had privily called the wise men, enquired of them diligently what time the star appeared.

And he sent them to Bethlehem, and said, Go and search diligently for the young child; and when ye have found him, bring me word again, that I may come and worship him also.

When they had heard the king, they departed; and, lo, the star, which they saw in the east, went before them, till it came and stood over where the young child was.

When they saw the star, they rejoiced with exceeding great joy.

And when they were come into the house, they saw the young child with Mary his mother, and fell down and worshipped him: and when they had opened their treasures, they presented unto him gifts; gold, and frankincense, and myrrh.

Unison
And being warned of God in a dream that they should not return to Herod, they departed into their own country another way.
—*Matthew 2:1-12*

12 Holy Spirit

And when the day of Pentecost was fully come, they were all with one accord in one place. And suddenly there came a sound from heaven as of a rushing mighty wind, and it filled all the house where they were sitting.

And there appeared unto them cloven tongues like as of fire, and it sat upon each of them.

And they were all filled with the Holy Ghost, and began to speak with other tongues, as the Spirit gave them utterance.

And they were all amazed, and were in doubt, saying one to another, What meaneth this? Others mocking said, These men are full of new wine.

But Peter, standing up with the eleven, lifted up his voice, and said unto them, Ye men of Judaea, and all ye that dwell at Jerusalem, be this known unto you, and hearken to my words:

For these are not drunken, as ye suppose, seeing it is but the third hour of the day. But this is that which was spoken by the prophet Joel;

And it shall come to pass in the last days, saith God, I will pour out of my Spirit upon all flesh: and your sons and your daughters shall prophesy, and your young men shall see visions, and your old men shall dream dreams:

And on my servants and on my handmaidens I will pour out in those days of my Spirit; and they shall prophesy:

Now when they heard this, they were pricked in their heart, and said unto Peter and to the rest of the apostles, Men and brethren, what shall we do?

Unison

Then Peter said unto them, Repent, and be baptized every one of you in the name of Jesus Christ for the remission of sins, and ye shall receive the gift of the Holy Ghost.

—*Acts 2:1-4, 12-18, 37, 38*

13 Love

Though I speak with the tongues of men and of angels, and have not charity, I am become as sounding brass, or a tinkling cymbal.

And though I have the gift of prophecy, and understand all mysteries, and all knowledge; and though I have all faith, so that I could remove mountains, and have not charity, I am nothing.

And though I bestow all my goods to feed the poor, and though I give my body to be burned, and have not charity, it profiteth me nothing.

Charity suffereth long, and is kind; charity envieth not; charity vaunteth not itself, is not puffed up,

Doth not behave itself unseemly, seeketh not her own, is not easily provoked, thinketh no evil;

Rejoiceth not in iniquity, but rejoiceth in the truth;

Beareth all things, believeth all things, hopeth all things, endureth all things.

Charity never faileth: but whether there be prophecies, they shall fail; whether there be tongues, they shall cease; whether there be knowledge, it shall vanish away.

For we know in part, and we prophesy in part. But when that which is perfect is come, then that which is in part shall be done away.

When I was a child, I spake as a child, I understood as a child, I thought as a child: but when I became a man, I put away childish things.

For now we see through a glass, darkly; but then face to face: now I know in part; but then shall I know even as also I am known.

Unison

And now abideth faith, hope, charity, these three; but the greatest of these is charity.

—*I Corinthians 13*

14   Thanksgiving

Give thanks unto the Lord, call upon his name, make known his deeds among the people.

Sing unto him, sing psalms unto him, talk ye of all his wondrous works.

For the Lord thy God bringeth thee into a good land, a land of brooks of water, of fountains and depths that spring out of valleys and hills;

A land of wheat, and barley, and vines, and fig trees, and pomegranates; a land of oil olive, and honey;

A land wherein thou shalt eat bread without scarceness, thou shalt not lack any thing in it; a land whose stones are iron, and out of whose hills thou mayest dig brass.

When thou hast eaten and art full, then thou shalt bless the Lord thy God for the good land which he hath given thee.

Beware that thou forget not the Lord thy God, in not keeping his commandments, and his judgments, and his statutes, which I command thee this day:

Lest when thou hast eaten and art full, and hast built goodly houses, and dwelt therein; and when thy herds and thy flocks multiply, and thy silver and thy gold is multiplied, and all that thou hast is multiplied; then thine heart be lifted up, and thou forget the Lord thy God.

And thou say in thine heart, My power and the might of mine hand hath gotten me this wealth.

But thou shalt remember the Lord thy God: for it is he that giveth thee power to get wealth.

Now therefore, our God, we thank thee, and praise thy glorious name.

Unison

. . . . for all things come of thee, and of thine own have we given thee.

—*I Chronicles 16:8, 9; Deuteronomy 8:7-14a, 17, 18a; I Chronicles 29:13, 14b*

15   Salvation

For I am not ashamed of the gospel of Christ: for it is the power of God unto salvation to every one that believeth;

For with the heart man believeth unto righteousness; and with the mouth confession is made unto salvation.

For whosoever shall call upon the name of the Lord shall be saved.

(For he saith, I have heard thee in a time accepted, and in the day of salvation have I succoured thee: behold, now is the accepted time; behold, now is the day of salvation.)

Wherefore, my beloved, as ye have always obeyed, not as in my presence only, but now much more in my absence, work out your own salvation with fear and trembling.

For it is God which worketh in you both to will and to do of his good pleasure.

But let us, who are of the day, be sober, putting on the breastplate of faith and love; and for an helmet, the hope of salvation.

For God hath not appointed us to wrath, but to obtain salvation by our Lord Jesus Christ.

For the grace of God that bringeth salvation hath appeared to all men,

Teaching us that, denying ungodliness and worldly lusts, we should live soberly, righteously, and godly in this present world;

Looking for that blessed hope, and the glorious appearing of the great God and our Saviour Jesus Christ;

Unison

Who gave himself for us, that he might redeem us from all iniquity, and purify unto himself a peculiar people, zealous of good works.

—Romans 1:16a; 10:10, 13; II Corinthians 6:2; Philippians 2:12, 13; I Thessalonians 5:8, 9; Titus 2:11-14

16   Praise

Bless the Lord, O my soul: and all that is within me, bless his holy name.

Bless the Lord, O my soul, and forget not all his benefits:

Who forgiveth all thine iniquities; who healeth all thy diseases;

Who redeemeth thy life from destruction; who crowneth thee with lovingkindness and tender mercies;

Who satisfieth thy mouth with good things; so that thy youth is renewed like the eagle's.

The Lord executeth righteousness and judgment for all that are oppressed.

He made known his ways unto Moses, his acts unto the children of Israel.

The Lord is merciful and gracious, slow to anger, and plenteous in mercy.

He will not always chide: neither will he keep his anger for ever.

He hath not dealt with us after our sins; nor rewarded us according to our iniquities.

For as the heaven is high above the earth, so great is his mercy toward them that fear him.

As far as the east is from the west, so far hath he removed our transgressions from us.

Like as a father pitieth his children, so the Lord pitieth them that fear him.

For he knoweth our frame; he remembereth that we are dust.

Bless ye the Lord, all ye his hosts; ye ministers of his, that do his pleasure.

Unison

Bless the Lord, all his works in all places of his dominion: bless the Lord, O my soul.

—Psalms 103:1-14, 21-22

17 Holiness

Having therefore these promises, dearly beloved, let us cleanse ourselves from all filthiness of the flesh and spirit, perfecting holiness in the fear of God.

Know ye not, that to whom ye yield yourselves servants to obey, his servants ye are to whom ye obey; whether of sin unto death, or of obedience unto righteousness?

But God be thanked, that ye were the servants of sin, but ye have obeyed from the heart that form of doctrine which was delivered you.

Being then made free from sin, ye became the servants of righteousness.

What fruit had ye then in those things whereof ye are now ashamed? for the end of those things is death.

But now being made free from sin, and become servants to God, ye have your fruit unto holiness, and the end everlasting life.

Furthermore we have had fathers of our flesh which corrected us, and we gave them reverence: shall we not much rather be in subjection unto the Father of spirits, and live?

For they verily for a few days chastened us after their own pleasure; but he for our profit, that we might be partakers of his holiness.

Now no chastening for the present seemeth to be joyous, but grievous: nevertheless afterward it yieldeth the peaceable fruit of righteousness unto them which are exercised thereby.

Wherefore lift up the hands which hang down, and the feeble knees;

And make straight paths for your feet, lest that which is lame be turned out of the way; but let it rather be healed.

Unison

Follow peace with all men, and holiness, without which no man shall see the Lord.

—II Corinthians 7:1; Romans 6:16-18, 21, 22; Hebrews 12:9-14

After this manner therefore pray ye: Our Father which art in heaven, Hallowed be thy name.

Thy kingdom come. Thy will be done in earth, as it is in heaven.

Give us this day our daily bread.

And forgive us our debts, as we forgive our debtors.

And lead us not into temptation, but deliver us from evil: for thine is the kingdom, and the power, and the glory, for ever. Amen.

For if ye forgive men their trespasses, your heavenly Father will also forgive you:

But if ye forgive not men their trespasses, neither will your Father forgive your trespasses.

Ask, and it shall be given you; seek, and ye shall find; knock, and it shall be opened unto you:

For every one that asketh receiveth; and he that seeketh findeth; and to him that knocketh it shall be opened.

Or what man is there of you, whom if his son ask bread, will he give him a stone? Or if he ask a fish, will he give him a serpent?

If ye then, being evil, know how to give good gifts unto your children, how much more shall your Father which is in heaven give good things to them that ask him?

Unison

The effectual fervent prayer of a righteous man availeth much.

—*Matthew 6:9-15; 7:7-11; James 5:16b*

Grace be to you and peace from God our Father, and from the Lord Jesus Christ.

For our rejoicing is this, the testimony of our conscience, that in simplicity and godly sincerity, not with fleshly wisdom, but by the grace of God, we have had our conversation in the world, and more abundantly to you-ward.

For all things are for your sakes, that the abundant grace might through the thanksgiving of many redound to the glory of God.

We then, as workers together with him, beseech you also that ye receive not the grace of God in vain.

For ye know the grace of our Lord Jesus Christ, that, though he was rich, yet for your sakes he became poor, that ye through his poverty might be rich.

And God is able to make all grace abound toward you; that ye, always having all sufficiency in all things, may abound to every good work:

My grace is sufficient for thee: for my strength is made perfect in weakness. Most gladly therefore will I rather glory in my infirmities, that the power of Christ may rest upon me.

Unison

The grace of the Lord Jesus Christ, and the love of God, and the communion of the Holy Ghost, be with you all. Amen.

—*II Corinthians 1:2, 12; 4:15; 6:1; 8:9; 9:8; 12:9; 13:14*

20 Divine Guidance

Unto thee, O Lord, do I lift up my soul.

O my God, I trust in thee: let me not be ashamed, let not mine enemies triumph over me.

Yea, let none that wait on thee be ashamed: let them be ashamed which transgress without cause.

Shew me thy ways, O Lord; teach me thy paths.

Lead me in thy truth, and teach me: for thou art the God of my salvation; on thee do I wait all the day.

Remember, O Lord, thy tender mercies and thy lovingkindnesses; for they have been ever of old.

For thy name's sake, O Lord, pardon mine iniquity; for it is great.

What man is he that feareth the Lord? him shall he teach in the way that he shall choose.

His soul shall dwell at ease; and his seed shall inherit the earth.

Unison

The secret of the Lord is with them that fear him; and he will shew them his covenant.

—Psalms 25:1-6, 11-14

21 Practical Exhortations

Therefore let us not sleep, as do others; but let us watch and be sober. For they that sleep sleep in the night; and they that be drunken are drunken in the night.

But let us, who are of the day, be sober, putting on the breastplate of faith and love; and for an helmet, the hope of salvation.

For God hath not appointed us to wrath, but to obtain salvation by our Lord Jesus Christ, who died for us, that, whether we wake or sleep, we should live together with him.

Wherefore comfort yourselves together, and edify one another, even as also ye do.

And we beseech you, brethren, to know them which labour among you, and are over you in the Lord, and admonish you; and to esteem them very highly in love for their work's sake. And be at peace among yourselves.

Now we exhort you, brethren, warn them that are unruly, comfort the feebleminded, support the weak, be patient toward all men.

See that none render evil for evil unto any man; but ever follow that which is good, both among yourselves, and to all men.

Rejoice evermore. Pray without ceasing.

In every thing give thanks: for this is the will of God in Christ Jesus concerning you.

Quench not the Spirit. Despise not prophesyings. Prove all things; hold fast that which is good.

Abstain from all appearance of evil.

Unison

The grace of our Lord Jesus Christ be with you. Amen.

—I Thessalonians 5:6-22, 28

22   Heaven

And I saw a new heaven and a new earth: for the first heaven and the first earth were passed away; and there was no more sea.

And I John saw the holy city, new Jerusalem, coming down from God out of heaven, prepared as a bride adorned for her husband.

And I heard a great voice out of heaven saying, Behold, the tabernacle of God is with men, and he will dwell with them, and they shall be his people, and God himself shall be with them, and be their God.

And God shall wipe away all tears from their eyes; and there shall be no more death, neither sorrow, nor crying, neither shall there be any more pain: for the former things are passed away.

And he carried me away in the spirit to a great and high mountain, and shewed me that great city, the holy Jerusalem, descending out of heaven from God,

Having the glory of God: and her light was like unto a stone most precious, even like a jasper stone, clear as crystal;

And I saw no temple therein: for the Lord God Almighty and the Lamb are the temple of it.

And the city had no need of the sun, neither of the moon, to shine in it: for the glory of God did lighten it, and the Lamb is the light thereof.

And the gates of it shall not be shut at all by day: for there shall be no night there.

Unison

And they need no candle, neither light of the sun; for the Lord God giveth them light: and they shall reign for ever and ever.

—Revelation 21:1-4, 10, 11, 22, 23, 25; 22:5b

23   The New Year

Therefore, my brethren dearly beloved and longed for, my joy and crown, so stand fast in the Lord, my dearly beloved.

Rejoice in the Lord alway: and again I say, Rejoice.

Let your moderation be known unto all men. The Lord is at hand.

Be careful for nothing; but in every thing by prayer and supplication with thanksgiving let your requests be made known unto God.

And the peace of God, which passeth all understanding, shall keep your hearts and minds through Christ Jesus.

Finally, brethren, whatsoever things are true, whatsoever things are honest, whatsoever things are just, whatsoever things are pure, whatsoever things are lovely, whatsoever things are of good report; if there be any virtue, and if there be any praise, think on these things.

Those things, which ye have both learned, and received, and heard, and seen in me, do: and the God of peace shall be with you.

Brethren, I count not myself to have apprehended: but this one thing I do, forgetting those things which are behind, and reaching forth unto those things which are before,

I press toward the mark for the prize of the high calling of God in Christ Jesus.

Unison

Let us therefore, as many as be perfect, be thus minded: and if in any thing ye be otherwise minded, God shall reveal even this unto you.

—Philippians 4:1, 4-9; 3:13-15

Peace I leave with you, my peace I give unto you: not as the world giveth, give I unto you. Let not your heart be troubled, neither let it be afraid.

Behold, how good and how pleasant it is for brethren to dwell together in unity!

Unison

And the peace of God, which passeth all understanding, shall keep your hearts and minds through Christ Jesus.

—Isaiah 2:2-4; John 14:27; Psalms 133:1; Philippians 4:7

24   Peace

And it shall come to pass in the last days, that the mountain of the Lord's house shall be established in the top of the mountains, and shall be exalted above the hills; and all nations shall flow unto it.

And many people shall go and say, Come ye, and let us go up to the mountain of the Lord, to the house of the God of Jacob; and he will teach us of his ways, and we will walk in his paths: for out of Zion shall go forth the law, and the word of the Lord from Jerusalem.

And he shall judge among the nations, and shall rebuke many people: and they shall beat their swords into plowshares, and their spears into pruninghooks: nation shall not lift up sword against nation, neither shall they learn war any more.

25   Sanctification

Sanctify them through thy truth: thy word is truth.

And for their sakes I sanctify myself, that they also might be sanctified through the truth.

And God, which knoweth the hearts, bare them witness, giving them the Holy Ghost, even as he did unto us;

And put no difference between us and them, purifying their hearts by faith.

I am crucified with Christ: nevertheless I live; yet not I, but Christ liveth in me: and the life which I now live in the flesh I live by the faith of the Son of God, who loved me, and gave himself for me.

But unto every one of us is given grace according to the measure of the gift of Christ.

And he gave some, apostles; and some, prophets; and some, evangelists; and some, pastors and teachers;

For the perfecting of the saints, for the work of the ministry, for the edifying of the body of Christ:

Till we all come in the unity of the faith, and of the knowledge of the Son of God, unto a perfect man, unto the measure of the stature of the fulness of Christ.

But as he which hath called you is holy, so be ye holy in all manner of conversation; because it is written, Be ye holy; for I am holy.

And the very God of peace sanctify you wholly; and I pray God your whole spirit and soul and body be preserved blameless unto the coming of our Lord Jesus Christ.

Unison

Faithful is he that calleth you, who also will do it.

—John 17:17, 19 : Acts 15:8, 9 ;
Galatians 2 :20 ; Ephesians 4 :7, 11-13 ;
I Peter 1 :15, 16 ; I Thessalonians 5 :23, 24

26   Affliction

Therefore seeing we have this ministry, as we have received mercy, we faint not;

For God, who commanded the light to shine out of darkness, hath shined in our hearts, to give the light of the knowledge of the glory of God in the face of Jesus Christ.

But we have this treasure in earthen vessels, that the excellency of the power may be of God, and not of us.

We are troubled on every side, yet not distressed; we are perplexed, but not in despair;

Persecuted, but not forsaken; cast down, but not destroyed;

Always bearing about in the body the dying of the Lord Jesus, that the life also of Jesus might be made manifest in our body.

For we which live are alway delivered unto death for Jesus' sake, that the life also of Jesus might be made manifest in our mortal flesh.

Knowing that he which raised up the Lord Jesus shall raise up us also by Jesus, and shall present us with you.

For all things are for your sakes, that the abundant grace might through the thanksgiving of many redound to the glory of God.

For which cause we faint not; but though our outward n.an perish, yet the inward man is renewed day by day.

For our light affliction, which is but for a moment, worketh for us a far more exceeding and eternal weight of glory;

Unison

While we look not at the things which are seen, but at the things which are not seen: for the things which are seen are temporal; but the things which are not seen are eternal.

—II Corinthians 4 :1, 6-11, 14-18

Blessed be the God and Father of our Lord Jesus Christ, which according to his abundant mercy hath begotten us again unto a lively hope by the resurrection of Jesus Christ from the dead.

To an inheritance incorruptible, and undefiled, and that fadeth not away, reserved in heaven for you,

Who are kept by the power of God through faith unto salvation ready to be revealed in the last time.

Wherein ye greatly rejoice, though now for a season, if need be, ye are in heaviness through manifold temptations:

That the trial of your faith, being much more precious than of gold that perisheth, though it be tried with fire, might be found unto praise and honour and glory at the appearing of Jesus Christ:

Whom having not seen, ye love; in whom, though now ye see him not, yet believing, ye rejoice with joy unspeakable and full of glory: receiving the end of your faith, even the salvation of your souls.

Beloved, think it not strange concerning the fiery trial which is to try you, as though some strange thing happened unto you:

Unison

But rejoice, inasmuch as ye are partakers of Christ's sufferings; that, when his glory shall be revealed, ye may be glad also with exceeding joy.

—*I Peter 1:3-9; 4:12, 13*

Let not your heart be troubled: ye believe in God, believe also in me.

In my Father's house are many mansions: if it were not so, I would have told you. I go to prepare a place for you.

And if I go and prepare a place for you, I will come again, and receive you unto myself; that where I am, there ye may be also.

And whither I go ye know, and the way ye know.

And I will pray the Father, and he shall give you another Comforter, that he may abide with you for ever;

Even the Spirit of truth; whom the world cannot receive, because it seeth him not, neither knoweth him: but ye know him; for he dwelleth with you, and shall be in you.

I will not leave you comfortless: I will come to you.

These things have I spoken unto you, being yet present with you.

But the Comforter, which is the Holy Ghost, whom the Father will send in my name, he shall teach you all things, and bring all things to your remembrance, whatsoever I have said unto you.

Unison

Peace I leave with you, my peace I give unto you: not as the world giveth, give I unto you. Let not your heart be troubled, neither let it be afraid.

—*John 14:1-4, 16-18, 25-27*

29 New Birth

There was a man of the Pharisees, named Nicodemus, a ruler of the Jews:

The same came to Jesus by night, and said unto him, Rabbi, we know that thou art a teacher come from God: for no man can do these miracles that thou doest, except God be with him.

Jesus answered and said unto him, Verily, verily, I say unto thee, Except a man be born again, he cannot see the kingdom of God.

Nicodemus said unto him, How can a man be born when he is old? can he enter the second time into his mother's womb, and be born?

Jesus answered, Verily, verily, I say unto thee, Except a man be born of water and of the Spirit, he cannot enter into the kingdom of God.

That which is born of the flesh is flesh; and that which is born of the Spirit is spirit.

Marvel not that I said unto thee, Ye must be born again.

If I have told you earthly things, and ye believe not, how shall ye believe, if I tell you of heavenly things?

And no man hath ascended up to heaven, but he that came down from heaven, even the Son of man which is in heaven.

And as Moses lifted up the serpent in the wilderness, even so must the Son of man be lifted up:

That whosoever believeth in him should not perish, but have eternal life.

Unison

For God so loved the world, that he gave his only begotten Son, that whosoever believeth in him should not perish, but have everlasting life.

—*John 3:1-7, 12-16*

30 Victory

Whosoever believeth that Jesus is the Christ is born of God: and every one that loveth him that begat loveth him also that is begotten of him.

By this we know that we love the children of God, when we love God, and keep his commandments.

For this is the love of God, that we keep his commandments: and his commandments are not grievous.

For whatsoever is born of God overcometh the world: and this is the victory that overcometh the world, even our faith.

Who is he that overcometh the world, but he that believeth that Jesus is the Son of God?

Who shall separate us from the love of Christ? shall tribulation, or distress, or persecution, or famine, or nakedness, or peril, or sword?

As it is written, For thy sake we are killed all the day long; we are accounted as sheep for the slaughter.

Nay, in all these things we are more than conquerors through him that loved us.

For I am persuaded, that neither death, nor life, nor angels, nor principalities, nor powers, nor things present, nor things to come, nor height, nor depth, nor any other creature, shall be able to separate us from the love of God, which is in Christ Jesus our Lord.

Unison

But thanks be to God, which giveth us the victory through our Lord Jesus Christ.

—I John 5:1-5; Romans 8:35-39;
I Corinthians 15:57

31   Immortality

. . . I would not have you to be ignorant, brethren, concerning them which are asleep, that ye sorrow not, even as others which have no hope.

For if we believe that Jesus died and rose again, even so them also which sleep in Jesus will God bring with him.

For this we say unto you by the word of the Lord, that we which are alive and remain unto the coming of the Lord shall not prevent them which are asleep.

For the Lord himself shall descend from heaven with a shout, with the voice of the archangel, and with the trump of God: and the dead in Christ shall rise first:

Then we which are alive and remain shall be caught up together with them in the clouds, to meet the Lord in the air: and so shall we ever be with the Lord.

Wherefore comfort one another with these words.

For God hath not given us the spirit of fear; but of power, and of love, and of a sound mind.

Be not thou therefore ashamed of the testimony of our Lord, . . . but be thou partaker of the afflictions of the gospel according to the power of God;

Who hath saved us, and called us with an holy calling, not according to our works, but according to his own purpose and grace, which was given us in Christ Jesus before the world began.

Unison

But is now made manifest by the appearing of our Saviour Jesus Christ, who hath abolished death, and hath brought life and immortality to light through the gospel.

—I Thessalonians 4:13-18;
II Timothy 1:7-10

32   The Sabbath

Thus the heavens and the earth were finished, and all the host of them.

And on the seventh day God ended his work which he had made; and he rested on the seventh day from all his work which he had made.

And God blessed the seventh day, and sanctified it: because that in it he had rested from all his work which God created and made.

Remember the sabbath day, to keep it holy. Six days shalt thou labour, and do all thy work:

But the seventh day is the sabbath of the Lord thy God: in it thou shalt not do any work, thou, nor thy son, nor thy daughter, thy manservant, nor thy maidservant, nor thy cattle, nor thy stranger that is within thy gates:

For in six days the Lord made heaven and earth, the sea, and all that in them is, and rested the seventh day: wherefore the Lord blessed the sabbath day, and hallowed it.

If thou turn away thy foot from the sabbath, from doing thy pleasure on my holy day; and call the sabbath a delight, the holy of the Lord, honourable; and shalt honour him, not doing thine own ways, nor finding thine own pleasure, nor speaking thine own words:

Unison

Then shalt thou delight thyself in the Lord; and I will cause thee to ride upon the high places of the earth, and feed thee with the heritage of Jacob thy father: for the mouth of the Lord hath spoken it.

—Genesis 2:1-3; Exodus 20:8-11
Isaiah 58:13, 14

33   Trust

Preserve me, O God: for in thee do I put my trust.

O my soul, thou hast said unto the Lord, Thou art my Lord: my goodness extendeth not to thee; but to the saints that are in the earth, and to the excellent, in whom is all my delight.

Their sorrows shall be multiplied that hasten after another god: their drink offerings of blood will I not offer, nor take up their names into my lips.

The Lord is the portion of mine inheritance and of my cup: thou maintainest my lot.

The lines are fallen unto me in pleasant places; yea, I have a goodly heritage.

I will bless the Lord, who hath given me counsel: my reins also instruct me in the night seasons.

I have set the Lord always before me: because he is at my right hand, I shall not be moved.

Therefore my heart is glad, and my glory rejoiceth: my flesh also shall rest in hope.

For thou wilt not leave my soul in hell; neither wilt thou suffer thine Holy One to see corruption.

Unison

Thou wilt shew me the path of life: in thy presence is fulness of joy; at thy right hand there are pleasures for evermore.

—Psalms 16

34 The Word of God

The Revelation of Jesus Christ, which God gave unto him, to shew unto his servants things which must shortly come to pass; and he sent and signified it by his angel unto his servant John:

Who bare record of the word of God, and of the testimony of Jesus Christ, and of all things that he saw.

Blessed is he that readeth, and they that hear the words of this prophecy, and keep those things which are written therein: for the time is at hand.

I am Alpha and Omega, the beginning and the ending, saith the Lord, which is, and which was, and which is to come, the Almighty.

I am he that liveth, and was dead; and, behold, I am alive for evermore, Amen; and have the keys of hell and of death.

Write the things which thou hast seen, and the things which are, and the things which shall be hereafter;

For I testify unto every man that heareth the words of the prophecy of this book, If any man shall add unto these things, God shall add unto him the plagues that are written in this book:

And if any man shall take away from the words of the book of this prophecy, God shall take away his part out of the book of life, and out of the holy city, and from the things which are written in this book.

All scripture is given by inspiration of God, and is profitable for doctrine, for reproof, for correction, for instruction in righteousness:

That the man of God may be perfect, throughly furnished unto all good works.

He which testifieth these things saith, Surely I come quickly. Amen. Even so, come, Lord Jesus.

35   Missions

Comfort ye, comfort ye my people, saith your God.

Speak ye comfortably to Jerusalem, and cry unto her, that her warfare is accomplished, that her iniquity is pardoned: for she hath received of the Lord's hand double for all her sins.

The voice of him that crieth in the wilderness, Prepare ye the way of the Lord, make straight in the desert a highway for our God.

Every valley shall be exalted, and every mountain and hill shall be made low: and the crooked shall be made straight, and the rough places plain:

And the glory of the Lord shall be revealed, and all flesh shall see it together: for the mouth of the Lord hath spoken it.

Let the wicked forsake his way, and the unrighteous man his thoughts: and let him return unto the Lord, and he will have mercy upon him; and to our God, for he will abundantly pardon.

Declare his glory among the heathen, his wonders among all people.

Say among the heathen that the Lord reigneth: the world also shall be established that it shall not be moved: he shall judge the people righteously.

Ask of me, and I shall give thee the heathen for thine inheritance, and the uttermost parts of the earth for thy possession.

Unison

So shall my word be that goeth forth out of my mouth: it shall not return unto me void, but it shall accomplish that which I please, and it shall prosper in the thing whereto I sent it.

—*Isaiah 40:1-5; 55:7; Psalms 96:3, 10; 2:8; Isaiah 55:11*

36   Testimony

With my lips have I declared all the judgments of thy mouth.

I have declared my ways, and thou heardest me: teach me thy statutes.

Make me to understand the way of thy precepts: so shall I talk of thy wondrous works.

Let thy mercies come also unto me, O Lord, even thy salvation, according to thy word.

So shall I have wherewith to answer him that reproacheth me: for I trust in thy word.

I will speak of thy testimonies also before kings, and will not be ashamed. And I will delight myself in thy commandments, which I have loved.

Be not thou therefore ashamed of the testimony of our Lord, nor of me his prisoner: but be thou partaker of the afflictions of the gospel according to the power of God;

But sanctify the Lord God in your hearts: and be ready always to give an answer to every man that asketh you a reason of the hope that is in you with meekness and fear:

And I heard a loud voice saying in heaven, Now is come salvation, and strength, and the kingdom of our God, and the power of his Christ: for the accuser of our brethren is cast down, which accused them before our God day and night.

Unison

And they overcame him by the blood of the Lamb, and by the word of their testimony; and they loved not their lives unto the death.

—*Psalms 119:13, 26, 27, 41, 42, 46, 47; II Timothy 1:8; I Peter 3:15; Revelation 12:10, 11*

37   Obedience

If ye love me, keep my commandments.

He that hath my commandments, and keepeth them, he it is that loveth me: and he that loveth me shall be loved of my Father. and I will love him, and will manifest myself to him.

Judas saith unto him, not Iscariot, Lord, how is it that thou wilt manifest thyself unto us, and not unto the world?

Jesus answered and said unto him, If a man love me, he will keep my words: and my Father will love him, and we will come unto him, and make our abode with him.

He that loveth me not keepeth not my sayings: and the word which ye hear is not mine, but the Father's which sent me.

Not every one that saith unto me, Lord, Lord, shall enter into the kingdom of heaven; but he that doeth the will of my Father which is in heaven.

. . . Hath the Lord as great delight in burnt offerings and sacrifices, as in obeying the voice of the Lord? Behold, to obey is better than sacrifice, and to hearken than the fat of rams.

Unison

Children, obey your parents in all things: for this is well pleasing unto the Lord. Servants, obey in all things your masters according to the flesh; not with eyeservice, as menpleasers; but in singleness of heart, fearing God.
—*John 14:15, 21-24; Matthew 7:21; I Samuel 15:22; Colossians 3:20, 22*

38 Motherhood

Who can find a virtuous woman? for her price is far above rubies.

The heart of her husband doth safely trust in her, so that he shall have no need of spoil.

She will do him good and not evil all the days of her life.

She seeketh wool, and flax, and worketh willingly with her hands.

She riseth also while it is yet night, and giveth meat to her household, and a portion to her maidens.

She stretcheth out her hand to the poor; yea, she reacheth forth her hands to the needy.

She is not afraid of the snow for her household: for all her household are clothed with scarlet.

She maketh herself coverings of tapestry; her clothing is silk and purple. Her husband is known in the gates, when he sitteth among the elders of the land.

Strength and honour are her clothing; and she shall rejoice in time to come.

She openeth her mouth with wisdom: and in her tongue is the law of kindness.

She looketh well to the ways of her household, and eateth not the bread of idleness.

Her children arise up, and call her blessed; her husband also, and he praiseth her.

Many daughters have done virtuously, but thou excellest them all.

Unison

Favour is deceitful, and beauty is vain: but a woman that feareth the Lord, she shall be praised.
—*Proverbs 31:10-13, 15, 20-23, 25-30*

39 Faith

Now faith is the substance of things hoped for, the evidence of things not seen.

For by it the elders obtained a good report.

By faith Abraham, when he was tried, offered up Isaac: and he that had received the promises offered up his only begotten son,

Of whom it was said, That in Isaac shall thy seed be called:

He staggered not at the promise of God through unbelief; but was strong in faith, giving glory to God;

And being fully persuaded that, what he had promised, he was able also to perform. And therefore it was imputed to him for righteousness.

By faith Moses, when he was come to years, refused to be called the son of Pharaoh's daughter;

Choosing rather to suffer affliction with the people of God, than to enjoy the pleasures of sin for a season; esteeming the reproach of Christ greater riches than the treasures in Egypt.

Therefore being justified by faith, we have peace with God through our Lord Jesus Christ:

Unison

By whom also we have access by faith into this grace wherein we stand, and rejoice in hope of the glory of God.

—Hebrews 11:1, 2, 17, 18;
Romans 4:20-22; Hebrews 11:24-26a;
Romans 5:1, 2

40 Communion

Now when the even was come, he sat down with the twelve.

And as they did eat, he said, Verily I say unto you, that one of you shall betray me.

And they were exceeding sorrowful, and began every one of them to say unto him, Lord, is it I?

And he answered and said, He that dippeth his hand with me in the dish, the same shall betray me.

The Son of man goeth as it is written of him: but woe unto that man by whom the Son of man is betrayed! it had been good for that man if he had not been born.

Then Judas, which betrayed him, answered and said, Master, is it I? He said unto him, Thou hast said.

And as they were eating, Jesus took bread, and blessed it, and brake it, and gave it to the disciples, and said, Take, eat; this is my body.

And he took the cup, and gave thanks, and gave it to them, saying, Drink ye all of it;

For this is my blood of the new testament, which is shed for many for the remission of sins.

Unison

But I say unto you, I will not drink henceforth of this fruit of the vine, until that day when I drink it new with you in my Father's kingdom.

—Matthew 26:20-29

41 Adoration

The heavens declare the glory of God; and the firmament sheweth his handywork.

Day unto day uttereth speech, and night unto night sheweth knowledge.

There is no speech nor language, where their voice is not heard.

Their line is gone out through all the earth, and their words to the end of the world. In them hath he set a tabernacle for the sun,

Which is as a bridegroom coming out of his chamber, and rejoiceth as a strong man to run a race.

His going forth is from the end of the heaven, and his circuit unto the ends of it: and there is nothing hid from the heat thereof.

The law of the Lord is perfect, converting the soul: the testimony of the Lord is sure, making wise the simple.

The statutes of the Lord are right, rejoicing the heart: the commandment of the Lord is pure, enlightening the eyes.

The fear of the Lord is clean, enduring for ever: the judgments of the Lord are true and righteous altogether.

Unison

Let the words of my mouth, and the meditation of my heart, be acceptable in thy sight, O Lord, my strength, and my redeemer.

—*Psalms 19:1-9, 14*

42   Christ

In the beginning was the Word, and the Word was with God, and the Word was God.

The same was in the beginning with God.

All things were made by him; and without him was not any thing made that was made.

In him was life; and the life was the light of men.

And the light shineth in darkness; and the darkness comprehended it not.

There was a man sent from God, whose name was John. The same came for a witness, to bear witness of the Light, that all men through him might believe.

He was not that Light, but was sent to bear witness of that Light.

That was the true Light, which lighteth every man that cometh into the world.

He was in the world, and the world was made by him, and the world knew him not.

Unison

He came unto his own, and his own received him not. But as many as received him, to them gave he power to become the sons of God, even to them that believe on his name.

—*John 1:1-12*

43   Easter

In the end of the sabbath, as it began to dawn toward the first day of the week, came Mary Magdalene and the other Mary to see the sepulchre.

And, behold, there was a great earthquake: for the angel of the Lord descended from heaven, and came and rolled back the stone from the door, and sat upon it.

His countenance was like lightning, and his raiment white as snow:

And for fear of him the keepers did shake, and became as dead men.

And the angel answered and said unto the women, Fear not ye: for I know that ye seek Jesus, which was crucified.

He is not here: for he is risen, as he said. Come, see the place where the Lord lay.

And go quickly, and tell his disciples that he is risen from the dead; and, behold, he goeth before you into Galilee; there shall ye see him: lo, I have told you.

And they departed quickly from the sepulchre with fear and great joy; and did run to bring his disciples word.

And as they went to tell his disciples, behold, Jesus met them, saying, All hail. And they came and held him by the feet, and worshipped him.

Unison
Then said Jesus unto them, Be not afraid: go tell my brethren that they go into Galilee, and there shall they see me.
—Matthew 28:1-10

44 Stewardship

Trust in the Lord with all thine heart; and lean not unto thine own understanding.

Honour the Lord with thy substance, and with the firstfruits of all thine increase: so shall thy barns be filled with plenty, and thy presses shall burst out with new wine.

Bring ye all the tithes into the storehouse, that there may be meat in mine house, and prove me now herewith, saith the Lord of hosts, if I will not open you the windows of heaven, and pour you out a blessing, that there shall not be room enough to receive it.

Give, and it shall be given unto you; good measure, pressed down, and shaken together, and running over, shall men give into your bosom. **For with the same measure that ye mete withal it shall be measured to you again.**

For ye know the grace of our Lord Jesus Christ, that, though he was rich, yet for your sakes he became poor, that ye through his poverty might be rich.

But this I say, He which soweth sparingly shall reap also sparingly; and he which soweth bountifully shall reap also bountifully.

Every man according as he purposeth in his heart, so let him give; not grudgingly, or of necessity: for God loveth a cheerful giver.

Unison
And God is able to make all grace abound toward you; that ye, always having all sufficiency in all things, may abound to every good work.
—Proverbs 3:5, 9, 10; Malachi 3:10; Luke 6:38; II Corinthians 8:9; 9:6-8

45 The Will of God

Furthermore then we beseech you, brethren, and exhort you by the Lord Jesus, that as ye have received of us how ye ought to walk and to please God, so ye would abound more and more.

For ye know what commandments we gave you by the Lord Jesus. For this is the will of God, even your sanctification,

For God hath not called us unto uncleanness, but unto holiness.

He therefore that despiseth, despiseth not man, but God, who hath also given unto us his holy Spirit.

But as touching brotherly love ye need not that I write unto you: for ye yourselves are taught of God to love one another.

And that ye study to be quiet, and to do your own business, and to work with your own hands, as we commanded you;

That ye may walk honestly toward them that are without, and that ye may have lack of nothing.

Now we exhort you, brethren, warn them that are unruly, comfort the feebleminded, support the weak, be patient toward all men.

See that none render evil for evil unto any man; but ever follow that which is good, both among yourselves, and to all men.

Unison

Rejoice evermore. Pray without ceasing. In every thing give thanks: for this is the will of God in Christ Jesus concerning you.

—*I Thessalonians 4:1-3a, 7-9, 11, 12 ;*
5:14-18

46   Atonement

Who hath believed our report? and to whom is the arm of the Lord revealed?

For he shall grow up before him as a tender plant, and as a root out of a dry ground: he hath no form nor comeliness; and when we shall see him, there is no beauty that we should desire him.

He is despised and rejected of men; a man of sorrows, and acquainted with grief: and we hid as it were our faces from him; he was despised, and we esteemed him not.

Surely he hath borne our griefs, and carried our sorrows: yet we did esteem him stricken, smitten of God, and afflicted.

But he was wounded for our transgressions, he was bruised for our iniquities: the chastisement of our peace was upon him; and with his stripes we are healed.

All we like sheep have gone astray; we have turned every one to his own way; and the Lord hath laid on him the iniquity of us all.

He was oppressed, and he was afflicted, yet he opened not his mouth: he is brought as a lamb to the slaughter, and as a sheep before her shearers is dumb, so he openeth not his mouth.

Yet it pleased the Lord to bruise him; he hath put him to grief: when thou shalt make his soul an offering for sin, he shall see his seed, he shall prolong his days, and the pleasure of the Lord shall prosper in his hand.

He shall see of the travail of his soul, and shall be satisfied: by his knowledge shall my righteous servant justify many; for he shall bear their iniquities.

Unison

Therefore will I divide him a portion with the great, and he shall divide the spoil with the strong; because he hath poured out his soul unto death: and he was numbered with the transgressors; and he bare the sin of many, and made intercession for the transgressors.

—*Isaiah 53:1-7, 10-12*

47 Worship

How amiable are thy tabernacles, O Lord of hosts!

My soul longeth, yea, even fainteth for the courts of the Lord: my heart and my flesh crieth out for the living God.

Yea, the sparrow hath found an house, and the swallow a nest for herself, where she may lay her young, even thine altars, O Lord of hosts, my King, and my God.

Blessed are they that dwell in thy house: they will be still praising thee.

Blessed is the man whose strength is in thee: in whose heart are the ways of them.

Who passing through the valley of Baca make it a well; the rain also filleth the pools.

They go from strength to strength, every one of them in Zion appeareth before God.

O Lord God of hosts, hear my prayer: give ear, O God of Jacob. Selah.

Behold, O God our shield, and look upon the face of thine anointed.

For a day in thy courts is better than a thousand. I had rather be a doorkeeper in the house of my God, than to dwell in the tents of wickedness.

For the Lord God is a sun and shield: the Lord will give grace and glory: no good thing will he withhold from them that walk uprightly.

Unison
O Lord of hosts, blessed is the man that trusteth in thee.

—Psalms 84

48 God's House

I was glad when they said unto me, Let us go into the house of the Lord. Our feet shall stand within thy gates, O Jerusalem.

Jerusalem is builded as a city that is compact together: whither the tribes go up, the tribes of the Lord, unto the testimony of Israel, to give thanks unto the name of the Lord.

Pray for the peace of Jerusalem: they shall prosper that love thee. Peace be within thy walls, and prosperity within thy palaces. For my brethren and companions' sakes, I will now say, Peace be within thee.

One thing have I desired of the Lord, that will I seek after; that I may dwell in the house of the Lord all the days of my life, to behold the beauty of the Lord, and to enquire in his temple.

For in the time of trouble he shall hide me in his pavilion: in the secret of his tabernacle shall he hide me; he shall set me up upon a rock.

How amiable are thy tabernacles, O Lord of hosts! My soul longeth, yea, even fainteth for the courts of the Lord: my heart and my flesh crieth out for the living God.

Yea, the sparrow hath found an house, and the swallow a nest for herself, where she may lay her young, even thine altars, O Lord of hosts, my King, and my God.

Unison
Blessed are they that dwell in thy house: they will be still praising thee.

—Psalms 122:1-4, 6-8; 27:4, 5; 84:1-4

INDEX of RESPONSIVE READINGS

TOPICAL INDEX

GENERAL INDEX
Titles and First Lines

Index of "Hymn-Orchestration"